HISTORY OF
THE UNITED STATES
VOLUME IV

THE WEST FRONT OF THE CAPITOL

Illuminated during the Conference for Limitation
of Armament

THE MARCH OF DEMOCRACY

A
HISTORY OF THE UNITED STATES

By

James Truslow Adams

Volume IV

AMERICA AND WORLD POWER

NEW YORK

CHARLES SCRIBNER'S SONS

CONTENTS

vii

CONTENTS

ILLUSTRATIONS

ILLUSTRATIONS

ILLUSTRATIONS

ILLUSTRATIONS

ILLUSTRATIONS

ILLUSTRATIONS

ILLUSTRATIONS

ILLUSTRATIONS

ILLUSTRATIONS

ILLUSTRATIONS

END OF VOLUME

GREAT SCENES AND PERSONAGES
OF OUR HISTORY

xix

ILLUSTRATIONS

VOLUME IV

AMERICA AND WORLD POWER

CHAPTER I

WE ENTER THE NEW ERA

THE mounting surplus, the temptation to legislative extravagance, the excess taxation, the need for reform, had all properly weighed heavily on Cleveland's mind. Whatever else he may not have accomplished, he had created at last a clear-cut issue for the two parties in the campaign of 1888—the first real issue since slavery in 1860.

Had not Blaine, who was spending the year in Europe, absolutely declined to have himself nominated by the Republicans, he would unquestionably have again been their candidate. At St. Louis, where the Democratic Convention met on June 5, Cleveland had been unanimously renominated, with Senator A. G. Thurman of Ohio as his running-mate, Vice-President Hendricks having died in office. When the Republicans met at Chicago on the 19th, nineteen candidates were balloted for, and it was only after three days that the choice fell on General Benjamin Harrison, of Indiana, a grandson of old "Tippecanoe," with Levi P. Morton of New York for Vice-President.

The issue of the tariff was squarely met by both

I

parties in their platforms, though in the campaign the Republicans unfairly misrepresented the Democratic position and Cleveland's own views. He believed that "unnecessary taxation is unjust taxation," that the surplus obviously called for the reduction of taxes, and that for the benefit of the farmers and other elements in the nation who suffered from the high costs resultant from excessive duties, there should be downward revision of the worst schedules in the old war-time tariff. Cleveland made it clear that he in no wise advocated free trade, but the Republicans raised the cry that he did, and that he would ruin the country. On the other hand, they declared in their platform that "we are uncompromisingly in favor of the American system of protection," and protested against "its destruction."

Rather illogically the Republicans also declared their "opposition to all combinations of capital . . . to control arbitrarily the condition of trade among our citizens," and claimed to favor legislation to "prevent the execution of all schemes to oppress the people by undue charges on their supplies." The mixture of opinion between the two parties is interestingly indicated by the Republicans' coming out against "trusts," and also in the plank on money, in which they demanded the use of silver and denounced Cleveland for his stand in favor of the gold basis!

The tariff, however, for the first time in our history, overshadowed all else in the campaign, and enabled the

Republicans to raise a huge corruption fund. The manufacturers who had been growing rich by the excessive duties were "put under the fire to have the fat fried out of them," as a Pennsylvania politician phrased it. John

PRESIDENT CLEVELAND.

AN ILLUSTRATED POEM.
By H. CLAY PREUSS.

Respectfully dedicated to the Members of the New York Delegation to the National Democratic Convention, at St. Louis. June 5th, 1888, as a just tribute to a noble son of the old "EMPIRE STATE."

When like Diogenes of old,	And by the magic power of gold
The people ruled by power of gold,	Our ruling men were bought and sold.
Cried out aloud on every hand,	'Twas then you took your noble stand,
"Oh! God, for a true and honest man!"	To weed corruption from the land:
They found in you what they had sought,	To bravely face the coming storm,
A man too honest to be bought.	And introduce all true reform:

© 1888.

A TRIBUTE TO CLEVELAND BY A MARYLAND ADMIRER
From the Library of Congress.

Wanamaker, for the Republican National Committee, in a circular letter to the manufacturing interests, put it more elegantly but with no less directness, asking them what they would pay "to be insured" against a lower tariff? Their responses were all he could have desired, in all the manufacturing States.

3

There were the usual tricks and misrepresentations in the campaign, and Cleveland lost some votes by an incident which cost the far from astute British Minister at Washington his post. A Republican in California, who pretended to be an Englishman naturalized as an American, wrote to the minister, Sackville-West, asking which Presidential candidate would probably be more friendly to England if elected. The minister, with incredible stupidity, forgetting that a diplomat has no right to meddle in the domestic affairs of a country to which he is accredited, advocated Cleveland to his correspondent. The Republicans published the letter broadcast, and tried to prove that Cleveland truckled to England and was attempting to commit us to free trade for the benefit of that country and not ourselves. The unhappy minister was at once handed his passports, but it was too late to undo the damage. On the whole, however, the campaign was much cleaner than the preceding one, and no personal scandals were raked up.

THE ELECTION OF HARRISON

The result of the election was a victory for Harrison who received 233 electoral votes to Cleveland's 168, although the latter received a plurality of apparently about 100,000 over his rival in the popular vote. It was the tariff question, and the large electoral votes of the manufacturing States which had defeated him. His friends had warned him not to send in his tariff message but to await re-election and then act, but this suggestion he

A COPY OF SACKVILLE-WEST'S LETTER TO BAYARD ADMITTING HE HAD BEEN DUPED, AND A LETTER FROM BAYARD TO THE PRESIDENT COMMENTING ON IT

From the Division of Manuscripts, Library of Congress.

had thrust aside as dishonest. He felt, he said, that this would not be fair to the country, and that the people should know before they elected him just where he stood.

The people had voted for him, but in the wrong

States, and, as has several times happened, in our peculiar system, we were again to have a President elected by a minority of the voters. As a Republican House was returned to Congress, the majority for Cleveland may be considered as a personal triumph. It is a fact worth pondering by politicians that an electorate will insist upon a weak man following *them,* but they admire a strong man, and if a man is strong enough they may follow *him*. Perhaps so many congressmen follow, in fear for their seats, because they realize they are not strong enough to lead. In this they are usually right.

Harrison had slight claim to national distinction when he entered the White House, and gained none afterward. A creditable career in the war, always valuable for a Republican candidate, one term in the Senate, and an unblemished personal record as an able lawyer in a small city, an ability to charm audiences by his oratory and an unfortunate frigidity of manner in personal intercourse, were the most notable attributes of the new President. He failed to understand the new currents in the life of his day, had no quality of leadership, and the entire story of his term can be made up of the activities of members of his Cabinet and of Congress without mention of his own. For the first time in more than a dozen years the President and both Houses of Congress were of the same party, and the way seemed open for the enactment of important legislation if the party so willed. Unfortunately about all the party wanted was to distribute money and favors. The administration was to prove utterly reckless, and was to pay the penalty.

Harrison chose an undistinguished Cabinet, with the exception of his Secretary of State, Blaine, whom he did not want but who could not be ignored. Blaine had made Harrison President by refusing to run himself, and the next highest post in the administration obviously belonged to him. John Wanamaker, who had been so useful in "frying the fat" in the campaign, was made Postmaster-General, and a leading business lawyer of New York, Benjamin F. Tracy, went to the Navy Department.

The party had been elected on the tariff issue, but the situation was not simple, and the tariff bill to be passed had to depend on other elements as well as on the Eastern manufacturers. Although Harrison was inaugurated in March, 1889, it was not until the next year that important measures began to be put through with the help of the new Republican House.

In that, there were two men, Thomas B. Reed of Maine, and William McKinley of Ohio, who like Blaine were much more important than the President, whose very lack of achievement, and thus of enemies, had made him a compromise candidate.

One of the dangers of "government by the people" is that of substituting endless talk for action. The lower House of Congress had become a body in which a few resolute obstructionists could hold up the public business indefinitely. Although when the Republicans had been in a minority, Reed had declared himself in favor of such possibility of obstructionist tactics, when he was elected Speaker of the House which assembled in December, 1889, he had made up his mind to end them by introducing new rules.

One of the most important innovations made by him early in 1890 was the counting of the members actually in the room, instead of merely those responding to the roll-call, to determine whether a quorum were present. Another was that the Chair might decline to entertain motions which it considered offered solely for the purpose of delaying business. These and other new rules, which gave him his title of "Czar," while unquestionably strengthening the power of the majority in the House, were really called for in the interests of the public business. When the Democrats later secured a majority in the House they continued to enforce the "Reed Rules." At the time of their introduction, however, the rules met with a storm of opposition, and although they greatly assisted the Republicans to pass their legislation in the next two years, they also were a factor in the turning out of the party in the mid-term elections.

For some years the situation in the South had been considered a sore grievance by the Republicans. Legally the negro had the vote, but the Southern white, determined at all costs to keep a white government in power, had, in one way and another, practically nullified the

Fourteenth and Fifteenth Amendments. The problem, as we have said, was racial, but the negro vote was Republican, and it is hardly open to question that such staunch Republicans as Henry Cabot Lodge would have seen less iniquity in the Southerners' refusal to live under negro governments had the negro vote been as largely Democratic as it was Republican!

It may have been unjust to deprive the negro of his vote, though that is open to question considering the history of the amendments, but when Lodge demanded "protection" for the negro in his rights he well knew that it could only be gained at the expense of depriving the white American of *his* "rights," which would have disappeared promptly on a return to the negro-carpet-bag domination system. The population figures according to the latest available statistics at that time were those of the Census of 1880 which showed the comparisons noted below for some of the Southern States.

	WHITES	BLACKS
South Carolina	391,000	604,332
Georgia	198,328	243,266
Alabama	662,185	600,103
Mississippi	479,398	650,291
Louisiana	454,954	483,665

If the Republican Party could force the South to count negro votes, the advantage to the party and the disaster to the South were both clear as noonday.

Under the new Reed Rules, a bill passed the House by

9

the narrow partisan vote of 155 to 149 designed to prevent interference with the "right" of the negro to vote. This would have had the happy result of returning many more Republican members to Congress, and the less happy one of throwing the South back into a condition of political barbarism. There were no Reed Rules in the Senate, and senators could talk and obstruct in relays as long as lungs and the dictionary held out. A minority in the Senate refused to look kindly on a Republican tariff bill as long as the Republicans threatened to set up a carpet-bag régime in the South again with the aid of Federal supervisors, and this was the first obstacle that McKinley met in the effort to redeem his party's campaign pledges and to reimburse the manufacturers for the tortures to which they had been put when the "fat" was fried out of them.

A disadvantage of the protectionist system is that if certain manufacturers are to be awarded pickings by government favoritism, other interests will also want their share at the public trough. Some of these others were the silver mine owners. If they voted the Republican ticket and Eastern manufacturers got high tariffs, which the mine owners cared nothing about, the latter considered it only reasonable that if they voted for tariffs they should get in exchange something they did care about.

Their ranks had gained much in Congressional influence owing to the fact that four new States,—Montana, Washington, and the two Dakotas,—had just been admitted to the Union. The Secretary of the Treasury, William Windom of Minnesota, was a silverite, President Harrison was favorable to bi-metallism, and the

AS THE CARTOONISTS REGARDED THE SHERMAN SILVER BILL
From the Library of Congress.

Westerners thought the time had come to insist on the free and unlimited coinage of that metal. Largely because Cleveland had been for gold, the Republicans had come out for silver, and on July 14, 1890, Congress passed the bill known as the Sherman Act, as it was fathered by the former Treasury head, John Sherman.

11

The Act provided for the purchase by the government of 4,500,000 ounces of silver each month, to be deposited against Treasury notes which were to be legal tender for all payments, including those of duties at the Custom Houses. The Act also committed the United States to the impossible and highly dangerous task of maintaining the two metals on a parity with one another. In view of the campaign of 1896 it is interesting to note that not a single Democrat voted for the fatal bill and not a single Republican against it.

The 54,000,000 ounces of silver which Congress thus ordered the Treasury to buy annually was practically the entire output at that time of the American mines. There was no more reason why the government should be required by law to buy the entire output of the silver miners than the entire wheat output of the farmers, and many Eastern Republicans must have had some realization of the danger entailed to our whole currency and financial system. However, as one of the Massachusetts Republican representatives said: "all there is in this silver bill is pure politics."

The politics were based on the tariff. The Eastern manufacturers had not paid "insurance" for nothing, and they were determined to get something for it at any cost. For most of them it was a matter of dollars and cents, as free silver was for the mine owners, but for the chairman of the Ways and Means Committee of the House (who was also a free-silverite), William Mc-

Kinley, it was a tenet of faith. He believed as firmly
that protection was for the good of the whole people as
some agitators believed in free silver for the same assumed reason.

As early as May, 1890, the Tariff Bill which had
emerged from his committee, and which embodied the
most radical extension of the protective system yet offered, was passed by the House on a strictly party vote.
In the Senate, however, it encountered opposition. Two
bargains had to be made to get it through, and in order
to do so the tariff senators agreed to buy the votes of
Southern senators by abandoning any effort to enforce
the Fourteenth and Fifteenth Amendments, and of the
Western senators by passing the silver purchase Act.
The "rights" of the negro, of which so much had been
heard, suddenly became transformed into higher duties
on woollens and hemp, and if, as McKinley said, "cheap
merchandise means cheap men," we were saved at the
added price of buying 54,000,000 ounces of silver a year
to debase the currency and bring on a panic.

The problem of the surplus was not long to remain.
The same Congress which passed the tariff also passed
the Dependent Pension Bill, vetoed by Cleveland, under
which applications for pensions at once multiplied ten-
fold, and Harrison watched the annual payments to the
combined forces of worthy veterans and political crooks
rise from $81,000,000 to $135,000,000. "Rivers and Har-
bors" fared royally in the "pork barrel," and the reck-

13

less session won its nickname of the "billion-dollar Congress."

On the other hand, in spite of his appointment of Roosevelt as Civil Service Commissioner, Harrison, with the exception of McKinley, was the most reactionary President who has held office since reform was inaugurated under Arthur. Even such hide-bound partisans as Lodge had to complain publicly of the abuse of the spoils system, and Roosevelt wrote that Boss Platt seemed "to have a ring in the President's nose," as he never gave the Civil Service Commission "one ounce of real backing."

The recklessness that the administration had shown brought about a revulsion in public sentiment, and in the mid-term election of 1890 the Republicans were disastrously defeated in a veritable landslide. Although the party managed to hold on in the Senate, only one third of the members of which are elected every two years, the overturn in the House effectually stopped further extreme Republican legislation.

Outside of Congress, the leading figure of the administration was Blaine. Even in Congress, though occupying the office of Secretary of State, he did not hesitate to wield influence as though he were still in the Senate. In the Department of State he was intensely interested in fostering relations with the countries, too often neglected by us, of South America; and when the Tariff Bill was being considered he urged with all his strength that provision be made for a system of reciprocity. Against much opposition he won his point, in an amendment to the bill, and as a result negotiated treaties with a dozen West Indian and South American countries, which he hoped would win us a far larger part of the trade to the South in which, considering our geographical and economic position, we then shared only to a nominal amount.

Blaine's conduct of his office was spirited, and he was perhaps more genuinely interested in foreign policy than any other Secretary of State between Seward and John Hay, but there is little of lasting importance to record. A settlement with Germany of a dispute over Samoa was chiefly interesting as indicating a willingness on our part to consider it our right to intervene in the affairs of a far distant land quite outside the sphere of all our activities hitherto. An effort to settle the troublesome question of the seal fisheries in the Behring Sea was determined against us but had an importance as being the second warm dispute which we settled amicably with England. Another hot controversy, with Chili in 1891, which threatened what might have been the only war in our history with a South American nation, was also adjusted peacefully.

Of more significance than these, because of the prominence which it again gave to one of the weak and dangerous features of our Constitution, was the difficulty which arose with Italy in the same year. It may be recalled that in 1840 the possibility of the execution of the English subject, McCleod, had brought about the threat of war from Lord Palmerston if the Federal Government could not control the State of New York. Now a similar case arose.

For some time there had been much violence and a number of murders in New Orleans, due, it was suspected, to the operations of the Mafia, an Italian secret society, and many of the victims had been Italians. The Chief of Police, David C. Hennessy, had done his best to track the murderers, when he was himself murdered. Eleven persons, three of them Italian subjects, and the rest naturalized, were indicted for the crime but appeared to be likely to be acquitted on account of the fear of the jury that vengeance would be wreaked on them if a verdict of guilty were found. A mob of several thousand persons then stormed the jail, and lynched the eleven suspects.

The United States had a treaty with Italy guaranteeing Italian citizens in our country "constant protection and security," but the Federal Government had no control over the Louisiana government. Italy adopted a high tone, demanding the immediate punishment of the offenders. This, of course, no government could guarantee until they had been proved guilty, and fortunately, although diplomatic relations were broken for about a year by the mutual recall of ministers, Italy had placed herself in a weak position by demanding too much.

DESIGN FOR A SMALL BUT BEAUTIFUL VILLA

To be executed in the quiet and charming village of Rhinebeck on the Hudson.

A CALIFORNIA RESIDENCE

Another dwelling of the period, at San Francisco.

From "Croft's Progressive American Architecture," 1875, and University of California, Extension Division.

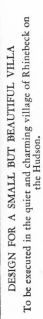

NEW YORK (FORTY-SECOND STREET) IN THE EIGHTIES

Horse car lines came into use in New York about 1832. The last was abandoned July 26, 1917. Cables were substituted for horses in 1893 and followed by electric propulsion in 1901.

TYPE OF EARLY HORSE CAR USED IN NEW YORK

Built in 1862. The body turned on the truck to avoid switching.

By courtesy of W. F. Reeves, Esq.

Eventually, the Federal Government settled the matter by the payment of 125,000 francs to the families of the three murdered Italians. In spite of the fact that Governor Nicholls of Louisiana showed himself more accommodating than Governor Seward of New York had in the preceding incident, the weakness of our theory of divided sovereignty had again appeared.

On June 4, 1892, four days before the Republican Convention was to meet to nominate a candidate for the Presidential campaign, Blaine suddenly resigned office. But before we continue the political narrative, we must glance at what had been happening in other parts of the national life.

CHANGES IN AMERICAN LIFE

America in the late '80's and early '90's seems almost incredibly different in thought, surroundings, and ways of life from the America of our own day. It is true that the age of steam and machinery had wrought great changes, some of which we have already noted, in the social and economic life of the people. Those changes, however, had been slight compared with such as were to come within another few decades. Labor-saving machinery had done away with much drudgery and had increased leisure and productivity—the cable, telegraph, and improved printing-presses had brought the modern newspaper into existence; factory production, replacing home crafts, had forced a rapid urbanization of the population; and such a list of changes could be long extended.

Yet with all of them, life for most people had not altered greatly, and their list of wants had not been much extended. They travelled more rapidly and often, read more widely, and had more conveniences, such as gas lights and friction matches, than their fathers had had in their early days, but there had been no great revolution in our life and its ways. Except for the very poor in the very largest industrial centres, a home still meant for almost every American a house of his own in which the family lived its own life in privacy. The "apartment" was scarcely known.

Family activities and friendships were largely confined to the immediate neighborhood of the home. In the cities, there were no subways, few electric cars, and for the most part busses and horsecars jogged along at about four miles an hour. There was not an automobile in use in the country, and even the "safety" bicycle was not invented until 1884, and pneumatic tires somewhat later. Every one, in city and country, relied upon a horse and carriage, if he had a conveyance of his own. There was not a mile of concrete road in the whole United States, and most of the roads were of dirt, and bad. The household of the farmer was isolated to an extent it is almost impossible to conceive today.

Although the telephone had become practical it was not in wide use and was to be found in few city homes

Copyright, Grabhill, 1889.

THE OMAHA BOARD OF TRADE IN THE MOUNTAINS NEAR DEADWOOD, APRIL 26, 1889

EVOLUTION OF THE STEEL SKYSCRAPER

Left: Old Home Insurance Building, Chicago, 1885, designed by Jenney and Mundy, the world's first skyscraper. *Centre:* the Flatiron Building, New York, 1902, designed by D. H. Burnham. *Right:* the Woolworth Building, New York, 1913, designed by Cass Gilbert.

© *Ned Van Buren.*

even of the well-to-do, and scarcely at all in the country. Not even all the offices of New York Stock Exchange firms found it necessary to have one in the early '80's. The radio, of course, was utterly unknown, and even the phonograph was put on the market, in very crude form, only in 1886. Two years later came the invention of a portable camera. In looking back, one is forcibly struck with the simplicity of life and its lack of "apparatus." The typewriter was coming into use, but when Cleveland first became President he did not feel the need of employing even a single stenographer and there was but one telephone for all the White House business, which he would answer himself when the clerks had gone for the day.

The skyscraper had scarcely appeared, and although some experiments were made with steel-frame buildings, notably by Louis Sullivan, John W. Root, and Daniel Burnham in Chicago, it was not until past this period, in 1902, that the twenty-story Flatiron Building in New York marked the real beginning of a general architectural transformation, with its accompaniment of soaring prices for city real estate. Although much good and competent work was being done in the arts, chiefly by the men who were noted as beginning their careers in the preceding decade, the one original and virile contribution which the nation made was in the skyscraper, now being experimented with, and it is notable that it was one in which feminine influence was wholly lacking.

The rest of the arts were still very strongly under that influence as exerted by the woman of the day. Nudity in painting or sculpture was still looked at askance as "not nice," and the most realistic, and in some ways the best, literary craftsman of the period, W. D. Howells, carefully skirted away from anything more realistic in life than could be considered proper reading for a girl in her 'teens. Public taste was sentimental and romantic, and in the '90's such books as Doctor Weir Mitchell's *Hugh Wynne,* Booth Tarkington's *The Gentleman from Indiana,* and James Lane Allen's *Choir Invisible* enjoyed a great vogue.

The period, however, was not without its literary effort to get beneath the parlor aspects of American life, which contained plenty of elements not quite suited for discussion in that room. Henry Adams in *Democracy* had laid bare the shoddiness of the national government and politics, and novels began to deal with "problems," while such men as Henry Demarest Lloyd were forerunners of the "muck rakers" of the years immediately after 1900.

Underlying the surface of our life there was deep and justified discontent which we shall discuss presently, and America was maturing. In 1890 the frontier was officially declared at an end, and although this did not mean that there was no more free or unoccupied land, it did mean that the old dream of being able to grow up with a "new country" from the start by the simple process of moving to a frontier had passed. Discontented Americans, to a far greater extent than ever before, would henceforth have to face their problems instead of dodging them by going off into the "great open

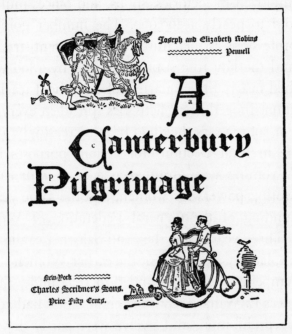

TITLE–PAGE OF A BOOK WRITTEN AND ILLUSTRATED BY
JOSEPH AND ELIZABETH PENNELL IN 1885
From the Rare Book Room of the Library of Congress.

spaces." Expansion, if there were to be any more, would have to take place outside the well-defined boundaries of the United States.

After the set-back of the Civil War, what may be called generally the woman's movement had taken on renewed vigor, and under such leaders as Elizabeth Cady Stanton, Carrie Chapman Catt, Doctor Anna Howard Shaw, and others, made rapid progress. In the two decades after 1870 the number of women over sixteen employed in factories, shops, and offices multiplied threefold to nearly 1,200,000. The number going into such professions as the church ministry, dentistry, medicine, and the law rose suprisingly and by 1890 women furnished nearly three quarters of the school teachers in the nation. Indeed, their activities spread in every direction. For some years they had been increasingly granted suffrage in local elections for certain purposes but in 1890 Wyoming was admitted as a State with full and equal voting powers for women, and the same year saw the founding of the General Federation of Women's Clubs. Three years later the Anti-Saloon League began its work, largely as a result of the earlier Women's Christian Temperance Union founded in 1874 under the lead of Frances E. Willard. By 1893 eight States had adopted absolute prohibition, and twelve were partly dry under local option legislation.

One of the great changes in the short period was in the character of the addition to our population by immigration. Until 1880 almost all our immigrants had come from northern and western Europe, and although they had affected our national life and formed large racial groups, notably the Germans, Irish, and Scandinavians, they had been assimilated to the population at

22

large with comparative ease as contrasted with those now about to arrive. Until 1870 those coming from eastern and southern Europe,—Italy, Russia, Hungary, and other States,—had been negligible. Between 1870 and 1880 the proportion rose to over seven per cent of the total and in the succeeding decades it became approximately eighteen per cent, fifty-two per cent, and seventy-one per cent, falling off somewhat again after 1910. Although in part this sudden change in the character of our population, which had received in four decades over 9,000,000 immigrants of racial stocks not allied to our own, was due to conditions in the countries from which they came, it was more largely the result of the demand for cheap labor in America.

This point brings us to a consideration of the economic conditions prevailing during the final decade of the last century, which had such resounding effects on politics.

Let us try to plot out in simple diagrammatic outline the chief groups and forces which were to come into conflict.

Most strikingly in the public eye were the great Titans of the new business era, the coal and meat "barons" and the copper, railway, steel, and other "kings," men of the type of the elder J. P. Morgan, of James J. Hill, William H. Vanderbilt, Carnegie, Frick, William H. Clark, and Rockefeller. Such men had certain broad traits in common, differ as they might from each other as individuals. They were men of wide economic but intensely narrow social vision, and of colossal driving power and iron wills. They could lay their economic plans with imperial vision in time and space, but for the effect of their acts on society they cared nothing whatever. They claimed the right to rule the economic destinies of the people in any way that would enure to their own personal advantage. Illogically, they insisted upon the theory of *laissez-faire* for all except themselves, while they demanded and received every favor they wished in the way of special privileges from the government, as in the tariff and the silver purchase Act. The whole machinery of government must be at their disposal when desired,—legislation, court decisions, and Federal troops. They combined their business units into "trusts" and combinations of almost unlimited power, yet they insisted on "freedom of contract" when dealing with labor, whose organization in any form they almost wholly refused to sanction.

There were two other groups, far more numerous, though less powerful and spectacular—the farmers and the industrial laborers. Although times had in general been good for some years after 1879, when recovery from the great panic of 1873 had fully set in, by 1890 they had been becoming much less so. For various reasons, the prices of farm products had been falling, and particularly in the South and West the agricultural class was beginning to suffer severely. Efforts were also being made to reduce wages in manufacturing and other industries, and there were much discontent and numerous strikes among the employees.

Gradually and quite naturally, there grew up the belief in a great conspiracy on the part of the very rich to ruin the poor. The farmer, for example, found himself at the mercy of the railroads while he saw a railway magnate like Vanderbilt enlarge his private fortune from about $10,000,000 to more than $100,000,000. Appeal to the law seemed hopeless. When the possible interest of the public was suggested to the younger Vanderbilt, who was associated with his father, his famous answer, which rang through the land, was "The public be damned." When the law was pointed out to the coarse and vulgar older man, with his tricky little eyes and heavy sensual mouth, he answered in much the same way, "What do I care about law? Hain't I got the power?" Such were the men whom the small shipper saw in control of the nation's transportation system while at the same time he saw big shippers, like Rockefeller, spreading ruin right and left among his competitors while he drove his own freight-rate bargains with these rail magnates, and was amassing tens of millions.

The iron and steel industry was one of those benefiting most from government favoritism under the tariff, and the labor unions in that industry were also the strongest of all in the United States. In 1889 H. C. Frick, the largest coke manufacturer and a bitter enemy of organized labor, became chairman of Carnegie Brothers & Co., and bad feeling at once developed between the owners and the workmen. In 1892 the wage contract expired and after fruitless conferences the owners delivered an ultimatum to the men that if the wages offered were not accepted the operators would no longer deal with the union but only with the men as individuals. The men then went on strike to save their union.

Frick had already arranged to have 300 Pinkerton detectives sent to the plants to act as guards, and this embittered the operatives who had threatened no violence. When the imported detectives reached Homestead on July 6, a pitched battle ensued in which a number were killed on both sides. The strike spread to the other Carnegie plants, and the State militia was called out and remained for several months, although there was no further disorder. By November 20 the funds of the strikers were used up, and the men, facing winter without work, were forced to go back, giving up their union. Organized labor was broken in practically the whole steel industry, the other mills following the example set by the Carnegies, and labor had learned that its strongest organization was powerless before organized capital.

That summer there were also strikes in other industries and sections, the most violent being at the silver mines of the Cœur d'Alene district in Idaho. The price of silver, like that of most commodities, had been steadily falling, and although the silver-mine owners, unlike the farmers, had forced the government to come to their aid as we have seen, by buying a very large proportion of their annual output, they had forced several wage reductions when at last the workmen struck. The owners imported strike breakers and there was a good deal of violence, including the blowing up of a mill. The Idaho militia proving ineffective, Harrison was called upon and sent Federal troops to suppress the strike.

It began to seem that the power of the government was always on the side of the rich. The high-tariff men talked about protecting the standard of living of the American workmen but the steel industry gave the lie to this. Entrenched behind their high duties and with the new abundance of cheap immigrant labor to pick from, so far from handing on the benefits of protection to the men, the owners of that industry seemed bent on beating the wages down and even destroying what effectiveness in bargaining and self-defense the men might gain from organization. As between an individual workman, out of work and with a family to support, and the Carnegie Steel Works, it was sheer hypocrisy to destroy the union as a means of upholding the right of the individual to make such contracts as he might choose. It was the same in the silver industry. The American people were being forced to relieve the mine owners by buying a large part of the output at nearly double its market price, yet none of the benefit was passed on to labor.

When cases involving working conditions or wages came into the courts, labor found the same favoritism. The Supreme Court of the State of New York declared that the law making it illegal to manufacture cigars in tenement-house homes was unconstitutional because it depreciated the value of property without compensating public advantage. This was but one of the many decisions in which the courts appeared to set the rights of property above those of man. The New York decision just mentioned, which so roused the ire of Roosevelt, struck that note of sanctimoniousness which we have found before and shall again, and which was so irritating to those whose interests were involved. The law had been aimed to break up in part the system of "sweated" labor under which families lived, ate, slept, and worked in vile conditions, often in one room; but the judges declared they could not see how the health or morals of the worker would be benefited by forcing him to labor outside the "hallowed associations and beneficent influences" of his own home!

There was, indeed, no general conspiracy of "the rich" (who fought fiercely enough among themselves for government favors and private profits), but if the masses of farmers and industrial workmen were mistaken as to the great conspiracy they were right enough as to there being something radically wrong with the system. The masses were not economists and for the most part their knowledge and views were limited to the range of their own daily needs and woes. The intelligence of the nation, unfortunately, was almost wholly busy in making money as fast as possible, and was on the side of the larger capitalists. The leadership of the masses thus had to come mainly from their own ranks.

What the masses saw was a government granting huge

A TILT BETWEEN THE KNIGHTS OF LABOR AND THE TRADES UNIONS, WITH CAPITALISM THE ARBITRATOR
A cartoon by Nast from "Harper's Weekly," June 12, 1886.

favors to men and groups who were amassing enormous fortunes while screwing down wages and taking heavy toll on all products. Political parties, Congress, and the courts seemed to be on the side of the magnates and against the "people." Moreover, as prices declined in terms of gold, and debts contracted in paper became harder to pay when demanded in gold, and when government bonds which had been bought with paper were repaid to the capitalists in gold, the conspiracy to de-

29

fraud the poor man and make the rich richer and more powerful appeared to the former to be unquestionable.

Many movements and organizations arose from this seething discontent. In the ranks of industrial workers the Knights of Labor declined but in 1886 with the organization of the American Federation of Labor there was initiated the most important workingmen's organization in our history, which was to weather the storms of this period and exert lasting influence. Started by Samuel Gompers, a cigar maker, it developed in him one of the greatest of American labor leaders, who was to remain in control and exert a beneficent power for nearly forty years.

The Federation of Labor worked through economic pressure for immediate aims of higher wages and better conditions, and meddled but little in politics. For the most part the workers' particular grievances were such as could be remedied only by State and not by Federal legislation, if relieved by legislation at all. The farmers, however, could gain nothing by organizing as unions and striking, and their grievances, which sprang largely, as they thought, from abuses of the currency, from the "money-power," trusts, and from interstate commerce freight rates, could be most rapidly remedied by legislation, largely Federal. By 1890 many separate political parties had arisen, in addition to the Farmers' Alliance, to elect legislators and exert political pressure.

In the South the Alliance worked through the only white man's party in that section, the Democratic, but in

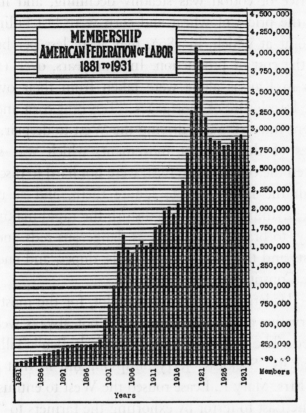

MEMBERSHIP
AMERICAN FEDERATION OF LABOR
1881 TO 1931

FROM THE REPORT OF THE ANNUAL CONVENTIONS OF
THE AMERICAN FEDERATION OF LABOR

the West the various new parties worked independently, such as the People's Party in Kansas, the Industrial Party in Michigan, or the Independent Party in South Dakota, and in the elections of 1890 they managed to

31

send two senators and eight representatives to Congress.

Their success was not to be wondered at. In the South the price of cotton was steadily declining, and in the West the prices of wheat and corn were fast falling to the point at which, in 1893, they were less per bushel than the cost of production. In four years, over 11,000 farms in Kansas alone were taken from their owners under foreclosure of mortgages. "Ten cent corn and ten per cent interest" were driving the West to despair. The sources of the Populist movement, which was so to frighten the conservative East, were not hard to discover, though the East chose to ignore them, and as usual, when anything threatens to disturb the rapid making of money, to brand the leaders as dangerous reds and anarchists and their followers as fools, dupes, and enemies to the Constitution.

The leaders were a picturesque lot, for the most part conservative and honest enough, if not always well informed. The South had its "Pitchfork Ben" Tillman, Kansas its "Sockless" Jerry Simpson, and in that same State Mrs. Mary E. Lease roused the West to enthusiasm and the East to terror by exhorting the farmers to "raise less corn and more hell," extremely wise advice under the existing economic and political conditions.

Nor, by the time the campaign of 1892 came round, was the East itself confident of its own position. The Republican tariff measure had been bought at a terrific price, and the evils of the Sherman Act for the purchase of silver were becoming appallingly manifest. By the end of 1892, after having rapidly dwindled, the import duties were being paid ninety-six per cent in silver and only four per cent in gold. Gold was being hoarded, and the solvency of the national government, further weakened by the wild extravagance of the Harrison administration and Congress, was seriously in danger.

Our trade balance was, for practically the first time since the war, becoming adverse instead of heavily in our favor. Our railroads and other enterprises had been loaded down with watered stock for the benefit of speculators. Partly from the fears aroused in Europe by the threatened default of the great English banking house of Barings on $100,000,000 obligations in 1890, partly from other European conditions, and partly from fear of our continued ability to pay in gold, Europe began to draw that metal from us in payment of debts in large amounts. The Eastern banks had to curtail credit, and it looked as though our whole financial structure might collapse, and the bankers and magnates follow the farmers into the bankruptcy courts.

Such was the atmosphere in which the Presidential campaign of 1892 was fought, and such the depressing prospect for any candidate who might be elected.

THE CAMPAIGN OF 1892

The Republican Convention met at Minneapolis on June 7, and as was always customary until the Democratic Convention of 1912, adopted its platform before voting for candidates. With the sublime disregard of facts which can be compassed only by politicians in a campaign, the platform pointed to the prosperity of the country and claimed that the tariff was its cause. It "reaffirmed" the "American" doctrine of protection, and straddled the money issue by demanding at once bimetallism and the maintenance of the parity of gold and silver.

Although Harrison had aroused no enthusiasm, and Blaine had a considerable following who wished, in spite of his ill health, to see him nominated for the Presidency, there was little question but that Harrison would secure renomination, as he did. Marcus A. Hanna, who was not a delegate, had gone to Minneapolis to help along the political fortunes of McKinley, who was made Chairman of the Convention. The episode is chiefly interesting in the light of later events, and Hanna, who had made a fortune as an iron manufacturer, was not at that time a national figure. Harrison was easily given the nomination in lukewarm fashion, and Whitelaw Reid, the owner of *The New York Tribune,* received second place.

In spite of the boast of the prosperity of the country, the record of the Republicans in the previous four years clearly gave the Democrats an unusual opportunity to come back to power, but the problem of a candidate was more serious for them than for their rivals. Some months before the convention met at Chicago on June 21, it had seemed as though the strongest candidate was Senator David B. Hill of New York, who had twice been governor of that State. Cleveland was unquestionably the strongest man in the party, but he had made many enemies, had apparently definitely retired from politics, and had been subjected to scurrilous abuse by even such Democratic papers as *The New York Sun*.

Moreover it had been thought that an incident of February, 1891, had lost him his last chance to be again the leader of his party. Both parties and most professional politicians with ambitions hedged on the silver question as adroitly as they could. Cleveland was asked to address a meeting of business men at the Reform Club in New York which had been called for the purpose of opposing an unsound currency. Although his friends advised him not to express himself strongly he declined to accept the advice, and, unable to be present in person, wrote a brief, clear-cut letter in which he stated that he considered the "experiment of free, unlimited, and independent silver coinage" then before Congress to be "dangerous and reckless." As in his previous pronouncement on the tariff, he insisted that the people should know where he stood even if it involved complete defeat.

The result was interesting. Almost every practical politician at once decided Cleveland was dead politically. Hill, who was a consummate politician, used every political trick known, including the attempt to call a "snap convention" four months before the meeting of the National Convention, to nominate delegates from New York. In Chicago, Bourke Cockran's eloquence and the whole power of Tammany were put forth to defeat Cleveland, who, nevertheless, won the nomination on the very first ballot taken. Without minimizing the exceedingly able work done for him in the preceding months by William C. Whitney and others, it must be conceded that it was Cleveland's own strength of character and his complete independence in saying what he thought, instead of "pussyfooting," which gained for him the support of the rank and file of voters, and it was this popular demand that determined the votes of the delegates with their ears to the ground. They tried to soften the effects of Cleveland's forthrightness by nominating Adlai E. Stevenson of Illinois as his running-mate.

The platform was also trimmed to suit varied tastes. It did, indeed, "denounce the Republican protection as a fraud," which was straight enough, but the currency question was handled with gloves and a concession to the cheap-money advocates was made in the suggestion that the ten per cent prohibitory tax on the notes of State banks should be repealed. However, the Republican Convention had been equally timorous whereas the Democratic candidate himself had spoken clearly.

From the various parties of discontent which we have

mentioned emerged the national Populist Party, which held its convention at Omaha on July 2, and nominated General James B. Weaver of Iowa for President, and James G. Field of Virginia for Vice-President. The platform demanded free and unlimited coinage of silver at sixteen to one, and that the amount of currency in circulation be increased at once to not less than fifty dollars per capita of the population. In addition to the dangerous cheap-money planks, there were others which seemed to the conservatives almost as heretical and radical. Many of these latter, however, have been enacted into law since then and are now commonplaces of our own time. Among them we may mention the establishment of Postal Savings Banks, restriction of immigration, a graduated income tax, and the popular election of senators.

THE RE-ELECTION OF CLEVELAND

Although the record of the Republicans appeared to give the Democrats an excellent chance to win, the outcome of the election was considered to be far more doubtful than it should have been. For this reason, in a number of States, such as Colorado, Idaho, Kansas, North Dakota, and Wyoming, the Democrats fused with the Populists, and in the South the Populists fused with the Democrats, so that it is impossible to judge of the real strength of either as shown by the figures, inaccurate in any case, of the popular vote. The campaign,

37

which was a rather dull and quiet one, resulted, however, in an overwhelming victory for Cleveland, who secured 277 electoral votes to Harrison's 145 and Weaver's 22. In the popular vote the figures were approximately, Cleveland 5,566,000, Harrison 5,175,000, and Weaver 1,040,000.

On Cleveland's second accession to office, his position was at once strong and weak. In the House of Representatives his party numbered 220 against only 126 Republicans and 8 Populists, but on the other hand there was scarcely a move he could make which would not disgruntle a large part of the people. That the Republicans would be bitterly hostile to tariff revision in itself and to everything which he did as a Democrat was, of course, a foregone conclusion. But the condition of the currency and finances demanded immediate action with regard to silver, and that would be almost equally displeasing to many of his own party and to the Populists to whom, in part, he owed his election. If he did his duty wisely, it would seem that his doing so would inevitably alienate him from what, with the rising tide of Populism, would, unfortunately but probably, be the main currents of thought in the nation's opposition to the Toryism of the Republicans.

The Cabinet members whom he chose for advisers formed a strong group, among them being John G. Carlisle at the Treasury, Daniel S. Lamont in the War Department, and Richard Olney as Attorney-General.

38

The chief position, that of Secretary of State, went to Judge Walter Q. Gresham, until recently a Republican. It was Cleveland himself, however, who throughout his second term dominated the policies of the administration.

The President was at once confronted with an alarming situation which he had inherited from Republican rule. Well before he assumed office the folly of the Sherman Silver Act of 1890 had made itself evident. In the national currency there were the $346,000,000 of paper money, the old "greenbacks." By early summer under the Sherman Act the government had already been obliged to buy $147,000,000 of silver, of which over $135,000,000 had gone into circulation as silver notes, and there were also, under the Bland Act, $328,226,000 as Treasury notes. We have already mentioned the hoarding of gold and the failure to pay customs duties in that metal under Harrison.

At the same time that the Treasury had been accumulating the $147,000,000 of silver, each "dollar" of which was worth only about 60 cents in gold, the amount of the latter metal in the Treasury's possession had been lessened by $132,000,000. Against the combined total of $809,716,000 of paper and depreciated silver, the government had tried to keep a gold reserve, for exchange on demand, of $100,000,000. Just before the end of Harrison's term, this amount was threatened with impairment, and the Republicans had made preparations to issue bonds to buy gold, but New York bankers came to the rescue, and Harrison left Cleveland just a trifle over the $100,000,000 when the latter came in.

The "endless chain," however, was working rapidly. Greenbacks could be presented for payment in gold. Then the government was forced to reissue them again, and the next holder could again present them for gold. Also, the purchase of $54,000,000 a year of depreciated silver had to continue. People both in America and abroad had become frightened at the probability that the government would not be able to continue to pay in gold, and the more frightened they became, the more gold they demanded. Clearly a step of the first importance was to repeal the Sherman Purchase Act. The danger to the country, as many could see, was great. There was another which was not guessed at the time.

Cleveland could be counted on to defend the gold standard, but the Vice-President, Stevenson, was a silverite. Just before Cleveland's inauguration, the Philadelphia & Reading Railroad had failed. Toward the end of April, the government reserve fell below $100,000,-000. A week or so later came a devastating panic, initiated by the failure of the great National Cordage Company, followed within a few weeks by a great number of banks and important commercial concerns. On June 30 the President sent out a call for a special session of Congress to repeal the Sherman Act, but, for reasons not then understood, it was not to meet until August 5.

The unknown reason was that the President was in danger of his life from the development of a cancer on the roof of his mouth, and a critical operation was immediately essential. On the day he issued the call for Congress, he went aboard E. C. Benedict's yacht in New York harbor to undergo the operation in complete secrecy. With a Vice-President who believed in free silver, the nation faced bankruptcy if Cleveland died, and the truth could not be told or the panic already raging would have become instant destruction. Fortunately the surgeons were successful, and it was not until many years later that the nation knew how critical that June 30 had been.

In the message which Cleveland sent to Congress he clearly stated the situation into which the Sherman Act had brought us, and demanded its repeal after "the ordeal of three years' disastrous experience." With the aid of about 100 Republicans—a large part of the President's own party voting against the measure—repeal passed in the House by 239 to 108, the most determined and eloquent opponent of the President being a young congressman named William J. Bryan. In the Senate, the Democrats were equally divided for and against, but there also the bill was passed with Republican help, and on November 1 was signed by Cleveland.

Meanwhile the panic was raging. The Erie Railroad had defaulted on July 25, and the number of commercial failures in 1893 was three times as large as in 1873 with liabilities half again as great. Among financial institutions, 158 national banks failed (almost all of them in the West and South), 172 State banks, 177 private banks, 47 savings banks, 13 trust companies, and 16 mortgage companies. Recovery did not begin until 1895, and in the meantime the Atchison, Union Pacific, Northern Pacific, and other roads, great and small, had followed the Reading and Erie into receiverships until 169 of them, with a mileage of 37,855 miles and a capitalization of over $2,400,000,000, were bankrupt. Union Pacific stock sold at $4 a share, Northern Pacific at 25 cents, and the stockholders of both were assessed $15 a share for the privilege of participating in the reorganization. The nation seemed prostrate, and unemployment and labor troubles were universal.

Bands of workless men wandered about the country, and one of these, under the lead of a certain Jacob Coxey of Ohio, gave the nation a genuine thrill of terror by marching from that State to Washington early in 1894 to demand, among other things, that the government at once issue a half-billion of paper money. This episode ended in a farcical anticlimax when the remnant of the "army" which reached Washington was quietly arrested for not "keeping off the grass" of the White House grounds!

LABOR TROUBLES

The grievances of labor, however, were deep and real, as were its sufferings, and in 1894 about 750,000 workmen were involved in disturbances of one sort or another. In the early summer the panic was punctuated by one of the most serious and important strikes the country has known. George M. Pullman, head of the Pullman Palace Car Company, was a "hard-boiled" example of the type of the great business magnate then in economic power. He had built a town, Pullman, in which his workmen were to be housed in "model" dwellings. The men felt constrained to dwell there whether they wished to or not, and the philanthropic corporation charged from twenty to twenty-five per cent higher rents than the workmen could find comfortable houses for elsewhere. In May, 1894, the company cut wages twenty per cent, although salaries were untouched, and the grievances of the men were treated with brutal indifference. On the 11th a strike at the shops began, without violence.

Two months earlier, many Pullman men had joined the American Railway Union. In June the Union threatened to go on strike also, and to stop moving any trains with Pullman cars attached unless the company would arbitrate with its men. This it refused point-blank to do, although the mayors of about fifty cities urged Mr. Pullman in fairness to consent. Eugene V. Debs, head of the Railway Union, gave orders to start a railway strike on June 26, and to avoid all violence. The governor of Illinois was John P. Altgeld, whose name was anathema to the larger business interests, partly on account of his support of those trying to get better laws regulating factories and largely because, on reviewing the case of the anarchists still confined in jail for the Haymarket affair of 1886, he had decided they were innocent and had pardoned them.

The Haymarket riot had been one of the sporadic outbreaks of violence in its period, but bomb-throwing was new to America, and the word anarchist sent a shudder down every one's spine. The public had been in much the same state of nervous terror as it was to be later over the "reds" at the time of the Sacco-Vanzetti case after the World War, and although some men were undoubtedly guilty (four were condemned and hanged), the best opinion today supports Altgeld in his conclusion that those whom he pardoned in 1894 were innocent of the crime alleged against them. Altgeld, however, was denounced with extreme rancor and was considered by business men as an enemy of society.

In fact, Altgeld, although strongly in favor of a square deal for labor, was a conscientious public officer who was prepared to maintain law and order, who posted State militia where called for, and had a force in Chicago. How violence began in the strike, which soon spread over a large territory, it is impossible to say. As in the Homestead strike, the employers,—in this case the Railway Managers' Association,—engaged their own guards, selecting and paying for 3600 deputy marshals, and the larger business interests were anxious not only to see the

44

MISS JESSIE COUTHOUI READING "THE PROPHECY, 1492"

The opening of the World's Fair, Chicago, May 11, 1893. Immediately behind her is President Cleveland.

ADMINISTRATION BUILDING, WORLD'S FAIR, ON CHICAGO DAY

BOUND DOWN THE RIVER.

RIVER TRAVEL IN 1870

A Currier and Ives lithograph in the Library of Congress.

strike broken with discredit to the men but also to take
revenge on Altgeld. Chicago, full of lawless characters,
and especially so with the riff-raff left over after the
World's Fair which had ended a few months before,
offered ample opportunity at the moment for a flare-up
of any sort.

Although the railway men had obeyed Debs's orders
to keep the peace, violence suddenly broke out, and there
was mobbing and destruction of railroad and other property on a large scale. The worst of this occurred after
the Federal Government had obtained an injunction
from the courts forbidding any one to interfere with the
moving of trains and the transportation of the United
States' mails. This had been done by Olney, the over-
bearing Attorney-General who had appointed a railway
attorney as special counsel for the government. Cleveland himself, sensing in the case only the maintenance
of law and order, backed Olney, and made his famous
pronouncement that he would see that the mails were
carried if it took every soldier in the army and every
dollar in the Treasury to deliver a single postcard in
Chicago. Federal troops were sent to that city and after
their arrival on July 4 there were serious clashes with
the mobs. Debs and three other labor leaders were arrested for conspiring to restrain trade, and were tried
for contempt of court in disobeying the injunction.
When the president of the American Railway Union
had been sent to prison for six months, the strike col-
lapsed.

45

Altgeld had protested against the sending of Federal troops into a State against the wishes of its governing authorities, claiming that there was nothing left of the Constitution if the President on his own initiative could interfere with the internal affairs of a State by the use of the United States Army. Cleveland was honest in his intentions but had it been only a question of transporting mails, mails were not carried in Pullman cars, and trains carrying mail only could probably have been run without interference. That was not tried, and by the use of the injunction and Federal troops, the whole power of the national government was thrown on the side of Pullman and the railway owners to break the strike. The employees had a sound case, and at first public opinion was with them. They had offered to arbitrate their grievances, and it had been the obstinate injustice of Pullman which had brought about a situation in which many lives were sacrificed, about $80,000,000 in property and wages lost, and an extremely ugly feeling engendered between capital and labor.

The use of the injunction was declared legal soon after by the Federal Supreme Court in an amazing decision, and the owners of property were thus given an enormously powerful weapon in labor disputes. The strike was a landmark in the rising tide of opposition to wealth and "big business" among the laboring class.

Another incident, which seemed to indicate to the farmers and workmen that the Federal Government, including the Supreme Court itself, was on the side of the rich and against the poor, had arisen in connection with the effort of the administration to redeem its campaign pledge and reform the tariff. In the Wilson Tariff Bill, passed by a very large majority in the House, duties had been materially reduced and many articles put back on the free list. As usual, it met its end in the Senate, where a handful of senators forced over 600 amendments to be added, making a less well-balanced measure with scarcely lower duties than that which Representative McKinley had sponsored in the previous administration of Harrison.

Cleveland, disgusted with the bill, which special interests had completely wrecked by their selfish demands and trading of votes with each other, allowed it to become a law without his signature. As a sop to the increasing discontent of the country there had been added to the bill a clause levying an income tax of 2 per cent on all incomes over $4000. But here again the Supreme Court intervened, and, as it seemed to the people at large, on the side of wealth. Although that tribunal had decided by a unanimous vote fifteen years earlier that an income tax was constitutional, it now decided, in the case of Pollock *vs*. Farmers' Loan & Trust Company, that such a tax was unconstitutional as being "direct."

The three facts, that a previous unanimous decision was reversed, that it was now decided by a vote of five to four, and that one of the justices had changed his vote at the last moment, not only made it appear that the court had changed to the side of capital but lessened also the public respect for its decision, which appeared to be based not on legal principles but on prejudice or political views.

DEPRESSION AND PANIC

Meanwhile no improvement in business had appeared, and the depression continued throughout the country, with the usual increasing hopelessness and decreasing confidence. Everything that Cleveland had done had been unpopular, and in 1894 the Congressional elections went heavily in favor of the Republicans. The bad business conditions alone would have accounted for an overturn, and they had been getting worse even before the election.

The drain on the gold in the Treasury, for which the Republicans, and not Cleveland, had been to blame, continued with increasing menace to the reserves. By January, 1894, these had dwindled to $70,000,000 instead of the customary $100,000,000. The Treasury sold $50,-000,000 of government bonds at a price of about 117, thus securing somewhat over $58,660,000, but the "endless chain" was still working and by November the reserve was down again to less than $62,000,000. The sale of another $50,000,000 was of no permanent avail. In the year 1894, over $172,000,000 in gold had been withdrawn against only $117,000,000 gained by the bond issue.

PROHIBITION PROPAGANDA OF 1895

This temperance poem would seem to have been very much in the spirit of an even earlier day.

THE ORIGINAL "COXEY'S ARMY"

A cartoon by W. A. Rogers showing the public's belief in Government favoritism of special interests.

From "Harper's Weekly," May 12, 1894.

Issuing bonds while Treasury notes could be handed in to the Treasury to be paid in gold, and then, having been re-issued according to the requirements of the law, be presented again for more gold, was obviously pouring precious liquid into a vessel which was leaking faster than it could be filled. As lack of confidence in the government's ability to keep up this game increased, the game itself went on with accelerated swiftness. In February, 1895, the reserve was down to $41,000,000.

On the 7th of that month, Cleveland had an interview in the White House with J. P. Morgan, the leading banker of the country. Merely to issue another block of bonds as the President had done before would be futile. He had asked Congress to pass a law by which the Treasury notes when presented and paid in gold could be cancelled instead of being re-issued. Congress had refused. The President now arranged with a syndicate headed by the Morgan firm to sell to them bonds to the extent of about $62,300,000 at a premium of four and one-half per cent, which the syndicate re-sold to the public at 118.

A howl of rage went up from the country, and the President was accused of having sold the country to Wall Street. There is no question, however, that he was justified. The syndicate had done more than buy the bonds. By their management of the gold market and foreign exchange they stopped, for a while, the "endless chain," which Congress had refused to stop. They made a loss on their own business to keep gold from flowing to Europe, as called for by the rate of exchange. They provided the government with $15,000,000 more gold than they had agreed to.

Confidence slowly came back, and in January, 1896, when $100,000,000 more was needed, and the last bond issue was floated, it could be offered directly to the public and was taken at a premium of over eleven points. Much gold was still hoarded by the people but the danger had passed. Nevertheless, Cleveland had scarcely a political friend left. The Republicans, who had done their best to ruin the country by refusing to assist him, hated him for his action. The rank and file of his own party, who were growing more and more opposed to gold and Wall Street, were as hostile to him as were the Republicans. Few men who have rendered so great a service to their country have been so bitterly reviled for it.

Among Cleveland's outstanding characteristics were independence, honesty, and courage, but he had nothing of the jingo in his make-up, which renders it somewhat difficult to understand the famous sally into international affairs which he made toward the end of his term. Detesting imperialism and the "big stick" methods with which we were to become familiar later, he had blocked the attempt to annex Hawaii which had started under Harrison. Indeed, the treaty of annexation of the new Hawaiian Republic, which had been prepared for submission to the Senate by the previous administration, was pigeon-holed by Cleveland because he felt that we had not been honest in so far as we had helped to foment trouble in the islands for our own ultimate benefit.

In another and more important affair, however, he

PUBLIC APPROVAL OF CLEVELAND'S ATTITUDE TOWARD JINGOISM
From a cartoon from "The Evening Telegram" in the Library of Congress.

was to wield the big stick with a vengeance, and gain, for a moment, the applause of even such Republican imperialists as Roosevelt and Lodge. In South America, the British colony of Guiana lay next to the republic of Venezuela, and for decades a boundary dispute had been dragging its weary length. At Venezuela's request we had offered to mediate in 1887, but England had declined to accept our offices. The Venezuelan claims were too sweeping to be justified, but, on the other hand, there were somewhat delicate questions involved, in view of our assertion of the Monroe Doctrine, in allowing a European nation to enforce demands for a considerable extension of its own territory on the American continent.

The Doctrine, of course, was mere assertion on our part and had no place in international law. Bismarck had in fact referred to it as an "international impertinence," and the only sanction it might possess would be our physical power to enforce it. In 1895 our navy did not include a single first-class battleship. Cleveland wished to have the Anglo-Venezuelan dispute settled by arbitration, but having failed in that in the spring of 1895 there is no entirely satisfactory reason known for his allowing Olney, the Secretary of State, to dispatch such a note to the British Government as would almost certainly have brought on war between any other two nations.

Olney brusquely demanded a settlement of the Venezuelan dispute which should be satisfactory to us, and claimed our right to intervene. After a long and somewhat erroneous interpretation of what the Monroe Doctrine was intended to be, the Secretary indulged in some extraordinarily brutal jingoism. "Today," he wrote to Lord Salisbury, "the United States is practically sover-

eign on this continent, and its fiat is law upon the subjects to which it confines its interposition. Why? It is
not because of the pure friendship or good will felt for
it. It is not simply by reason of its high character as a
civilized state, nor because wisdom and justice and equity
are the invariable characteristics of the dealings of the
United States. It is because, in addition to all other
grounds, its infinite resources combined with its isolated
position render it master of the situation and practically
invulnerable as against any or all other powers."

Such an extraordinary challenge would have involved
us in war with England, whose naval power at that time
was about five to one as compared with ours, had it not
been that England genuinely wished to keep the peace
with us. Salisbury did not reply for four months, and
our own public was not aware of the seriousness of the
situation until Cleveland submitted all the correspondence to Congress in December, with a war-like message.
There was almost a panic in Wall Street, and general
consternation in both countries.

Fortunately, to the sane public opinion in each of them
it appeared to be the height of criminal folly to bring
on war between the United States and the British Empire over a minor imperial boundary dispute. Luckily,
also, at the beginning of January, the German Emperor
sent his famous telegram to old Kruger in South Africa
congratulating him on having captured the Englishman
Doctor Jameson, and this insult, as it was considered,

offered to England by the Kaiser, acted as a lightning-rod to ground some of the very natural anger felt against the United States.

In his message to Congress, the President had asked for the appointment of an American commission to determine for ourselves the boundary in dispute, after which the force of the United States was to be pledged to keep England from advancing beyond such a line as we should determine. England, of course, could not consent to that, but after a good deal of diplomacy and a marked show of friendliness by leading English statesmen, the whole question was finally submitted to arbitration, as a result of which most of England's claims were conceded.

The episode undoubtedly brought to the attention of Europe with startling suddenness the fact that the United States was no longer a fourth-rate and negligible power, but this was accomplished at terrific risk and by our assuming a position that was not logically tenable. Fortunately it also brought to light the very strong feeling in both countries against their ever again engaging in war for any reason whatever if there were any other way out. That was probably the most valuable by-product of the incident. In a few years England was to have her energies absorbed by her war in South Africa, and we were to have our thoughts forced into wholly new channels by our war with Spain and all the results flowing from it. The whole affair of Venezuela and Olney's jingoism left much less lasting impression than might have been expected, but the lurid danger which played over the destinies of both peoples for some months was more or less in accord with the whole of the stormy period of Cleveland's second term.

CHAPTER II

THE REPUBLIC BECOMES AN EMPIRE

THE year 1896 was a peculiarly interesting one from many standpoints, and from none more so than that of studying the relation between politicians and the unknown laws or accidents of the universe. Cleveland, by his strength and honesty, had antagonized almost every interest and prejudice of his followers and opponents. In time his reputation among both was to be raised high, there being, perhaps, no better touchstone for it than the contemporary and subsequent opinions of such a bitter Republican partisan as Senator Lodge. Writing in 1897 to Roosevelt, Lodge "took a kind of grim satisfaction," as he said, in noting that to the very end (in his veto of an immigration bill) Cleveland had continued "to injure the country as much as he could." Many years later Lodge wrote, in comment on this remark of his own, that he had become "very certain" that Cleveland "was not only a strong but an honest man and thoroughly American."

But in 1896 the President was reviled on all sides, and had got hopelessly out of touch with his own party on account of his defense of the gold standard. The two important questions in the campaign of that year were to be prosperity and free silver, with the tariff as a subsidiary one. The irony of the situation was that prosperity was returning in any case, and that free silver was almost at once to lose importance as an issue, both

THE FREE TRADE BIRD BUILT ITS NEST ON EVERY CHIMNEY
A Republican National Committee cartoon, by Leon Barritt, used in 1904.

of these happenings coming from causes with which parties and platforms had nothing to do.

Periods of business depression come in cycles of about twenty years, and that which was due in the early nineties had run its course by 1896, recovery being ensured by Cleveland's stopping the operation of the "endless chain." Prosperity had begun to return before the campaign in the fall of that year, and, although no one knew it, the nation was at the beginning of the greatest period of speculation and business advance it had yet experienced.

Apart from the recovery which might have been anticipated from the law of cycles, there was to be another factor operative which was greatly to increase business, expand credit, and for forty years to lay the ghost of the silver menace. This was the discovery in several parts of the world of immense and hitherto unknown deposits of gold. For the twenty years preceding 1891 the world production of that metal had never again reached the figure of 6,270,000 ounces mined in 1870, and in five of the years had been well below 5,000,000 ounces. This had been one of the causes, if not the leading one, in making the low prices for agricultural and other products, and thus of much of the hardships suffered by primary producers and debtors. From 1891, however, the annual gold production began to rise. There was a big jump in 1897 to 11,420,000 ounces and by 1912 it had reached 22,600,000.

THE CAMPAIGN OF 1896

As there were no great wars in the period, practically all of this enormous increase was available for the needs of normal business, and consequently resulted in a general rise in prices. The tremendous political fight for free silver approaching in 1896 was thus staged just at the very moment when underproduction of gold was ceasing to be a menace to the classes which feared it. The Democratic Party repudiated Cleveland on what was for many decades thereafter to be merely an academic question.

But there was nothing academic about it in the campaign of 1896. The fact is that by that year the question of the gold standard had become infinitely more than a problem in economic theory. Gold had become the symbol in the eyes of vast numbers of our people of the "money power," of Wall Street, of a plutocracy riding rough-shod over the happiness and rights of the ordinary man. At the centre of the vast wave of emotion which was to overtake the nation and make the campaign almost a religious crusade, there was, however, the fact that the failure of the gold supply to keep pace with expanding commercial needs had in truth been in large part the cause of low prices and of the troubles of the farmers South and West.

There was also the other truth that the common man was not getting what Roosevelt later called the "square deal" from his government. The Republican Party, being that of the bankers, manufacturers, other business magnates and of wealth in general, was particularly vulnerable to suspicion and attack on that score. It seemed as though the rich and powerful could get any favor wanted, whereas both in Congress and the courts the ordinary man believed his interests were increasingly sacrificed. There were great cancers of corruption in the Democratic Party also, such as Tammany Hall in New York City, but Croker was no worse than the Republican Boss Platt, and the ordinary people of the country believed rightly that, whether wisely or not, the Republican Party laid more stress on the rights of property whereas the Democrats laid it on the rights of man, and that that broad distinction had been true from the days of Hamilton and Jefferson.

We must not be blinded by the gold issue in the campaign of 1896 to what the real issue was. That was, in the opinion of many millions who voted for Bryan, precisely what we have stated, a belief that the candidate stood for the rights of the plain man as against the powers of a plutocracy which was threatening to make the plain man a slave and the government a mere machine for increasing the wealth of its plutocratic controllers.

As we have said before, a nation to progress sanely and safely requires both a conservative and a liberal party of more or less equal strength and ability, just as society needs both the counsel of age and the optimistic courage of youth. Unfortunately we in the United States have suffered from having only a conservative party which has tended to run constantly to special privilege for its supporters, and a liberal party which has been wanting in the broad-minded leadership which would keep it from running after all sorts of "isms."

The situation in 1896 was interesting in this regard. Twice before, in 1800 under Jefferson, and in 1828 under Jackson, the democratic elements in the population had risen and won. They were to fail in 1896 in spite of a tremendous fight. They were to do so in large part because they fought for their cause under the symbol of a wrong and dangerous idea, that of free coinage of silver. The campaign showed that there was tremendous resentment against what we may call the conservatives and their theories of economic and social government, but the rank and file of the liberals were largely ignorant and there was not a sufficient leaven of wise leaders in the party to keep it straight.

This lack of sound leadership has been an extremely serious one for liberalism in America. By leadership I do not mean merely a few outstanding national figures, but men in all communities and in all ranks of life who adopt the liberal attitude. To a considerable extent our lack of such leadership and of an intellectually sound liberal tradition may have come about from the fact that to a degree not known in any other country we are business men and our ablest men tend to be great business leaders or associated with business on a large scale.

Two results have come from this. Large-scale business, and this was particularly true of the era on which our story is now entering, demands a government from which it can get favors and which will be amenable to it. Secondly, as a rule, the successful business man is extremely conservative and fearful of trying anything politically that may in the slightest endanger his position. By the time we have now reached, not only were a preponderant number of the ablest and most powerful men in the nation heads or owners of great business concerns—railroads, banks, manufacturing, and other enterprises—but in law and some of the other professions the ablest men were drawn into close alliance with what was coming to be known as "big business."

It is all too easy for any class, as we have learned from the experience with socialistic as well as plutocratic governments, to think of national welfare in terms of what affects their personal power and profit. Joseph H. Choate, for example, was an able and honest man as well as one of the leading lawyers of this period, yet he could denounce the attempt of the Democrats to enact an income-tax law as "anarchy." Almost any law which threatened the profits or entire freedom of action of the magnates was considered by them, and probably in good faith, as extremely dangerous radicalism, whereas the people at large merely saw the Republican Party as providing all sorts of favors to the magnates and blocking reforms which might help lesser men.

Nor were the people wrong. There had in truth grown up a combination of the ruthless and unsocial-minded big business men with the dishonest political bosses which seemed too strong for honest men to struggle against. Writing to Lodge in 1897, Roosevelt, who was as strong a Republican partisan as ever lived, said, "The ugly feature in the Republican canvass is that it *does* represent exactly what the Populists say, that is corrupt wealth. The Pierpont Morgan type of men forced Fitch on the ticket; and both Platt and Tracy represent the powerful, unscrupulous politicians who charge heavily

SKETCHES MADE AT THE "POPS" CONVENTION IN ST. LOUIS IN 1896, FOR *THE CHICAGO JOURNAL*

From the Library of Congress.

for doing the work, sometimes good, sometimes bad, of the bankers, railroad men, insurance men, and the like." If a Republican like Roosevelt could write in confidence in that way to a Republican like Lodge, it is easy to understand the rising resentment of the ordinary citizen.

How thoroughly entrenched the system was may be seen from the necessity which even Roosevelt found himself under of working with the corrupt bosses whom he denounced in private. In 1895 he wrote, again confidentially, that "Platt's influence is simply poisonous. I cannot go in with him; no honest man of sincerity can." Yet three years later when Roosevelt was running for Governor of New York he wrote to the same correspondent that "Senator Platt and Congressman Odell are doing all they can for me, and I could not wish the canvass to be in better hands"! It is needless to say that the ordinary Democratic politician was no better, and where, from local conditions, a Democratic boss had become firmly established, big business dealt with him or his henchmen just as readily as with the Republicans of the same stripe.

There was, however, a marked difference between the parties. The Republican was that of the rich men and the Democratic that of the poor. This had its evil effects on both. Any class, as we have said, tends to look at affairs through the lens of its own self-interest, and the world is rapidly increasing in complexity, especially economically. If the plutocrats had too little interest in the larger social implications of what they were doing, so the small men—farmers, laborers, factory employees —although they recognized the social injustice about them, had too little knowledge of the complex forces which were operative in society, and were too easily captured by false doctrines.

In Cleveland, the Democracy had had a sound leader, but aside from the fact that he had already run for President three times, he was considered too subservient to high finance to be longer acceptable to the people at large. During 1895 and early 1896 the young Congressman Bryan, who had opposed Cleveland's stand on gold, had been going up and down the country preaching his economic doctrines. Also a little book on free silver, by W. H. Harvey, called *Coin's Financial School,* had been selling at the rate of 100,000 copies a month.

ONE OF THE ILLUSTRATIONS FROM *COIN'S FINANCIAL SCHOOL*
ON THE RISING VALUE OF THE DOLLAR

Bryan's views on gold and silver were as erroneous as those of Harvey, but it is a mistake to think of the young orator whose voice and appearance won him literally millions of devoted admirers as a mere spell-binder or demagogue. Now that the passions of the day have faded somewhat it is possible to appraise him more fairly, and I think it may be said that few men in public life have been guided more consistently in all their actions by morality as they have seen it or by a more genuine desire to serve the people. Unfortunately, he had an almost unbelievably restricted mind. Starting with a certain stock of ideas, many of them erroneous, he scarcely grew at all mentally during a long public career. Unluckily, the ideas which he had were those of millions of his fellow-countrymen, and his very possession of them seemed to his followers to make him an ideal leader as being one of themselves.

In some respects, on the other hand, he was broader-minded than any of his Presidential opponents during that career except Roosevelt. He cannot be very heavily blamed for his advocacy of free silver in 1896, for he had distinguished company. William McKinley, who was to be the Republican candidate, was himself a free-silverite, as were also such Easterners of distinction as Brooks and Henry Adams and E. Benjamin Andrews, the president of Brown University. But Bryan saw something more in the campaign than silver, and it was precisely that "something more" which most Republican leaders, except Roosevelt, refused to see, and which maintained Bryan's hold on the public for a score or so of years.

In one of his speeches he clearly stated that "this is not a contest for the supremacy of one of two metals—it is not a miners' campaign." The fight, he added, was to save the American people from being "dominated by the financial harpies of Wall Street . . . to make money the *servant* of industry, to dethrone it from the false position it has usurped as master." This he believed could be done only by preventing the continued fall in prices due to the gold standard and the scarcity of gold, and by fighting the increasing concentration of wealth in the hands of the few who manipulated business, the currency, and the government for their own benefit. In another decade,

MISS DEMOCRACY IN A QUANDARY AS TO WHICH WAY TO GO
BEFORE THE 1896 CONVENTION
A cartoon in "The New York Advertiser."

Roosevelt was to fight the corrupt power of wealth with greater wisdom, and in 1931, with the world again overwhelmed with debts, personal and international, the gold question was again to come to the fore.

The party conflicts in the 1896 campaign were unusually complicated. The Prohibition Party, which was the first to hold its convention, split into two factions, each putting a ticket in the field. The Republicans, meeting at St. Louis on June 16, nominated McKinley on the first ballot, with Garret A. Hobart of New Jersey as Vice-President. Platforms are not very important usually in American campaigns but in this year they proved so. Not only McKinley himself but a considerable wing of the Republicans had been for free silver, and although all delegates could unite in proclaiming that the business depression had been due solely to the Democrats; that the reduction in pensions deserved the "severest condemnation"; that America sympathized with the Armenians and the Cubans; that the Monroe Doctrine should be upheld; and the rest of the usual bunkum, there was a real struggle over the money plank.

The candidate himself became converted to the gold standard, and the platform declared that all money must be maintained on a parity wth gold, but a sop was thrown to the silverites by adding the phrase "except by international agreement with the leading commercial nations." The gold Republicans felt themselves safe, for, although they pledged themselves to promote such an agreement as might permit the free coinage of silver, they knew perfectly well that no such international agreement could be made. The silverites considered the concession as of no value and after 110 had voted against the plank, without avail, 34, including 4 Republican members of the United States Senate, bolted the convention and withdrew, most of them going over to the Democrats.

The latter held their convention at Chicago on July 7,

where a fierce fight took place over the money question, the national committee being in the control of the gold Democrats whereas the majority of the delegates were for silver. It soon became evident that the silverites would have things their own way, and when Bryan made his famous speech (much of which he had often delivered before) the convention was in a frenzy.

Pleading for the little business man, the farmer, the country-store-keeper, the wage-earner, as against the big business man, Bryan claimed that he spoke in their name. "We have petitioned," he said, "and our petitions have been scorned. We have entreated, and our entreaties have been disregarded. We have begged, and they have mocked when our calamity came. We beg no longer; we entreat no more; we petition no more; we defy them!" In his peroration he repeated a phrase of his congressional speech which had attracted little attention when first used but which was now to stir the whole nation. "Having behind us the producing masses of this nation and the world, supported by the commercial interests, the laboring interests, and the toilers everywhere, we will answer their demand for a gold standard by saying to them: 'You shall not press down upon the brow of labor this crown of thorns—you shall not crucify mankind upon a cross of gold.'" The wildest excitement seized the delegates.

In the platform as finally adopted the convention came out squarely for free and unlimited coinage of silver, declared the money question the paramount one in the campaign, and refused to pass the usual vote endorsing the administration of the retiring President. On the fifth ballot Bryan was nominated for the office, with Arthur Sewall, a rich free-silverite of Maine, as running-mate.

Almost immediately the gold Democrats, who felt they could neither vote for Bryan nor turn Republican, organized the National Democratic Party, which on a platform declaring for sound money put another ticket in the field with John M. Palmer and General S. B. Buckner as candidates. Meanwhile both the People's Party and the National Silver Party had also held conventions, both endorsing free silver and the nomination of Bryan.

The ensuing campaign was an extraordinary one, perhaps best described by Mrs. Lodge, the wife of the Republican senator, in a letter to Sir Cecil Spring-Rice. Immediately after the result was known she wrote: "The great fight is won and a fight conducted by trained and experienced and organized forces, with both hands full of money, with the full power of the press—and of prestige—on the one side; on the other, a disorganized mob at first, out of which burst into sight, hearing and force —one man, but such a man! Alone, penniless, without backing, without money, with scarce a paper, without speakers, that man fought such a fight that even those in the East can call him a Crusader, an inspired fanatic, a prophet! It has been marvellous. . . . We acknowledge to $7,000,000 campaign fund against his $300,000. We had during the last week of the campaign 18,000 speakers on the stump. He alone spoke for his party. . . . It is over now but the vote is 7,000,000 to 6,500,000."

The Republicans had indeed had the money. Marcus Alonzo Hanna, the Ohio iron magnate who was responsible for McKinley's nomination, had seen to that. Ordinary business men and the great corporations were properly frightened at the possibility of a debased currency, and their fright was easily coined into campaign contributions. Much of the vast sum collected was spent honestly and it was estimated that the Republicans distributed a quarter of a billion of pamphlets and other printed matter in a score of languages to educate the voter. Much was also spent dishonestly, as it always is. Speaking of the primary elections in New York in February, Roosevelt had confided to Lodge that the Republican frauds were "so unblushing as to be comic. On examining the rolls of their voters there were found over 600 from vacant lots, from houses where no such men lived, from houses of ill fame, and the like. . . . In certain streets the Platt people simply took the names on the signs of all the shops along the streets and voted under them right in order." Such a large number of decent men were disgusted, he wrote, that it is "pretty difficult for me to keep them from bolting."

It is evident that $7,000,000 thrown into that sort of politics might be very effective. Other methods of influence were used. Farmers were offered a five-year renewal of mortgages on easy terms if McKinley were elected. Factory hands were paid off the day before election with the notice that there would be no further work for them if Bryan won. He did not, although so great was the polling owing to public interest, and so great was his own popularity and that of the fight he was making against corrupt wealth, that he polled almost 1,000,000 more votes than Cleveland had four years before, and was beaten by about 600,000, the vote being approximately 7,110,000 to 6,510,000.

THE ELECTION OF McKINLEY

The fervor which Byran aroused, comparable only to that of the old religious revivals, and the huge vote he polled, not only among Western farmers but Eastern industrial workers, were not in the last analysis mere endorsements of free silver. That indeed became, and properly, the foremost issue in the campaign, and with a party committed to it, it would have been a calamity for the country had Bryan been elected. But the great uprising under Bryan was an uprising against the growing injustices, as the ordinary American saw them, of the combined economic and political system as it was then developing. Free silver was merely the weapon he had unwisely been taught he could use to bring about reform. He sensed in Bryan his genuine moral fervor and his devotion to the ordinary man.

Unfortunately these cannot balance intellectual errors,

and of those in Bryan's teaching the ordinary man was unaware. Also, unfortunately, however, Bryan's opponents, who should have sensed the real issue, did not do so. They were content to call him an "anarchist" and point to his economic heresies. It was not until nearly a decade later that Roosevelt took up the same fight as Bryan had fought, and became almost as much hated by his own party as Cleveland had been by his. The campaign of 1896 taught big business and the Republicans generally nothing, and because of their large majority they felt no need to try to remedy abuses.

Back of the new President stood the figure of Hanna, who was to become the symbol of the "trust" and of plutocratic wealth, made familiar to the people through the medium of bitter cartoons. Hanna, who had backed McKinley for years and was genuinely devoted to him, was typical of both the best and the worst of the new business leaders. In personal intercourse he was kindly and loyal. He treated his employees well and was liked by them. He did not consider himself corrupt and that he did not do so was in itself one of the best indices of the outlook of big business of his day. A strong-willed, self-made man, "neither very far-sighted nor very broad-minded," as Roosevelt said, he was imperious and autocratic. There was no difference between his business ideals and methods and his political. In business when he wanted to control an enterprise he manœuvred and bought it, and when he wanted the votes of the public or a legislature he bought them in precisely the same way. If he was acquiring a street railway, he apparently saw no difference between buying the stock from one set of people and a favorable franchise and legislation from

BRYAN—"A SUGGESTION FOR THE 53-CENT DOLLAR"
From a cartoon in "The New York Press."

another set. Yet on the whole he stands out very favorably among the crowd of similar magnates in that period.

McKinley wished to have him in his Cabinet, but as Hanna preferred the Senate, a deal was concluded by which the venerable John Sherman, also of Ohio, was made Secretary of State, and Hanna elected senator in his place. Sherman, who had had a distinguished career but was now almost senile, was not fit for the post and was soon replaced by William R. Day, who, in turn, in about a year was succeeded by John Hay. Among other Cabinet members were Lyman J. Gage, a Chicago banker, who went to the Treasury, C. N. Bliss, a New York banker, in the Interior Department, Russell A. Alger in the War Department (an unfortunate appointment), and John D. Long in the Navy, with Roosevelt as assistant secretary.

In spite of the fact that the election had been fought and won on the question of the gold standard, legislation in regard to that issue was to be postponed for three years, and McKinley preferred to consider the tariff as paramount. During the campaign he had been proclaimed as "the advance agent of prosperity," and the pernicious practice began (to be raised to its most absurd and disastrous height in the case of Hoover) of regarding the President of the United States not as the head of our government but as the purveyor of prosperity to the business of the nation. The prosperity following 1896 was even less due to McKinley than was the economic débâcle of 1929 due to Hoover.

McKinley's idea of prosperity was a higher tariff, and the administration at once set to work to secure one. The two houses of Congress were Republican and there was little difficulty about passing a bill, though there were the usual log-rolling and tinkering in the Senate. In their platform the Republicans had advanced far beyond their views on protection of even a decade earlier. They had unqualifiedly proclaimed protection to be the foundation of American prosperity and had denounced the repeal of certain reciprocity agreements by the Democrats as "a national calamity." The Dingley Bill, which was now enacted, raised duties to the highest point they had ever reached—an average of approximately 50 per cent, with some duties collected much higher than that, such as 91 per cent on woollen goods, 97 per cent on sugar, and 119 per cent on tobacco. Although some of these would have been reduced by reciprocity agreements with other nations, such agreements were killed in the Senate when introduced. The "interests," as they were beginning to be called, were in the saddle and meant to ride.

Purely economic questions, however, were quickly to be overshadowed by an adventure into world politics that was to change the United States more profoundly than any other single event between the Civil and the World Wars.

THE SPANISH-AMERICAN WAR

Cuba and Porto Rico were the last remaining possessions of Spain in the New World. There had long been unrest in the larger of the islands where the situation was difficult. Much of the capital used in Cuba had been provided by the American and English owners of the sugar estates. Other than the comparatively few American and English residents, the population was made up of some pure-blood Spanish, and a mass of negroes and mixed-bloods, to a great extent illiterate. There was no "public," in the Anglo-Saxon sense, educated and fit for self-government, but there were plenty of the unfortunate type of South Americans who take naturally to political agitation and insurrection.

On the other hand, the government by Spain was inefficient, weak, and venal. In 1895 a new insurrection had broken out, under Maximo Gomez, a Santo Domingan, and General Weyler was sent from Spain to quell it. The "insurrectos" kept up a guerrilla warfare, killing the Spanish from ambush, burning sugar cane and levying tribute on American and English planters, who had to pay the patriots large sums to save their crops, while the Spaniards were not above levying the same tribute for "protection."

Weyler's policy was one of ruthless suppression, and in the course of carrying it out he adopted the plan of gathering the people from certain country districts into "reconcentration camps," leaving him free to deal with the rebels outside. The problem was a difficult one. Owing to the absence of a large organized force of rebels, it was impossible to strike a vital blow at them, most of them being mere civilians who alternately worked when they felt like it and fought when they felt like it. Due partly to the basic impossibility of Weyler's plan, partly to the natural inefficiency of the Spanish authorities, and partly to other causes, there was much suffering among the *reconcentrados* herded into the camps. Sickness and insufficient food took a large toll of life, though the number of deaths, like all else in the situation, was enormously exaggerated for propaganda purposes by the rebels and the American newspapers committed to a war policy.

Near the end of his term, Cleveland had offered to intervene but the offer had been refused by Spain. The President, however, realized that strenuous efforts were being made to embroil us in the affair, even by our own Consul-General, Fitzhugh Lee, and to avoid war Cleveland had asked Frederic R. Coudert, the noted international lawyer, to go on special mission to Spain to try to adjust matters, agreeing to get McKinley's approval, as Cleveland himself had then only a few days more of office. Mr. Coudert declined. Such was the situation when McKinley was inaugurated, with as great and as honest a desire to avoid war as Cleveland had felt.

The United States, however, as well as Cuba, was full of combustible material in 1897. There were four chief factors involved. In the first place there was the genuine idealism, combined with the "under-dog complex" of the great mass of the American public. The average American seldom has very accurate knowledge of conditions in foreign lands or clear notions of the difficulties as well as the abuses, real or seeming, of administration in them, but for reasons already suggested, it is always easy to rouse our sympathy for any people which appears to be struggling for its liberty. We also have a rather naïve belief that all peoples and races are capable of orderly self-government, a belief scarcely lessened at all by our insistence that the Filipinos are not. Emotionally based on an expansive good-nature and our own history, rather than on knowledge or reason, this belief is a force to be reckoned with, and both parties in their 1896 platforms had expressed sympathy with the Cubans, the Republicans throwing in the Armenians also, as we have seen, for good measure.

Moreover, there was at work in New York a Cuban junta of no mean ability which expended much of the money it extorted from the American and English sugar planters under threats of destroying their property, in clever propaganda, doing its best to enlist the sympathy mentioned above.

There were, again, a good many Americans in high places in government or business who desired a war and imperial expansion for their own several ends. For example, powerful business interests were chafing because we did not annex Hawaii. Senator Lodge had his eye on Porto Rico and the Philippines. Assistant Secretary of the Navy Roosevelt was anxious for something to do with his ships. All of these, and others with their own axes to grind, well understood the background of our idealism which could be depended upon.

In the summer of 1897 Roosevelt confided to Lodge that "it would be everything for us to take firm action on behalf of the wretched Cubans. It would be a splendid thing for the Navy, too." After Lodge had been parading the woes of the Cuban patriots in the Senate for a year or so until war came on, he wrote Roosevelt, then in Cuba in the midst of it, "From everything I hear I get a very poor impression of the insurgents, and if you get time I wish you would write me about them." If it had not been that he had helped to plunge the country into war and imperialism for the sake of Porto Rico and the Philippines, rather than for that of the "patriots," this would be rather amazing. One might have expected that the time for the distinguished senator from Massachusetts to find out something about the insurgents was before, and not after, he had done his best to bring the war on in their alleged behalf.

Lastly, there was the newspaper situation. The decade of the nineties saw a great change in journalism. Although there had been "yellow" journalism before, notably due to the efforts of James Gordon Bennett on *The Herald,* it was about 1890 that the format of the modern paper, with big headlines and the attempt to make sensational news of everything from a murder to the stock market, became general, and at that time *The World* and *The Journal* were fighting one another to win as large a following as possible by sensational news and methods among the new reading public.

Prosperity was returning, and failures and strikes as sources of headlines were beginning to disappear. Companies beginning to earn dividends again and men going soberly to work were insignificant news items for selling papers as compared with mobs, and defaults of great railroad and industrial enterprises. The newspapers were

"LITTLE CUBA;"

OR,

CIRCUMSTANTIAL EVIDENCE.

BEING

A TRUE STORY OF LOVE, WAR, AND STARTLING ADVENTURES.

The Massacre of the Young Students!

SHOOTING THE MEN FOUND ON THE AMERICAN SHIP "VIRGINIUS."

SPANISH DEEDS OF BLOOD-CHILLING ATROCITY!

SPANISH CRUELTIES AND INTRIGUE IN CUBA FORMED THE PLOT OF A THRILLER PUBLISHED IN PHILADELPHIA IN 1873
From the Rare Book Room in the Library of Congress.

looking about for something to create excitement. Mr. Pulitzer, owner of *The World,* remarked "that he rather liked the idea of a war—not a big one—but one that would arouse interest and give him a chance to gauge the reflex in circulation figures." Meanwhile Mr. Hearst was making the new public spin like a whipped top with

81

all sorts of sensational and heart-rending stories from Cuba, many of them without the slightest foundation.

Incidentally in the previous decade we had advanced from twelfth to fifth place as a naval power and were rather proud of our new "white squadron," with Roosevelt as anxious to use it as a boy with a new shot-gun.

Such, then, were the conditions:—an idealism in the people at large that could be easily aroused in favor of any people supposed to be oppressed and struggling for freedom; a really bad and difficult situation in Cuba; a group of powerful business men and politicians bent on imperial expansion; a group of newspapers callously searching for sensational news which could be translated into circulation; and a shiny new gun in our hands of which we were proud. A spark thrown into such a collection of combustible material would be bound to cause an explosion.

On June 27, 1897, the old and distinguished Secretary of State, John Sherman, whose unhappy senility was soon to be so grossly manifested as to cause his replacement to become an obvious necessity, sent a note of protest to Spain against Weyler's inhumanity. The Spanish Government replied with a denial, and a hint that Weyler's conduct in Cuba under the necessities of the case was no more inhumane than had been that of the American Secretary of State's brother, General Sherman, on his famous march through Georgia.

If the Cubans were not satisfied with the Spanish Government, neither were many of the Spaniards themselves at home, and soon after the above note was received by the indignant old Secretary, the reactionary Spanish Premier, Canovas, was assassinated and the Liberal Sagasta became head of the government. Weyler in Cuba was replaced by an abler and more humane general, Blanco, and autonomy was promised to the island. Our minister at Madrid, General Stewart L. Woodford, was working hard for peace and affairs looked more hopeful.

However, there were powerful forces that did not want peace. Senator Proctor of Vermont, who had gone to Cuba, painted a lurid picture of conditions there. Our consul-general, who Cleveland had feared would precipitate a war if he could, was sending despatches alarming to our people and demanding the presence of American war-ships at Havana. The newspapers were fanning our idealism and emotions into a blaze which was sending their circulation rapidly mounting. The battle-ship *Maine* was ordered to pay a "friendly visit" to Havana.

Meanwhile, an unfortunate incident had occurred. The Spanish Minister in Washington, Señor Depuy de Lôme, had written a private letter to a friend in Cuba, in which he expressed a very unfavorable opinion of McKinley, as was within his right in personal correspondence. The letter was stolen from the Havana post-office and published both in a Cuban newspaper and in *The New York Journal,* arousing a storm of resentment. His usefulness obviously over, de Lôme at once resigned, though protesting against the publication of a stolen private letter.

The letter had been published on February 9, 1898. Before the public excitement over this incident had had time to cool, on the morning of February 16 the public read in the papers the ghastly news that the previous evening the battle-ship *Maine* had been blown up by an explosion and sunk in Havana harbor with the loss of 260 officers and men.

It has never been satisfactorily determined what caused the explosion. An American board of naval experts examining the sunken hull claimed that the vessel had been blown up from the outside. A Spanish board, who were not allowed to examine the hull but who did examine the bottom of the harbor, determined that the explosion must have been internal. Thirteen years later, the hull was raised and examined afresh by our own naval experts. They decided that the first board had been wrong as to the part of the ship where the explosion had occurred, a majority still claiming, however, that the explosion had been external and a minority that it had been, as the Spaniards claimed, internal. As the ship was then towed out into deep water and sunk, no one can examine her again and the truth will always remain uncertain and the verdict suspicious. We refused to allow any one but ourselves to examine the evidence and then destroyed it.

That, however, made no difference in 1898. The newspapers and the public at once decided that the ship had been blown up by the deviltry of the Spaniards, and the

AS *THE NEW YORK JOURNAL* VIEWED THE SITUATION
ON MARCH 8, 1898

Cartoon by Davenport.

war-cry of "Remember the *Maine*" swept the country. Three weeks after the sinking, Congress voted $50,000,-000 for the national defense. On March 29 McKinley sent an ultimatum to Spain demanding the immediate rescinding of the order for the reconcentration policy, and an armistice in Cuba. Spain complied immediately with the first demand, and on April 9 to the second. Two days earlier, the six greatest European powers had offered their services to intervene and bring about a peaceful solution. Woodford from Madrid reported that the Spanish Government was moving as rapidly as possible to comply with all our demands without bringing on revolution, the overthrow of the dynasty, and chaos.

**ARMED INTERVENTION   SPAIN PLANTS 40 MINES
    IF M'KINLEY DODGES.   IN HAVANA HARBOR.**

THE NEWSPAPERS HAD DECLARED FOR WAR
"The World" of April 4, 1898.

McKinley himself had desired peace, but the pressure on a man who was honest and amiable but not strong had become overwhelming. The powerful groups who wanted war were determined on it. The newspapers fanned the fury of the populace to a roaring blaze. The President decided to throw the decision on Congress, and on April 10 had his message ready. That day he received despatches from Woodford stating that Spain conceded practically anything we might ask.

It was too late. The next day, McKinley sent his message to Congress with merely a casual reference at the very end to Woodford's despatch and Spain's offer. On the 19th, Congress passed a resolution declaring Cuba independent, calling on Spain to withdraw from her colony, authorizing the President to enforce this demand with the army and navy, and finally declaring that we would ourselves withdraw from Cuba as soon as we had

THE PLIGHT OF THE CUBAN PATRIOTS ROUSED THE PATRIOTISM
OF CONFEDERATE VETERANS

From the original card in the Confederate Museum, Richmond.

secured her independence and would leave her to govern herself. Five days later, Spain declared war. We declared war on April 25.

At this stage, the idealism of the American people was in full flood. The Cuban patriots had been painted in glowing colors, the ferocity of the Spaniards in deepest black. We were on a crusade to help a glorious little people win their freedom from oppression, and we had guaranteed that we would altruistically leave them their independence when we had helped them achieve it. How immensely finer we thought ourselves than the empire-grabbing States of Europe who, particularly since about 1880, had been seizing territory all over the world and subjecting alien races to themselves because of markets or raw materials! If the thoughts of newspaper owners were on circulation and profits, and those of certain astute statesmen and captains of industry were strongly flavored with plain European imperialism, it is only fair to emphasize that the people at large who favored the war did so at first in a fine spirit of unselfishness.

They immediately, however, received something of a shock. The island of Cuba was definite enough. It was almost at our doorstep, a few miles only from our coast. The job seemed to be to go down there and put the Spaniards out, if they did not get out voluntarily. The President called for 200,000 volunteers. If, in more than a month, only 120,000 had come forward, that did not make much difference. They were a good many more than our incompetent War Department knew what to do with anyway, and ample for the Cuban job.

If the people had been thinking only of Cuba, others had wider views, the "large policy" which Lodge, Roosevelt, and others had been trying to educate McKinley up to adopting. Roosevelt had sent Dewey to the Far East, and the day before we formally declared war, on April 25, that officer at Hong-Kong received orders to proceed to the Philippine Islands and to destroy or capture the Spanish Oriental Fleet. So the American nation, with its eyes on Cuba, on May 6 was stunned to hear that five days earlier Dewey had destroyed ten Spanish men-of-war at Manila, killed or wounded 381 men, without the loss of a single American, and with no damage to our ships. He had then settled down to the blockade of Manila with the intention of taking the Philippine Islands.

Hardly any of us knew where the islands were and it all seemed remote from the patriots whom we were supposed to be rescuing in Cuba. That island, in fact, was more remote in policy than the Philippines in space, though the idealism of the people had not yet grasped that fact. In May, Lodge was writing to Roosevelt, now Lieutenant-Colonel of the Rough Riders in Texas instead of in the Navy office, that "we are not lugging that monitor across the Pacific for the fun of lugging her back again. They mean to send not less than 20,000 men to the Philippines. As to Cuba I am in no sort of hurry . . . Porto Rico is not forgotten and we mean to have it. Unless I am utterly and profoundly mistaken the Administration is now fully committed to the large policy that we both desire." A week later he added, "for various reasons I am not anxious to see the war jammed through. . . . Let us get the outlying things first."

The Cuban patriots and America on crusade had overlooked the desirability of the "outlying things," but the war was to be in many ways a surprise. It was a short and, as far as America was concerned, an almost bloodless one. We had only about 379 men killed or died of wounds, though the toll of sickness, largely due to the colossal inefficiency of the War Department, was heavy in comparison. Perhaps no other war has had such amazing results at so slight a cost in life. The Spaniards were brave and showed themselves chivalrous, but the fighting at all points was thousands of miles from Spain, and her navy was made up of antiquated ships in bad condition. The fight in Manila Bay was about as exciting and glorious as killing a deer which walks out of the woods to look at you.

Although Dewey could take the city of Manila he had no troops to hold it and had to await the reinforcements of which Lodge wrote to Roosevelt. While waiting, a British, French, Japanese, and two German ships of war arrived to look after the rights of their nationals. All behaved with exemplary courtesy except the German Admiral, Von Diedrich, who blustered and threatened until Dewey, after accusing him of gross discourtesy and suggesting that if he wanted a fight he could have it at once, brought him to some sense of decency. The chief result of this otherwise unimportant incident was the beginning of a far more friendly feeling for England in America owing to the fact that the British commander, Chichester, had made it obvious to the Germans that if they did try a fight he would be on the side

ENTRENCHMENTS AND UTAH LIGHT BATTERY IN ACTION

Near Chinese Church, Caloocan, February 10, 1899. Smoke on left is from the 3d Artillery, engaged as infantry.

RECRUITING FOR THE SPANISH–AMERICAN WAR

From photographs in the War Department.

OREGON VOLUNTEER INFANTRY RETURNING TO MANILA AFTER THE FIGHT OF
FEBRUARY 5, 1899

OFFICERS' MESS OF THE ROUGH RIDERS IN SAN ANTONIO, TEXAS, 1898

Col. Leonard Wood and Lieutenant-Colonel Theodore Roosevelt at head of table. Cadet Haskell,
badly wounded in the San Juan fight, at the left.

From photographs in the War Department.

of Dewey. After our troops had arrived, an assault was made on the city and on the 12th of August the capital of the islands passed into our possession. Meanwhile, Congress by joint resolution had annexed the Hawaiian Islands on July 7, as a valuable naval base and a handy stepping-stone to our embryo Oriental empire.

In the West Indian theatre of operations we had been trying to locate the Spanish fleet under Admiral Cervera. For a while it could not be found, and there was tremendous excitement up and down the Atlantic coast lest it should appear and bombard one summer resort or another. After the game of hide-and-seek had gone on for some time it was found that Cervera had taken refuge in the harbor of Santiago in Cuba. Although he had sailed into the harbor on May 19 and Rear-Admiral Sampson had ordered Schley to blockade him there with the American fleet, it was not until the 29th, and after inexplicable backing and filling, that Schley got there.

The troops destined for the island had been gathered at Tampa, Florida, where the confusion due to the incompetence of the higher military authorities was almost beyond belief, as it was to continue throughout the brief struggle. No attempt was made to improve the single-track railroad; the food was bad, when there was any; troops had to move by themselves without orders and capture their own freight cars to get to docks nine miles off to reach the embarkation point; lighters had to be seized by energetic officers for their men to get on board transports; cavalry regiments were shipped without their horses; orders to sail were given and countermanded; men herded like cattle on the decks of ships were left there for days in the tropical sun. Roosevelt wrote to Lodge begging him to bring pressure to get some one to bring order out of the chaos. Lodge replied soothingly, saying, "I am devoting all my strength to get the annexation of Hawaii," adding that there was no longer any doubt we must have Porto Rico and that the administration was coming round to the annexation of the Philippines. The Cuban "patriots" had ceased to count.

Finally, however, troops did reach the coast of their island, and on June 24 won against the Spanish at Las Guasimas, and on July 1 assaulted the heights around Santiago. The most noted minor engagement was that at San Juan Hill where Roosevelt under Colonel Leonard Wood led the Rough Riders on foot (their horses were still in Florida), against the enemy. The American charge against fortified positions was magnificently carried out, and much valor was shown on both sides.

Santiago itself had not yet been captured but was in imminent peril, although sickness was taking a heavy toll of the Americans, and General Shafter was inclined to withdraw the troops. On July 3 Admiral Sampson had steamed to Siboney, where the sick general had his headquarters, to confer with him, and had been gone from the blockading squadron only about half an hour when the Spanish fleet made an effort to escape from the harbor. No braver man or more courteous enemy has ever commanded at sea than Admiral Cervera. He had known from the start, when ordered overseas by the government in unfit and unprepared vessels, that only surrender or destruction could await him.

Realizing that when Santiago fell, his fleet would be bombarded from the heights, he preferred to dash out to sea and end in glorious fight. There was never any chance for him, and one after another his ships were destroyed, Cervera himself leaping from the burning deck of the *Maria Teresa* into the sea, to be picked up by the Americans, as they rescued hundreds of others from the blazing and exploding vessels. The fact that Sampson, who outranked Schley, had been absent at the beginning of the fight, and the jealousy between them and their partisans, resulted in one of the most notable and unedifying controversies in our history, which divided the American people and lasted for years.

Ten days after the battle, General Toral surrendered Santiago to Generals Shafter, Miles, and Wheeler, and on the 25th, Miles, who had proceeded to Porto Rico, received the surrender of that island. The war was over.

In the meantime, American sentiment had suffered a profound change. Whatever many leaders had had in their minds, when the people had applauded the war at the beginning the people had thought only of freeing Cuba. But as we gathered islands into our arms in the Atlantic and Pacific, a wave of imperialistic ambition swept the nation. Men who believed that America as an empire, governing alien and subject races, would change its character from that of the great self-governing Republic, were denounced as unpatriotic fools or worse. The conventions of the Republican Party all over the country were passing resolutions declaring that "where the flag once goes up it must never come down." McKinley wrestled with the problem of whether or not to demand the Philippines while imperialists like Lodge and large business interests which wanted materials and markets, and clergymen who dreamed of saving the souls of natives, all brought pressure on him. Finally he decided it was destiny that we must keep the islands.

The Peace Commission which met the Spanish Commissioners in Paris secured all that the most ardent imperialist could have wished. Spain gave up her sovereignty over Cuba, ceded Porto Rico and Guam to the United States, as, for $20,000,000, she also surrendered the Philippine archipelago to us. The Treaty further provided that Congress should be empowered to determine the rights of the inhabitants of the ceded territories.

The Treaty, however, met with strong opposition in the Senate, where many senators felt that the constitutional and other problems involved in our becoming an empire were bound to have serious and unhappy results. Oddly enough, in view of his stand on another Treaty twenty years later, likewise negotiated in Paris, Lodge insisted that not to accept it would "be a repudiation of the President and humiliation of the whole country in the eyes of the world." Bryan, who was opposed to imperialism but who wished also to end the war, voted in favor of the Treaty, which was ratified by a majority of only one vote.

On April 11, 1899, peace was declared. We had acquired 8,500,000 "subjects"—about 1,000,000 Spaniards and negroes in Porto Rico, and 7,500,000 Filipinos, a large part of the latter being savages. Many, however, were not so but were civilized and educated, and under their leader, Emilio Aguinaldo, had, like the Cubans, been fighting for independence. This insurrection was now directed against us instead of Spain, and it took us three years to suppress it.

It was not until the spring of 1900 that we began to provide forms of government for our new dependencies, but Cuba received attention more promptly. We had pledged ourselves to her independence, so the main problem was settled. Much to the mortification of the Cubans, however, we tied a string to their sovereignty, and forced them to add an amendment to their Constitution by which the United States could in part control their foreign policy and finances. The Platt Amendment, as it is called, also gave us the right to intervene at any time to maintain an "adequate" government for the protection of life, property, and liberty; and forced Cuba to cede us a couple of coaling stations on her coast.

It should be added that the American army of occupation, under General Wood, did extraordinarily good work in sanitary and other improvements in the island before they withdrew and Wood handed over the government to the first elected President, Estrada Palma, on May 20, 1902. It was a fine piece of colonial administration, and the efficiency displayed, in notable contrast to the muddle of the war, was of lasting benefit to the island. The Platt Amendment was also for the good of the Cuban people, and if we threw to the winds the idealism with which we had started the war, we at least maintained it with regard to Cuba, and gave an example of restraint in leaving the rich "Pearl of the Antilles" to work out its own destiny in comparative freedom if it could.

Little by little, since the Peace of 1783 we had been extending our territory, but now for the first time we found ourselves a world power, and were so recognized by both our own people and foreign statesmen. This did not come about from our having defeated a decrepit and tottering second-rate European nation with a glorious past. That was not a great feat in itself, and at least the ostensible cause of the quarrel had been conditions just off our own coast in Cuba, and had had nothing to do with world politics. Nor did the recognition of our new status come altogether from our having become an Asiatic power by the acquisition of the Philippines, though that did indeed mark a great departure from our traditional policy and might presage almost anything.

It came, rather, from the sudden recognition of what had been largely overlooked until the war turned the spotlight of the world's interest on us, the fact of our colossal economic growth. In the new world system then developing, wealth and economic resources had begun to spell power as never before, and the world all at once discovered that there were 75,000,000 of restless and energetic people, possessing the richer half of one of the richest continents in the world, who were beginning to emerge from their self-centred isolation and to spread out in trade and conquest. Small and short as the war had been, it had also fired the enthusiasm of most of our own people for taking a place among the nations of the world.

If one overlooked the almost pathetic weakness of our foe, the naval victories at Manila and Santiago had certainly been smashing ones, and the people suddenly developed an immense pride in their navy. Atlases had been in much request during the war, and great numbers of citizens whose interest before had scarcely gone beyond their "Main Street" found themselves thinking in terms both of Europe and the Far East. Minds were opened and victory brought a sense of power. For the next twenty years, until we shut ourselves up again, it seemed as though we were destined to play that rôle in international affairs which all expected that we should.

In 1899, when the Czar of Russia sent out invitations to the powers to meet at The Hague to discuss the problem of the economic burden of armaments, breaking with our traditional policy of isolation, we accepted, and sent an able delegation with Andrew D. White at its head. They were not mere "observers," and it was chiefly owing to American influence that the Conference agreed to establish the permanent Court of Arbitration, before

This Government is animated by a sincere desire that the interests of our citizens may not be prejudiced through exclusive treatment by any of the controlling Powers within their so-called "spheres of interest" in China, and hopes also to retain there an open market for the commerce of the world, remove dangerous sources of international irritation, and hasten thereby united or concerted action of the Powers at Pekin in favor of the administrative reforms so urgently needed for strengthening the imperial Government and maintaining the integrity of China in which the whole western world is alike concerned. It believes that such a result may be greatly assisted

OFFICE COPY OF INSTRUCTIONS OF JOHN HAY TO AMBASSADOR
CHOATE IN LONDON, RELATIVE TO THE "OPEN DOOR" POLICY
Courtesy of the State Department, Washington.

which, three years later, the United States and Mexico were the first nations to appear to settle a serious dispute by amicable methods.

Our delegates were scarcely home from The Hague, when Secretary of State Hay took the lead in endeavoring to save the Chinese Empire from practical dismemberment, in the guise of concessions, by competing European powers. On September 6, 1899, he initiated the policy which became known as "the open door," by ask-

GOOD MEDICINE

The
BRONCHO PHILOSOPHER

MAY 18 1907

LOVE, SONG AND LAUGHTER

SAY! LISTEN!

When a bit of sunshine hits ye' after passin' of a cloud,
An' a fit of laughter gits ye' an' yer spine is feelin' proud,
Don't forgit to up an' fling it at a soul that's feelin' blue
For the minit that ye sling it, it's a boomerang to you.

From a sacred song— **FAITH***—Copyrighted*

I have no regrets to offer, I have no desire to stay,
But I want to scatter sunshine ere my soul has passed away,
Oh, I want to tell the story to the friends I love today
I shall tell it to my Saviour in the morning,
In the morning, in the morning, with the halo of His love
my soul adorning.
I am clinging to His hand, I shall know and understand,
When I meet my blessed Saviour in the morning.

What are you? What am I? But a stew and a fry,
A broil and a siz, and a scramble for biz,
And six feet of earth when we die.

"THE POET SCOUT"

PRESS OF GEORGE SETON THOMPSON, CHICAGO

Copyright, 1907.

JACK CRAWFORD—THE LAST OF THE POET PHILOSOPHERS

Famous as a scout and composer and reciter of verses from the late seventies until his death in 1917.

TROOP L, 6TH U. S. CAVALRY, AT THE GREAT WALL OF CHINA, NEAR THE MING TOMBS

From a photograph in the War Department.

ing France, England, Russia, and Germany that each should make no discrimination against other nationals in the spheres of their "concessions," to which they all acceded,—a distinct liberalizing of the older imperialism. Some months later there was again a serious threat of the dismemberment of the empire. Floods, famines, and hatred of the foreigners stirred a revolt, and the revolutionists, or "Boxers," threatened to destroy the foreign legations at Peking. A complete massacre of all the foreigners and their families in the beleaguered city was feared, and the world was in suspense until a rescue was effected by a force made up of 2500 American troops, 3000 British, 800 French, and 8000 Japanese.

Such an incident under the old imperialism was considered an opportunity to acquire territory as a means of punishment, and the European nations were ready to dismember China by securing large punitive grants. Hay blocked this plan by claiming that the rebellion was a domestic one against the Chinese Government, and that all that foreigners could claim would be the proper punishment of offenders and the payment of a cash indemnity for actual losses. America placed hers at $24,-000,000 and it was only with much difficulty that the European nations were induced to place theirs at $110,-000,000, secured by Chinese taxes and duties. America, however, had saved the territorial integrity of the empire, and five years later, when it was found that our actual loss had not been much more than half the sum first named, we remitted $11,000,000 of the payment, which China in gratitude put aside as a fund to send Chinese students to American universities.

THE CAMPAIGN OF 1900—McKINLEY AND ROOSEVELT

Although the issue of the bitter campaign of 1896 had been free silver, it was not until March 14, 1900, that an Act ensuring the gold standard was finally passed and signed. This established that all forms of our money must be redeemable in gold on demand, created a redemption fund of gold metal to the amount of $150,000,000, and provided that paper notes, when presented for payment in gold, should not be issued again except for gold. The endless chain, which Cleveland had pleaded to have broken, was at last shattered.

The rapid increase in the annual production of gold, of which we have spoken, and a series of unusually fine harvests, had brought abounding prosperity to the United States. There was, however, much dissatisfaction with the distribution of its fruits, and Roosevelt noted in 1899 that "the agitation against trusts is taking an always firmer hold," and that he was surprised to find how many workmen in New York State who had been strongly Republican in 1896 were now grumbling. But on the whole there was little doubt of the outcome of the election of 1900.

There was no doubt at all as to candidates for the Presidency. McKinley might, as Roosevelt somewhat unjustly said, have "no more backbone than a chocolate éclair" but he had got on well with Congress, had been dignified in office, and was popular and respected. In the Democratic Party, Bryan had made himself practical dictator and the attitude of the rank and file toward him was rather that of the followers of a prophet than of a mere political leader. In their eyes he stood for the cause of humanity rather than for any particular policy, but the exigencies of a campaign demanded specific issues, and there was none in 1900 on which he could rouse the country.

He came out strongly against imperialism and our governing subject races, but with the exception of a comparatively small group of intellectuals, the mass of the people were proud of the war and of our new acquisitions, and the issue, both in its constitutional and ethical aspects, was rather above the head of the average voter. Besides, it had been Bryan's influence which had made possible the ratification of the treaty by which we acquired the Philippines, and this fact made a weak point in his armor. With abounding prosperity, both the tariff and the free-silver issues roused comparatively little interest, and it was probably Bryan's attacks on the trusts and corporate wealth which brought him the greatest number of followers.

To a certain extent Hanna, who was again manager of the campaign, afforded Bryan ammunition. Whether Hanna was becoming a bit tired or merely lazy, he found it much easier to get contributions to the $2,500,000 he wanted to elect McKinley from a comparatively few rich men and corporations than from the people at large, and the election of 1900 was financed more exclusively by the "interests" than any one previously had been. On the other hand, full revelations of the scandals of big business had not yet been made, and Hanna was able to make effective use of the slogans of "Republican prosperity" and the "full dinner pail."

As it was to turn out, the most important event in what would otherwise have been a rather stale political season was the choice of McKinley's running-mate.

In many respects there has been no other figure in American public life to compare with Theodore Roosevelt. After a rather sickly youth he had become a man of almost incomparably abounding physical as well as mental vigor. Never a profound and often not a logical thinker, the range of his intellectual interests was wide and his memory unusual. Standing firmly for the ideals, which he was fond of preaching, of the ordinary, clean, honest American, he also delighted to describe himself as a "very practical man," a combination which sometimes brought him into strange combinations with political bosses. He was essentially pragmatic, and believed in working with what tools one had, even if they were pretty filthy at times.

Of his patriotism, ideals, and ability both in politics and statesmanship, there can be no doubt. He had an extraordinary capacity also for making himself popular, which he used as an actor does, but apart from this, there were genuine qualities in the man himself which enormously interested people of the most varied sorts. No other American, if any statesman anywhere, has ever aroused the world-wide interest in himself and his doings which attended Roosevelt in the fifteen years after the Spanish War.

He had a way of making himself, or at least of becoming, the centre of every scene in which he figured, a characteristic popularity commented on in the saying that if he attended a funeral he would insist on being the corpse. In the Spanish War he had promptly abandoned his desk to raise a regiment of Western cowboys, and although he was only second in command, Wood being the colonel, the spotlight of publicity was always on Roosevelt. He did good work but when the regiment got to Cuba, the impression created was that there was almost no one on the island but Roosevelt, and his ordinary brave part in the charge at San Juan Hill was magnified into one of the glories of the ages. As McKinley remarked, no one else had got so much out of the war as Roosevelt had, and even before his return he was being boomed for governor of New York.

He was accepted by Platt, and elected, but his honesty and energy in office antagonized the larger business interests, who preferred to know just what a legislature cost rather than to indulge in purity in politics, and they were anxious to get rid of him. In view of his enormous popularity as "Teddy" throughout the country, the safest thing seemed to be to kick him upstairs to the innocuous office of Vice-President, and although McKinley was not desirous of having this political *enfant terrible* and erratic human dynamo as his running-mate, it was arranged among the bosses that he should be given the nomination. Roosevelt himself swore that he did not want it and would not take it, but although warned that if he went to the convention he would be nominated by acclamation, he went, in Rough Rider hat and red bandanna, and received and accepted the nomination

The popular enthusiasm is one side of the picture but we may look at another, for the nomination of Roosevelt is as good an example as any for the study of the National Convention as an expression of the choice of the people for candidates. It had been hoped that such a system of nomination by delegates chosen by State conventions, delegates to which in turn had been chosen by district conventions, delegates to which last had been chosen by "the people," would express the people's choice. In fact, to a very great extent, the National Convention system, although none better has yet been suggested, had come to descend to and rest upon, through the hierarchy of delegates, not "the people" but the local and State bosses.

According to as shrewd an observer of politics as the old Joe Cannon, what happened at the Philadelphia convention was something quite different from the people's choosing Roosevelt. Platt, the boss of New York, wished to rid himself, as did big business, of Roosevelt as governor. The simplest method, as we have said, was to "kick him upstairs" to the seemingly innocuous office of Vice-President. On the other hand, the powerful party boss, Hanna, was strongly opposed to having the irrepressible governor as the running-mate for the less picturesque McKinley. There was, however, another factor in the situation. Matthew Quay, the boss of Pennsylvania, had conceived the notion that if the number of delegates to the National Convention were based on party strength instead of population in each State, his own position as controlling the delegates from the overwhelmingly Republican State of Pennsylvania would be much increased. He wished to have the rules changed to compass this desirable result. Such a change would in many ways be beneficial to the country, and was later advocated by Taft, but Hanna, controlling the delegates from the Democratic South, naturally had no wish to have his own power shorn for the benefit of Boss Quay. Platt, however, had agreed that he would vote for Quay's change of rules in exchange for the promise that Quay would have his delegates vote for Roosevelt.

As between Roosevelt and a change in the rules, Hanna considered Roosevelt the lesser of the two evils, as less permanent. He therefore split the Platt-Quay alliance by promising Platt his own backing of Roosevelt if Platt would oppose Quay's plans. This was what was going on behind the scenes, while the delegates applauded Roosevelt's red bandanna, and is much the sort of thing which goes on in all National Conventions. As

THE PRODIGAL'S RETURN

A cartoon by Coffin in the Isabella Solomons's Collection, Library of Congress.

between Platt and Quay as political bosses there was not much to choose, but Quay's plan, although proposed for the purely selfish purpose of strengthening his own corrupt power in a notoriously corrupt State, was really constructive in its more permanent effects. No one was thinking, however, in terms of statesmanship, but all three,—Hanna, Platt, and Quay,—in terms of immediate political advantage. So, amid vast enthusiasm, the hero of San Juan Hill was put on the ticket with Major McKinley.

Although, in the ensuing campaign, there was an unusual number of parties in the field, the real contest, as always, was between the Republicans and Democrats, and, as had been anticipated, the ticket of McKinley and Roosevelt easily won, 7,219,000 to 6,358,000 in the popular vote and 292 to 155 in the Electoral College. Apparently Roosevelt had been respectably buried as presiding officer of the Senate, and big business sighed relief. It did not dream of assassination.

CHAPTER III

THE ROOSEVELT ERA

THE last year or more of McKinley's life as President, both before and after his second election, was chiefly notable for the adjustment of our relations to our new dependencies. In a series of cases which reached the Supreme Court in 1900 and 1901, it became all too clear that the overseas possessions, "the outlying things" of Senator Lodge's phrase, had no legitimate place in our constitutional system. Unlike the areas acquired in the course of our steady continental expansion, these islands inhabited by alien races, many of them savage and all speaking languages other than our own, could not be passed through a "Territorial" stage to be admitted within a reasonable time as States of the Union.

We had, however, acquired them, and the Supreme Court was faced by a condition and not by a theory. If the logic of its decisions was far from clear, that was chiefly because the situation itself was not logical. The new possessions were declared not to be foreign countries but on the other hand neither were they parts of the United States, and their citizens were left suspended in a sort of Mahomet's coffin of an anomalous status. What mainly came out of the decisions was the verdict that Congress had the power to legislate for the possessions and to do about as it chose, subject to revision by the Court, which reserved the right to decide on each topic as it might come up without laying down any general principles.

At first, largely owing to the insurrection, the Philippines had to be placed under strict military rule, but Aguinaldo surrendered to General Funston in March, 1901, and the backbone of the revolt was broken, though the islands were not entirely pacified. We may note that although we paid Spain only $20,000,000 for the archipelago, and had complained of her inability to put down the Cuban revolution upon our immediate demand, it took us four years and cost us $170,000,000 to quell the Philippine one. An adjustment of disputed land titles with the friars cost us over $7,000,000 more, so that our new possession really cost us about nine times the sum first contemplated by the imperialists.

Civil governments of different forms were set up in all the newly acquired islands, in both the Atlantic and the Pacific, before the end of McKinley's term, following in many respects the precedents of the old British colonial governments before the American Revolution. It is interesting to note that in ruling our own dependencies we have found it necessary to do not a few of the things of which we so bitterly complained as being tyrannical in

1776. It is the old story of the different viewpoints of those in opposition and those in power with the responsibilities of office. In Porto Rico, for example, we erected a government in which both the governor and members of the Upper House were appointed by the President of the United States, and the Lower House was elected by the qualified voters in Porto Rico. As Congress had also the power to legislate for the welfare of the island, we reproduced the old type of Royal colony, merely substituting the President for the King, and Congress for Parliament.

In April, 1900, both Hawaii and Porto Rico were made Territories, but although their populations warranted Statehood, they have never received that status, and it is uncertain if they ever will. The United States undertook its obligations of governing in good faith, and all of our possessions have improved greatly in such matters as public health, education, and order. There has been much advance in building of roads, in the sanitation of cities and the establishment of hospitals, in water supplies and many other fundamentals of modern life, while our administrative services have been freer from graft and scandal than have our own domestic governments. They have, indeed, beginning with Wood in Cuba and William H. Taft in the Philippines, developed a series of administrators of whom we may well be proud.

Nevertheless, it is improbable that these possessions can be absorbed as integral parts in our self-governing system for a long time, if ever. How completely outside our normal course of expansion they were was shown at once in the disputes over levying tariff duties on the products imported from them. It would be as unthinkable as it would be unconstitutional to lay duties on the import of products of any of the continental States or Territories into the rest of the country, but both Congress and the Supreme Court decided that we could do so on the products of even Hawaii and Porto Rico after they had become "Territories," and we did so also in the Philippines. Of course we could not do so if they ever became States, and this fact has large political significance.

ROOSEVELT BECOMES PRESIDENT

McKinley was chiefly concerned with these insular questions in the early months of his second term in 1901 when he attended the Pan-American Exposition at Buffalo in September. He was not a great man, but he was an able, gentle and lovable one, and since he had been in the White House he had endeared himself in an unusual degree to the American people. He had also developed as a statesman, especially in his views of international relations and policy. As a small-town congressman he had believed in a Chinese wall of tariffs around protected American industries; as President he had come to realize that, as he said in a speech on September 5, at Buffalo, we cannot "forever sell everything and buy little or nothing." He had come to regard the tariff not as protection for American industry but, in reciprocity treaties, as a means of expanding American commerce. The nation applauded the speech, and with three and a half years yet to serve, McKinley seemed to have a great and useful future before him.

The next day, at a reception, he held out his hand to shake that of a young Pole, one of whose hands, apparently injured, was done up in linen. Instantly a flash of flame came from the bandage, followed by another, and the President fell back, shot through the stomach by a madman. Rallying from the operation which was immediately performed, his recovery was looked upon as certain, but a week later he began to sink and died on the 14th. Roosevelt, the man of whom the bosses and the big business interests had thought to have rid themselves by burying him as presiding officer of the Senate, was President of the United States.

The mourning country, which now so unexpectedly found the young Roosevelt,—he was yet but forty-two,—at its head, had changed much in the preceding decade. Not only had it become a world power but there had been a similar change of scale in many other aspects of its life. We were on the threshold of the era in which we are still living, in spite of the vast changes which have occurred since.

A BYGONE ERA

Fifth Avenue, looking north from 11th Street, New York, 1898.

ALL SET FOR THE RIDE

A Haynes-Apperson automobile of 1901.

By courtesy of W. F. Reeves, Esq.

Wood engraving, circa 1880, in the J. Clarence Davies Collection, Museum of the City of New York.

Top, First car in world operated by cable, on Greenwich Street, from Battery Place to Cortlandt Street, New York, 1867; it was the first passenger car on an elevated railroad; Charles T. Harvey, designer and engineer of the Ninth Avenue Elevated Railway, New York, is in car. Centre, the first Grand Central Terminal, New York, 1871–1910; Grand Union Hotel (right), and the end of the Elevated spur in use from 1878 to 1923, between the two. Bottom, Subway secretly built in the early seventies on Broadway from Murray to Warren Streets, New York. The tube was 9 feet in diameter, built mostly of brick with the car designed to be operated by compressed air. No franchise could be obtained and the company went out of existence. The work of building a new subway nearly fifty years later brought the tunnel and car to light.

A NEW ERA

The age of electricity, after many experiments, had come, and its effect was being felt in many directions. In 1900 there were about 2500 power stations, and their number was increasing rapidly every year. The first trolley cars had been installed in 1898, and in a few years were to be common everywhere. In that year, Boston had built the first subway in America, and New York followed in 1900. Roosevelt's Presidency was to see the electrification of the great railroad systems well begun, and the tunnels built connecting New York with Long Island and New Jersey.

The transmission of electric power from central stations to homes and offices quickly brought into the market innumerable sorts of electrical appliances, such as irons, dish-washers, and so on, as well as electric lights. The cheaper power made the elevator more practicable, and with the elevator came the apartment house and the skyscraper. The Flatiron Building in New York rose to its twenty stories in 1902, and in a few years was followed by the great Metropolitan Tower, the Singer Building and the Municipal Building, as well as the beginning of the super-skyscraper in other cities, and, in just a decade, by the Woolworth Building, in New York, 785 feet high. As part of the change, we may note that in the late '80's about 1300 private houses were built annually on Manhattan Island, but that by 1904 only 40 were put up whereas apartment houses were rising rapidly, completely altering not only the physical form of the old "home" but the life of the women and children within it.

The new architecture marked a profound change in the mentality of the people. One has only to contrast the low, small and exquisite City Hall in New York, perhaps the most perfect of the early nineteenth-century buildings in America, with the soaring bulk of its neighbor, the Municipal Building, to realize the psychological as well as the architectural gulf that separates the builders of each. There was profound significance in the fact that we Americans had suddenly started to build our communal and public edifices on a scale equalled only by the Egyptian and the Roman. Not only the office skyscraper but the vast railway stations of this decade were symptomatic of the change. While Europe was content with small, grimy, and purely utilitarian structures, the Americans undertook that series of great marble buildings, unsurpassed save by Rome in vastness and satisfying dignity, beginning with the Union Station at Washington, completed in 1907, and reaching the summit in the Pennsylvania (1910) and Grand Central Stations (1913) in New York.

In other respects we were also standing at the threshold of a new era in 1901. In America, at least, perhaps no other mechanical invention has so altered the entire life and ways of living and of thought as has the automobile. In 1895 there were but four motor cars registered in the whole country. By 1900 there were 8000, and the flood of production was soon to be let loose. In 1903 the Wright brothers in North Carolina made the first flight in the air in world history in a machine which had raised itself by its own power, and eight years later Glenn Curtiss made the first successful hydroplane. A new world was indeed coming into being.

The change of scale and the growing interest in communal rather than personal life was as notable in the field of letters as in that of architecture. Improvements and reduction of costs in printing and illustrating, as well as the discovery of the great profits in advertising, doubled and trebled the circulation of the new types of popular, low-priced magazines, such as *Collier's, Munsey's, McClure's, The Cosmopolitan* and others. *The Saturday Evening Post,* bought for $1000 in 1897, was soon to rise to amazing figures of circulation. Among books, the best sellers were also sold in hitherto unheard-of quantities,—such as, in 1901, 275,000 copies of *Janice Meredith,* 320,000 of *The Crisis,* 420,000 of *Richard Carvel,* and 520,000 of *David Harum.*

It was not merely, however, the increase in scale which was notable in publishing. In the decade after the war, the attention of both authors and readers was almost wholly concentrated on the American scene, as is shown by glancing over the list of titles of such leading writers of the period as Booth Tarkington, Jack London, Mrs. Wharton, Hamlin Garland, Harold Frederic, John Fox, Frank Norris, Miss Wilkins, Owen Wister, and others. Moreover, increasingly after 1901, the articles which helped to sell the popular magazines were those dealing with the evils and scandals of our economic and political régime, exposed also in such books as *The Octopus* (1901) and *The Pit* (1903) by Norris, *The History of the Standard Oil Company* (1904) by Ida Tarbell, *The Shame of the Cities* (1904) by Lincoln Steffens, or *The Jungle* (1906) by Upton Sinclair, and *The Iron Heel* (1907) by Jack London. These and such authors also as Burton J. Hendrick and Ray Stannard Baker, although imitated by a host of mere sensation-mongers, did careful and able work in uncovering the corruption and injustice which were eating into our national life from the Atlantic to the Pacific. Their popularity testified to the deep discontent and mistrust of the people with their leaders.

Both emotions were wholly warranted. Although as we have seen, the "trust" and large corporation had appeared before the war, the change in scale and the tendency toward consolidation were most notable immediately after. Between 1898 and 1900 more than two score combinations took place in the iron and steel industry alone, and in those years were formed such huge companies as the Amalgamated Copper, the American Smelting & Refining, the larger Standard Oil, and the

Consolidated Tobacco, to be followed in 1901 by the United States Steel.

The last, which was characteristic of all them in the extent of its over-capitalization, issued securities of a par value of over $1,400,000,000 though its actual assets were estimated at only about $682,000,000 so that a large part of its 7 per cent preferred stock, as well as its whole issue of more than $500,000,000 of common, was water. Huge quantities of water were also similarly injected into the new railway and other combines. The only way to make profits on all this gigantic mass of capital, issued for the benefit of those who floated it, and much of which represented no tangible property or earning power, was to keep expenses, including wages, to their lowest point, to charge unwarranted and sometimes outrageously high prices for services or products, and to utilize all possible means of controlling markets and prices.

Both the consumer and the wage-earner had begun to feel completely helpless before these colossal aggregations of wealth and power. Such a railroad man as E. H. Harriman boasted openly of being able to buy both legislatures and courts for whatever he needed. The word of these financial titans, and not of the people's representatives and judges, appeared to have become the law of the land. They seemed, and felt themselves to be, all-powerful. Harriman did magnificent work in rehabilitating the broken-down Union Pacific railroad system, but on the other hand he considered himself a czar in the vast

Western territory which he ruled. The people of Oregon complained bitterly that they could not develop their State, in which there was a section as large as Ohio without a mile of railroad, because Harriman was not ready to build himself and would allow no one else to do so.

The great change in the scale of business, the vast opportunities for sudden and incalculably great riches from stock watering and market operations, had gone to the heads of these leaders who were corrupting and threatening the whole of American life, growing colossally rich while wages were being lowered. Speaking of them five years after the Steel Trust had marked the advent of billion-dollar companies, Roosevelt wrote that "in their hearts they take the ground that to take legal proceedings against them when they violate the law and to endeavor to have them pay their proper share of the taxes is as much of an outrage as to excite the mob to plunder the rich. As you know, in San Francisco many of the big corporations have deliberately stood by the labor union party, saying with utter cynicism that they preferred the chance of occasional violence if they could temper it with corruption, to an honest government that would permit neither corruption nor violence." It was the old story of corrupting governments, municipal, State, or national, in order to obtain special privileges which would enable their possessors to crush competitors, and make profits on bogus capital.

Free silver as an issue was dead, but what had been the

underlying issue of the 1896 campagn was not. Neither the Republican Party nor the great business leaders had learned anything. Having downed Bryan they had merely become more reckless and cynical than ever. On the other hand, the discontent of the people had become more profound, wide-spread and intelligent. The question of a sound currency was settled. The question in 1901 was of a sound national life and of the rights of the tens of millions of ordinary citizens as against the new concentrated power of a few dozen.

By 1904, 164,500 miles of railroad, practically all that was worth anything, was controlled by six groups of individuals, who by means of their own wealth, and yet more by the control they held over banks and life insurance companies, were coming to dominate the life of the people in every department. The organization and control of the business concerns were, in truth, concentrating so rapidly that by 1910 an investigating committee of Congress could report that the two banking groups in New York, known generally as the Morgan and the Rockefeller groups, held 341 directorships in 112 companies with aggregate resources of $22,245,000,000. In the face of this situation the old political system of government appeared to have become useless.

On the other hand, the people were becoming very much alive to the evils, though they did not know how to cure them, and the spiritual forces of the nation were gathering strength. For the first time, the women, who had been given a great increase of leisure in many classes by the change in the type and management of the home, began to take their part in forming public opinion. The women's clubs throughout the country tended rapidly to become not merely blue-stocking reading circles but aggressive centres in their communities for the militant improvement of local conditions. Here and there, in such cities as Cleveland, Toledo, Milwaukee or San Francisco, efforts, more or less successful, were made to clean up the municipal governments, such efforts in the last city in particular bringing out clearly that the power of the great corporations was wholly on the side of graft and bribery and against any attempt to cleanse the filth.

Not much good was accomplished permanently, for the system of building up, by corruption, political machines dominated by a boss whom the corporations believe essential to them for corrupt purposes of their own, is too deeply entrenched even yet in our national life. Every link in the chain that runs from the corporation desiring political favors down to the policeman on the beat levying his toll on the prostitute or the apple-seller is too strong to have been broken yet. Roosevelt was right. Big business does not want honest government, and so long as government is not honest, and the laws are not justly and impartially administered, every business man, even if he desires to be honest, finds himself caught in the system of great or petty graft and bribery.

In 1901, however, among a very large and steadily increasing part of the ordinary people, there were developing a vast disgust and a vast fear. The magnates believed even more firmly than old Vanderbilt had a generation earlier that they had the power, and refused to accede to any demands of the public. In truth they were living over a smouldering volcano which might blow them into the air at any moment if no vent were provided for the forces of discontent.

The Democrats had understood that much in 1896 but they had been able to find no leader save Bryan, who, honest and well-meaning as he was, could lead them only into the wilderness because he was not intellectually capable of understanding the economic forces and tendencies of his time. He had been, however, no more dangerous to the peace of the nation than were the great business leaders and the Republican politicians who were equally blind to the social forces, and as to whither their own economic policies were carrying the nation.

The shot that killed McKinley had by chance installed in the White House a Republican leader who did understand both the social discontent and the inevitability of large aggregations of capital under the conditions of the new economic era. It was Roosevelt's sympathy with all classes, his love of fairness, and his ability as a statesman that led him to undertake, not the leadership of the forces of discontent but the reconciliation of the conflicting parties on the basis of what he called the "square deal" in what was promising otherwise to become serious social upheaval.

Roosevelt was far from being a perfect character, and there are not a few traits and episodes in his career which even his most ardent admirers have to deplore. One has only to consider his character in terms of a Washington to realize vividly some of his shortcomings, but his general love of honesty, his devotion to the people as a whole and not to any one class, his practicality, his fighting spirit, and his equal courage when faced either by labor unions or entrenched wealth, together with the extraordinary popularity which he possessed, made him the best possible leader in the struggles of the next eight years and the commanding figure in the entire nation.

It had been McKinley and not himself who had been chosen President by a great majority, and Roosevelt declared that he would continue his predecessor's policies, as he did his Cabinet. The latter had been an unusually distinguished one, including John Hay as Secretary of State, Lyman J. Gage in the Treasury, Elihu Root in the War Department, and Philander C. Knox as Attorney-General. It was impossible, however, that Roosevelt should merely carry on the policies of another. The most dynamic and explosive personality that has ever crossed the stage of American public life, he could be no one but himself. During his service as President he made no less than twenty-three changes in his Cabinet, and in his first message to Congress, on December 3, 1901, he went at once to the attack of the economic problems of his day.

It was, in truth, a distinctly conservative message, decrying any rash attempts to destroy the existing delicate economic machinery of the nation. Nevertheless it seemed radical to the business men who had considered

Fifty-first Congress of the United States of America;

At the *First* Session,

Begun and held at the City of Washington on Monday, the *second* day of December, one thousand eight hundred and eighty-*nine*.

AN ACT

To protect trade and commerce against unlawful restraints and monopolies.

Thomas B Reed
Speaker of the House of Representatives.

Approved July 2 ᵗʰ 1890
Benj Harrison

Levi P Morton
Vice-President of the United States and President of the Senate

HEADING AND SIGNATURES TO THE SHERMAN ANTI-TRUST ACT,
PASSED IN 1890
From the original in the Department of State, Washington.

themselves above the law, because the President suggested that corporations should be amenable to the law and subject to investigation and, "within reasonable limits," controlled by the government in the interest of the people. The addition of another member to the Cabinet, a Secretary of Commerce and Industries, was also suggested, and the extraordinarily long document of about 20,000 words laid down all the principles on which

Roosevelt was to act for the next eight years. Reasonable as most of it would seem today, it sent a shiver down the spine of big business, which waited, in considerable fear and anger, to see what the new President might do in acts rather than words.

Meanwhile, the Sherman Anti-trust Law had been almost wholly neglected since its passage in 1890, and the great combinations had given it scant attention, if any, as court decisions appeared to have shown that it was a mere toothless bogey. Suddenly, in the spring of 1901, all Wall Street, and a good deal of the country, were made to realize how powerful for good or ill had become the forces wielded by the super-business men who could play with the rest of us like pawns on a chess-board. It was as though a terrific flash of lightning had made us realize the strength of the electrical forces in the sky.

The Hill-Morgan group controlled the Great Northern and Northern Pacific lines in the northwest, and wished to obtain control of the Burlington, running out of Chicago. The Harriman-Kuhn, Loeb and Company group owned the Southern and Union Pacific lines, and wished to block the purchase. Hill and Morgan won, securing control of 97 per cent of the Burlington stock, which they divided between the two northern roads. Thinking themselves secure, Hill went home and Morgan went to Europe. The ambition of the comparative newcomer, Harriman, however, would not be balked, and, backed by Kuhn, Loeb, he suddenly began to buy

Northern Pacific stock in the expectation of wresting control from Morgan, and so getting not only that line but half of the Burlington stock with it.

Sensing what was being attempted by the action of Northern Pacific stock in the market, Morgan cabled to buy 150,000 shares. Ordinarily selling for about $100 a share, many brokers had sold it short as it rose, and as

NEW YORK STOCK EXCHANGE.							
Complete Transactions in Stocks—Thursday, May 9, 1901.							
—Closing— Bid	Asked	Sales		First	High	Low	Last	Net Change.
50	51	5,400	Norfolk & West.....	50⅝	51⅝	47½	50	+7
78	86	800	North American	85	85	80	80	—5½
350	..	11,170	Northern Pacific	170	700	170	325	+165
		8,700	Northern Pacific cash	190	1000	200	320	.....½
105½	106½	7,600	Northern Pacific pf..	106	106¾	104½	106	— ½
32½	35	8,250	Pacific Mail	36	36	30½	32	—6⅜
143¾	144	72,400	Pennsylvania R. R....	145½	146	137½	144	— ⅞

PART OF *THE NEW YORK TIMES* FINANCIAL PAGE OF MAY 10, 1901, SHOWING NORTHERN PACIFIC AT $1000 A SHARE

the violent fight for control between Morgan and Harriman reached its climax, the brokers were unable to deliver. On May 9, Northern Pacific soared to $1000 a share, bid up by frantic "shorts" who were trying to make good their contracts and avoid bankruptcy. As that stock rose, others fell with appalling rapidity, Standard Oil dropping 150 points between sales. By noon there would have been scarcely a Stock Exchange house which would have been solvent if it had to settle at the prices then prevailing. The chief contestants, to save the whole banking structure, had to call a truce, and allow the shorts to settle.

Each side claimed to have approximately half the stock of the Northern Pacific, having in fact purchased from short-sellers 78,000 shares more than existed. As a way out of the difficulty, a great holding company, capitalized at about $400,000,000, under the hospitable laws of New Jersey, was formed to take over the stocks of the Great Northern and Northern Pacific, with their joint ownership of the Burlington. As the Harriman-Kuhn, Loeb interests would have heavy representation on its board and already owned the other two Western transcontinentals, it seemed as though the entire Western railway system would come under one control, and the West was immediately up in arms.

This had been done in November, less than a month before Roosevelt sent his first message to Congress, and those who were waiting to see what he would do had not long to wait. In February, the government brought suit for the dissolution of the holding company under the Sherman Act, and in a little less than two years had won its suit and dissolved the company. By his action, Roosevelt had antagonized practically all the greatest leaders in finance and industry, but in the summer, after his Attorney-General had started the suit, the President made a speaking tour of the country. The wild enthusiasm of the audiences in response to his reiterated statements that there should be no one in the nation so great or powerful as to be above the law and that he intended to enforce it, showed clearly that the people stood behind him.

Roosevelt was no demagogue but he had grasped the fact that the time had come to control irresponsible power for the interests of society as a whole. On the other hand,

IT WONT FLY.
ROCKY MOUNTAIN NEWS
DENVER - JUNE 09

TAFT'S KITE IN 1906 COULDN'T RISE VERY FAR BECAUSE OF
THE SHERMAN ACT

*A cartoon by Gilbert in "The Rocky Mountain News," by courtesy of the
Roosevelt Memorial Association.*

the business leaders, used to riding rough-shod toward their ends, denounced the suggested right of control as socialistic demagoguery, destructive of the business interests of the nation. This attitude was to appear rather brutally in another contest between Roosevelt and the business leaders in the autumn of the same year, 1902.

The condition of the coal-mining industry had been scandalous for many years, both legally and socially. Contrary to law in some States the great railroads, such as the Reading, owned mines, the products of which they carried, and contrary to social justice the owners treated their employees shamefully. Kept on low wages, forced to live at exorbitant rents in houses belonging to the mine-owners, required to buy even the tools of their trade, such as blasting powder, at more than double cost from the companies whose own coal it was that was to be blasted, and receiving in many cases the bulk of their wages in certificates good only for purchases of supplies at the companies' stores, the status of the worker in the mines had come to be that of economic slavery.

There had been a flare-up in 1900, when the miners had offered to submit their grievances to fair arbitration and to abide loyally by the decision. This the owners refused, but to avoid serious trouble and scandal just before the Presidential election, Hanna had patched up a truce. There was no real redress of grievances, however, and in the early summer of 1902 the storm broke.

The leader and spokesman for the miners was John Mitchell, one of the finest and broadest-minded of the labor leaders we have had in America. On the other hand, the leader of the owners was George F. Baer, president of the Reading Railway, one of the most reactionary, narrow-minded and arbitrary of the inner ring of big business magnates. Refusing to consider complaints, to arbitrate or to recognize the union, his attitude was summed up in his incredible statement that "the rights and interests of the laboring man will be protected and cared for, not by the labor agitators, but by the Christian men to whom God in his infinite wisdom has given the control of the property interests of this country." One scarcely knows whether to wonder most at the ignorance, arrogance or blasphemy of such a view of the relations of the new coal barons to their new serfs. Unfortunately the view was accepted as natural by the owners, the great bankers and all the small group of big business leaders. These resented any assertion of rights by labor or the ordinary citizen which might challenge their own absolute control, reducing their personal profits or limiting their entire freedom of action.

Almost 150,000 desperate men had gone on strike in May, and as the cold of autumn approached without any settlement, the price of coal to consumers had risen to $30 a ton. Even such a man as Stuyvesant Fish, who a few years later was to be financially murdered by Harriman and other leaders because of his firm stand on the reform of the life insurance companies, warned Roosevelt that the coal owners had the right to make all they could out of the situation and that nothing should be done by the government to end the strike and interfere with the "legitimate" increase in profits. In view of the enormous suffering in store for the people at large, as well as the miners, when winter should come, the President wrote that "the only analogy" to Fish's suggestion "I could think of would be a protest by the undertakers against the improper activity of the government quarantine officers in preventing the admittance of Asiatic cholera."

As President, Roosevelt had no constitutional power to do anything beyond maintaining order by force, if necessary, in the mining districts, but he undertook personally to bring about a settlement. Calling a conference at the White House of Mitchell and some of the representatives of the owners, he asked them to reach some agreement which, for the good of the suffering nation, might result in resumption of mining. Mitchell immediately offered to arbitrate, but the owners flatly refused, and the meeting broke up in anger, Mitchell, according to the President, being the only one of all, including Roosevelt himself, who kept his temper.

The public, however, which had been on the side of the men, was deeply aroused and alarmed, and the owners began to take fright. Moreover the President was considering taking over the mines with Federal troops and operating them for the benefit of the people regardless of the owners. At last the latter agreed to the appointment of a Commission of Arbitration, and although they absolutely refused to allow a representative of labor on the Commission they agreed to it if he should be designated as "an eminent sociologist"! As Lodge wrote, "the business man dealing with a large political question is really a painful sight."

Mining was at once resumed and the nation was saved unthinkable suffering. Four months later the Commission decided largely in favor of the miners, who received a ten per cent increase in wages, recognition of the Union, and other advantages. The willingness of the owners to entail any amount of suffering on the people rather than yield an inch on the side of fairness and justice had taught the public again how completely it was coming under the control of a small and arrogantly arbitrary group. Roosevelt's able handling of the situation enormously increased his popularity as a leader.

An episode at the very end of the same year was to do so yet further, as well as to give him prestige abroad, although the details were not disclosed for many years after. Venezuela, which, under its dictator Castro, owed considerable sums to several European nations, had been involved in disputes over payments for a long time, when England and Germany, working in harmony, broke off diplomatic relations, and both sent some war-ships to the Venezuelan coast. Roosevelt had no objections to the European nations' bringing Castro to book, but he became convinced, apparently justly, that Germany intended to use the incident to acquire at least a permanent naval base in the Caribbean. This we would not have allowed in any case under the Monroe Doctrine, but in addition, as we shall see, we had begun negotiations looking to the building of the Panama Canal. The President had no intention of allowing Germany to establish a fortified base commanding its eastern end.

England, which had no such intention and had no

UNCLE SAM—THAT'S A LIVE WIRE, GENTLEMEN!

A CARTOON ON THE MONROE DOCTRINE
From *"The New York Herald,"* December 16, 1902.

wish to pull Germany's chestnuts out of the fire, withdrew her ships and there was no trouble on that score. Germany, however, refused arbitration with Venezuela, and contented herself with denying that she intended "permanent" occupation of any Venezuelan territory. Roosevelt pointed out to von Holleben that "permanent" was a very vague word, and that Germany had seized the Chinese port of Kiauchau on a ninety-nine-

year lease. Meanwhile, the President had ordered
Dewey, with a fleet of over fifty ships, including every
battle-ship and torpedo boat in the American navy (at
that time more powerful than the German), to "man-
œuvre" in the West Indian waters, with secret orders to
have the fleet ready to sail to Venezuela at an hour's
notice. The German Ambassador was then informed that
if Germany did not agree to arbitrate within ten days,
Dewey would be ordered to Venezuela.

According to Roosevelt's version, unfortunately the
ambassador advised his government that Roosevelt was
bluffing. When some days passed and no word came
from Germany, the President asked von Holleben if he
had any answer. Roosevelt's story is that when von
Holleben replied "No," he was informed that, in that
case, Dewey would receive his orders twenty-four hours
earlier than had been planned. Recent research has
thrown grave doubt on Roosevelt's tale; but it is certain that von Holleben miscalculated his purpose.

The Emperor agreed to arbitration and von Holleben
was dismissed from the service. It was a wound to the
Kaiser's prestige and self-esteem that must have cut deep,
but in a public statement Roosevelt gave the German
praise for his offer of arbitration and let him off easily.
Although the Emperor had asked Roosevelt himself to
be the arbitrator, the President declined, and strengthened the position of the Hague Tribunal by having all
the nations take their cases to that Court. Although the

full story of the negotiations was not to be revealed for more than a decade, it was clear that the President had scored a heavy diplomatic victory over the Emperor, and between his defense of American rights abroad and his defense of the ordinary small citizen at home, Roosevelt was attaining a degree of enthusiastic popularity which has fallen to the lot of no other President.

Few, indeed, have had such a successful year as Roosevelt had in 1902. Perhaps the most important and beneficent policy which he initiated in it, and which Congress embodied in the Newlands Act, was that of the much-needed conservation of our national resources. For generations we had been recklessly wasteful of them. Private ownership had destroyed the forests of State after State, with no replanting, so that the vast forest areas which under proper management might have lasted us a thousand years had disappeared almost in one generation. But we had also been wasteful of our water power and other resources, the government having taken little or no interest in preventing their rapid dissipation in private hands.

Cleveland had made a beginning, and a few Acts, such as the Forest Reserve Act of 1891, and the Carey Act of 1894, had been passed, but fraud, graft, and greed, combined with lack of aggressiveness on the part of the authorities, had largely made them dead letters. Roosevelt initiated a wholly new era and indeed changed the current of national thought on the subject. He not

THE FAMOUS FLORODORA SEXTETTE

Florodora opened November 12, 1900, at the Casino Theatre and ran to five hundred and forty-seven performances in New York. The original members of the sextette were: Margaret Walker, Vaughn Texsmith, Marie Wilson, Marjorie Relyea, Agnes Wayburn, Daisy Green.

A FARO GAME IN FULL SWING AT THE ORIENT SALOON, BISBEE, ARIZONA, IN 1903

Recognized: *Left to right:* Tony Downs (standing with derby—part owner of saloon); Doyle, a concert-hall singer, at the corner of table sitting, with derby. Back of him standing is Dutch Kid. Sleepy Dick, the porter, to right with light felt. Charlie Bassett, wearing soft felt, in rear, next wall; dealer is Johnny Murphy. Smiley Lewis is in silk hat.

AN ADVERTISEMENT OF ABOUT 1908, INSPIRED, APPARENTLY, BY A
GOVERNMENT RULING

From the Library of Congress.

only withdrew 85,000,000 acres of public lands from sale until their mineral resources could be examined, but, whereas under the Act of 1891 former Presidents had set aside about 30,000,000 acres each of forest land, he formed a national forest preserve of nearly 150,000,000 wooded acres, out of the 200,000,000 that existed when he became President. Moreover, by the building of dams and the utilization of our Western water powers for the irrigation of "desert" lands, the results of Roosevelt's policy and foresight are crops now valued at about $250,-000,000 a year. In this, as in all else, he encountered the strong opposition of private interests of one sort or another, who much preferred the old opportunities for making money by exploiting the resources of the moment to considering their value for future generations.

Although 1903 was chiefly notable for the acquisition of Panama at its close, it began less spectacularly with continued social legislation. In February an Act was passed by Congress creating the Department of Labor, and another giving precedence in the courts to cases against the trusts, such as that against the beef combine which was won by the government in May. The Elkins Act, although it did not give the government control over railway rates, made an important step forward by making illegal any secret rebates from published rates, and making the receiver as well as the giver of such rebates liable to punishment.

Fear, mistrust, and hatred of Roosevelt were increasing almost as rapidly in Wall Street as was his popularity outside of it. The brief, but rather sharp, depression in business in 1903, which was due to the reckless way in which the bankers had floated enormous amounts of "undigested securities" in capitalizing their new consolidations, was, of course, attributed to the President, either because the financiers believed it or because they wanted a scapegoat for their own misdeeds. Even so extraordinary a judge of values as Morgan had lost his head, and in throwing together the International Mercantile Marine combination had displayed an utter disregard of realities in the prices paid for the White Star Line and other constituents.

BUILDING THE PANAMA CANAL

Whatever other things he accomplished, and they were both many and great, Roosevelt himself always believed that the greatest was the building of the Panama Canal. It is certain that no other action of his life brings out more clearly both his qualities and their defects.

The background of the situation in 1903 may be briefly described in its essential points. For at least a decade, Roosevelt had been deeply interested in the project of an isthmian canal, which, owned, controlled, and fortified by us, he deemed essential to our security and naval policy, and which he was most keen to have as the chief claim to glory of his own administration. To accomplish what he wished, it was necessary to abrogate honorably the old Clayton-Bulwer Treaty of 1850 with England, and after a couple of years' negotiation this was done amicably by the signing of the Hay-Pauncefote Treaty, February 21, 1902.

There was a question whether the route across Nicaragua or that across Panama was the more suitable, the decision finally being in favor of the latter. A French company had long before secured a concession, terminating in 1904, from the Colombian Government, and had done some work but had been unable to make a success of the undertaking. In January, 1902, the company offered to sell out to the United States for $40,000,000.

There was also in the background an old treaty made in 1846 between Colombia (then called New Granada) and the United States. For nearly sixty years this had been interpreted by both parties to mean that we should protect the neutrality of Panama (a province of Colombia) against foreign attack; preserve freedom of transit across the isthmus; maintain Colombia's sovereignty over it; and avoid interference with any effort of Colombia to suppress insurrection, indeed to assist her in so doing.

In March, 1902, negotiations were begun with the Colombian Minister in Washington for a treaty which should serve as the basis for our undertaking to build the Canal. On January 22, 1903, a Convention was signed by John Hay and the Colombian *chargé d'affaires,* Thomas Herran. The terms on which the United States had insisted had been so repugnant to the Minister from Colombia and his government that the former had declined to sign the Convention and had left Washington. The terms were, in brief, that there could be no negotiations between Colombia and the French company; that the United States should have full control over a strip of land six miles wide across the isthmus, Colombia renouncing her sovereignty; and that for these and other considerations we should pay Colombia $10,000,000 in gold, and after nine years $250,000 a year. On the 17th of March the American Senate ratified the agreement.

On the other hand, the Colombian Government did not. There had been a dictatorship in that country for five years, and the politicians were unquestionably difficult to deal with, but popular sentiment upheld the Colombian Senate in its contention that Colombia should not give up its sovereignty and that the $10,000,000 offered to that country for all it was asked to yield was too little compared with the $40,000,000 paid to the almost defunct French private company. In August, the Senate rejected the proposed treaty.

There is no question that however useful the Canal might prove to us and to the world, and however anxious Roosevelt may have been to link his name with it, Colombia was entirely within her rights in declining to ratify the treaty, precisely as our own Senate has declined to ratify innumerable treaties. It is also almost certain that although more time would have been involved, a satisfactory treaty could have been made by the use of more courteous negotiation and by the payment of a larger sum. It was none of our business what might become of the money after we paid it to the Colombian Government, and in truth what we offered was very small. Within a few years after the opening of the Canal our annual net profits from its operation, quite apart from its strategic value to us, were about fifty per cent more, not allowing for capital charges, than the total capital sum we offered Colombia for the Zone.

However, Roosevelt, always impatient, would brook no delay. Powerful interests had become involved in the possible payment of $40,000,000 to the French company, and so careful was the protection accorded to it that although its charter had only one year to run, we insisted, by prohibiting all negotiations between it and Colombia, that the Colombians could get none of the $40,-000,000. Moreover, no Vice-President who had succeeded to the Presidency had ever been subsequently elected, and the Presidential election was only a year off. Roosevelt preferred therefore to wield "the big stick," and throughout the negotiations there was an air of haste and bullying which was most unusual in diplomatic intercourse.

The Province of Panama itself naturally wanted the Canal built, and when Colombia declined to sign the treaty and we declined to negotiate further, it was not difficult for those interested in the $40,000,000 payment to the expiring French company, and others, to stage a revolution. There is no evidence that Roosevelt took an active part in bringing it about. He did not have to, but he was aware that it was coming, and was prepared to act. He had already contemplated seizing the Canal Zone by force and declaring war against Colombia, but the revolution offered a simpler way out. Although by our Treaty of 1846 we were supposed to uphold Colombian sovereignty, Roosevelt gave a different and wholly new interpretation to that document, and as a result of the intervention of our naval forces we established the independence of the revolted province as the Republic of Panama. We then made a treaty with that new State, getting all we wanted in the way of a Canal Zone for ourselves at our own price.

The evidence points to the almost certainty that if we had agreed to give Colombia $7,500,000 more, we could have got all we wanted from her, but it seems to have been less a question of money than of time—time which was growing short for those interested in the French company with its expiring concession and for Roosevelt with only a year or so more of his term. The consequence of the way the affair was handled was that not only did Colombia become our bitter enemy, and justly so, but fear of the "big stick" and of the brutal aggressiveness of the great American Republic spread throughout the whole of South America. Roosevelt's later statement, "I took the Canal Zone," was all too clearly understood by our southern neighbors, and in spite of the fact that in 1922 tardy justice was done to Colombia, partly under pressure from American oil interests on Congress, by the payment to her of $25,000,000, or more than three times what we would have had to pay extra in 1903, irreparable harm had been done to our reputation for friendly and honest dealing.

In the treaty with Panama we reserved to ourselves the right to intervene to maintain order in that new "sovereign" state, as we had done in the case of Cuba, and, largely as a result of our interest in the Canal, we were in succeeding years to develop further the theory of our "protectorate" over the countries of the Caribbean. Most of them were unstable in government and in debt to Europe, a situation which, in order to prevent European occupation, might cause us, as Roosevelt pointed out in his message to Congress in December, 1904, to exercise "an international police power."

This, within a few weeks, he proceeded to do in Santo Domingo, which had become bankrupt, owing money to France, Italy, and Belgium, which nations had announced their intention of extorting payment by force. Roosevelt made a treaty with the small republic under which the United States was to take over the finances and assets of Santo Domingo in the capacity of a receiver and to administer them for the benefit of that nation and its creditors. Although the Senate declined to ratify the treaty and denounced Roosevelt's usurpation, the President went ahead and carried out his plan by Executive action only. The plan worked well, and the treaty was ratified three years later, but the extension given to the Monroe Doctrine by Roosevelt marked an important, and perhaps dangerous, step in the interpretation of that

EXPANSION LED TO THIS CARTOON BY LEON BARRITT, USED BY THE REPUBLICAN NATIONAL COMMITTEE OF 1904

From the Library of Congress.

very vague policy. On the other hand, until the Drago theory of non-intervention by force to collect international debts is generally accepted by the nations of the world, probably Roosevelt's policy of our acting as policeman in the Caribbean is the lesser of two dangers.

It was a policy, however, that by no means approved

itself to all Americans, many of whom had also been shocked by the way we acquired the Canal Zone. The settlement of the Alaska boundary dispute with England and Canada in 1903, the courageous handling of the coal strike the year before, and above all the President's attitude on the trust problem, had won him enormous popularity. On the other hand, the last two points had also made him a host of powerful enemies among the leaders of business and his party, to which were now added many who had formerly approved of his course but who objected to our wielding the "big stick" in foreign relations.

THE CAMPAIGN OF 1904

Mark Hanna, who had made Roosevelt's predecessor President, and was now himself spoken of for the office, was one of the bitter enemies to be reckoned with, but his death in February, 1904, cleared the path, and made Roosevelt's nomination practically a certainty. When the Republican Convention met at Chicago on June 21, Roosevelt was unanimously acclaimed as the candidate, with Senator Charles W. Fairbanks of Indiana for Vice-President. The Democrats at their convention at St. Louis, July 6, were torn between the radical section under Bryan and the conservatives under Cleveland, finally uniting on a respectable but weak candidate, Judge Alton B. Parker of New York. There was no doubt of the result of the election. Roosevelt, in resisting the demand of trades unions when pushed too far against public interest, just as he resisted the trusts, had made some enemies in the labor ranks but he had made for himself a place in public opinion comparable only to that of Andrew Jackson.

His personality was the issue in the campaign, which was carried on in the returning flood-tide of prosperity after the set-back in 1903, and Roosevelt was overwhelmingly elected by 336 electoral votes against only 140 for Parker, who polled about a million less popular votes than Bryan had in the previous campaign. Roosevelt was now at last President in his own right, and consequently in a much stronger position. The independence of this he also strengthened by announcing that "the wise custom which limits the President to two terms regards the substance and not the form, and under no circumstances will I be a candidate for, or accept, another nomination," a statement which was to plague him later.

Whatever else may be said of Roosevelt, it must be conceded that in spite of the "big stick" and big business, the idealism and aspiration of the American people were steadily rising with him as leader, and they were growing more determined to set their own house in order and to play a distinguished part in the international life of the world. Oddly enough, one of the marked features of the decade and a half before the World War was to break upon the world, to its destruction, was the increase in many countries of the sentiment for peace. Peace societies multiplied, and America was one of the leading nations in favor of arbitration and the resort to the Hague Court.

The Russo-Japanese War, which had been going on

A CONTRAST—A 1904 CAMPAIGN CARTOON

Returning prosperity led to "Don't give the Democrats another chance," as campaign material.

From the Library of Congress Collection of Cartoons.

since February, 1904, with heavy losses and with no apparent termination, gave Roosevelt a great chance, which he seized, to lead both the world movement for peace and to bring his own country into the larger life of nations in a beneficent way. In June, 1905, he urged on both warring governments that they should send repre-

145

sentatives to negotiate peace, and after many delays and much adroit statesmanship on his part, representatives of the two nations did meet at Portsmouth, New Hampshire. Over and over in those sweltering August days, it seemed as though his efforts had been in vain, but to the relief of the entire world, a treaty was signed on the 5th of September.

The other nations gladly acknowledged the part which America had played, and America only, for European diplomacy had wholly broken down in the effort to end the strife. In America, the entire credit must go to Roosevelt, who displayed statesmanship of a high order and an unexpected degree of patience and tact. John Hay, the Secretary of State, was dying, and Taft, who had become Secretary of War, was temporarily in the Philippines. In any case, Roosevelt was always very much his own foreign secretary, and the entire burden of reconciliation fell upon him.

Not only had America, almost ignored a decade before, played a great part in world affairs but the President had gained a standing as one of the leading statesmen of the entire world, a position which was to be enhanced the following year by his entrance again into European affairs, although his full part was not realized until the publication of documents some years later. In the summer of 1905, war was imminent between France and Germany over the advance of the former in creating what was practically a protectorate over Morocco. The

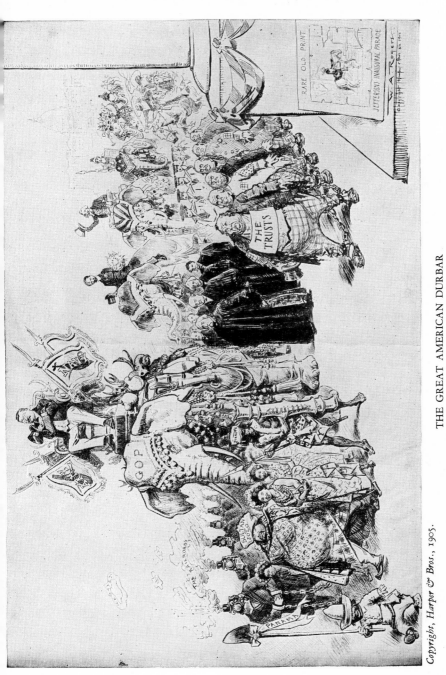

THE GREAT AMERICAN DURBAR

As W. A. Rogers pictured Roosevelt's Inauguration, for *Harper's Weekly* of March 4, 1905.

UNITED STATES SUPREME COURT

The first session was held in the Royal Exchange, New York (*bottom, left*), in 1790. From 1791 to 1800, sessions were held in the Old City Hall, Philadelphia. The Old Senate Chamber (*lower, right*) has been its home since 1859. *Top*, the new home of the Court, opposite the Capitol, Washington, D. C.

Kaiser, who was then claiming for his country that "place in the sun" which was to cost it dear, was bellicose, and the French Foreign Minister, Delcassé, had manœuvred France into a position from which it could not easily retreat. The despatch of the German warship *Panther* to Agadir made the situation so tense as to make it appear that a Franco-German war was inevitable.

Through the good offices of Roosevelt, a conference was arranged to meet at Algeciras, January, 1906, in which the United States was represented by Henry White and S. R. Gummere, and in which what had appeared as insuperable difficulties were smoothed away. Even more important than the Portsmouth Conference, the credit again was almost solely Roosevelt's. When we consider the part which America was playing in international affairs in Roosevelt's second term with that of her "unofficial observers" and almost complete refusal to participate officially from 1920 onward, we can realize better the immense reaction which was to come in America's international feeling. Both our growing power and the transition through which we had been passing from a nation chiefly agricultural to one largely manufacturing, with the need of overseas markets, had led Roosevelt to grasp the idea that, as he said, "we cannot sit huddled within our own borders and avow ourselves merely an assemblage of well-to-do hucksters who care nothing for what happens beyond."

In 1906, work actually began on the Panama Canal, and in eight years and at a cost of about $375,000,000 it was opened for traffic. The two American continents had been cut apart from each other by one of the greatest engineering feats yet attempted. Great as that was, however, it was scarcely greater than the sanitary and medical work of Colonels Gorgas and Goethals who transformed our tropical jungle, ravaged by diseases, into a healthful land for white men. Whatever may be objected to our method of acquiring the Canal Zone, we completed in record time the digging of the Canal where the French had failed, and also, what they had not even dreamed of doing, we made an almost magic transformation of the Zone both physically and morally. In those respects we have everything to our credit.

In the same year that dirt began to fly at Panama, we were called upon to intervene again in Cuba, at the request of the Cuban authorities. The government had been lax, and had allowed much of the sanitary and other work of improvement we had bequeathed the island from our former occupation to be undone. Moreover the electorate, largely illiterate, had shown itself more apt at revolution against its own government than at governing. Elections became a farce, and in 1905 the actual number of qualified voters, about 300,000, was increased in registration by approximately 150,000 fictitious names, a fraud on so colossal a scale as to make the operations of our political bosses seem almost morality itself.

Taft was in charge of administration in this second occupation, which lasted about two years, and although supported by a small body of American troops, no force had to be used. The intervention had been entered upon with genuine reluctance on our part, and when an orderly election had been held in the autumn of 1908, we withdrew on the inauguration of the new President in the following January and again turned the island over to the Cubans.

Roosevelt's first message to Congress in 1901 had outlined practically all his views and policies, and these he continued to carry out throughout his two terms. Both the "muckraking" and public dissatisfaction with big business methods reached their climax between 1903 and 1906, the year 1905 being marked by the investigations of the great insurance companies in New York. Charles E. Hughes, who was in charge of the probe, conducted it with such skill and success as to give him a national reputation, and surprising and disgusting scandals and graft were disclosed on the part of men who had stood high in the business life of the country. One of the astounding features of the investigation was the pettiness of much of the graft to which men whose wealth was reckoned in millions and even tens of millions had been willing to stoop, and the belief they seemed to hold that the great companies over which they presided were private preserves for themselves.

The public resentment, emphasized by the feelings of

hundreds of thousands of policy-holders, who felt themselves personally injured, was intense, and Roosevelt's
opprobrious term, "malefactors of great wealth," took on
new meaning. Congress, conscious of the strength of
public opinion, continued to place new social legislation
on the statute books. In 1906, the disclosures which had
been made with regard to patent medicine frauds, involving the dishonesty of the advertising pages of not a few
great newspapers, and the facts which had been given
to the public about conditions in the stockyards, led to
the passage of the Pure Food Act, which has proved of
great protective benefit to American households. In the
same year, laws were passed forbidding the corporations
to make campaign contributions, and also an employer's
liability Act.

Big business, however, seemed to be learning little or
nothing. In 1907, it was found that the American Sugar
Refining Company had been deliberately, and for years,
defrauding the government on the collection of customs
duties, and over $4,000,000 was recovered from it in the
courts. In spite of the law against rebates, it was likewise
found that the Chicago & Alton Railroad was giving and
the Standard Oil Company receiving them. The absurd
fine of almost $30,000,000 levied by Judge Landis on the
latter corporation did not obscure the fact that apparently some of the richest business men in the nation were
still defying the laws and adding to their wealth by de-
liberate fraud. Although the sugar and oil company scan-

dals were the most spectacular of those unearthed in
1907, they were far from the only ones,—the New York
Central, for example, also being convicted of rebating,
—and the people felt with steadily mounting enthusiasm that Roosevelt was almost the sole champion of the
doctrine of one law for both rich and poor.

The financial situation by 1907 had become distinctly
unstable. A series of good harvests had brought prosperity but this had been recklessly over-capitalized by financiers in the flotation of new enterprises, and there was
heavy strain on credit. The stock market had risen rapidly and attracted a large public following, quite willing
to share in the profits made for them by the very men
whose methods they were denouncing. On the other
hand, the succession of scandals had really undermined
confidence in these men, and in the institutions which
they controlled and operated. Panic would seize the public quickly if they came to suspect any crack in the
strength of the general position.

In the spring of 1907 the banks, over-extended, had
to call loans and the stock market began to tumble. There
was a sharp break, and throughout the summer confidence became more and more undermined. In October
the crash came, precipitated by the failure of the great
Knickerbocker Trust Company of New York and ten
other financial institutions in that city within a few days.
It was with great difficulty that others were saved, and
currency went to a premium of five per cent. Business

throughout the country received a very severe shock, and it was not until the Pennsylvania Railroad floated a successful loan in the following March that confidence began to revive.

Although Roosevelt used every legitimate means in his power to assist business, efforts were made by the larger interests to propagate the belief that it was his reckless meddling with business affairs and men and his wild radicalism that had brought the business structure crashing. A President usually has to suffer the onus of bad times if they come in his administration, but outside of Wall Street Roosevelt suffered less than might have been expected. His hold on the imagination of the ordinary citizen and the long succession of scandals, aired in magazines and courts, smudging the reputation of one great business man after another, made the President's word appear more reliable than that of big business.

The rigidity of the old bond-secured currency system of the nation had been again revealed by the panic of 1907, and the following year a commission, with Senator Nelson W. Aldrich at its head, was appointed to consider the whole problem of our banking system. Meanwhile, as a stop-gap, the Aldrich-Vreeland Act, authorizing the Treasury to lend emergency currency to the banks in time of stress, secured by approved collateral, marked the first step toward reform and a more elastic currency system.

While we were in the midst of the panic, an episode

occurred which, for the third important occasion, called attention to the dangers of our Federal system. Racial

HE GOT HIS BUMPS

From the time you start to toddle
'Till you're called a Mollycoddle
 You,ill find this rocky road is full of stumps,
And a bunch of bum disaster
Like a piece of porous plaster
 Keeps a trying hard and fast to give you bumps

Mr. Harriman Got his bumps
'Cause Teddy Roosevelt held the trumps
 You can bet he got his bumps —he got his bumps

※ ※ ※ ※ ※

When Willie Randolph Hearst
Tried to land on Mackie first
 He didn't count on Democratic slumps
But your uncle Charley Hughes,

Gave the grafters all the blues
 And Willie got his bumps—got his bumps

Yes little Willie got his bumps
And calls McCarren—Croker chumps,
 But he surely got his bumps—he got his bumps

Billy Bryan as a boy,
Filled his little heart with joy
 When the funny—nologist felt his lumps,
And the bets were ten to one
That he'd land in Washington
 But Billy got his bumps—got his bumps
Yes, Mark Hanna gave him dumps
And then Roosie held the trumps.
 It's a shame but the same got his bumps.

© *Charles H. Walker.*

PART OF A PHILOSOPHIC POEM OF 1907 TOUCHING ON PERSONALITIES
AND POLITICS
From the Library of Congress.

feeling in California had been steadily growing more intense against the Japanese for some years, when in 1906 the San Francisco Board of Education issued an order segregating Japanese school-children from the whites. A sensitive and proud nation, Japan promptly resented what she considered an insult, and what was unquestionably an infringement of her treaty rights with the United States. As in the previous cases of New York and Louisiana, however, the Federal Government had no power to coerce a State, and a dangerous international situation developed. It was saved, though with only partial allayment of Japan's resentment, by the negotiation with her of the Root-Takahira Treaty and a "gentleman's agreement," the two covering the problems of the school-children, immigration into the United States, and the larger questions of the Pacific and the Orient.

By the end of 1908 prosperity was returning, the Canal was being built, we were preparing to withdraw in a few weeks from Cuba, and an immense amount had been accomplished to purify the business life of the country. Roosevelt was at the summit of his popularity and prestige at home and abroad. A President would have to be chosen in November, but Roosevelt had declared that he would not accept another nomination.

CHAPTER IV

THE NEW FREEDOM

THERE was little or no doubt in advance as to who would be the candidates of the two major parties in the campaign of 1908. Each party was wholly dominated by its leading personality, the Democratic by Bryan and the Republican by Roosevelt. Either could have received the nomination without effort, but whereas Bryan intended to accept it, and did, from the Democrats, Roosevelt, in view of his two terms and his self-denying pronouncement of 1904, made it clear that he would not accept, and that he intended to have the nomination go to William H. Taft.

Roosevelt was at the very height of his popularity, though possibly not of his power, for the rebellions against him in Congress of "Old Guard" Republicans like Senator Aldrich and Speaker Cannon had been increasing in bitterness and strength. It is an interesting but superfluous question as to how far the retiring President would have succeeded in the fights of a third term had he accepted it. But the very hostility to him of "the interests," inside and outside Congress, had served only to increase the idolization of him by the people at large, and there was no doubt that he could nominate his successor in the convention which met at Chicago on June 19.

The man whom he had chosen was apparently extraordinarily well trained both to make a great President and to carry out Roosevelt's policies. At fifty-five years of age, Taft had had a distinguished career as a judge in the Federal service, as a member of the Philippine Commission, as first civil governor of the Philippines, 1901-4, as Secretary of War in Roosevelt's Cabinet, 1904-8, as temporary governor of Cuba, 1907, and as head of diplomatic missions to various courts, from that of the Pope at Rome to the Mikado in Japan. He had acquitted himself with marked ability in every post he had occupied, had been one of Roosevelt's closest friends, was in sympathy with the President's social policies, was incorruptibly honest, and was genial and popular.

There were, however, two points as to which Roosevelt miscalculated. One was a flaw in Taft's training, which has been exemplified again in the case of Hoover. The two cases, both of honest men with apparently exceptional preparation for the Presidency, are interesting. Neither had ever been in the rough and tumble of American political life, and did not know how to get on with politicians in the legitimate sense in which a President has to get on to get things done. Shortly after Taft's inauguration, Lodge wrote to Roosevelt saying that Taft was all they had thought but that "I am surprised that he has not, in all his years of public life, learned more about politics . . . as one of the conditions with which a man has to deal."

The Hit of the Campaign
as sung by UNCLE SAM.

"SWEET BILLEE"
(COPYRIGHTED 1908.)
BY CHAS. A. PENNELL
(air Sweet Marie)

Respectfully dedicated to the Republican Party

1. What's this racket that I hear? Sweet Billee.
   Something's broken loose I fear, for I see
All the voters in the land, have resolved to take a stand
And they will throw you on the strand. Sweet Billee.
For your platform it is weak. Sweet Billee.
   Braced and patched with rotten timbers, don't you see?
And with Roosevelts help and rine, you tried to steal some
                    planks of Bryan.
But you missed them every time. Sweet Billee.
CHORUS.
Oh William Taft just come to me and I'll whisper unto thee,
 William Bryan is on your trail don't you see?
He is a daisy from the Platte and he will knock you out quite flat,
When November winds come back. Sweet Billee.

© *Charles A. Pennell,* 1908.

A 1908 CAMPAIGN SONG
From the Library of Congress.

The other point which had escaped Roosevelt was the fact that although Taft was not a reactionary and was in full sympathy with the President's own aims, his ap-

157

proach to the practice and theory of government was quite different. If there was one quality more lacking than another in Roosevelt, it was the judicial mind. Although he so often insisted upon the execution of the law impartially, he was so convinced of the rectitude of his own intentions and of the rightness of his own aims, that when, in his impatience, he found the law obstructing or delaying him, he was almost as contemptuous of it as the leaders of big business themselves. His later advocacy of the popular recall of judicial decisions was alone enough to indicate how little he had of the legal or judicial temper.

Taft was essentially judicial, and although liberal in his political and social outlook was extremely conservative when it came to questions of legal or constitutional methods of approach to them. These two points—his lack of political knowledge and finesse, and his judicial conservatism of mind—were to shipwreck him amid the swirling currents of American political life in the next four years, but were as hidden from the people as they were from the man who almost alone made him President.

THE CAMPAIGN OF 1908

In their conventions the Democrats chose Bryan on the first ballot and the Republicans Taft, the latter with James S. Sherman as his running-mate for the Vice-Presidency. The campaign, so tamely begun, continued without marked interest. Smaller parties, such as the Socialists running Eugene V. Debs, and the Independence League which nominated Hearst, were as usual in the field, but Taft polled about 7,700,000 of the popular vote to Bryan's 6,500,000, and was easily elected, together with a Republican Congress.

If the campaign was comparatively quiet, there were nevertheless a good many features in it to give the politicians pause. Not much attention was paid to party platforms, and the contest was really between the popularity of Bryan and that of Roosevelt, embodied in his candidate Taft. Issues, however, were not wholly ignored, and the fact that Taft ran far ahead of his ticket in all the States, and that many of those which elected him at the same time elected Democrats as governors and members of legislatures indicated that there was much unrest and also dissatisfaction with Republican rule, notably in the matter of the tariff.

Although wages had risen in the preceding decade they had far from kept pace with the rising cost of living, and the working class had shared to only a small extent in the prosperity of the great corporations. While the United States Steel Corporation, for example, had been rapidly changing the sea of water, which was all the common stock was originally, into the terra firma of a sound dividend-paying investment security, the workmen had demanded in vain most of the improvements in their condition which they had sought.

The business leaders appeared no more willing to share their prosperity or privileges than they ever had been, whereas the scandals revealed in the insurance and other

Republican Campaign Song for 1908,
Entitled

THE G. O. P.

I

Stand by the G. O. P. boys, stand by the crowd,
Stand by the G. O. P. makes a nation strong and proud,,
Stand by the G. O. P., our opponents they have split
And when the election's over they'l surely have a fit.

CHORUS.

Not without your wondrous story, G. O. P.,
Can be writ the nation's glory, G. O. P.,
On the record of the years
Abraham Lincoln's name appears,
McKinley, Logan and our tears, G. O. P.

II

Stand by the G. O. P., Teddy and his nag,
Stand by the G. O. P. our opponents we will bag,
Stand by the stars and stripes that wave so clear and
bright,
They'll carry the nation's problems thro' the darkest
night.

© 1906 by Lewis T. Watkins.

A 1908 CAMPAIGN SONG
From the Library of Congress.

investigations, the suits against the sugar and other trusts, the mass of information and misinformation which the public had derived from the muckraking magazines, had all aroused both a deeper and a more intelligent resentment. It was realized that the Old Guard

Republican leaders were making an effort to recapture control of the party and its policies, and the conflict between the reactionaries and the Progressives which was to split the party four years later was already foreshadowed.

In many directions the increasing lack of confidence of the rank and file of the people in the older organizations and forms of government was becoming manifest. Distrust of the Senate, the death-chamber of tariff reform and the stronghold of special privilege, was bringing on an ever stronger demand for a change in the Constitution which would permit of the popular election of its members. The experimentation in many Western States with the initiative, the referendum, and the recall, as well as the acceleration in the movement for woman's suffrage, all were symptoms of the same mistrust of old ways of governing, and the belief that conditions could be improved by bringing the governments into closer relations with a widening electorate.

The rise, from 1905, of the extreme radical groups in labor, such as the Industrial Workers of the World (I. W. W.), betokened likewise a menacing increase of unrest among the labor class, which in its Left Wing was now preaching violence as the only means of cure. On the other hand, the ultra-conservatives, whether in business or politics, instead of trying to remedy conditions were merely digging in to resist change.

If, in the situation, Taft failed to work out a policy

which satisfied any one, it is far from certain that Roosevelt, facing conditions more difficult than any he had himself had to meet, would have succeeded any better. Having secured Taft's election, the former President, still the most popular man in the country, disappeared from the American scene to hunt big game in the wilds of Africa, in order that his successor should have a free hand. If there was a certain amount of egotism in his feeling that Taft could not be free unless he himself got out of America, there was also much truth in his belief. Other Presidents have been able to retire to the seclusion of private life with dignity, but Roosevelt's abounding energy, his inability to keep out of a fight or the limelight of publicity, combined with the hero-worship of him by the people, would have made the rôle of a retired elder statesman practically impossible for him in 1909. Unfortunately for his own reputation it was one he would never be able to play.

The rising resentment in the country against the tariff had forced the Republicans to put a plank in their platform promising revision in a special session of Congress to be called immediately following the inauguration of their President if elected. When Congress, called together by Taft, met to consider the problem, the new tariff bill proceeded through all the usual stages with which the nation had become all too familiar. As passed by the House it embodied in considerable degree a genuine downward revision. Both there and in the Senate it was subjected to the influence of the lobbyists of the special interests who would benefit by high rates, about the only interest not having a lobbyist to represent it being the American people.

In the Senate, under the lead of Aldrich, 847 amendments were made, mostly raising duties, in spite of the efforts of the group of Progressive Senators, including La Follette, Beveridge, Cummins, Bristow, and Dolliver, who were gradually emerging as insurgents from the Republican Party. When the bill finally went to Taft for his signature, it was evident to the people that there had been no downward revision to give them relief. The publicity given to the pressure brought to bear by particular interests made the whole thing appear more baldly than ever a raid on the public for the benefit of a few. To the disgust of the Democrats and the steadily more influential Progressive element among the Republicans, the President not only signed the bill, but in a speech in Minnesota defended it as the best tariff bill the Republicans had ever enacted.

The disappointment of the Progressives throughout the country was intense, and the fear that the man who had been elected to carry out Roosevelt's forward policies had gone over to the reactionaries was increased by the reliance placed by Taft upon Cannon in the House and Aldrich in the Senate, both of whom, with all they stood for, were the objects of determined opposition by the Progressives.

Balked of tariff reform, and suspicious of the President's alliance with Cannon and Aldrich, the Progressives were in no mood to reason calmly about the rights and wrongs of a bitter personal quarrel between officials which now broke out, and which was used to indicate that Taft was going back on one of Roosevelt's most important policies, that of the conservation of our natural resources.

Taft was as thoroughly in sympathy with the policy as was Roosevelt, but the difference between the two men came out clearly in connection with their attitude toward the legal questions involved. The problem was a confused one, both as to legislation and organization. Congress, which to some extent had fought Roosevelt on the point, had never passed proper conservation laws, and in the organization of the government the Land Office was in one Department, the Forestry Service in another, and there was as yet no Bureau of Mines at all, that being established only in 1910. For the working out of his plans, Roosevelt had relied chiefly on his young Secretary of the Interior, J. R. Garfield, and on the Chief Forester, Gifford Pinchot, both ardent followers of the President. Pinchot in particular was fanatically devoted to the cause of conservation at all costs and a reformer of the impractical type.

Taft had replaced Garfield, when forming his Cabinet, by R. A. Ballinger, an Iowa lawyer, whose father had studied law in Lincoln's office. On examination of some of the withdrawals which had been made and of claims in connection with others, Ballinger was by no means as convinced of their legality as had been the ardent Garfield and Pinchot. At once, when Ballinger began to move slowly, the cry went up from the Conservationists that he was impeding the work and that he was even on the side of private interests as against the government. An employee of the Interior Department, L. R. Glavis, made charges against his chief in a letter to Senator Dolliver, and was dismissed. Pinchot also took the quarrel to the newspapers, and was removed for insubordination. A Congressional committee was appointed to investigate the charges, and although Glavis was represented by Louis D. Brandeis, later member of the Supreme Court, and Pinchot by George W. Pepper, the committee found that the charges brought by them were groundless, and that there was not a single fact to indicate that Ballinger had been actuated by any motive other than the public interest.

Under ordinary circumstances, the dismissal of two unimportant public officials might not have had serious results, but the circumstances were not ordinary. In the first place, Pinchot was a close friend of Roosevelt, and, like a small boy running to his mother, he hurried off to Europe to wait for Roosevelt's emergence from the African wilderness to be on hand to tell him all his woes. As his was the first personal account which Roosevelt received of the affairs of the Taft administration, the impression was important. In the second place the Ballinger-Pinchot controversy was used with great effect by the Progressives to emphasize the growing belief, due to the tariff and other matters, that Taft had betrayed the cause of liberalism and had gone over to the "interests."

There is ample evidence to disprove this, and even in the matter of conservation distinct progress was made in his administration. The taking over of the coal lands which Roosevelt had impulsively reserved without legal sanction was, at Taft's request, lawfully authorized by Congress. He also began the reservation of oil lands, and established the Bureau of Mines. In the same year, 1910, the passage of the Mann-Elkins Act greatly strengthened in some respects the Hepburn Act of the Roosevelt administration, giving to the Interstate Commerce Commission jurisdiction over the telegraph and telephone companies as well as railways, and authorizing it to suspend rates which it considered questionable pending investigation.

In his direct attacks on the great corporations, Taft was much more energetic than Roosevelt had been, the government during his four years bringing 67 bills and indictments against the trusts as compared with 43 during Roosevelt's seven and a half years. It was Taft's Attorney-General, George W. Wickersham, who secured the dissolution of the Standard Oil and Tobacco companies, and the government was successful in winning many of its other cases.

166

As a "trust buster," indeed, Taft was much more of a crusader than his sponsor, but it was already beginning to be recognized that in the new economic structure

"Jingle bells, jingle bells, jingle all the day !
Oh, what fun it is to ride in a one-horse open sleigh !"

A CARTOON BY F. OPPER IN *THE NEW YORK AMERICAN,*
JANUARY 10, 1910
Showing popular idea of the power of the Trusts of the period.

arising everywhere in the world, justice for the ordinary man would not be secured by the simple process of breaking up great aggregations of capital. By 1911 the Supreme Court was introducing into the conception of "restraint of trade" under the Sherman Act the qualifying adjectives "undue or unreasonable."

The fact is that Taft had to contend with a far more difficult situation than Roosevelt had, part of the difficulty having been made by Roosevelt himself. The tendency toward building up great national units of business, which had been a marked feature of our economic life ever since the Civil War, was a natural one. The population, which had numbered about 38,000,000 in 1870, and 76,000,000 when Roosevelt had been elected in 1900, had risen to 92,000,000 by 1910 when he returned from Africa. There had been a corresponding increase in national wealth, and in the aggregations of corporate capital.

Enormous abuses had crept into our political and social life in this progress of growth. Roosevelt had rendered a most useful service in arousing the people to a sense of these, and in serving as a leader. He had performed brilliant special feats, as the settlement of the coal strike and the Russo-Japanese War, and the building of the Canal. The people had come to regard him as a Moses to lead us into the Promised Land of justice for the common man. But Roosevelt himself had no map of the way into that land. He had fumbled his way along with the trust problem, and in truth he did not have, as no man could, a policy which would quickly cure the fundamental evils of the new economic order. Having led the people to believe that a hero could save them, his term had come to an end, he had presented Taft to his followers as that saving hero, and then disappeared into the jungle.

When Taft failed to save them, the people murmured mightily. They did not realize, and there is no evidence that Roosevelt did, the magnitude of the incomprehensible forces which were changing the face of the world and society.

In the year that McKinley was first elected the world production of gold had been less than 10,000,000 oz. During Taft's four years it averaged about 22,000,000 oz. The shortage of gold which had brought about the hardships which had made possible Bryan's campaign of 1896 had changed into a plethora which was bringing to the front new problems and hardships for other classes. The rapid rise in prices was depreciating even increasing wages and salaries. The increased scale of big business was creating huge wealth and incomes for lucky individuals. The whole social structure seemed to be getting out of gear, and the resentment against dishonesty and injustice, which had been fanned by Roosevelt, sought an outlet in some quick remedy. Taft could not supply it, and was thus considered a failure and a reactionary. No one else, however, has done so as yet.

Roosevelt returned from Africa in June, 1910, after an extraordinary tour of Europe in which he had been fêted by many of the sovereigns in a manner hitherto unheard-of for a private citizen. He found a Republican Party rapidly splitting, with much bitterness, into Insurgents and Old Guard, and, although his self-appointed successor was not half through his term, Roosevelt could not resist the appeal of a fight. Within a few weeks he was making political speeches through the country, clearly showing his preference for the Insurgent wing of the party, hostile to Taft.

It cannot be said that Roosevelt had any specific programme to offer, and many of his suggestions were those of the Democrats of the seemingly far-off days of 1896. The chief point in the "New Nationalism" which he preached appeared to be the injection of more democracy as a cure for our ills, notable in his appeals for an extension of the primary election as a means of nominating candidates, and in his demand for the recall of elected officials during the term for which they were elected if the people wished. The latter would, of course, make officials even more subject than they are now to the momentary whim or wrath of a temporary majority balloting for a recall. There was no doubt, however, of the dissatisfaction of the people with the world as it was, and the election returned 229 Democrats to 161 Republicans and 1 Socialist in the lower House of Congress, while of the 10 Republican majority left in the Senate enough were Insurgents to nullify the apparent advantage. Taft's administration, like so many others under our system, had to face its second two years hamstrung by having the legislature of a different party.

In April, 1911, however, the President had the temerity to call Congress into special session to pass a bill

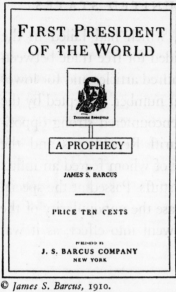

FIRST PRESIDENT
OF THE WORLD

A PROPHECY

BY
JAMES S. BARCUS

PRICE TEN CENTS

PUBLISHED BY
J. S. BARCUS COMPANY
NEW YORK

© James S. Barcus, 1910.

A PROPHECY OF 1910

From the Rare Book Room, Library of
Congress.

"WE NEVER SPEAK AS WE PASS BY"

From a cartoon in "Puck," February 19,
1912.

Courtesy of Roosevelt Memorial Association.

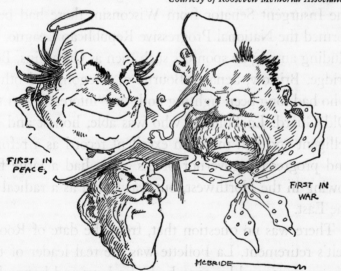

FIRST IN PEACE, FIRST IN WAR, FIRST IN THE HEARTS OF
HIS COUNTRYMEN

From a cartoon by McBride. Courtesy of Roosevelt Memorial Association.

171

for reciprocity with Canada, which had failed in the regular session. The bill provided for free trade between the countries in about one hundred articles and for lower duties on about four times that number. Accepted by the low-tariff Democrats, it had encountered strong opposition from the Eastern big-tariff Republicans and the Western Insurgents, the latter of whom feared an influx of Canadian lumber and foodstuffs. Passed at the special session, it served only to increase the unpopularity of the President, although it never went into effect, as it was defeated in Canada.

THE RISE OF THE PROGRESSIVES

In January, under the organizing lead of La Follette, the Insurgent Senator from Wisconsin, there had been formed the National Progressive Republican League, including among its sponsors such men as Cummins, Beveridge, Bristow, Senator Bourne of Oregon, and others who had long been fighting both the "interests" and the Old Guard. La Follette, who was able, honest and intelligent and had made an excellent record as a reform and progressive governor of his State, had a large following in the Northwest, but was feared as a radical in the East.

There was no question that, from the date of Roosevelt's retirement, La Follette was the real leader of the Progressives, and by 1911 he had a long and honorable record of successful fighting for fair play for the ordinary man. During the special session of Congress, the split in the Republican Party became complete, and in the Senate La Follette worked with the Democratic leader in the House, Oscar Underwood, to put through a new tariff bill, lowering duties, which barely failed of passage even over the veto of the President.

For the rest of Taft's term, the interest shifts from Congress to the Departments. That of Justice continued busy with suits against the trusts, while the State Department had its hands full with the relations to our neighbors on the south.

The building of the Canal and the policies connected with it initiated by Roosevelt had practically developed into the theory of our exercising a protectorate over all the Caribbean governments, except that of Mexico. Coupled with the practice of "dollar diplomacy," that is of using our diplomatic service for the purpose of promoting loans and other economic interests in foreign, and mostly backward, countries, the theory of protectorates quickly took further tangible form.

In 1911, as part of the terms of securing a loan from New York bankers, the custom house in Nicaragua was placed in charge of an American. The following year, we landed marines there to quell disorder, and, with a brief interval, they have been there ever since. In 1913, we supervised the elections in Santo Domingo, followed by the marines three years later. In 1915 (looking for

173

a moment forward into the next administration), we established with marines a forcible protectorate over Haiti. Unquestionably much good work has been done during the American occupations, and we could not afford complications with European nations arising from lack of order in these ill-governed small countries. On the other hand, although the problem is understood by many in the greater nations of South America, there is no doubt that the southerly advance of the "colossus of the North" has caused much ill-feeling and alarm in that continent.

A far more serious problem was raised by the situation in Mexico. Owing to a revolution led by Francisco Madero, the long rule of the strong Dictator Diaz came to an end in May, 1911. There had been a good deal of fighting just over the line from the United States in which Americans on our side had been killed, and Western blood was hot for revenge. The President despatched 20,000 troops to patrol the border, and although affairs quieted down, the pot boiled again at the end of Taft's term and when he left office he was to bequeath, as we shall see, a difficult problem and an army mobilized on the frontier to his successor.

In spite of some excellent achievements of the second half of his term (such as the establishment of the parcel post, his support of the Constitutional amendments providing for an income tax and popular election of senators, and his wide extension of Civil Service reform), he

had completely lost the confidence of the Progressives.
What seemed our new foreign policy, although initiated
by Roosevelt, was also giving serious concern. The "dollar diplomacy" of Secretary Knox was greatly disliked
and mistrusted by many. Whatever might be said for the
necessity of administering small Caribbean states, the
seeming willingness of the government to shut the "open
door" in China and to pronounce blessing on the participation of American bankers in the "Six Power" loan
of $300,000,000 to that country with various entering
wedges for the acquisition of its territory, appeared to be
a complete reversal of our former high-minded policy. It
began to look as though the Department of State were
being used as a Wall Street office to get profits and commissions for bankers. By the time the question came up
of Presidential nominations, Taft had seemingly lost almost all of the popularity and prestige with which he
had begun his term.

With the opening of the Presidential year of 1912, it
was clear that there would be a terrific struggle for control within the Republican Party between the Progressives and the Conservatives. If the latter, who were already in control of the machinery of the party, won they
would undoubtedly nominate Taft, but if the former
won, who would be the candidate? If Roosevelt had been
killed by a lion in Africa, the answer would have been
simple: La Follette, the man who more than any other
had kept the Progressive banner flying the past four years

and stood the heat and burden of the day. Roosevelt was not lying in an African grave but was in America, bursting with energy, and with the unanswered question as to what to do with a particular ex-President. He still had an immense public following, not diminished by the limelight which played over his every action. It might have been difficult to avoid it, for everything which he did had been, for long, "news" in an extraordinary degree. But he certainly did nothing to avoid it, and by his constant writings and his speaking tours of the country he kept the spotlight on himself.

What would be his attitude toward the political complications of his party and nation? That had been the great American political enigma since the cables had announced in 1910 that he was safely out of the jungle with his trophies. He had stood on such a pinnacle of popularity at home and fame abroad as no other American had ever before occupied, and had come to consider himself as the only American capable of leading the people and solving their problems. Given his character and temperament, there was really but one answer, however he might deceive himself. Roosevelt would run again for President. On the 21st of February, 1912, he gave out his political creed of the moment, a programme which could not be distinguished from that of La Follette and the Progressive League. Three days later he announced that he would accept a nomination if offered.

With Roosevelt's immense popularity in all parts of

the country, the contest for the regular Republican nomination had now evidently been narrowed to that between him and Taft. La Follette had been eliminated. The nation was genuinely shocked when Roosevelt, speaking of the man who was then President of the United States, announced that "it is a bad trait to bite the hand that feeds you." Probably no other remark has ever been made by a man of Roosevelt's standing so insulting both to the nation and to its elected head. But for the rest of his career, Roosevelt's megalomaniac belief in himself as the savior of America was to scatter not a few unhappy recollections for his admirers on what had been a most distinguished career.

THE CAMPAIGN OF 1912

When the Republican Convention met at Chicago on June 18, the question of the validity of the elections of about 200 delegates, about one fifth of the total, was, as always, settled by the Republican National Committee, and practically all in favor of the Taft delegates. Although Roosevelt had himself on previous occasions backed similar decisions when in his favor, he and his followers now raised the cry of fraud and "steamroller" in the convention, and when unable to get their way, finally bolted the party, which chose Taft for re-election.

The schism in the Republican ranks appeared to make a Democratic victory certain, and the interest in that party's convention at Baltimore on June 25 was unusu-

177

ally keen. Bryan was still the most powerful individual leader but the contest for the nomination was between J. B. ("Champ") Clark, Speaker of the lower House of Congress, Oscar Underwood, Chairman of the Committee on Ways and Means of that House, and Governor Woodrow Wilson of New Jersey. The political career of the last had been extraordinary. A college professor who had become president of Princeton, his forceful personality and determined views had led to conflicts between him and some of the wealthy trustees of the university, and finally to his retirement.

What seemed like a break in one career, however, was but the opening to another. The Democratic Party in New Jersey, normally a Republican State, had been casting about for a dignified figurehead to run as governor, and had chosen the president of Princeton. Wilson had not only won the election but had made such a record as governor as to fasten himself upon the attention of liberals and Progressives throughout the nation.

The contest at Baltimore, however, was long and bitter, with many dramatic moments. It was only on the forty-sixth ballot, after Bryan had thrown down the gauntlet to both Tammany Hall and the great bankers in New York, and given his full support to Wilson, that this former president of Princeton was nominated for the Presidency of the nation.

It was not until August 5 that Roosevelt and the bolting Republicans held their convention at Chicago to nominate the ex-President as head of the ticket put forward by the newly organized Progressive Party. It was an extraordinary gathering even for American national

SWEEPING THE COUNTRY

From a cartoon by Herbert Johnson in "The North American," September 25, 1912.
Courtesy of Roosevelt Memorial Association.

conventions, Roosevelt being cheered for a whole hour, and the members marching round the hall while singing "Onward Christian Soldiers," and finally ending, after the nomination of Roosevelt and Hiram Johnson of California, with singing the "Doxology."

In spite of the religious fervor instilled into the Roosevelt campaign, and his unquestioned popularity, there was something about it all that rather rang hollow. He had himself announced most solemnly that the sound tradition of a President's not serving more than two terms looked to the substance and not the form, and though he now tried to explain that away by saying he had meant serving *successively* more than two terms, the problem of the substance and not the form remained. If Roosevelt's new application of his statement were to hold, what would there be to prevent a man of such vast popularity, or even greater, serving two terms, then putting in his own nominee as he had done with Taft to keep the seat warm, and serving himself for another eight years, and keeping it up indefinitely? Moreover, was there no alternative, as has sometimes been denied, for his action, granted his adherence to Progressive principles?

As far as principles were concerned, there was practically nothing to choose between the platform of the Democrats and that of the Progressives, or "Bull Moose Party" as it came to be called. The Democrats had nominated not Bryan but a man who had already become nationally known for a sane defence of those principles. Astute politician as Roosevelt was, he must have known that the only result of his splitting the Republican Party wide open would be to elect the Democrats, and leave his own party broken and full of bitterness. Throughout his life he had insisted that parties must be reformed, if necessary, from the inside, and had preached the need of party loyalty, and of acquiescence in what the organization might do. In fact, his action did nothing to increase the Progressive spirit within the party, and when it was

A SIMPLE EQUATION

A Cartoon in "Puck," August 13, 1912. Courtesy of Roosevelt Memorial Association.

eventually to return to power after eight years it was with a Harding at its head.

THE ELECTION OF WOODROW WILSON

The result of the campaign, which was less exciting than might have been anticipated, was to give Wilson a popular vote of about 6,300,000, Roosevelt 4,125,000 and Taft 3,500,000. As his leading two opponents alone thus polled 9,800,000 votes to Roosevelt's 4,125,000, it was evident that the nation had not insisted that he should save it. The wave of Progressivism was at its height, as was that of discontent with things as they were, evidenced by the polling by the Socialist Party of its highest recorded vote. Of the two Progressive candidates Wilson

181

received nearly 60 per cent more votes than Roosevelt. With him, were elected a strong majority in the House of Representatives and a small majority of six in the Senate. The general Democratic landslide throughout the country in both local and national elections reflected the deep dissatisfaction of the people.

It was to this dissatisfaction, characteristically and not untruly interpreted by Wilson spiritually, that he turned in his first inaugural address, the shortest in our history. In moving words he spoke of the greatness of the nation in spiritual and material goods, but added that "evil had come with the good, and much fine gold has been corroded. . . . We have been proud of our industrial achievements, but we have not hitherto stopped thoughtfully enough to count the human cost, the cost of lives snuffed out, of energies overtaxed and broken, the fearful physical and spiritual cost to the men and women and children upon whom the dead weight and burden of it all has fallen pitilessly the years through. The groans and agony of it all had not yet reached our ears, the solemn, moving undertone of our life, coming up out of the mines and factories and out of every home where the struggle had its intimate and familiar seat. . . . The great government we loved has too often been made use of for private and selfish purposes, and those who used it had forgotten the people. . . . There has been something crude and heartless and unfeeling in our haste to succeed and be great. Our thought has been 'Let every man look

182

out for himself, let every generation look out for itself,'
while we reared giant machinery which made it impossible that any but those who stood at the levers of control
should have a chance to look out for themselves. . . .
This is the high enterprise of the new day: To lift everything that concerns our life as a Nation to the light that
shines from the hearthfire of every man's conscience and
vision of the right. . . . We shall restore, not destroy.
We shall deal with our economic system as it is and as it
may be modified, not as it might be if we had a clean
sheet of paper to write upon. . . . This is not a day of
triumph; it is a day of dedication. Here muster, not
the forces of party but the forces of humanity. Men's
hearts wait upon us; men's lives hang in the balance;
men's hopes call upon us to say what we will do."

It is one of the misfortunes, as I have pointed out, of
a weak opposition party, seldom attaining to power, that
when it does so at long intervals it has comparatively few
men of marked ability and rich public experience to draw
from for its chief posts. Wilson had no slight difficulty
in filling both the chief diplomatic posts and his own
Cabinet with men of the highest grade.

For the Cabinet, however, he managed to get on the
whole a competent, though not a distinguished group.
Unfortunately the necessity of placing Bryan at its head
as Secretary of State was too obvious to be ignored. Not
only did the President owe the nomination to him but
his influence in a large section of the party was as yet so

great as to make essential his loyalty to the administration if the Presidential policies were to be carried out by Congress. Only two other Cabinet members, W. G. McAdoo in the Treasury and Franklin K. Lane in the Interior Department, could be considered as even minor national figures. Both President Eliot of Harvard and former Secretary of State Olney declined the appointment to England, but that ambassadorship, always the most important in our service, and of supreme difficulty as it was to prove in the next few years, was at last happily filled by Walter Hines Page.

In the short list of problems with which Wilson in his inaugural address had promised to grapple he had placed first the tariff and the reform of the antiquated banking system. He at once called Congress in special session to consider both of these.

Under the lead of Oscar W. Underwood in the House, a bill was rapidly drafted which, although still keeping the protective principle, raised the duty on only 86 articles, left them unchanged on 307, and reduced them on 958. Any reduction in government income was provided for by taxes on incomes of over $3000 for single and $4000 for married persons, this provision having been made possible by the Sixteenth Amendment to the Constitution which had been declared operative on February 25, just before Taft's retirement.

The first genuine effort made to reduce the tariff for a generation was promptly successful in the House, where it was passed early in May by 281 to 139 votes, but it still had to run the ruthless gauntlet of the Senate, where the Democrats had a majority of only six. As usual, every entrenched interest was represented, and the emasculation of the bill commenced. Although Louisiana produced only about 500,000,000 of the 8,000,000,000 pounds of sugar which the American public consumed, the two senators from that State were adamant as ever against allowing us to get our sugar cheaper by putting it on the free list, and all the other industries "protected" likewise at the expense of the public started the customary "log rolling," agreeing to vote for somebody else's absurd duty if that somebody else would vote for theirs.

Into this maze of corrupt bargaining Wilson threw a bombshell when he appealed directly to the people with the statement that a "numerous, industrious, and insidious lobby" was at work trying to prevent a reduction in the tariff. In answer to this charge, which might have been as true of any other tariff measure in the past two generations, Congress had to appoint an investigating committee. The public attention thus focussed was undoubtedly the means of eventually securing the passage of the bill through the Senate so that it could at last receive the President's signature on October 3. He had won his first round and carried out his first pledge.

As may be recalled, our banking system had been evolved during the exigencies of the Civil War, and our bank-note currency, being based on government bonds as security, bore a direct relation to the amount of bonds available profitably at any time but none whatever to the shifting demands of trade activity. One result had been an annual scramble for money in the autumn when the crops were being moved, and a succession of minor and major "money panics" or crises. On occasions, reputable New York banks might be charging 6 per cent on call loans to one customer and 120 per cent to another, or even the two rates on different loans simultaneously to the same customer. Founded by the Republicans, that party had made no effort to amend the system for fifty years, save for the appointment of the Aldrich Commission to investigate the subject and the passage of the stop-gap Aldrich-Vreeland Bill in 1908 after the devastating money panic of 1907. The commission had made exhaustive investigations, the results of which had been published in nearly forty volumes, but nothing further had been done.

Wilson now undertook this second task, and the result of his efforts was the great Federal Reserve Act under which the banking system of the nation now functions, and without which we could not have gone through the ensuing twenty years without meeting colossal financial as well as economic disaster.

The bill itself was drafted by the President, by McAdoo, and the chairmen of the Committees on Banking and Currency in the two Houses of Congress, Carter Glass and Senator R. L. Owen, with, of course, help from many sources. There has been no little effort made to spread the belief that the Federal Reserve system as we now have it varied but little from what Aldrich had proposed, but that can hardly be maintained. Aldrich, in fact, declared it to be "revolutionary, socialistic and unconstitutional," and most of the leading bankers who had been in favor of the Aldrich plan were bitterly opposed to the Wilson one.

The chief point of contention was that the bankers insisted upon a highly centralized institution which should be in the control of private bankers, whereas the Wilson administration insisted that it should be largely decentralized and under the control of the government. In his autobiography, McAdoo gives an amusing list of the opinions of leading financiers of the country with regard to the dire evils that the Federal Reserve system would inevitably bring upon us.

In general the plan called for twelve regional Federal Reserve Banks to be located in various parts of the United States, under the control of a central Federal Reserve Board to be made up of the Secretary of the Treasury, the Comptroller of the Currency and other members (now six), to be appointees of the President. Two of the principal objects to be attained, and which have been, were to establish regional banks in which the individual commercial banks could safely keep their reserves, and to provide an elastic currency which would expand and contract with the varying demands of business. Wilson took a leading part in helping the bill through both Houses of Congress, and it was no small feat of statesmanship that it could be passed for him to sign by December 23, less than ten months after he had taken office. Although J. R. Mann, the Republican leader in the House, had asserted that after all, it did not make any difference how bad the bill was because none of the national banks would go into the system, within a week after the bill's passage 767 had applied for admission.

With a successful revision of the tariff accomplished, —that reef on which so many Presidents have foundered, —and with the great reorganization of the banking system of the nation to his credit, Wilson might well take pride in the accomplishment of his first few months in office. Unfortunately some other matters were not going so well. He had never given much attention to or had much interest in diplomatic or foreign affairs. His teaching and his writings had been almost wholly devoted to the constitutional aspects of the history of his own country, and he had entered upon office with the burning desire to readjust the economic and social life of that country to conform more closely to the new spiritual vision of what it might be which he had suggested in his inaugural. Before leaving his home at Princeton to go to Washington he had remarked to Professor Conklin that "it would be the irony of fate if my administration had to deal chiefly with foreign affairs." It was to be not only the irony but the tragedy of it.

RELATIONS WITH MEXICO

Wilson was an idealist, perhaps the greatest idealist in the history of the world who has held the post of a responsible statesman of such surpassing importance in any crisis of world history. Had he been called upon to deal only with American affairs, as he hoped he would, during his terms of office, his idealism would have been wholesomely kept in touch with practicality by his knowledge of the psychology and history of his own countrymen. But when he had to do with foreign nations, his lack of sound knowledge let his idealism fly loose, like a balloon whose string has been cut and which floats away from the solid earth. His first test was the Mexican situation which he inherited from Taft, and of that he wrote to a friend "I work hard. . . . But it is not that that tells on a fellow. It's the anxiety attending the handling of . . . affairs in which you seem to be touching quicksilver,—matters (in) which your own judgments and principles furnish no standards." That was the great tragedy of Wilson. At the flood tide of American revolt and idealism he was precisely the leader we needed in our own affairs. Instead of that, he was forced to a position of world leadership for which nothing in his career had previously prepared him.

Wilson had a profound belief in morality, and also believed that a government could not govern usefully or efficiently unless its acts were moral. He believed, again, profoundly in democracy, and in the ability of the ordinary human being to govern himself wisely. Knowing only American conditions—though even those might have given him pause—he extended this belief to the entire world and to peoples of all races and conditions. It was with this background of rigid beliefs that he undertook to solve the Mexican problem.

Briefly the situation was that the new dictator, Madero, after he had gone through the forms of a popular election as President, had been assassinated, and the government overturned, by a new faction under a ruthless general of Indian blood, Victoriano Huerta. Opposed to Huerta was yet another faction under Carranza, and Mexico was plunged in civil war, in so far as the struggle between rival leaders with their followers could be dignified by that name. In any case, conditions were so disturbed as to make life and property unsafe.

Mexico is a country of the richest natural resources, and American capitalists, whose investments had been estimated by Taft at over $1,000,000,000, and European capitalists were heavily interested in the establishment of stable conditions. The English oil concessions, belonging to companies headed by Lord Cowdray, were alone colossal, and tied up with the British navy. Huerta might be considered not unreasonably by any one as a bloody usurper, but he was strong, and capitalists and foreign governments believed that rule by him offered the best chance at least of maintaining order in a nation in which, owing to illiteracy and the depressed economic condition of the mass of the people, genuine democracy could not be expected to exist. Huerta was promptly recognized by England and other European countries, but Wilson refused to recognize a government which he declared did not represent the people and which was founded on bloody crime.

He insisted that "just government rests always upon the consent of the governed, and that there can be no freedom without order based upon law and upon the public conscience and approval." Unfortunately, as far as Mexican conditions were concerned, this was merely an ideal gyrating in a vacuum. Among the mass of Mexicans there were much suffering, ignorance, and injustice, but it was impossible for almost any one except Wilson to think of them in terms of an American or British electorate. To insist, in Mexico, upon a democratic government based on the consent of the governed and an intelligent public opinion and conscience was to dream of building a skyscraper on a quicksand.

Wilson drifted along, largely ignoring the State Department officials, goaded by the business interests which felt that hundreds of millions of dollars were being sacrificed to his impracticable policy of "watchful waiting," and thwarted by a political situation which he simply did not understand. There was no doubt that Huerta was unspeakably bad, but even the Mexicans themselves resented our not acknowledging their government, and so far from appreciating Wilson's desire for their welfare as he saw it, were maddened by what appeared to be our officious interference with their internal affairs.

On April 9, 1914, a boatload of American sailors with one or two officers, who had gone ashore at Tampico for supplies for the U. S. S. *Dolphin,* were arrested by the Mexican authorities, and although they were released, Huerta declined to offer the salute to the American flag which Admiral Mayo demanded as an apology. We were slipping into deeper water, and about two weeks later, to prevent a German vessel from landing arms for Huerta, Wilson cabled Mayo to seize the port of Vera Cruz, later sending General Funston with 6000 men to hold the city.

It looked like war, and the three great South American powers, Argentine, Chile and Brazil, offered their mediation, which was accepted. The negotiations were only partly successful, but by July Huerta abdicated and sailed to Europe. In February, Wilson had abandoned neutrality by lifting the embargo on arms for Carranza, although he had not allowed arms to go through for Huerta, and his policy toward the latter prevented the dictator from getting loans abroad. Wilson had thus drifted into actively intervening to overthrow a government which did not suit his own constitutional and moral ideals, and had incurred the enmity of Mexico and the suspicion of all South America by doing so.

SIXTH INFANTRY AT EL VALLE, MEXICO, 1916

Adobe shelter for two men in semi-permanent camp after active pursuit of Villa had ceased.

GENERAL PERSHING AND STAFF, PUNITIVE EXPEDITION

Left to right: Captain W. O. Reed, 6th Cav., M.I.D. 1st Lt. J. L. Collins, 11th Cav., A.D.C. Col. DeR. C. Cabell, 10th Cav., Chief of Staff. Brig.-Gen. J. J. Pershing, Commanding. Major John L. Hines, Adj. Gen. Col. G. O. Cress, Div. Inspector. Capt. L. B. Kromer, 11th Cav. Div., Q. M.

From photographs in the War Department.

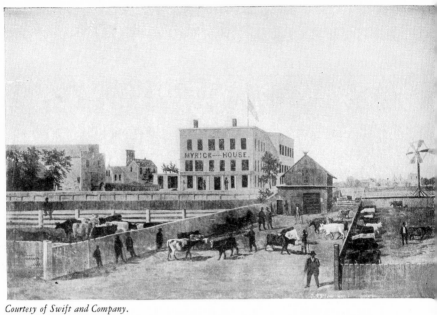

Courtesy of Swift and Company.

CHICAGO STOCKYARDS OF SWIFT AND COMPANY IN 1861

Courtesy of Mrs. Joseph Pennell.

CHICAGO STOCKYARDS OF ARMOUR AND COMPANY IN 1917

From the lithograph by Joseph Pennell in the Joseph and Elizabeth Robins Pennell Collection, Library of Congres.

Nor did the accession to power of Carranza settle the Mexican question. He was well-meaning, but the uprising against him of the bandit Villa continued disorder in Mexico, and with Carranza's permission the United States despatched General Pershing across the Mexican border to capture Villa, without success. Wilson, by 1916, had 150,000 militiamen from various States patrolling the frontier, and we seemed as far as ever from having a Mexican policy. Our troops were withdrawn in January, 1917, when Carranza proclaimed a constitution for Mexico, but three years later he himself was to be assassinated.

If Wilson had muddled rather than solved the Mexican problem, his anti-Huerta policy had one important result. Under the Hay-Pauncefote Treaty of 1901, the United States had agreed that all vessels of all nations should be allowed to use the Panama Canal on a perfect equality. This agreement had been lived up to, and American vessels had been charged the same tolls as those of foreign nations, with one exception. For a very long period no foreign ships had been allowed to engage in our purely domestic coastwise business, a rule of many other nations as well as of our own. As there was thus no question of competition in this traffic, both parties in Congress had considered that the exemption from tolls of our own ships when merely passing from one coast to another and not engaging in foreign trade was not an infringement of the Hay-Pauncefote Treaty, and in 1912 this business had been granted exemption from tolls.

England, however, bitterly denounced the exemption as a breach of good faith, and was probably right, although it had certainly not been deliberately intended as such. The fact that the Canal had been built by American enterprise with American money, and that the only shipping exempted from tolls was local American business in which foreigners could not lawfully compete in any case, obscured for many honest Americans the fact that the exemption was in its larger aspects a genuine infringement of England's treaty rights. A good deal of irritation had been aroused on both sides of the water, and the question had become so tinged with emotion as to make it difficult of adjustment.

Suddenly, on March 5, 1914, Wilson appeared before Congress, and asked for a repeal of the exemption clause in the Act of 1912, not only because it was in violation of our solemn pledge but also, he added, because if Congress did not grant him confidence "in ungrudging measure" and repeal the clause without further delay he would not "know how to deal with other matters of even greater delicacy and nearer consequence." No one knew what important complication in our foreign affairs might be signified by these cryptic words, but the clause was promptly repealed, and it seems possible that what Wilson intended was to secure the co-operation of England in his Mexican policy against Huerta. In this he was successful, for Lord Cowdray's oil interests ceased to dominate the British Foreign Office, and in less than four months Huerta had fled.

Although it seems certain that the repeal was asked for in connection with the Mexican policy, it has also been said that it was on account of the complicated and threatening situation in which Wilson found himself with regard to Japan. This arose again from the form of our Federal Government. About eleven months before Wilson appeared before Congress, the Japanese Ambassador had protested against the law then being considered in California forbidding aliens from owning land, a law directly aimed at Japan and which appeared to be in contravention of her treaty rights with us.

The feeling against the Japanese had continued strong in California, and indeed, was not friendly throughout the nation. Laws relating to land ownership were within the legislative jurisdiction of the individual States and not of the Federal Government, which nevertheless was responsible for making treaties and for foreign relations. Theoretically a treaty, as the "supreme" law of the land, supersedes local law, but in practice, when feeling is strong, it does not. California declined to change her policy, passed the law, and with a jingo press in both countries doing its best to exacerbate instead of to smooth over the situation, the affair began to appear extremely serious. We could not afford war with Japan while getting more and more mired in Mexico and with a quarrel with England on our hands. With reference to the tolls, the Mexican and Japanese situations may perhaps thus be regarded as one.

In April, 1914, Wilson also made an effort to adjust the old Panama dispute with Colombia by negotiating a treaty which expressed "regret" for the incident and which gave Colombia $25,000,000 in lieu of all claims. Roosevelt at once proclaimed that the administration had forfeited all right to the respect of the American people, and called the payment "belated blackmail." It is probable that his subsequent bitter hatred of Wilson was in no small measure due to what seemed to him this suggested placing of a stigma on his own acts. In any case, the treaty failed in the Senate, and the matter had to wait until a Republican administration finally made amends to Colombia, without expressing regret other than in terms of cash.

Absorbed as the President was in the spring of 1914 with these foreign entanglements, which he had so much dreaded, he continued to push forward his programme of internal reform. He was urging on Congress the creation of a Federal Trade Commission, which should collect information as to industrial organizations and take the initiative in securing the enforcement of the Sherman Anti-Trust Law. He was also outlining the Clayton Act, which diminished the evils of interlocking directorates; declared that labor and agricultural organizations were not in restraint of trade; and prohibited the issue of injunctions in labor disputes unless it were clear that irreparable damage would otherwise be done. Both of these were passed by Congress in the early autumn. Meanwhile, the swift occurrence of unpredictable events in Europe had relegated Japan, Mexico, and our domestic policies to positions of almost negligible interest.

Glancing ahead for a moment we may note two other important accomplishments of Wilson's administration. The Farm Loan Act of 1916 was epochal in its effect on the farmers, always as a class likely to suffer from the incubus of debt. Local banks had not seldom charged them as high as ten per cent for accommodation. The Farm Loan Act provided means for their borrowing from the government at rates as low as six and even five per cent, thus saving nearly half their interest charges. Whether or not this sudden facility in borrowing should be wisely used or induce unwise increase in obligations would naturally depend on the wisdom and restraint of the individual farmer. That it came as a blessing to many cannot be denied.

Another Act, the so-called La Follette's Seamen's Act of 1915, was directed at ameliorating the condition of another class of workers, though its beneficent influence may be questioned. In the opinion of some it is "the charter of liberties for America's seamen" which "freed the men in the forecastle from the tyranny of the bridge," whereas others consider that it "prescribed such rules for the wages, food and accommodations of sailors as made it impossible to compete with foreign shipping." There would seem to be more truth, if less emotion, in the latter statement. With England operating her ships at twenty-five per cent lower costs and Japan hers at fifty per cent less, and with the high wages offered American workmen in other employments, there was in any case little hope ahead for an American merchant marine unless heavily subsidized. Both these Acts, however, marked a proper and growing interest in the welfare of the ordinary man as contrasted with the larger business interests which had formerly considered government aid as rather peculiarly a perquisite of their own.

The vast economic changes in the preceding forty years or more which had been developing problems for Americans to solve had also been altering the entire world. The race for overseas possessions, which had made the period from 1880 onward so markedly imperialistic, had been but one expression of the new demands for sources of raw materials and for markets as outlets for manufactured products. The European balance of power, always rather delicately poised, had been subjected to new stresses and strains, although the individuals in each nation had continued to live their lives with little realization of the instability in which they were placed.

BEGINNINGS OF WORLD WAR

In determining the "causes" of the war which was now to burst on the world, one may go back many decades to trace the growing tension among nations or may consider merely the events of the few weeks following the assassination of an Austrian archduke and his wife by a Serbian. If we consider the broader "causes," those tensions which sooner or later would have caused an upset of the unstable equilibrium of the great powers, it is difficult to apportion the blame among nations for bringing the catastrophe about. If we consider the events of the last few weeks before the conflagration blazed, Germany and Austria must bear the heaviest part of the responsibility.

It is impossible here to give a detailed narrative of those momentous days between the murder on June 28 and the first week in August when war had actually started with Germany and Austro-Hungary on one side and Russia, Serbia, Belgium, France, and England on the other. Before the war, Austria, Germany, and Italy had been united in the Triple Alliance, and France, Russia, and England in the Triple Entente, and when Russia came to the aid of her fellow Slav state of Serbia, which Austria claimed the right to chastise, Germany had realized that France would go to the aid of Russia. Counting on disposing of the French quickly before the great Russian war machine could get into motion, Germany invaded France by way of the neutral state of Belgium, breaking the treaty, nearly a century old, guaranteeing the neutrality of that little country.

The act shocked the world, but we had had nothing

199

to do with the treaty or guaranty, and at this stage we were in no way concerned with the causes of the conflict. We were not international policemen to defend the injuries of the weak or to enforce treaties to which we were not parties. Nor had other nations in the past undertaken such duties. In 1866, for example, England had made no move when Prussia made a war of aggression against Denmark and took from her the province of Schleswig and Holstein, nor had she moved when Germany attacked France in 1870.

For us, in 1914, there were special reasons for trying to maintain neutrality. Not only had it been, for more than one hundred years, our traditional policy to avoid European entanglements, but under the Monroe Doctrine we had demanded a free hand for ourselves in the New World and had coupled that assertion many times with the counter declaration that we should keep out of the local quarrels of the Old. Moreover, of our people, literally several tens of millions were immigrants or children of immigrants from the races now locked in a death struggle, and their sympathies were naturally divided between the two groups of contestants. It was right, therefore, that on August 4, 1914, Wilson should proclaim our complete neutrality.

In view of the claim raised later in so many quarters, both at home and abroad, that it had been "our war" from the start and that we shirked our duty for a long time, it is well to bear these facts in mind. Even Roosevelt, more than six weeks after the war began and Belgium had been raped, wrote in *The Outlook* that it was desirable and right for us to remain neutral, and that we had "not the smallest responsibility" for what had happened in Belgium.

It was one thing, however, to proclaim neutrality, and another to maintain it. Gradually the conflict took on the aspect of a world war. In the summer and autumn, Turkey joined the Central Powers and Japan the Allies, other smaller nations also being drawn in. Italy, in spite of her alliance with Austria and Germany, hesitated for ten months, and then, after securing a treaty guaranteeing her additions to her territory, joined their enemies, the Allies, in May, 1915.

Meanwhile, our whole life had been changed by the sudden upheaval in Europe. To avoid a fatal collapse of all values, the Stock Exchange had been forced to close on July 31 to remain closed for many weeks. On the other hand, the break-down of the economic life of Europe, and the colossal war-time demand for food stuffs, ammunition and goods of all sorts at any prices, brought quickly a feverish activity to American business life. Our excess of exports over imports rose by leaps, $470,653,000 in the year ending June 30, 1914, $1,094,000,000 in 1915, $2,135,000,000 in 1916 and $3,630,000,000 in 1917. In 1914 we had exported only $6,272,000 of explosives. In 1917 we exported them to the amount of $802,789,000. Our total exports, which had been $2,329,000,000 in

1914, were $4,272,000,000 by 1916 and $6,227,000,000 by 1917.

It was very far, however, from being a golden shower for all Americans. As usual in wartime, some grew immensely rich and many made fortunes from the profits of war contracts and opportunities. The daily wage earner had ample work at rapidly rising wages. But for a vast number of Americans, especially for those who were neither war-profiteers nor wage earners, the fast mounting cost of living, with incommensurate or no increase in salaries or other income, played havoc with family budgets.

As in the Napoleonic struggles of just a century earlier, when France and not Germany had been trying to overrun Europe, the United States was the most important neutral nation, and upon her rested the responsibility of maintaining neutral rights. The problem was an extremely difficult one, for the nature of war had completely altered whereas international law had not. We alone could not alter the latter in the midst of the struggle without being accused of being unneutral, and if both sides claimed at times that we took too narrow a legalistic view, that is perhaps as good proof as any that we were trying to steer a middle course.

The chief trouble came, as of old, on the sea. Within our own borders, though we might resent the propaganda of both sides, designed to stir up racial feeling among our mixed population, we could take care of the grosser forms of violation, such as the Austrian and German efforts to destroy ammunition and other plants to prevent supplies being sent to the Allies. In September, 1915, Wilson had to ask for the recall of the Austrian Ambassador, and not long after of two of the attachés of the German Embassy for connection with such plots.

But if there was no question as to the laws of our own land, there were many and difficult ones as to sea-borne commerce under the conditions of modern war. As the German navy had quickly been cleared off the sea, most of the earlier problems arose between us and England. They proved so delicate that had Germany not undertaken her submarine campaign it is not impossible that there might have been a new "War of 1812."

The nature of war, as we have said, had changed greatly in a century. In 1909, in what was known as the Declaration of London, ten of the greatest maritime powers had signed a convention modifying the international law relative to contraband, seizures at sea, and other such matters. England had signed this but Parliament had refused to adopt it. Through the summer of 1914, England, by the Orders in Council of which we had such unpleasant recollection from the Napoleonic Wars, had added thirty-two articles to the list of contraband which had not been specified in the Declaration of London, and which included some of our most important products, such as cotton and various metals. When Wilson asked both sides to adhere to the Declaration of

1909, the Central Powers naturally agreed but the Allies refused.

According to international law we had a right to export goods as a neutral nation to other neutral nations. To the north of Germany were the neutral states of Holland, Denmark, and Sweden, and our trade with them increased at such a rate, about fivefold in a year, that it was evident our exports to them were in reality going to Germany. As the Allies were not in a position to stop the trade over the German borders, from those countries, the only thing they could do was to prevent it on the high seas. This England, as the chief naval power on the Allied side, did, stopping our ships, which were heavily laden with essential war material for her enemies, confiscating cargoes and even capturing our mails. Such action was necessary to win the war but was against international law, and as immensely valuable cargoes of cotton, meats, and other goods were seized and confiscated, although with promise of eventual payment, the wrath of the American shippers grew, precisely as the wrath of English merchants would have been aroused had the position been reversed.

Just as, a century before, Napoleon and England had answered each other with orders and blockades, now Germany declared, February 4, 1915, that she would answer the Allied effort to cut off her food supplies by the arbitrary extension of the contraband list of the Declaration of London and by illegal seizures, with the proclamation of a war zone around the British Isles within which zone German submarines would sink enemy vessels without attention to the international law that demanded the placing of the crew and passengers in safety.

When we notified the German Government that this was illegal and that we would have to hold them to "strict accountability," the reply was that the government would reconsider its action if we would insist upon England's observing the terms of the Declaration of 1909. Later, Germany also demanded that we stop supplying the Allies with munitions, which they were getting from us in huge quantities and which she, from her position, could not get. This, as a highly unneutral act which would have given the victory almost at once to Germany, we promptly declined to do. Germany claimed, however, that if we were supplying the Allies with all they needed, and that if they illegally stopped goods destined for her, she would also adopt illegal methods. With that the submarine campaign was on.

What Germany did not realize was the difference between life and property. In about two and a half months the submarines sank over sixty ships belonging to different countries, including an American steamer, the *Gulflight,* with a total loss of 250 persons, of whom one was an American. On the very day the *Gulflight* was sunk, a notice appeared, signed "Imperial German Embassy," in the New York papers warning Americans not to sail that day on the *Lusitania.* Few, however, cancelled their passage, and the great English liner, with war supplies and 1250 passengers on board, sailed as usual. Six days later she was torpedoed off the Irish coast and sank

OCEAN STEAMSHIPS.

CUNARD

EUROPE VIA LIVERPOOL

LUSITANIA

Fastest and Largest Steamer
now in Atlantic Service Sails
SATURDAY, MAY 1, 10 A.M.
Transylvania, Fri., May 7, 5 P.M.
Orduna, - - Tues.,May 18, 10 A.M.
Tuscania, - - Fri., May 21, 5 P.M.
LUSITANIA, Sat., May 29, 10 A.M.
Transylvania, Fri., June 4, 5 P.M.

Gibraltar—Genoa—Naples—Piraeus
S.S. Carpathia, Thur., May 13, Noon

NOTICE!

TRAVELLERS intending to embark on the Atlantic voyage are reminded that a state of war exists between Germany and her allies and Great Britain and her allies; that the zone of war includes the waters adjacent to the British Isles; that, in accordance with formal notice given by the Imperial German Government, vessels flying the flag of Great Britain, or of any of her allies, are liable to destruction in those waters and that travellers sailing in the war zone on ships of Great Britain or her allies do so at their own risk.

IMPERIAL GERMAN EMBASSY

WASHINGTON, D. C., APRIL 22, 1915.

THE *LUSITANIA* ADVERTISEMENT IN *THE NEW YORK HERALD*
OF MAY 1, 1915

with over 1150 men, women, and children, of whom 114 were Americans.

The country, however, was not ready for war. In the vast Mississippi Valley and over the mountains on the Pacific slope, thousands of miles from Europe, and with a population a considerable part of which was of Teutonic descent, the *Lusitania* sinking, although it carried a thrill of horror, did not appear to most as a cause for plunging a nation of 110,000,000 people into war, if any other way out could be found. It was frequently said that if a few Americans wished to take the risk of travelling through the war zone on an armed ship of a nation at war loaded with ammunition, they had no right to demand that their own nation go to war to avenge them. Whatever the justice of this pacifist doctrine, the general

THE WORLD HEADLINES OF MAY 8, 1915

disinclination of the people for war had to be taken into account by Wilson.

Instead of declaring war, he demanded that Germany make reparation, and stop the illegal submarine sinkings. Although two more American lives were lost in the sinking of the *Arabic* on August 18, on the 27th of the same month the German Government solemnly agreed that liners would not be sunk without observing the laws of war, and later offered an apology and indemnity for the sinking of the *Arabic*. In the following February, although unwilling to avow the illegality of the *Lusitania* sinking, Germany also offered indemnity for that.

In January, Wilson went on a tour of the Middle West to rouse the people and to gain support for preparing for war, pointing out that the national honor must be upheld and could not be without adequate preparation. His own ideas as to what that might be, or what the people would support, was nevertheless so far below that of his Secretary of War, Lindley M. Garrison, that the latter had resigned, as, for the exact opposite reason, had Secretary of State Bryan who felt that Wilson was taking too strong a stand and endangering peace. When, on March 24, 1916, the Germans broke their pledge, and sank the *Sussex* without warning, Wilson refused to accept Germany's statement as to the circumstances, and wrote that unless such attacks immediately ceased for good and all, he would break off relations. For the next nine months they did stop.

RE-ELECTION OF WILSON

The election of 1916 clearly showed that the nation was divided. The Republicans nominated Charles E. Hughes on a platform which denounced Wilson's war policy and demanded preparedness and a more energetic attitude, whereas the Democrats, with Wilson as their candidate for renomination, praised his policy and adopted as their campaign slogan "He kept us out of war." The election was one of the closest in our history, Wilson carrying the whole South and Far West, and Hughes most of the East. At first it was thought the latter had been elected, the result not being certain for two days. It was then found that Wilson had polled 9,128,836 votes to 8,536,380 for Hughes, and had won.

America was still primarily interested in her domestic affairs, and it is probable that the apparent lack of interest shown by Hughes in progressive policies at home, as well as his somewhat evasive speeches on all topics, had gained as many votes for Wilson as the slogan that he kept us out of war. As the results of the campaign reached Europe, however, it was the latter which made the most impression. The Germans had heard it, and giving much too great significance to it, were to act upon their interpretation of it to their ruin.

CHAPTER V

THE WORLD WAR

THERE is no doubt that for at least a year and a half before we actually entered the war, Wilson had clearly recognized the possibility of our having to do so. On his Western tour to stir up the people as early as January, 1916, he had told them that they had laid two duties upon him, one to keep out of war if possible and the other to preserve the honor of the United States. There might come the time, he had added, arguing for preparedness, when he could not any longer preserve both honor and peace.

As the months of what seemed to be the interminable nightmare which had engulfed a large part of the human race went on, he ceaselessly turned over in his mind what might be the noblest and most useful service to all humanity which the United States could render. Wilson was neither a weak nor a timid man. If his dealings with Mexico had shown too much of the dreamer and idealist, his years at Princeton and his career since he had become governor of New Jersey showed equally that he could be a hard and determined fighter. That he should think of the possibility of himself playing a great rôle in bringing about peace, such as Roosevelt had played in 1907, only on a far vaster stage, was legitimate, but it is only fair to him to believe that he was not swayed in his course by personal ambition.

Apart from the wish of America to remain neutral if possible, there was the importance of limiting the already vast field of slaughter and madness and impending bankruptcy of civilization as much as might be. Finally, there was Wilson's belief—that when peace might come America could play a better part as the one great neutral nation untouched by the hatreds of the conflict than she could as one of the war-maddened belligerents.

Slowly there had developed in his mind as there had also in the minds of such men as Taft, Hughes, Lord Robert Cecil, and others, the possibility of using the terrible war as the means to end all wars, and of building up through some League of Nations a better order than that based on the old nationalistic ambitions and diplomacy. As in the case of Mexico, Wilson did not give sufficient weight to the actualities of the real springs of action in men, and to the strength of historic factors and conditions, but he did see clearly and rightly that there was little hope for mankind if no better foundation for lasting peace could be found than the armed balance of the great powers of Europe, which broke of its own weight about once a century.

There had been the devastating wars, ending temporarily in the Peace of Utrecht in 1713. A hundred years later the balance had been upset by the insensate ambition of Napoleon and the militarism of the French, which had again drowned all Europe in blood, and involved America also. By 1913 a new balance, that of the Triple Entente against the Triple Alliance, all armed to the teeth, had become unstable. Had it not been for the alliances and the armaments, designed to preserve peace, we might not have had war, but in the world as it was there seemed nothing to do but to build up alliances.

The great underlying tensions in the world structure are rarely perceived by the average citizen, who in modern civilized countries is naturally a peace-loving person. For the most part, these citizens have to be moved by great ideals, such as patriotism, the belief in the absolute justice of their cause, or by profound emotions of hate or fear or opposition to injustice, to turn them into fighting men. Hence the need of propaganda in all modern nations under modern conditions of warfare. Hate becomes almost as essential as ammunition, and how hate is manufactured, any one can recall with shame who worked in the propaganda section of any nation in those years of war. On the other hand, the propaganda of the righteous cause has also to be circulated, and just as every nation prayed to God for the victory, so practically every citizen in all believed implicitly in the justice of his own side.

By December, 1916, the war had been going on for

nearly two and a half years, with no prospect of ending. Had it ended with a victory for the Prussian "Potsdam Gang," and the enforcement of their ideas on a large part of Europe, the result would have been as bad as would have been a victory by Napoleon and the French at Waterloo. Wilson had no doubt of that, but what he wanted was not merely to end the war, but to do so in such a way as to bring about the new order under a League. This he felt would have to be done if possible before the bitter hatreds, growing more bitter every day, would put the feasibility of such a new order out of the question. On December 18, therefore, he addressed notes to all the belligerents asking them to define their war aims, and on what terms they would be willing to consider the making of such a peace. All, in general terms, he said had defined what they were fighting for, but each had done so in much the same words to their own peoples.

If, he added, "million after million of human lives must continue to be offered up until on one side or the other there are no more to offer; if resentments must be kindled that can never cool and despairs engendered from which there can be no recovery, hopes of peace and of the willing concert of free peoples will be rendered vain and idle." He did not, in these all too-prophetic words of what was to come to pass, suggest either peace or mediation, but a mere statement of war aims by both sides to see how far apart they might be.

213

THE ALLIES AND THE CENTRAL POWERS

The notes aroused a good deal of bad feeling, particularly on the side of the Allies who complained that Wilson could not see the difference between what they were fighting for and what the Germans were. The Allies had the better case. If we look only to the immediate causes of the war, the events in the few weeks before August, 1914, the chief responsibility for toppling over the delicate balance of Europe belonged to Austria and Germany, though France, Russia, and England are far from being free of all responsibility. However, it had been Germany which had talked about the Belgian treaty as a "scrap of paper," and which had committed the crime of invading that neutral state. Moreover it had been Germany which had introduced the horror of the submarine war.

Wilson was looking not at the moral question of this particular war, however, so much as at the whole problem of war, its causes and its possible cure. To understand his policy, this fact has to be kept in mind. Whatever might be the immediate and ostensible causes of this one, he saw the *larger* causes. There had been for some centuries the nationalistic desires to expand and to exert power. Whether or not an archduke had been murdered, Austria and Germany wanted to extend their power toward the southeast into Asia Minor. But this

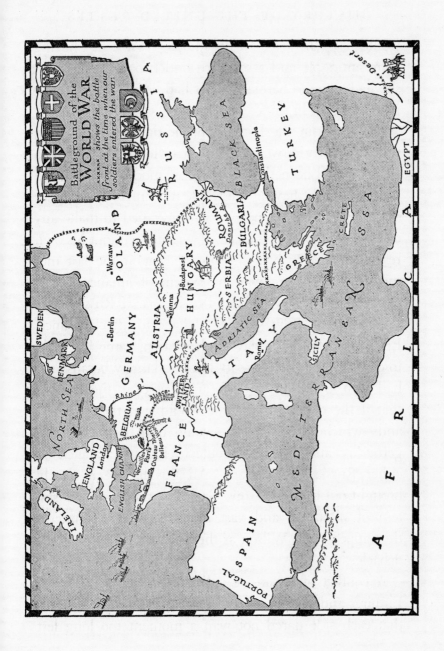

Battleground of the WORLD WAR. xxxx shows the battle front at the time when our soldiers entered the war.

215

would have thwarted Russia's hope of some day having Constantinople and a southern outlet to the sea. When she had come to Serbia's aid, it had been with this ultimate thought in mind.

Moreover, in the last few hectic days of July, 1914, when the world was frantically trying to patch up a peace, it had been the huge size of modern armies and the necessity of having the whole machinery move, once a button had been touched, which seemed to make any recall impossible; and the Czar was not without his own responsibility for bringing on the war at the last moment. Again, there was the system of alliances. England and France were bound to Russia. If Russia came in, Germany knew she would have to attack France. England, after some days of hesitation, came in partly to defend the Belgian treaty but also largely because she had been so bound to Russia and France in the Entente that if she did not go in she would win their enmity, and—whichever side won—would find herself in dangerous isolation, and the route to India threatened by either Russia or Germany. All this has been clearly brought out by Lord Grey. Greedy nationalism, the system of alliances, and vast and unwieldy armaments thus appeared to Wilson as the real causes of the world débâcle.

A conflict of expansive policies between the Central Empires and Russia; then such huge fighting machines that each side dared not wait a moment too long lest the advantages go to the other; then the necessity of extending the conflict to all allies lest the balance of power be overthrown;—so the war had begun, and after it had begun came the hope of spoil and the madness and hate of propaganda and war emotion. Italy, after ten months, deserted her former allies and made a secret treaty with her new ones which promised her additions to her territory on the Adriatic. Japan, likewise bribed with the promise of loot in Shantung and elsewhere in the East, joined the Allies. Others had been drawn in, and now it looked as though *we* might be, with every wish in the world not to be.

Wilson was pro-Ally in sympathy, but he was almost wholly concerned with how to prevent in future this recurring disaster to mankind. Even if the Allies won, and there was a redistribution of territory and a nominal peace, the President saw that if the old system of armed balance of power were set up again, there would be no guarantee of peace. It would be only a question of time when the whole thing would happen again, whatever the spark might be that next time would be called the "cause."

He came to believe with his whole soul that the only hope for humanity was the inauguration of a new order, of a genuine "society" of nations on the same basis of mutual trust and confidence as that on which citizens of the same country live with one another. But every month that the war went on with increasing bitterness then and to come, seemed to him to make such a plan less and less possible. It was this thought he had in mind when, on January 22, 1917, he addressed the Senate as to the result of his notes, and used the famous phrase, which aroused almost universal resentment, that there must be "peace without victory."

There must be in future, he said, not a "balance of power" but a "community of power," "only a tranquil Europe can be a stable Europe." The right state of mind is as necessary to lasting peace, he added, as "is the just settlement of vexed questions of territory or of racial and national allegiance." A victor's terms "would be accepted in humiliation . . . and would leave a sting, a resentment, a bitter memory upon which terms of peace would rest, not permanently, but only as upon a quicksand." The fifteen years following the Peace of Versailles, with their increasing tension of national animosities, their growing sense of instability, their mad increase of national jealousies and almost complete breakdown of economic civilization, were to prove Wilson a seer. We had a dictated victor's peace, a renewal of the old system of armed alliances, and—disaster.

Unfortunately it takes more than vision to make a statesman, and Wilson over-rated both the willingness of his own countrymen and of the world at large to assume the risks of trying to establish a new order in place of the old, while he under-rated the forces of nationalism. He also overestimated his own ability to solve the problem.

Before the Senate in January, he pleaded for no more alliances but for a concert of power beneath which all men could "live their own lives under a common protection." The rest of his own life, which he sacrificed to the cause, was devoted persistently and with a tragic disregard to actuality, to the attempt to make his vision

© *Press Publishing Company.*

GERMANY'S PROMISE!
From "The Evening World," New York.

real for all mankind. He failed, but he failed nobly, in perhaps the greatest effort that any statesman has ever made to bring content and lasting peace to all mankind.

Wilson was always a puzzle to the diplomats of the Old World, and Germany had interpreted the election of 1916 as indicating not that America was idealistic but that she was cowardly and would stand any amount of abuse. At once the building of new submarines had proceeded rapidly, and on January 31, nine days after Wilson had addressed the Senate as we have noted, Germany curtly told us that, in utter disregard of her former promise, she would thereafter sink at sight every vessel, neutral as well as belligerent, in the Mediterranean or in the waters adjacent to Great Britain.

The German Ambassador in Washington, Von Bernstorff, had been trying to influence his government against such a measure, and on January 23, cabled to Berlin that he had just received a formal offer from Wilson to act as mediator. Word came back, however, that the military operations already set in motion were of such magnitude that they could not then be halted. On February 3, the ambassador was given his passports by the American Government, and relations with Germany were broken.

WE ENTER THE WAR

Events now moved more swiftly. On January 19, the German Government had instructed its minister in Mexico to urge that nation to attack us if we attacked Germany, absurdly offering to Mexico as loot the American southwestern States. This precious document was made public by the British Intelligence Service on February 28, and a wave of indignation swept the United States. Meanwhile the German submarines had gone promptly and effectually about their dastardly work. In the month of February they sank 200 vessels, of which number three quarters were neutral although only two were American.

Two days before the Zimmerman note to Mexico was made public, Wilson had asked Congress for power to arm our merchant vessels with the idea of using the "armed neutrality" policy of a century earlier. The authority asked was granted by the House by an overwhelming vote of more than thirty to one, but in the Senate, where there was no rule limiting the time which a Senator could speak or for bringing debate to an end, twelve senators, about equally divided between the two leading parties, maintained a filibuster which prevented the passage of the bill before the session closed on March 3. The dozen senators had also prevented the passage of the Army Appropriation Bill, so that the President had to call Congress back into extra session to meet April 2.

Before that date, the Russian Government had fallen, and the revolution, believed, as they all are at first, to be controlled by the intelligent Liberals, had begun. With the Russian Czar as one of the principal three Allies, it had not been easy to make out a case for the war as a struggle of "free peoples" against "autocracy." But in the first days of the revolution, when it was believed that a great democratic and popular government might be established in the former Russian Empire, the war began to appear more as one of liberalism and liberation. Moreover, the submarines were sinking more

American ships, and forty-eight Americans had lost their lives.

When Congress convened, Wilson appeared before it and asked for a declaration of war against Germany, it having been shown to be impossible to deal with the government of that nation in any other way. We had, he said, no quarrel with the German people themselves, and the war on our part should not be for revenge but for human rights. It is well, in view of all that was to happen, for us to stress his very words, for the aims at which he was striving really changed not at all. Those aims had been, and continued to be, the safeguarding of the democratic way of governing and the inauguration of a new era of the *concert* instead of the *balance* of powers.

On April 2, before the crowded seats and galleries of the House, he again expressed these aims as clearly as any one could. "The world," he said, "must be made safe for democracy. Its peace must be planted upon the tested foundations of political liberty. We have no selfish ends to serve. We desire no conquest, no dominion. We seek no indemnities for ourselves, no material compensation for the sacrifices we shall make. . . . It is a fearful thing to lead this great and peaceful people into war, into the most terrible and disastrous of all wars, civilization itself seeming to be in the balance. But the right is more precious than peace, and we shall fight for the things which we have always carried nearest in our

222

hearts—for democracy, for the right of those who submit to authority to have a voice in their own government, for the rights and liberties of small nations, for a universal dominion of right by such a concert of free peoples as shall bring peace and safety to all nations. . . . The day has come when America is privileged to spend her blood and might for the principles that gave her birth and happiness and the peace which she has

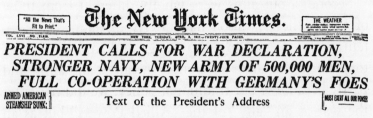

"All the News That's Fit to Print." **The New York Times.** THE WEATHER

VOL. LXVI...NO. 21,630. NEW YORK, TUESDAY, APRIL 3, 1917.—TWENTY-FOUR PAGES.

PRESIDENT CALLS FOR WAR DECLARATION, STRONGER NAVY, NEW ARMY OF 500,000 MEN, FULL CO-OPERATION WITH GERMANY'S FOES

ARMED AMERICAN STEAMSHIP SUNK; | Text of the President's Address | MUST EXERT ALL OUR POWER

FROM *THE NEW YORK TIMES*, APRIL 3, 1917

treasured. God helping her, she can do no other." That night the Resolution declaring war with Germany was introduced in both Houses and the Declaration of War received the President's signature on April 6, 1917.

Several points may be noted as to our entry into the war. First, the "causes" of our going in were not those which had led the "Allied Powers" to do so. Of them all, Belgium was the only one which had gone in solely on account of the attack on her neutrality. That had counted heavily with England, but so also had her alliances and her long-range policy. Russia had gone in to preserve her possible future in southeastern Europe, and France had been drawn in by her alliance with Russia.

In regard to the other greater powers, we have already spoken of the extremely practical motives which had influenced Italy and Japan. All these nations were, among themselves, partitioning the world anew if they should win.

Having had nothing to do with the original causes of the war, we had at last gone in solely because the attacks on neutral rights had become intolerable.

Secondly, our aims were wholly different from those of the "Allies." Wilson had utterly disclaimed any intention on our part to seek revenge, indemnities or territory. Partly for these differences in causes and aims, and partly because of our traditional policy, we did not enter the war as an "ally" of the "Allied Powers" but as an "Associated Power." We did not even go to war with all their enemies. We did, indeed, declare war on Austria on the 7th of the following December, but never declared war on Turkey, and did not even break off diplomatic relations with Bulgaria. All these points of difference were little regarded at the time, and because we had gone to war against Germany, our entry was proclaimed with wild enthusiasm in all the Allied countries.

OUR STUPENDOUS PROBLEM

We had not made adequate preparation for hostilities but the immediate assistance that we could give was to save the credit of the Allies, which had become exhausted. Mr. Balfour, who arrived with the governor of the Bank of England and other members of the British War Mission in Washington on April 22, assured the Secretary of the Treasury that the financial position was even more menacing than the submarine peril. Two days later, Congress passed the largest finance bill in the history of the world, authorizing the raising of $7,000,000,-000, of which $3,000,000,000 could be loaned to the Allied Powers. The next day McAdoo handed Lord Cunliffe for England a check for $200,000,000. Thus began the colossal financing of the struggle in America, and the loans to foreign nations, which latter, together with other causes, were to bring the world to the edge of collapse within fifteen years and to win for us the hostility of all our debtors.

The total face value of the loans we made to foreign countries before interest began to run was $9,466,000,-000, of which $2,170,000,000 was loaned after the Armistice. In order to make these and to pay our own governmental expenses and our own cost of the war, which was nearly $35,500,000,000, we increased our national debt by $21,439,394,500, and during the two war years raised in addition, nearly $11,300,000,000 by taxation. Had the war not ended in 1918, it was estimated by the Treasury that for the year ending June 30, 1919, we should have had to raise, for the needs of ourselves and the other nations, in that one year alone $24,000,000,000.

Before the war we could not possibly have raised any such sums, for we were ourselves a debtor nation, owing

Europe from $2,500,000,000 to $3,000,000,000. A new country always borrows from the older ones to develop its resources until such time as it has itself accumulated capital sufficient for the purpose. Until 1914 we had always been heavily in debt to the Old World, but the sudden demand for all our goods at war prices had, as has been noted, so increased our exports as to enable us to buy the $2,000,000,000 of our own securities which Europe dumped on us almost at the beginning of the struggle. By the time we entered it we had become, for the first time in history, a creditor nation, and able to finance both ourselves and the Allies. No one can help prices going up in a war, and when Europe sometimes scornfully points to the profits which we made in the first two years and more that she was fighting, it should not be forgotten that, had we not done so, there would have been no such reservoir of credit as Europe tapped on such a colossal scale after 1917.

Although the available man power in America for an army was obviously enormous, it had been the opinion of many that even if we should enter the war, our great value to the Allies would lie in the opening of credits and the production of the material resources for their armies rather than in any large army of our own. No nation under modern conditions had ever carried on a war of the first magnitude 3000 miles from its base. In view of the decreasing amount of shipping due to the submarine sinkings, and the dire need of transporting huge stores of supplies, not only for the armies already in the field but to keep the civilian populations of England and the other countries from starving, it was a question whether the sending over of a large army, with its additional need of food and other supplies, might not hinder rather than help. Germany believed the task impossible, and for that reason had looked with unconcern upon forcing us in.

Although our army was almost negligible in April, 1917, we had taken an important step in the organization of our resources by the creation of the Council for National Defense in the preceding August, and out of this organization there developed many of the great Boards which had to undertake the co-ordination of the entire industrial life of the nation. In the six months after our entry into the war, the United States had been transformed from a highly individualistic society of competing business concerns into what was almost a great socialistic State, in which the control of the whole industry, life, and purpose of the nation was directed from Washington. It was an amazing transformation, for nothing like it had ever been attempted before on any such scale, and the process was wholly antipathetic to our ordinary ways of doing things.

Volumes might be, and have been, written on the complex problems with which the complicated group of Boards had to grapple. Here we can only suggest in broad outline the magnitude of these. One of the early offsprings of the Council of Defense was the War Industries Board, which in turn was made up of many Divisions, such as the Price-Fixing Committee, the Allied Purchasing Commission, the Labor Division, Building Material, Chemical, Priorities Divisions, and many more. There were sub-committees for all sorts of products essential for the war,—acids, alkalis, copper, steel, pyrites, nickel, and some thirty others. The chief task of the War Industries Board was to rearrange the industry of the nation so that all war materials should be produced in sufficient quantities and supplied when and where needed.

All this involved in many cases the transformation of plants from producing things used in peace to those needed in war, and as new capital was suddenly required on a great scale, a War Finance Corporation was set up to provide it, and a Capital Issues Committee to pass on all new issues of stocks and bonds. Foreign trade had to be revolutionized, and so a War Trade Board was organized, which, for one thing, put the neutral nations on rations so that, while their legitimate needs should be supplied, there should be no surplus to be handed over to the enemy. America itself was rationed in essential foodstuffs, so that every bit possible could be shipped to the Allies, a work taken over by the Food Administration. It soon became necessary also to ration fuel to ourselves, and the Fuel Administration followed the Food Administration in economizing the use of coal

WAR POSTERS

The Recruiting Poster by James Montgomery Flagg; the National War Garden Commission by Leonebel Jacobs; the Red Cross by Harrison Fisher.

WAR POSTERS

The Victory Liberty Loan, drawn by Howard Chandler Christy; Veteran Relief, by James Montgomery Flagg; United States Shipping Board, by Charles Dana Gibson.

and other fuels, stimulating production and getting all possible shipments across to Europe. The forced stimulation of all our industries, including agriculture, was to cost us dear when deflation came after peace, but during the war there was nothing to be done but to increase all our means of production,—farms and factories,—to the fevered needs of a mad world, far beyond those of normal times of peace.

One of the most essential problems was that of transportation by land and sea. In a country as vast as the United States, 3000 miles wide, which it takes four days to cross by fast train, there could be no question of building emergency lines. The existing ones had to serve, and in order that they should all be co-ordinated to the one end of rushing supplies to Europe, 240,000 miles of lines, owned by several hundred private corporations, with 2,000,000 employees, were taken over by the government and operated by McAdoo, who added to his duties as Secretary of the Treasury, those of Director-General of the Railroads. In the midst of confusion, and with no time for careful planning, nearly a quarter of a million miles of railroad had to be operated by the Federal Government, the mere suggestion of which in peace times would have been regarded as the most dangerous of radical doctrines.

Before we entered the war, we had already felt the lack of shipping, and in 1914 the government had inaugurated a Bureau of War Risk Insurance to insure cargoes which could not be privately insured. In September, 1917, a United States Shipping Board was created to regulate and increase shipping, and immediately on our entry into the war, in April, 1917, Congress organized the Emergency Fleet Corporation which spent $1,000,000,000 and built ships faster than the Germans could sink them. We had not been a shipbuilding nation and almost everything had to start from nothing. During the war, however, we built 875 vessels and when the Armistice came 380,000 men were at work in the yards so that by 1919 our tonnage had risen from the 1,066,000 of 1914 to 6,665,000.

After a good deal of confusion and delay in the beginning, most of the work done by all these boards and committees, headed for the most part by the leading business men of the country, was excellent, although naturally there was much waste, including the inevitable profiteering by private firms. The only complete failure was that of the War Department in the matter of airplanes. Congress appropriated $640,000,000 in July, 1917, and the Secretary of War, Newton D. Baker, who had been against preparedness, declared that within a year we should have 20,000 planes in France. In fact not a single American fighting plane was shipped to France until May, 1918, and we had to rely on France and Italy for this branch of the service, the administration of which provided the leading scandal of the war.

The navy was far better prepared than the army. In

so small a regular land force as that of the United States, seeing active service only about once in a generation save for a bit of police duty now and then, the tendency to dry-rot and lax inefficiency is almost irresistible, and war usually finds us with a lot of dead wood in high places. The routine of an American army officer's life is conducive neither to ambition nor energetic work, and as we had not had a major war for a half century, and apparently had no enemies who could attack us on shore, planning for the possible use of an army of millions had lacked any real interest. The life of a naval officer, however, with its regular turns of sea duty, produces a much higher professional morale. The mistakes of an army officer, in command of a few hundred or thousand men in a well-appointed peace-time post, cannot have very startling results, but the mistakes of an officer in charge at sea of a cruiser or a battle-ship may be very startling indeed. The navy, therefore, was in shape to do its part immediately in European waters in blockading, mine-laying and other services.

Whatever may have been thought earlier of the possibility of sending large forces abroad, within three weeks after war was declared Congress passed the Army Bill which had been prepared by the General Staff. This provided for the immediate raising to their maximum strengths of the regular army (223,000 men) and of the militia (425,000) by voluntary enlistment, and for the raising of a new force by conscription of 500,000, or, if the President believed it necessary, of 1,000,000. The War Missions sent to us by the Allies begged for man-power as soon as possible, admitting that Germany was winning, that the courage of the French was giving way, and even a small force must be sent almost immediately to save the situation.

The problem was a difficult one. It was useless to send mere fresh recruits with no training, and our regular force was so small that if we sent any considerable part of that we should have few or no officers to train the millions of civilians who might have to be put into the service. Moreover, it was clear that in a nation so divided in its racial blood and sympathies, we could never raise millions by volunteering. To vast numbers in the great Mississippi Valley and the Far West, as well as to others in all sections, the war seemed almost as remote from their daily concerns as a flood in China. Moreover, with recollections of the draft riots in the Civil War, it was a question what might happen if we tried conscription on a large scale. Would all those who were opposed to the war and those millions whose German, Austrian, Hungarian and other racial descent and affinities bound them to the Central Powers rather than to the Allies, accept peaceably being drafted to go overseas to fight their own kin? It was freely predicted that conscription might mean for us torrents of blood and even civil war.

To the enormous relief and pride of America, the draft was carried out, as were subsequent ones, with per-

THE ANTS, 1917

*From the lithograph by Joseph Pennell in the Joseph and Elizabeth Robins Pennell Collection, Library of Congress
By permission of Mrs. Joseph Pennell.*

BUILDING ENGINES FOR THE ALLIES, 1917

From the lithograph by Joseph Pennell in the Joseph and Elizabeth Robins Pennell Collection, Library of Congress
By permission of Mrs. Joseph Pennell.

fect ease. Whatever the racial descent of our new citizens, they accepted their obligations to their new country as paramount and with an admirable spirit once the die was cast. The first draft included all men between the ages of 21 and 31, of whom over 9,500,000 registered in the 4557 registration districts into which the country had been divided. Each was given a number, and as these were drawn in Washington, the man in every district whose number was so drawn was drafted into the army. About 1,374,000 were taken on the first draft in July, of whom about half were accepted. These were distributed into thirty-two training camps, which were quickly built and equipped.

The President had decided, perhaps with memories of the Civil War in his mind, that this should be a war in the hands of experts, wholly unhampered in its military aspects by civilian meddling. He prevented, on the one hand, the formation of a Congressional Committee to supervise the conduct of the war, such as made so much trouble for Lincoln, and, on the other, he himself rigidly kept from meddling with his generals. He was, of course, technically Commander-in-Chief but he did not think, as Roosevelt appeared to with regard to himself, that that gave him adequate military knowledge for any post.

Roosevelt had asked to be allowed to start at once for France as commander of a division of 30,000 men, and was extremely resentful when not allowed to do so by

Wilson. Roosevelt's military career had been limited to a few weeks in the Cuban campaign of 1898. He was in

Your Song—My Song—Our Boys' Song

OVER THERE

With Both English and French Text as sung by ENRICO CARUSO

ONE OF THE MOST POPULAR OF THE AMERICAN WAR SONGS

SELF-CARICATURE OF ENRICO CARUSO MADE ABOUT 1916
From the collection of Erskine Hewett, Museum of the City of New York.

no way fitted for the post of chief command in Europe, and yet with his enormous prestige and popularity, with his ability always to make himself the centre of every

234

scene, most disastrous possibilities of friction might easily open up if he went as a subordinate in high position.

The command of all the American forces in Europe was given to General John J. Pershing, an officer of the regular army who had an admirable record in the Indian wars and later in the Spanish War and in the Philippines and Mexico. In response to the wish of the Allies, he had sailed for France the end of May, and within a few weeks was joined by several divisions,—the "Yankee," "Sunset," and "Rainbow,"—which formed the "American Expeditionary Force." On July 6, he cabled to the War Department that there should be at least 1,000,000 troops sent to France by the following May. That proved impossible, but in June, 1918, we did have in France 722,000 of the 2,112,000 total of the army, and on the Fourth of July we launched ninety-five ships in one day, the tonnage of which was more than equal to that of all American ships sunk by the Germans in four years.

Ships and ever more ships, however, were needed. Thanks to mine barriers—the United States Navy laid over 55,000 mines in the barrier in the North Sea— the submarine had ceased to be a serious factor. But the supplies of all kinds for the Allied nations, armies and civilians, and for our own growing foreign forces, had to be brought from all parts of the United States and from a few ports and carried the 3000 miles across the ocean. In France new docks had to be built, ports extended, and railways constructed to receive the swelling stream of goods and men.

The last great German offensive against the Allied lines was so threatening on June 2, 1918, that the Prime Ministers of England, France, and Italy cabled to Wilson that in the opinion of Foch the situation was of the utmost gravity, and that as the British and French could do no more to keep up their numbers, the war would be lost unless we could rush troops with all speed, at the rate of not less than 300,000 a month, across the ocean. This we did. In June we had had 722,000 men in France. In July we had just under 1,000,000, in August just under 1,300,000, in September, 1,576,000, in October 1,843,000, and in November, when the stream stopped early in the month owing to the Armistice, just under 2,000,000. Of the 1,200,000 troops carried overseas in less than five months, 49 per cent were transported in British vessels and 46 per cent in American, the American Navy supplying 83 per cent of the convoying warships, and American cargo vessels carrying 95 per cent of the supplies.

On August 31, to secure a greater reservoir of manpower, a new Draft Act had been passed by Congress, including, with the usual exemptions, all men between 18 and 45. This immediately added 13,000,000 men to the list of registrants, and preparations were made to raise the army to 8,000,000 by 1919, of whom 5,000,-000 were to be in France. Although these plans were

FIRST REGIMENT INFANTRY, ILLINOIS NATIONAL GUARD, LEAVING THE
ARMORY, CHICAGO, 1917

SECRETARY OF WAR NEWTON D. BAKER DRAWING THE FIRST NUMBER IN THE
SECOND MILITARY DRAFT, JUNE 27, 1918

From photographs in the War Department.

OUTPOST SENTRIES ON DUTY, MARCH 5, 1918
This post was destroyed by enemy shell fire a few minutes after this picture was taken.

GUN CREW OF THE 23D INFANTRY (2D DIVISION) FIRING 37M. GUN DURING
AN ADVANCE AGAINST GERMAN ENTRENCHED POSITIONS

From photographs in the War Department.

halted with unexpected and almost stunning suddenness by the Armistice, when that came we had 2,000,000
men overseas, another 2,250,000 in military service, and
nearly 11,500,000 civilians working at war jobs of one
sort or another.

So vast, complex and interwoven were the military
operations of the Western front, which stretched all the
way from Italy to Belgium, that it is impossible to disentangle the specific operations of the Americans from the
general maze to give an intelligent understanding of
their contribution. All that can be done in brief compass
is to point out some of the operations in which they were
engaged.

The hasty training which they received in America
before being sent across had to be supplemented by a
more intensive one in France, and the assistance, other
than psychological, which the American Army rendered
before the beginning of the great German drive in the
spring of 1918 was slight. Pershing had believed and
insisted, apparently wisely, that it would be best in the
end to organize a distinct American army rather than
merely to mingle our troops with the French, British or
Italians. So desperate, however, was the need for men
to resist the terrific onslaught of the Germans on the
war-weary Allies, that from April to August, 1918, he
consented to the use of our troops wherever needed to
strengthen the lines, and to this phase of our operations
belong the fights at Château-Thierry and Belleau Wood

where the Americans had their first chance to show their mettle, and acquitted themselves to the great admiration of the French.

By midsummer, however, the distinct American Army could be formed, and all the scattered troops were brought together from different sections and given the task of pushing back the Germans from the strongly protected indentation which they had made in the Allied lines in 1914 and held ever since, known as the St. Mihiel salient. The attacking force consisted of about 660,000 men, of whom 550,000 were Americans and 110,000 French, with some British aviators in addition. By September 13 the victory at this point was complete, and the enemy was driven back so as to restore 200 square miles of soil to France and free the Paris-Nancy railway and other lines of communications in such a way as greatly to assist the larger offensive against the Germans which was in contemplation. It was the beginning of the end.

The Germans had held also the Meuse-Argonne sector since early in the war. This was strongly fortified and of great importance to them from the standpoint of all their co-ordinated operations. The number of Americans available had been rapidly increasing, as we have seen, and in the operation in this sector Pershing had to handle more than 1,200,000 men. The struggle, which began on a front of 24 miles, and later extended to 90 miles, lasted for 47 days, and as Pershing wrote, was the "greatest, the most prolonged in American history." Steadily the Germans yielded to the pressure, retreating with heavy losses and with breaking morale. Similar

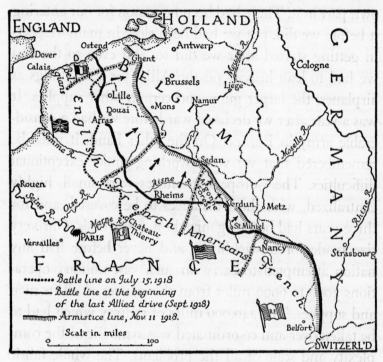

THE WESTERN FRONT

pressure was being brought on them along the whole front to the North by the Allied forces, and by the second week of November the retreat had become general. With such huge forces, with corresponding needs for communication and supplies, a retreat would certainly become a disastrous rout. It was all over, and on November 11 the Armistice was signed. The war had ended.

239

OUR PART IN THE WORLD WAR

We must neither over-estimate nor under-rate our own part in it. There had been no reason for our entering it before we did, but we had been slow in many respects in getting started after we did so, and even to the end we had to lean heavily on the Allies for such things as airplanes, the larger guns, and certain other supplies. It was a year after we declared war before we had a considerable army in Europe. On the other hand, it must be remembered that we were working under exceptional difficulties. The European countries were small, highly centralized, with short distances to be covered, and for three years had been organized on a war basis. Our very size made for unwieldiness, and never before had any nation attempted to carry on such vast military operations 3000 to 6000 miles from the sources of all its men and supplies. The 240,000 miles of railway which had to be taken over and co-ordinated was symbolic of the complexity and scale of all the problems. The whole fabric of one of the most populous and widely extended nations in the world had suddenly to be altered from its very foundations.

Without our fresh aid to the worn Allied countries it is quite evident from the despatches of both their military and civil authorities that they would have lost the war. At critical moments when all seemed over, we could throw in new supplies of financial credit, of material,

AIRPLANES ATTACKING TROOPS AT VIERZY DURING SOISSONS ATTACK

MARCHING IN ALONG A CAMOUFLAGED ROAD

From the lithographs by Lucien Hector Jonas. By permission of Wendell Westover, Esq.

THE MORNING WASH–UP

Sketched at Neufmaison, France, by Capt. Wallace Morgan, official artist of the A. E. F.

From the War Department.

NO MAN'S LAND

From the lithograph by Lucien Hector Jonas.   By permission of Wendell Westover, Esq.

and at last, in the final crisis, a supply of fighting men to overwhelm the enemy. Not having passed through the terrible ordeal of the earlier years, our troops were fresh and, as Foch exclaimed after the Argonne, "superb." But if, at the end, our added weight tipped the scales in favor of Allied victory, we must recall how heavy had been that heat and burden of the day which the other nations had borne year after year.

We can appraise our share, as well as the incredible magnitude of the calamity which had overtaken mankind, by a glance at some of the figures. Taking all the nations which had been engaged on both sides, over 65,000,000 men had been mobilized in the fighting services, 8,538,000 had been killed or died, 21,219,000 wounded, and at the end 7,750,000 were prisoners or missing. The table below gives the numbers of those who were killed or died in the armies of the chief belligerents:

Germany	1,773,700
Russia	1,700,000
France	1,357,000
Austro-Hungary	1,200,000
British Empire	908,371
Italy	650,000
Roumania	335,706
Turkey	325,000
United States	126,000

After the American Army was formed, the fighting in which it took part, especially in the Argonne, was so severe that the rate of casualties was high, and our low total was due to the short length of time in which our forces were engaged. The whole number of killed and wounded, about 360,000, may be contrasted, however, with the 500,000 a year which it is estimated are killed or injured merely in our industries in peace times.

Never before had soldiers been treated as well as were the Americans in this war. The pay of a private was raised to $33 a month, of which half could be held out for his family if he desired, and in addition allowances were made for certain classes of dependents. A man with a wife and two children, for example, received $50.50 a month. Vocational training was promised after the war for all those who might have been incapacitated in such a way as to prevent their taking up their former work, and, in the vain hope of avoiding the pension scandals of former wars, each soldier was given the opportunity to insure himself at the rate of $6.60 a month for $10,000. Over 4,000,000 men took advantage of this offer, the average policy being for $8744 and the total amount of insurance underwritten by the government was over $35,000,000,000, or $5,000,000,000 more than the total carried for civilians by all the companies in the country. The soldiers' comforts, as far as might be, were also catered to by such voluntary organizations as the Salvation Army, Knights of Columbus, Y. M. C. A., and Red Cross, the amounts spent probably running to well over $1,000,000,000, the Red Cross alone expending $400,000,000 in less than two years.

Y. M. C. A. THEATRICAL CORPS

Giving performance for 101st Machine Gun Battalion directly behind the lines, Bois de Rehanne, France, May 20, 1918.

HEADQUARTERS OF KNIGHTS OF COLUMBUS, DRAVEGNY, AUGUST 6, 1918

A sixteenth-century church was used for this purpose.

From photographs in the War Department.

RED CROSS CANTEEN AT SOUILLY, MEUSE, FRANCE, OCTOBER 13, 1918

SALVATION ARMY GIRLS SERVING MEN OF THE 26TH DIVISION, ANSAUVILLE, FRANCE, APRIL 9, 1918

From photographs in the War Department.

The basis on which the pension scandals were to be revived under the forms of "bonuses" and "adjusted compensation" was to be the claim for the difference between what the soldier received, when conscripted, and what his fellow who was not conscripted might have received at home in high wages. Except in the form of taxes and often illegitimate pressure to buy "Liberty Bonds," there had been no conscription of either capital or labor, and with the enormous war-time demands and scarcity of men, wages soared in all kinds of work, as did also almost equally however the cost of living, a cost that the soldier did not have to pay unless he had dependents, as many of the younger soldiers did not. Labor leaders, notably Gompers who was head of the American Federation, were given places on most of the War Boards, and many of the peace-time restrictions and demands were abrogated, labor agreeing to work wholeheartedly for the cause, to forego strikes, and in all cases of dispute to accept the verdict of arbitrations.

In spite of the fact that the war altered so greatly the ordinary daily life of tens of millions of Americans there was a curious unreality about it. The European participants suffered incomparably as contrasted with ourselves, but unprecedentedly horrible as it all was, there was a stark reality about it all for those in European countries which gave a normal outlet for the emotions. The actual fighting was, so to say, within sight, and the sick and wounded were to be cared for. So great, indeed, was the strain on the emotions that Europe was left almost exhausted emotionally.

In America it was different. The usual war propaganda, designed for that purpose, stirred the feelings of

RED CROSS BANDAGES POISONED BY SPIES

Startling Plot Reported by Director Staub in Urging Precautions by Philadelphia Workers.

Special to The New York Times.

PHILADELPHIA. March 28.—Albert W. Staub, Director of the Atlantic Division of the American Red Cross, addressing the local Red Cross organization today, said:

" You women of Philadelphia must clean house. Go over the list of your members and make sure of the loyalty of every one. Under no circumstances allow any one in your board rooms unless you know who they are. Keep persons out of the workroms who have no right to be there.

FIND DEBS GUILTY OF DISLOYAL ACTS

Socialist Convicted of Violating Espionage Act — Jury Out Six Hours.

SATISFIED WITH THE TRIAL

Rose Pastor Stokes Holds Defendant's Hand When the Verdict Is Announced.

(*Left*) ITEMS SUCH AS THIS WERE OF COMMON OCCURRENCE
In "*The New York Times*," March 29, 1917.
(*Right*) A VICTIM OF THE ESPIONAGE ACT
"*The New York Times*" of September 13, 1918.

fear and hate to a frenzy but there seemed no moral outlet for them. The enemy was so remote as to seem to innumerable Americans as unreal, lost in space. Wilson might talk about a war to end war and of making the world safe for democracy, but those phrases appeared insubstantial. Until the very last months before the Armistice, our participation in the fighting was slight, and even at the end our total casualties of all sorts of 360,000, scattered as they were among our population of 110,000,-000 in communities divided by thousands of miles, although they brought sorrow to individual homes, did not effect that purging of the heart of the whole nation as did the death tolls of Europe.

The fact that on the one hand our fears and hatreds were fanned into fierce flames, and on the other that our emotions did not have the outlets of fighting and sorrow, brought about, in a considerable degree, an abnormal psychology of the nation. On June 15, 1917, Congress had passed the Espionage Act which provided heavy penalties for any offenders who should be convicted of making false statements intended to interfere with the operation of our military forces or who should obstruct recruiting and in certain other ways interfere with the prosecution of the war. This was followed by an amendment, May 16, 1918, which extended the original offences to others in such broad and uncertain terms as to make prosecution possible by over-zealous or hysterical officials against citizens who might be honestly criticising the inefficiency of the government or its officials in conducting the war, who might object to the material war aims of the Allies,—as in proposed cessions of territory,—or say a word on behalf of the enemy. The punishment was set at a maximum of $10,-000 fine, twenty years in prison, or both. Enormous power was given to the Postmaster-General, who could exclude from the mails anything which "on evidence satisfactory to *him*" might be considered as constituting any of the offences named.

Freedom of speech and of the press was thus muzzled far more effectually than under Lincoln in the Civil War or than in any of the Allied countries. Public opinion both during the war and for several years after upheld the most drastic treatment of any one who, by the wildest stretch of the imagination, could be considered in the slightest degree unpatriotic or "radical." There was a veritable panic over the possible workings of German spies and later of the Russian Bolsheviks, which was part of the abnormal psychology of the times. About 2000 prosecutions were brought by the government, which imprisoned Eugene Debs and indulged in an orgy of attacks on people who might merely hold unorthodox opinions. Rose Pastor Stokes, for example, was sentenced to twenty years in prison for saying "I am for the people, and the government is for the profiteers," a statement that in view of such matters as the airplane scandals contained all too much truth.

But if America was abnormal and "jumpy," the morale of the German people was completely going to pieces in the late summer of 1918. Their losses and sufferings had been more than human beings could stand. Realizing that the whole structure of the state was fast crumbling, the German Government asked Wilson on October 4 to open negotiations for peace, based on his speech of January 8 and his subsequent utterances. This the President did only after the resignation of General Ludendorff and other evidences of a genuine change in the internal affairs of Germany had made it appear possible to base peace upon the sincere wishes of the German people themselves.

END OF THE WAR

Detailed terms for an armistice were drawn up by the Supreme War Council of the Allies and presented to the German representatives who had been brought, blindfolded, within the Allied lines. It is to be noted that the President had suggested to the Allied powers that the armistice could be arranged if they would make peace in accordance with the principles laid down by him and accepted by Germany. Although the terms of the armistice as presented by the military heads were extremely severe, there was nothing for the Germans to do but accept, which they did on November 11, the Kaiser having abdicated and fled to Holland two days before.

We have already indicated at length the views which Wilson held both as to the war and the possible peace. As far as America was concerned the armistice had been asked for by Germany and granted to her on the understanding that a peace treaty would be drawn up in accordance with Wilson's principles, notably as expressed in his speech before Congress, laying down his famous "fourteen points." He had, as we have seen, no trust in a peace negotiated on the basis of the old system of imperialistic diplomacy and national rivalries, and the publication by the Bolsheviks in Russia of some of the secret treaties of the Czarist régime proved all too clearly that the Allies, in spite of their idealistic propaganda, had made bargains among themselves for a division of territorial spoils based on the old system rather than on the broader basis of preparing for friendliness and co-operation among the nations of the world.

In brief, the "fourteen points" had laid down in the first five of them certain broad principles as the foundation of the future policy of the world. These were, speaking generally, that there should be no more secret diplomacy but "open covenants . . . openly arrived at," and no more secret treaties; that the seas of the world should be free to all to navigate in war as in peace; the removal, as far as possible, of all economic barriers between nations; the reduction of armed forces to the lowest point adequate for domestic safety; and an impartial adjustment of all colonial problems. The next eight points dealt with specific territorial changes in Europe, such as the restoration of Alsace-Lorraine to France, the re-establishment of Belgium, and the erection of an independent state of Poland, with "secure access to the sea." The final "point," which in Wilson's mind could alone be counted on to assure the new order, demanded the formation of a "general association of nations."

It had been on the basis of a peace wrought out somewhat on the lines of these points that Germany had offered to end the war, and although they had never been formally accepted by either the Allies or the American Congress, there had certainly been a tacit, if somewhat vague, assumption of them by the Allies in granting the armistice asked on the basis of them.

The task, however, which Wilson had set himself in proposing to alter the world order in accordance with the "points" was a stupendous and probably impossible one. It may be admitted, especially in view of the conditions in Europe since 1918, that a peace which merely renewed, in fresh combinations and with changed tensions and lines of cleavage, the old pre-war system of nationalistic jealousies and ambitions, and of armed balance of powers, could not be lasting. Wilson was right about that. On the other hand, in thinking out his new plan, the President, as he had done in Mexico, had flown too far above the actualities of the situation. To convert America to his views, he would have to alter our century-long fear of alliances and desire for isolation. To convert Europe, convulsed as she was by the bitterest of hatreds, with France especially burning for revenge and the desire of a new dominance, he would also have to alter human nature at a moment when it was not even sane. With regard to one point, the freedom of the seas, unjust as it may be that any one nation should set up a claim to rule them, it was most unlikely that the great maritime empire of England would consent to give up her private power for the sake of the public good.

Unfortunately, also, Wilson had made, and was to make, a succession of political blunders at home that rendered his defeat almost certain. To a very great extent, party politics had been laid aside during the war, and Republicans and Democrats had worked loyally for the sole purpose of helping the government to win. There was, however, much dissatisfaction with the way the war had been managed, and the President had powerful enemies, such as Lodge and Roosevelt, both within and without the government, and a considerable part of public opinion was naturally ranged against him.

Since the Civil War, our mid-term elections have frequently gone against the administration, and, in any case, it was likely that in 1918 the Congressional election would turn the Democrats out and put the Republicans in. Even so, however, they might have worked loyally with the President in international affairs, but Wilson made the extraordinary blunder of appealing to the nation before election to vote only for Democrats so as to strengthen his hand. The result was a howl of both rage and genuine disappointment from the public, and a sweeping victory for the Republicans, who now came in angered against the President instead of being ready, as far as they could, to work with him.

Had an election gone against the government in England, France, or other countries with a parliamentary system, and had Wilson been a European Prime Minister instead of an American President, he would have lost office with his party, but under our peculiar form the Executive continues, and for the second half of his term has to get along as best he can with a minority support in the legislature, though he still remains to a great extent, particularly in foreign relations, responsible for the conduct of affairs.

Wilson's second mistake, particularly in view of the strong and open hostility to him now to be expected in Congress, was not to appoint a senator a member of the delegation which set out for Paris on December 4, 1918, to negotiate peace. Nobody knows just what may be meant by the clause in the Constitution which provides that the President "shall have power, by and with the advice and consent of the Senate" to make treaties, but if the meaning of "advice" is uncertain, that of "consent" is not, and it was clear that no treaty negotiated by the President could be ratified unless two thirds of the senators present concurred when a vote was taken.

THE PEACE CONFERENCE

Wilson's decision to lead the Peace Commission at Paris in person was also a great and unfortunate innovation, arousing much criticism on several well taken grounds. Of the other four members only one, Henry White, was a Republican, and he, although he had done good diplomatic work in Europe, and was a close friend of Roosevelt, was not a national figure, and politically was a man of no importance whatever. Another member, the Secretary of State, Robert Lansing, had been a good Counsellor of the State Department but had been a mere figurehead since the resignation of Bryan and his own elevation to the Secretaryship. General Tasker H.

CONGRESS LEFT TO COPE WITH DOMESTIC DIFFICULTIES WHILE WILSON
WENT ABROAD TO NEGOTIATE PEACE

From "The National Republican."

Bliss was a strong man. Colonel House was not, although he had for some years occupied a position of peculiar confidence in his friendship with Wilson and had been abroad on many confidential missions before and during the war, and was supposed to have an intimate knowledge of the European situation. The make-up of the Commission did not indicate the slightest effort to gain the support or confidence of the Senate, and the inclusion of White as the only Republican was considered by some almost an insult to the party rather than a friendly gesture. It was clear that the President, in Paris in person, intended to dominate the Commission.

It was also clear, from the December elections in both France and England, that the Peace Conference intended to have as little as possible to do with any healing peace or change in the political order. In France, Clemenceau, one of the most reactionary of French statesmen, was re-elected on a platform of keeping to the old system of alliances and balance of power. In England, Lloyd George won by the most disgraceful appeals to mob passion, with such battle cries as promising to "hang the Kaiser" and to make Germany pay the entire cost of the war, shilling for shilling.

Thus it was that, leaving hostility behind him and sailing straight into a seething cauldron of hatreds ahead of him, Wilson landed at Brest on December 13. Whatever statesmen might think and promise, however, the peoples were heartily sick of war and of the old order. In the few weeks in which Wilson visited Italy, France, and England he was everywhere received with unparalleled enthusiasm as the savior of mankind from a recurrence of the overwhelming horrors of the past four years and as the herald of a new world. Then the Peace Conference got down to work.

The problems had to deal with almost every quarter of the globe, and thirty-two nations, though none of the enemy ones, were nominally represented. Even while the Conference was sitting, minor wars were still going on, and famine and Bolshevism were stalking over eastern Europe. It soon became evident that the real work would have to be carried on by the great powers alone, and for the most part decisions were reached behind closed doors

DISPATCH TO BE SENT.

*Date*___ February 19, 1919

*To*___ The President, USS GEORGE WASHINGTON.

*Prepared by*___ R A ___ *Approved*___ *Code*___ *No.*___

[Begin Dispatch below this line. Typewriter using double space.]

Secret for the President from Colonel House;

The following memorandum by the Chief of the British General Staff has just been sent me; QUOTE;

I had an interesting interview with Marshal Foch this morning, in which he expressed the following views;

As the result of his recent discussions with the German representatives at Treves, he is of opinion that under existing conditions we can dictate terms of peace to Germany. The German Government will agree to whatever terms we exact. But, he says, there is no time to lose.

PART OF THE FIRST PAGE OF A DISPATCH ON THE PEACE TERMS, FROM COLONEL HOUSE TO PRESIDENT WILSON, FEBRUARY, 1919

From the Manuscript Division, Library of Congress.

by the representatives of the United States, Great Britain, France, and Italy.

Little by little, Wilson, who had gone over with the hopes of negotiating a just and lasting peace, had to give way. He had trusted, like Lincoln, that he might bring healing as well as peace, but there was no healing, and many times it seemed as though there might be no peace.

Paris in that winter was the scene of perhaps the most virulent hatreds the world has ever known, and statesmen, who had come to power by promising their peoples impossible spoils, felt themselves on the edge of the volcanoes of revolution. The desire of the French leaders was not healing but revenge to the uttermost, and the ruin of the enemy. Japan held out for her promised plunder. Italy wanted her pound of flesh in extension of territory, and at one time her delegates left the Conference and threatened to plunge Europe again into war. Wilson himself, at one critical juncture, ordered the *George Washington* to be ready at Brest to take home the whole American delegation.

Much had to be surrendered of what he had hoped might redeem humanity from the curse of lasting hatreds and recurring wars, but he did save the League of Nations, which was written into the Treaty despite all the French strove to do to keep it out. It is impossible, as in an American history it is unnecessary, to follow the negotiations in detail or to describe the Treaty which itself fills a volume of 80,000 words. Many of the points for which the President fought would unquestionably have greatly helped the recuperation of the world had they been adopted. For example, he tried hard to have a definite sum named as that which Germany should pay in reparations, so that she and the world would know what had to be done. In the face, however, of the fantastic claims of France and England, Lloyd George demand-

255

ing, in view of his election pledges, the incredible sum of $120,000,000,000, that proved impossible.

We cannot exaggerate the aid which would have been

Paris, 29 May, 1919.

My dear Lansing:

I have the letter signed by yourself, General Bliss, Mr. White, and House about the desirability of calling a meeting of the Commissioners, technical experts, and advisors connected with the American Mission to discuss the German proposals about to be received, and am heartily in sympathy with the idea. Indeed, it is just what I myself had in mind.

Cordially and sincerely yours,

Woodrow Wilson

Hon. Robert Lansing,
Secretary of State.

LETTER FROM PRESIDENT WILSON TO SECRETARY OF STATE LANSING IN PARIS AT THE PEACE CONFERENCE, APPROVING THE MEETING OF THE AMERICAN DELEGATION TO DISCUSS GERMAN PROPOSALS

From the Manuscript Division, Library of Congress.

given to the economic recuperation of the world and to the restoration of confidence if the question of the reparations could have been settled, as Wilson urged, on a sane basis in 1919, instead of acting as a virulent cancer

in the whole world system for the years that were to follow. Had it been so, there might have been also a prompt
and reasonable settlement of the war debts to the United
States. There was no reason at that time for our cancelling

A SERVICE STRIPE FOR WILSON
With the subtitle—Why Not? Been there long enough.
From "The Republican" (Laramie, Wyoming).

the debts when the nations that owed us persisted, against
our strongest advice, in demanding for themselves the
huge sums which Clemenceau and Lloyd George insisted upon from Germany, and, as the years went by,
both questions were to become tinged with bitterness
and political jealousies.

In the midst of the Conference, immediately after the

League had been accepted, Wilson made a quick trip to the United States, in part, to consult prominent leaders of opinion, such as Taft, Root, and Hughes, and a number of suggestions made were later written into the Treaty by him. Meanwhile the opposition in the Senate was growing rapidly. Senators claimed that they were not being consulted or even kept posted as to what was going on, though we now know that Henry White, though loyal to Wilson, was keeping the chief opponent of the President, Senator Lodge, who was Chairman of the Committee on Foreign Relations, well informed of every move.

On the President's return to Paris, the work continued, and finally, on the 28th of June, the Treaty was signed at Versailles by Wilson, the Allies, and Germany, the latter complaining bitterly, and not without cause, of the extreme injustice of the terms, and that the whole document was contrary to the "fourteen points" which they had accepted as a preliminary to the armistice. On the 10th of July, the President submitted it to the Senate for ratification.

There at once it encountered, as was to have been expected, a storm of opposition. Lodge, twenty years before at the end of the Spanish War when defending the Treaty of Paris against its critics, had said that not to accept it as offered would "be a repudiation of the President and humiliation of the whole country in the eyes of the world." Now he fought bitterly to have this new treaty, negotiated by a President in person, rejected except with such reservations as Wilson would not accept. The Republican opposition was led by Lodge, but there was also a strong Democratic group, under the leadership of G. M. Hitchcock of Nebraska, which was equally opposed, as was the small but powerful group of "irreconcilables" led by Borah.

The President, who knew of the senatorial opposition, had counted on being able to offset it or to bring it to terms by appealing to the country and bringing the pressure of public opinion to bear. In pursuance of this plan, he started on a nation-wide tour to explain the Treaty directly to the people. The strain, however, of the last six years had been too great. The tour was undertaken against the advice of his physician, and while speaking in Colorado he suffered a paralytic stroke. He had staked all on his personal appeal to the nation, and had lost. Borne back to Washington a broken man, he recovered to some extent but was more or less shrouded in the mystery of a sickroom for the remainder of his term.

Meanwhile the interminable debate continued in the Senate, becoming more bitter. Much of the discussion centred about Article X, which it was held by some might force us to go to war merely to preserve the present territorial status of any of the countries in the League, though Wilson denied this. He also declined to accept the Treaty with any reservations, although it is more than probable that certain reservations would have been gladly accepted by the other nations as the price of our adhesion to the League. On November 19, a vote showed that the necessary two thirds could not be won in favor of the Treaty, either with or without the reservations, this being partly due to Wilson's known opposition to the Treaty with the reservations.

Under Hitchcock's lead, the Democrats themselves drew up a set of reservations, and in March the vote was again taken, with failure to ratify. The Presidential election was then less than eight months off, and political motives were becoming dominant. The groups became more stubborn, and in May, despairing of ratifying the Treaty, the two Houses of Congress, in order to put a technical end to the war, passed a mere joint Resolution declaring it at an end. This Wilson at once vetoed as a disgrace to American honor. Thus the deadlock continued. In the Senate there was opposition which could not be overcome unless reservations were added to the original Treaty. In the White House was the sick President, whose precise physical condition was a matter of uncertainty, and who stubbornly resisted the suggestion of any reservations whatsoever.

Whether Wilson would have succeeded in winning the country if he had been able to continue his tour can never be known. Once in the war, the nation had worked whole-heartedly for it, but it had not gone into it whole-heartedly, and, as we have said, the entire affair had always been somewhat unreal. We had no interest in the Old World and were more or less resentful at having been dragged into what had started as purely a European quarrel of the old sort. Many of the 2,000,000 soldiers who had been overseas had come back with no love for the Allies and with a wish to be done with Europe. On the other hand, had it not been for the stroke suffered by the President, with whatever influence it may have had on his mind, it may be conceived that Wilson might have accepted some reservations, and the deadlock have been broken in one way or another. He was stubborn but not as stubborn as many of his enemies made out, and at the Peace Conference had taken advice freely. But in his sickroom he was cut off from all contacts with the world and men, and no one can tell what thoughts passed through his partly broken mind.

Outside of that room, the whole current of American life had changed with amazing swiftness since the armistice, and the people whom the retiring President in the autumn of 1920 asked to take a "great and solemn referendum" on the Treaty and on our future part in the world, was a people anxious above all to forget the war and Europe and to take up again their old accustomed life.

CHAPTER VI

A MAD DECADE

THE "great and solemn referendum," which the President had asked for, was declined by the American people in a campaign and election which largely resembled a rush of a herd of ostriches to hide their heads in the sand in the hope of avoiding suspected dangers. The whole question of accepting the Treaty of Versailles centred about that of our entering the League of Nations, with or without reservations. Opinion cut across party lines, and leading Republicans such as Root, Taft, Hughes, and others were more favorable toward our joining with reservations than were many of the leading Democrats. The long discussion in the Senate and press had confused, rather than clarified, public opinion and had given time for the sentiments of nationalism and the desire for isolation to become dominant again.

Although the Treaty was one of the issues of the campaign of 1920, the fight was really between those of our citizens who realized that as a result of the war both we and the world were entering upon a new era of international relations and those others who frantically desired solely a return, which they did not realize was impossible, to our pre-war conditions of life and policies. The chief issue of the campaign was whether we should go forward boldly into the unknown and untried or pretend to go back to the old and accustomed. The referendum on that was to prove overwhelmingly in favor of trying to go back, of returning to what the successful Republican candidate was to term "normalcy."

The United States, as we have noted in the course of our story, had never been able to maintain its theory of complete isolation. Economically, however, we had appeared to ourselves to be self-sufficient to a large degree so long as we had exported chiefly foodstuffs which other nations had had to buy, and so long as we had allowed them to a considerable extent to pay for these by lending us the money which, as a rapidly developing debtor nation, was essential to the exploitation of our natural resources.

Of course, even economically, we had not been independent, but that fact had been more or less obscured until the years when the war, involving almost the entire world, dislocated all the accustomed exchange of commodities. Our moving-picture industry, for example, was dependent on a Japanese Government monopoly,—camphor,—for its films. Our great motor-car industry was dependent on foreign countries for the rubber which we could not produce in any of our own territory. In 1921 the United States Steel Corporation made up a list of forty commodities essential to manufacture which we had to import from fifty-seven foreign countries. The army discovered, if it did not know it before, that thirty commodities of one sort and another, necessary to the prosecution of modern warfare, could not be produced in the United States, or only in insignificant quantities.

Indeed, one of the underlying causes of the war itself had been the fact that for many years the political forces of exaggerated nationalism had been cutting across, and coming into conflict with, the economic forces of a commerce which had become world wide. No nation was any longer self-sufficient either in raw materials or markets for products. To be nationally prosperous involved exchanges with other nations, but the desire of each nation to be as prosperous as possible itself at the expense of any or all others brought about the conflict of wish and fact that had plunged the world into the Great War, as it might do again.

In addition to this general situation, that war had wrought changes for the United States which made the dream of isolation more difficult than ever of realization. Our industrial development had been rapid before the war, but the demands of that struggle had resulted in a colossal increase in our capacity for production. We *had* to export manufactures on a huge scale or to write off the cost of much of our new plant as dead loss. Such great new twentieth-century industries as the automobile and moving picture rested on the one hand, as we have seen, on essential imported articles, and, like all our mass-production industries, were dependent, on the other, on ever-expanding markets. Moreover, from a debtor nation we had suddenly become the world's largest single creditor. Besides the war debts of over $10,-000,000,000 we had invested in foreign countries by 1928 about $15,500,000,000 more. Our great corporations, such as the Ford Company, Standard Oil, General Electric, and many others built plants in other lands. Our banks were opening branches in the principal cities of Europe and South America. In a myriad ways our own prosperity was becoming linked to that of the world at large.

This sudden elevation to a position of dominance in world economics found us almost wholly unprepared. England had built up her foreign trade and her system of banking through centuries during which she had developed her technique and steadily grown in economic wisdom and knowledge. For us, the situation was much as though a branch-office manager had been called upon without notice to run the Steel Corporation as president.

As was pointed out in the previous chapter, a great revulsion of feeling as to Europe followed the end of the war, and by the election of 1920 the one great wish of the majority of our people was to avoid all responsibility and to get back to the days of 1913 before we had plunged into the maelstrom of the world outside. That it was impossible made no difference. We declined to see that we could not sell to others if we would not buy from them; that rapidly accumulating half the world's gold supply in our vaults we would force the world to a breakdown if we demanded more and more in payment of the debts due us if we would not take goods in payment; that by a thousand links we were at last bound to the rest of the globe whether we liked it or not. Like ostriches, we thought we would be safe if we stuck our heads in the sand.

THE ELECTION OF 1920

There was little doubt about the result of the 1920 election. At their convention which met in Chicago on June 8, the Republicans on the tenth ballot nominated Warren Gamaliel Harding for President after it had become clear that none of the three leading candidates, General Leonard Wood, Senator Hiram Johnson, or Governor Lowden, could receive the necessary number of votes. Calvin Coolidge, Governor of Massachusetts, was named as Vice-President. On the 28th the Democrats met for the first time in San Francisco, and it was only on the forty-fourth ballot, after a bitter fight between the forces of ex-Secretary McAdoo and Governor Smith of New York, that Governor James M. Cox of Ohio received the nomination for President, with Franklin D. Roosevelt of New York as his running-mate.

Although the question of the League was presumed to be one of those which divided the parties, Harding's straddling of the issue and the varying opinions of men in both camps undoubtedly justified Coolidge in saying that the election could not be taken as a mandate from the people on the subject. What had chiefly been decided was merely that the electorate was tired of Wilson and his idealism; that they wanted a change in the direction of "practicality"; that they wished to forget the war and all its problems; and that large numbers of persons of all shades of opinion were ready to unite against a man and a party that had of necessity aroused resentments during eight years of one of the most critical periods in the history of the nation. The quick disintegration of Harding's large majority showed that the backing he received came from a temporary situation and was not based on principles. Of these, Harding had none, but his majority was staggering, approximately 16,000,000 votes to 9,000,000 for Cox.

The new President had been a small-town newspaper man in Marion, Ohio, a party regular always, and with the help of Harry M. Daugherty, a local politician, had been elected in 1914 to the United States Senate for the term 1915–21. In the Senate he had rendered no distinguished service whatever, but had cast his vote in favor of Prohibition although he was himself then and always a heavy drinker. He was what is considered a "good mixer" in certain circles. He played poker, had dissipated habits, stuck by his friends, was untroubled by ideas or ideals, and was wholly commonplace in his mentality. On the other hand he often gained the liking of men who, at the same time, had no respect for him. Incapable and weak, the play of forces and passions which he did not understand, both in himself and others, made his rise to the Presidency a calamity for him. Of all our Presidents, except perhaps Grant, he was to be the most ill-served by his intimate friends, and the scandals of his régime were to spring from his own weakness and the rapacity of his "Ohio Gang."

His Cabinet was an odd assemblage of able men and of others who were much mistrusted. Charles E. Hughes as Secretary of State (the place had been offered first to George Harvey!), Andrew Mellon in the Treasury, and Herbert Hoover as Secretary of Commerce, were welcomed by the public as wise choices ,but those of Albert B. Fall, in the Interior Department, and of Will H. Hays as Postmaster-General, were not approved, while that of Harry Daugherty as Attorney-General was incredible in its unfitness. Some of the other appointments, such as Charles R. Forbes as head of the Veterans' Bureau and Thomas W. Miller as Alien Property Custodian, were equally bad.

In his inaugural address, the new President stressed the policy of keeping out of European affairs and of our own return to normal conditions, which were interpreted as being those prevailing before the Wilson administration. Although those had covered only eight years it seemed a century or more in looking back to the America of the days of Taft, due in part to the enormous accel-

AN EARLY MOVING PICTURE STUDIO IN CALIFORNIA
Established by Selig in March, 1908.

THE MOVIES IN 1932
Getting ready to "shoot" a scene from "Grand Hotel" (Metro-Goldwyn-Mayer). The actors stand beneath the "bungalow camera."

THE EFFORTS TO WIN SUFFRAGE

Top: An informal talk with the bathers at Long Beach, New York, 1912. *Centre:* Inez Milholland heading a parade in Washington in 1913. *Bottom:* Passing through Newark on the New York to Washington hike to present their cause to President Wilson, 1914.

eration which the war had given to various tendencies, many of which had long been in progress.

One of these had been the struggle for woman's suffrage, carried on since 1848, steadily gaining strength, but brought to a successful conclusion only by the war. The nineteenth amendment to the Constitution, proposed by Congress in 1919, had been approved by sufficient States to permit women to vote for the first time in a national Presidential election in 1920. The eighteenth amendment was likewise the result of the war psychology operating on a movement with a long history behind it. Adopted by thirty-six States by January 19, 1919, it was by its terms to go into effect a year from that date. By January 19, 1920, therefore, it had become illegal to manufacture, sell, or transport "intoxicating" liquor within the United States for beverage purposes. The definition of what might be intoxicating was provided in the Volstead Act (passed by Congress over President Wilson's veto October 28, 1919), which stated it to be one half of one per cent of alcohol. It is impossible to tell whether or not at the time the amendment was adopted it may have been approved by a majority of the voters, to whom it was never submitted.

When Wilson had been elected in 1912, the possibility of women voting for President seemed to belong only to a quite indefinite future, while no sane man would have dreamed of Federal prohibition. Other changes, however, had also come with equally unexpected swiftness.

After the turn of the century, H. G. Wells had made what then seemed the audacious prophecy that by 1950 airplanes would be used in warfare. By December 21, 1914, German planes were dropping bombs on English soil, and so rapid was the development of aeronautics that in the first year of peace, 1919, two Englishmen, Captain Alcock and Lieutenant Brown, flew the Atlantic without stop from Newfoundland to Ireland in sixteen hours, and another British plane had made the trip from England to Australia. In a few years more men were to be flying over the frozen waste of the North Pole (1926), and Lindbergh in "The Spirit of St. Louis" was to make his famous solo flight across the sea from America to France (1927). Although the general commercial use of flying belongs to the end of the decade, a new dimension had been given to men's thought and activity, and a new standard of speed had been established at its beginning.

Speed had also influenced the tempo of mind and life with the marvellous expansion of the motor-car industry. Ford had marketed his first car in 1903 but at the beginning of the war in 1914 the total sales of all motor vehicles was only about 500,000 a year. By 1920, however, over 8,000,000 passenger-cars were owned in America, a figure which grew to nearly 22,000,000, or one for every 5½ families, by 1928. Another industry of vast cultural influence, for good and bad, was that of moving pictures, which entered its real career only with the production of Griffith's "Birth of a Nation" in 1914. In

1920 perhaps about 30,000,000 persons were going to the movies once a week, and by 1930 100,000,000 were doing so. The radio, which had been used to some extent before the war for transmission of messages only, began to revolutionize the lives of the people with the erection of the first broadcasting station in 1921, and by the end of the decade probably 50,000,000 were daily "listening in" on the 10,000,000 receiving sets throughout the country.

One result of these inventions and of their extraordinarily wide use in America was to do away to a great extent with the difference which had always hitherto marked urban and rural communities. The car, and the better roads which followed it, permitted the country dweller to reach the nearest big town or city with ease, and to travel perhaps thousands of miles in his holiday season. The screen brought to his eye the same pictures seen by his fellows in the largest centres, and the radio brought to his ear the same music, news, and talk which all the nation heard simultaneously. That America owned approximately 80 per cent of all the motor cars in the entire world was merely an indication of how much further this urbanization of the provincial mind had gone with us than with any other nation, whatever its influences might prove.

As a result partly of the increased demand for opportunity by the laboring class and people of small incomes, we may note another phenomenon, the effect of which is difficult of appraisal. Between 1920 and 1926 the number of boys and girls at college increased from about 460,-000 to over 800,000. Minimizing, as we well may, the intellectual benefit which many derived from their experience, the social effects of taking the youth from home for four years and of bringing him into contact with those of other classes and regions cannot be neglected.

It is impossible to say how far the above changes, putting us so suddenly under the nervous strain of adjustment to a vastly quickened tempo of living and of a barrage of new sensations, and how far the war itself, may have been responsible for the abnormal mental condition in which the American nation found itself in the years following the coming of so-called peace. The two or three years immediately after were years of almost pathological unrest and mental panic.

One form which the panic took was a hysterical and almost sadistic persecution of innumerable individuals suspected of being radical or "red" in their political or social views. The Attorney-General of the United States, A. Mitchell Palmer, who had been transferred to that post, made himself notorious by his arrests and deportations, many of them on fantastically inadequate legal evidence. But local authorities also took a hand in what became a fanatical "witch hunt" on a national scale. Free speech came almost to an end and American Legionnaires and other "hundred per centers" indulged in defending what they considered American institutions by persecuting individuals with no due process of law. In the staid Commonwealth of Massachusetts, the case of Sacco and Vanzetti in 1920 was to bring an indelible stigma on our administration of justice, whatever may be thought of the guilt or innocence of the accused, and to have repercussions all over the world.

One of the most remarkable and cowardly of all the attacks on the constitutional freedom of the individual citizen was that made by great numbers of men, ranging from narrow-minded "hundred per centers" to mere ruffians, who enrolled themselves in what was called the Ku Klux Klan. This had no connection with the old Ku Klux of Reconstruction days, but its members adopted the same white-sheeted garb which effectually disguised them by covering the face, and in some respects the methods of the earlier Klansmen. Directed against Jews, Catholics, foreigners, and any to whom mistaken patriotic zeal, personal grudge, or religious bigotry might point as targets for persecution, the new Klansmen, by intimidation, flogging, and even murder, spread a veritable reign of terror throughout a large part of the country. From the narrowest mind of a country village, bent on rooting out any opinion with which it could not agree, to the highest legal officer of the United States, jailing and transporting suspects, the population seemed bent on suppressing every expression of thought which did not square with the standardized ideas of a Protestant Main Street.

273

The immediate post-war period was also marked by labor unrest in the form of strikes, of which that of the men in the Pittsburgh steel mills was the most bitter. The great prosperity of this tariff-protected industry had been but slightly handed on to the workmen engaged in it, and Chairman Gary of the United States Steel Corporation had resolutely fought against less than a twelve-hour day. A committee of the United States Senate, stronghold as that body is of corporation privilege, sided with the men on this point, and although the strike failed in its immediate results, working conditions were remedied a few years later. Troubles were general in other cities and industries, and in Boston the police force astounded the nation by going on strike, and gave Governor Coolidge a chance to make a belated gesture toward restoring order which somewhat absurdly gave him a national reputation as a defender of stability and won him the Vice-Presidential nomination.

Combined with a wave of passionate desire to withdraw from all world responsibilities and to reassume a rigid isolationist policy, there was felt equally strongly, and quite as irrationally, a dislike and mistrust of idealism and of all that had been considered progressive, before the war, under Roosevelt and Wilson. The people and the government seemed gripped by fears—fear of responsibility, fear of Russia, fear of whatever was foreign, of whatever was different, of whatever might take us farther on the road from the accustomed. So strong was the tide of reactionism that citizens quoted passages from even Jefferson and Lincoln at their peril, audiences, ignorant of their source, denouncing them as Bolshevik, Communistic, and traitorous.

In the midst of this mad distortion of genuine Americanism, Harding took office, pledged to lead the nation back to "normalcy," as he called it. This he appeared to think of solely as related to business. While his Attorney-General hunted "reds," and the President's friends hunted plunder for themselves from the public purse, Harding served big business. The railroads had been turned back to their owners under Wilson in 1920 by the terms of the Esch-Cummins Act, but there remained much to be done in liquidating the various Bureaus and other war organizations. The complete change in our position due to our having become a creditor and exporting industrial nation had been pointed out by Wilson the day before his retirement in his message caustically vetoing the tariff bill sent to him by Congress. That we could not continue to sell to the world if we declined to buy was obvious, but those who benefited by the tariff refused to see it. The first month of his term, Harding sent a message urging the immediate necessity of higher rates. An emergency tariff and, in 1922, a permanent one, were passed by Congress, raising duties to far the highest points yet attained.

The attitude of the people at large toward the great corporations had completely changed since before the war, and during the years from 1920 to at least the great crash of 1929, the big business man was to be America's hero, and business was to reign supreme. A number of causes may be assigned for the change, chief among them probably being the increased participation in stock ownership by the public. Over 21,000,000 persons had subscribed to the last Liberty Loan, and the great majority of them had become familiar with ownership of a security for the first time during the struggle. The fortunes made in stocks affected by war demands, the so-called "war brides," and the increasing newspaper publicity given to stock-market excitements, served to increase both the speculating and investing publics.

On the other hand, as we have seen, neither Roosevelt nor the other Progressive leaders had thought out any satisfactory plan for controlling corporations in the interest of the people, who had discovered that mere legal proceedings to break up a great combination brought no results to the ordinary citizen. The latter was tired of idealism, sceptical of government regulation or interference, rabid to make money for himself as he had seen others do, and was coming to care little about anything else provided he was allowed to do so. In that simple situation is the key to much of the history of the mad decade.

Moreover, the man in the street, whether laborer or capitalist, had got drunk on figures. Just as airplanes and automobiles had given us new standards of intoxicating speed, so the figures of war-time industry and debts had given us new and equally intoxicating standards of financial magnitude. In 1901 the United States Steel Corporation had seemed a malign colossus with its billion-dollar capitalization. In 1916 the entire debt of the United States Government had been only about $970,000,000. By the end of the war it was twenty-five and a quarter billions. Such incomprehensibly huge sums as this introduced a new standard of comparison and made the big corporation seem not so big after all.

Practically every great war of modern times has been followed by a business depression about two years later, and by a far more severe secondary depression about eight years after peace. The World War was to prove no exception, although the general failure of business leaders to forecast the situation properly was to result in a total collapse of that excessive confidence in their ability as leaders which was notable before war-time prosperity gave way.

By 1920 the primary depression had begun, brought on partly by general underlying conditions and partly by the "buyers' strike" entered upon by a public whose income had been deflated before the cost of living had been lowered. From being wildly extravagant during flush times, people suddenly held parades and formed organizations protesting against high prices, pledging themselves to wear old clothes and even overalls for the sake of economy. Retail prices soon fell, and the wholesale prices of commodities crashed from an index figure of 231 in 1920 to 125 in April, 1921. The great manufacturing companies, whose managements had been for the most part blind to what was historically inevitable, had to take huge losses in depreciated inventories, while the agricultural population was nearly ruined.

The corporations were to come back to a new and greater prosperity but the farmer was not. In 1921 he was getting only $1.19 a bushel for his wheat as compared with $2.14 two years before, 12.3 cents for cotton as compared with 29.6 cents, and much the same proportion for his other crops, whereas it has been estimated that one third of the farm income was taken for taxation. In the six years following 1920 the average value of his land fell from $108 to $76 an acre. In 1921 the so-called "Farm Bloc" was formed in Congress by representatives of the Middle Western States to secure relief specifically for the farmers, but the various panaceas proposed, such as the McNary-Haugen bill and others, have been more or less economically unsound, and during the wild period of stock speculation and inflation which was to follow the general business recovery after 1921, farming remained the dangerously unprosperous industry of the nation. The problem of markets and of the relation of agricultural prices to high wage scales and tariff-protected manufactured articles remains to be solved.

AN ERA OF GREAT PROSPERITY BEGINS

In spite of continued strikes, such as that of 300,000 railway shopmen in 1923, prosperity began to return with the huge gold imports which started in 1922. The Federal Reserve system which Wilson had given to the nation, after having stood the strain of war, unquestionably helped to pull us through the slough of deflation. But in the years immediately to follow, the fire of American prosperity, and more particularly of American speculation, was to blaze so fiercely as to astonish the whole world. The imports of gold, which did not stop until we had more than half the world supply, were but one of the forced draughts which made the blaze. Another was the first trial on a gigantic scale of national advertising which made its new and almost irresistible appeal to the potential buyer through his emotions skilfully played upon by psychological experts. The willingness of business men suddenly to increase so remarkably the sums spent in this way was largely due to the income tax. If, for example, the net income of a corporation was taxed 50 per cent it meant that the corporation could save 50 per cent on an increased expense. If it did not expend a million dollars on advertising the government would take a half million in taxes on earnings. If it did spend a million it would not have to pay the half million to the government on that particular million, and so it got a million dollars' worth of advertising for half that sum. The effect on the public of having their minds thus played upon at colossal expense and with consummate skill was, for the time being at least, immense. What a decade before had been luxuries, many of them unthought of in personal terms by a large part of the population, came to be considered necessities, under the insidious appeals to fear, pride, social prestige, duty to one's family, the lightening of work, or mere enjoyment.

The demand for goods made business, and the new economic theory, identified with the name of Ford, that high wages increased markets, seemed to open endless vistas of ever-rising purchasing power, broadening markets, and increasing production. Like the old legend of the Fountain of Youth, a new belief arose that we had discovered the way to eternal prosperity. If that were so, why wait until one had saved the money for anything one wanted? The introduction on a great scale, and in new fields, of the instalment-purchase idea became another forced draught under production and apparent prosperity. Mass-production methods, of which the full implications were not yet realized, also seemed to promise an indefinitely descending scale of prices for goods produced in ever-enlarging volume with attendant economies. The increasing market required would be created by increasing wages, and if wages were steadily to rise and prices to fall, the ordinary man saw a veritable New Jerusalem opening before him. If wise sceptics hesitated to accept the theory of a "new era," the actual increases in production, wages, and profits satisfied the more gullible, whether servant or captain of industry, and America

Attacks Instalment Buying.

Speaking before the State Secretaries Section, C. F. Zimmerman of the Pennsylvania Bankers' Association, said that the tremendous growth of local merchants' credit bureaus and of household loan companies during the last decade is convincing evidence of a "broad misunderstanding of right methods—to say nothing of profligacy—in the use of the family income." Country bankers in particular have occasion to listen day after day to stories of financial grief and need experienced by those who have been hopelessly improvident with their money, he said.

THE BANKERS' OPINION OF INSTALMENT BUYING
From "The New York Times," October 3, 1928.

had got started on the wildest debauch economically that she has ever enjoyed.

As the ordinary man became more and more anxious to make money, he cared less and less about the affairs of the world at large. Foreigners were to sell us raw materials, buy our mass-produced goods, and send us gold in payment, while we reserved our entire domestic market for our own manufactures. Although Harding, when a candidate for the Presidency, had made many contradictory statements as to his attitude toward the League of Nations, he became opposed to it after his inauguration, and in October, 1921, the Senate in passing the Knox resolution ratifying the treaty with Germany and declaring the war at an end, inserted a clause prohibiting the President from appointing any representative of the United States to serve on any body, commission, or agency set up by the Versailles Treaty (which meant, of course, the League of Nations), without the consent of Congress. For many years after, in the absence of that consent we have had to be represented on many European commissions by an "unofficial observer" only.

So far did our fear of the League go that it has been said our government at first would not even answer communications from it lest it become involved! Although successive Presidents, beginning with Harding, have endeavored to have the United States declare, with reservations as usual, its adherence to the World Court, the Senate was still blocking final action in 1932. As much of the international functioning of the nations of the world now proceeds through the League, we have, for the most part, either had to decline to take our proper place in conferences or do so in an undignified way.

In 1921, although anxious to take part in the movement for disarmament, which had always been an American ideal, we felt unable to do so with any body in any way connected with the League. As a result of both our desires and fears, Harding invited nine powers, including Great Britain, France, Italy, and Japan, to meet in Washington to discuss reduction of naval power, and on November 12 the meeting was opened by Secretary Hughes. A first beginning toward reducing naval expense was made by the agreement on the 5–5–3 ratio, which allotted equal strength of capital ships to the United States and Great Britain, and gave Japan three fifths of the strength of each of the others. Italy and France agreed to smaller percentages, but although sixty-eight capital ships were scrapped by the treaty, no progress could be made when other forms of naval weapons were discussed, France particularly objecting to limitation of her submarines. Submarines, however, were excluded as commerce destroyers.

Perhaps more important than the naval treaty were the two which were made at the same conference regarding affairs in the Far East. In place of a renewal of the British-Japanese alliance, the nine nations represented at the conference, including China, Holland, Belgium, and Portugal, as well as those named above, in what is called the "nine-power treaty," mutually guaranteed the integrity of Chinese sovereignty and the policy of the "open door" for trade. In a four-power treaty, Great Britain, France, Japan, and ourselves agreed to respect each other's possessions in the East, and to submit any question likely to cause trouble to the decision of a joint conference. Various minor matters were also adjusted in other treaties, and the conference was the one outstanding feature of Harding's term, probably due almost wholly to the Secretary of State, Hughes.

For twenty years before the war, restriction of immigration had been discussed, and several measures had been passed by Congress for the purpose, all of which had been vetoed. The unusual condition brought about by the war, however, gave added strength to the movement, and in 1917 a measure, based chiefly on a literacy test, was passed over Wilson's veto. The extreme nationalism aroused during the struggle and the danger, after its close, lest vast numbers of Europeans might rush to America to escape post-war poverty and unemployment in their native lands, led Congress to pass an Act in 1921 limiting immigrants to 3 per cent of the number of their several nationalities in the United States according to the Census of 1910.

Although this also was vetoed by Wilson, practically the same bill was approved by Harding in the special session immediately following his election. Under Coolidge the year chosen as a base was changed to 1890, which greatly favored emigrants of the north European nations as contrasted with those of the southeastern countries, but after 1927 it was provided that the total immigration should be not more than 150,000 persons a year, and that each nation might send only as many emigrants to us in proportion to that figure as the total number of its nationals in the United States in 1920 bore to our total population. This "national origins" system

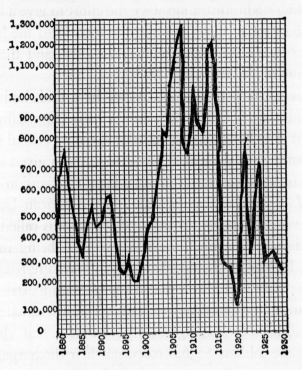

IMMIGRATION FROM 1880 TO 1930

did not go into operation, owing to various difficulties, until 1930, but is now the basis of our immigration policy. Although under it only 146 Japanese could enter the country each year as immigrants, Congress was so afraid of the California problem that it specifically excluded all Japanese entirely, to the natural irritation of

285

that proud nation, which had lived up to the spirit of the gentlemen's agreement made with Roosevelt.

The principal financial measures undertaken during Harding's administration were the effort to give a bonus to the ex-soldiers, the lowering of taxes with the beginning of cutting down the national debt, and the first funding of the European war debts.

Our soldiers in the war, as we have said, had been treated more liberally than those of any other nation or period. The high pay, the insurance, the vocational training, and the pay for disability, had all been given in the hope of doing away with the subsequent pension scandals following our other wars. The American Legion, however, soon began its demand for what is called "adjusted compensation," the word pension being in bad odor. In March, yielding as always to pressure from the "soldier vote," Congress passed a bill granting extra compensation to ex-soldiers to an amount estimated at $3,000,000,000, although the government had already given the soldiers $256,000,000 on their discharge, had paid out about $2,500,000,000 to the disabled, and was paying out $1,000,000 a day for soldiers and their dependents, besides carrying the low-rate war-time insurance for them. Harding vetoed the bill, but the House passed it over his veto by a majority of nearly five to one. The Senate narrowly defeated it, but it was clear that it was only a question of time when the old-time pension scandals would be renewed.

Mellon, who was to serve as Secretary of the Treasury longer than any other who has ever held the office, began at once his programme of tax reduction, much criticised by some sound financiers, but which he carried on for ten years, until the crash of American business in 1929 and the subsequent events afforded only too unhappy confirmation of the prophecies of his critics. The system of a national budget, which had been agitated for ten years, came into operation under Harding, but Congress continued to vote money lavishly, the national expenses in 1930 being nearly five times those of 1914. The prosperity which lasted from 1922 to 1929 enabled Mellon to play the wizard apparently, and continually to lower the rates of taxation, especially for the very rich (to which class he himself belonged), while at the same time reducing the total debt from $25,484,000,000 in June, 1919, to $15,922,000,000 in June, 1930. The steady reduction in taxation, however, begun under Harding and continued under Coolidge, gave the people at large a false sense of sound government finance, and disguised to a considerable extent the continued extravagance of government expense, a point which was to be most sharply brought to their attention by the staggering deficit left the moment "prosperity" could no longer be blown to a blaze by the forced draughts. The beginning of the policy may be noted here but the catastrophe was to occur under Hoover.

Another factor which gave a false sense of security in

expenditure was the belief that the European war debts could be funded and paid practically in their entirety. In 1922 Congress passed a measure designed to facilitate the refunding of the debts, almost nine tenths of which were owed by Great Britain, France, and Italy. The first, which owed much the largest sum, sent representatives to Washington in January, 1923, to arrange terms of settlement. The promptness with which Great Britain, with her unrivalled financial strength, agreed to pay $4,604,000,000 over a period of sixty-two years, lulled the average man into the belief that the entire amount of approximately $9,400,000,000 was a sound asset.

There was, indeed, a lack of sound basis for the whole of the "mad decade," and, as one looks back, men seem to move in a fog of abnormality and unreality. Unhappily by the end of his second year of office, the results of Harding's easy handing over of responsibility to others, and of his own personal habits and weakness, were beginning to involve him in a situation from which there appeared to be no escape. The newspaper reporters had been extremely considerate of him, both as a newspaper man himself and as President of the United States, so that the public at large knew practically nothing of his former mistress, his drinking parties in the White House, and his wilder ones outside. The doings, however, of the "Ohio Gang" and of other friends whom Harding had appointed to office could not be so well concealed.

On February 12, 1923, the Senate appointed a committee to investigate alleged irregularities in the Veterans' Bureau. Three days later, Harding's friend, Forbes, resigned as its head, though he could not stave off judicial proceedings, as a result of which he was convicted of defrauding the government and sent to Fort Leavenworth prison for two years. Thomas W. Miller, the Custodian of Alien Property, was also caught in fraudulent transactions, and, in 1927, finally likewise sentenced to prison. Daugherty, the Attorney-General and member of the Cabinet, was the centre of extraordinary intrigues which have never yet been cleared up. He was later to be forced out of office by President Coolidge, for obstructing the investigation of his own conduct, and appears to have been able to escape more serious results only by destroying his papers and records in several places. His explanation for the destruction of his bank records when he was later being tried in court was that their preservation would have deeply stained the memory of Harding.

Even a worse scandal, if possible, than that created by the character and conduct of Daugherty, involved two other members of the Cabinet. In May, 1921, at the request of Secretary of the Interior Fall, the President was induced to sign an order transferring the oil reserves of the navy from the custody of the Navy Department to that of the Interior. One of the reserves was located at Teapot Dome, Wyoming, and the scandal became known as "Teapot Dome," owing to the fact that it was that particular reserve which Secretary Fall, after having accepted a bribe of $100,000, leased to Harry F. Sinclair, the Elk Hills reserve being likewise leased to Edward L. Doheny. The leases, which were of colossal value, were made secretly and without competitive bids. Harding's own order had been wholly without constitutional authority, and Denby, the Secretary of the Navy, had no right to comply with it.

Under the lead of Senator La Follette, the Senate demanded an investigation, although Harding issued a statement approving of Fall's actions. Denby resigned under fire, and the investigation revealed the worst state of corruption which the nation had ever known. All of these various scandals were becoming ripe, and to some extent known or suspected, by the beginning of 1923, although it was to take longer to fathom them, and for obvious reasons Harding's successors were not anxious to air them. In the case of Secretary Fall it was not until October, 1929, that, after availing himself of every possible legal device for delay, he was finally sentenced to a year's imprisonment. Considering the position he occupied and the heinousness of his offence, this was assuredly light enough, but Doheny managed to get off altogether, and Sinclair with only a short prison term for contempt of the Senate and for using private detectives to shadow members of the jury sitting on his case.

How much or how little Harding may have known

of the utter rottenness of much of his administration it is as yet impossible to tell, as well as what such other Cabinet officers as Hughes and Hoover or Vice-President Coolidge, who sat with the Cabinet, may have known or thought about it all. At any rate it was not until long afterward that any one of them expressed abhorrence of the scandals or their authors.

DEATH OF PRESIDENT HARDING

There is good evidence that by the summer of 1923 Harding was becoming greatly worried over the situation of both his administration and himself, including his former relations to a certain Nan Britton. The results of his own weakness seemed to be closing in on him when he started on a trip to Alaska in June. A cipher message from Washington received by him in July nearly caused his collapse, though no one knows what was in it. Returning from Alaska to San Francisco, he was said to be suffering from ptomaine poison and on August 2 he died. Without accepting the most sensational of the stories of his death, it must be admitted that the mystery of it has never been cleared up, and as all of his papers were destroyed by Mrs. Harding before her own death, an unprecedented proceeding in the case of a President, there was evidently much that may now never be known.

One cannot but feel a certain pity for the man who, somewhat against his will and better judgment, allowed himself to be elevated to a position for which he was wholly unfitted and who let himself become surrounded by and dependent upon the worst gang of ruffians and grafters that have disgraced any administration in our history.

There is no real evidence that Harding himself profited financially by any of the corruption. He was merely a weak man of rather low tastes, who was comfortable chiefly in the society of men of inferior character and attainments. His own pleasures,—drink, women, or a poker game with the "crowd,"—were those of countless very ordinary men. The misfortune for himself and the nation was that when he had risen to the position of President, he was not able, as, for example, Chester Arthur had been, to rise also to the dignity and responsibility of his high office. At the time of his death the people at large realized little or nothing of the scandals, and knew only the rather likeable man as the newspapers made him appear to be. It was long before the public, or at least the Republican portion of it, could be brought to admit the truth.

The Vice-President was as yet but little known when, after Harding's death, he took the oath of office in his father's house at a cross-roads hamlet in Vermont. Like Hughes and Hoover, Coolidge had been wholly unsmirched by the dirt of the "Ohio Gang" and other malefactors of the Harding régime, and his accession to office and Harding's death were the most fortunate possible happenings for the Republican Party. He was to prove an extreme conservative, interested almost wholly in the economical running of the government, although with lavish Congresses he did not make the progress in that direction which was as needful for the nation as it was desired by him. His interests were narrow, and he apparently knew and cared little about international affairs or the larger problems of the post-war world. His comment on the debts when there was a question of their reduction,—"they hired the money, didn't they?" —gives a fair measure of the man.

Silent, without culture or intellectual tastes, a mind that in many respects was singularly ordinary and commonplace, he nevertheless had a certain hard-bitten Yankee shrewdness and common sense which made him appear to many as a wise and safe leader. As prosperity returned in steadily increasing measure under him, as it would have done under any one else, he became a legend, almost as closely identified with national economic well-being as the "good medicine" of the Indians. When, after more than a year of serving in Harding's stead, he ran for the Presidency in his own right, the campaign cry was "Coolidge or Chaos," and, absurd as this was, it expressed at once the chief interest of the people and the aspect in which the President was to be constantly presented.

By the latter part of 1923 it had become increasingly evident in Europe that the $33,000,000,000 of reparations which had been laid upon Germany were impossibly large and would require readjusting. Whether or not Europe had "hired" our money during the war, it realized that its ability to pay was closely linked with the payments which the debtor nations might or might not receive from Germany. The United States had declined to take part in European conferences, but in Europe it was thought it might be well if influential men in America knew and shared in the anxieties of the situation. The Reparations Commission thus asked General Dawes, a successful business man of the Middle West, who had served under Pershing in France and who had been the first director of the Budget Bureau under Harding, to head a committee which should study the problem of Germany's capacity to pay and the methods of her doing so. In April, 1924, the committee made public its findings and suggestions, which became known under the name of "the Dawes Plan," although in fact it was chiefly the work of Owen D. Young and not of Dawes. It brought the latter, however, prominently into the international limelight, and at the Republican Convention, which met at Cleveland on June 10, he was nominated for Vice-President on the ticket with Coolidge, who had received the Presidential nomination on the first ballot by an overwhelming majority. The platform on which the candidates stood called for rigid economy, further reduction of taxes, payment of war debts, and a high protective tariff.

THE ELECTION OF COOLIDGE

Fourteen days later the Democrats met in New York, but the long-drawn-out battle between Governor Smith

FRUEH'S CARTOONS ON THE CONVENTION IN *THE WORLD,*
JUNE 30, 1924

of New York and William G. McAdoo, which made it the lengthiest convention in American history, tired the country, created a bitter split in the party, and destroyed what chances John W. Davis, the candidate finally chosen as a compromise, might have had. The scandals of the Harding régime were scarcely used in the campaign, contrary to what might have been expected. This

295

was partly due to the fact that the public was curiously apathetic about them, and partly to the fear of the Democrats that the Republicans might reply by digging up such scandals of the war administration as might have been afforded, for example, by the air service. Moreover, Harding had been dead for more than a year and the Republican candidate could in no way be connected with the misdoings of his predecessor's appointees.

The Progressive Party, led by La Follette, interested the public only slightly, the minds of the people being far more concentrated on problems of money-making and prosperity than of social matters, and the Republicans won a sweeping victory, polling over 15,700,000 votes to about 8,400,000 for Davis, and 4,800,000 for La Follette. Only about 51 per cent of the total eligible voters took part in the election.

International affairs under Coolidge led the United States no further afield than they had done under Harding. Our Caribbean policy, which had developed around our ownership of the Canal Zone and the necessity of extending our sphere of influence over a wider and wider extent of neighboring territory for what was considered the necessity of defending the Canal, led us again to send troops to Nicaragua in 1926 to maintain order. They have remained there ever since.

Although the Republican platform, and Coolidge, like Hoover, advocated our joining the Court of International Settlement, the Senate continued, as we have noted, successfully to block such a participation by us in the life of the world. Also, although the League of Nations was at work upon plans for disarmament of the nations, we declined to have anything to do with such an effort, and in 1927 Coolidge issued invitations to Great Britain, France, Italy, and Japan to join us in another conference to make further progress beyond that achieved at Washington. Italy and France rejected the suggestion, France noting in her reply that her loyalty to the League, which was then at work on the same problem, would prevent her from undertaking the task through other channels. Even friendly Great Britain warned us that the relating of any conference with us would require careful adjusting to the proceedings of the League. Although Japan and Great Britain did send representatives to confer with our own at Geneva, the conference broke down and was a complete failure.

Throughout the latter part of 1927 and the first half of 1928, negotiations proceeded with Great Britain, Germany, Italy, Japan, and France with a view to a multilateral treaty, subsequently known in America as the "Kellogg Pact," from the name of our Secretary of State, although the first suggestion came from Briand in France and it is known in Europe as the "Pact of Paris." The object of the treaty was to "outlaw war" except in necessary self-defence, the definition of what constitutes both aggression and self-defence being left rather vague. As usual in the post-war years, although we were willing to make a gesture, we were unwilling to assume any international responsibilities in the way of sanctions, and it is questionable as yet just how important this verbal outlawry of war may prove to be. A certain moral effect it unquestionably has, but it remains uncertain how far this moral effect would withstand the strain of a genuinely serious international quarrel.

Coolidge's Cabinet had been made up of a number of new men, but Mellon had remained at the Treasury, and Hoover as Secretary of Commerce. The most characteristic portion of the history of the Coolidge administration was to be centred about the Treasury head.

The President in his inaugural address had truly said that "the collection of any taxes which are not absolutely required . . . is only a species of legalized larceny." Not a little of his popularity was to flow from his steady resistance to the quite opposite doctrine held by Congress, too ready to spend the people's money for the benefit of special groups who may be counted upon to help return a congressman to his office. The readjustment in business due to deflation had continued into 1922, which year witnessed the largest number, save for the preceding one, of big failures in our history up to that time. But after that, general business had picked up rapidly about the date of Harding's death, and in 1924 left the United States Treasury with the greatest surplus on record, over $500,000,000. Congress availed itself of this to pass a new bonus bill for the soldiers, over Coolidge's veto.

Within the three years after Great Britain had funded her debt with us, practically all the other nations had done the same, France delaying the longest of the great powers. Subsequent to the ready acceptance of our terms by the British it became evident that the other nations either could not or would not honor their bond in the same degree, and it became necessary to find some formula for treating them on a different basis, both as to the amount of the original principal and accrued interest which should be re-funded, and as to the terms of future payment. This was found in the alleged "capacity to pay," which it may be noted by 1932 had become a farce so far as the genuine capacity of the several nations was then concerned. Of the total amount funded of $11,671,-953,490, Great Britain had promised to pay us $4,600,-000,000 at 3.3 per cent interest, France $4,025,000,000 at 1.6 per cent, and Italy $2,024,000,000 at 0.4 per cent, the average rate for all loans being 2.1 per cent. That Great Britain paid heavily by being the first to come forward to settle with us is now generally acknowledged even by those who wish to collect every cent due.

The prosperity which returned to the United States, as might have been expected after the first post-war depression, followed a normal course up to about 1926 or 1927. The factors we have mentioned above did, indeed, supply forced draughts and to that extent emphasized the magnitude of the prosperity which might have been expected, and by doing so lent some plausibility to the insistence of many business leaders that all precedents should be scrapped and that American business had entered upon a "new era" in which the old economic laws no longer held sway.

The extraordinary earnings, especially of some of the new mass-production enterprises, and the generally excited condition of mind in the decade, had also greatly stimulated speculation, so that in the five years from 1921 to the close of 1926 the average price of twenty leading industrial stocks on the Stock Exchange had risen from $67 to $177. Brokers' loans had also steadily risen, $1,750,000,000 on January 1, 1925, $2,500,000,000 a year later, and $2,820,000,000 at the beginning of 1927. By the latter year, in which normally the secondary and greatest post-war depression might have been expected to appear, business had in fact begun to turn downward.

The unprecedented size of the loan account was seriously disturbing the minds of the more conservative students of business. In January, 1928, the leading financial journal, *The Commercial and Financial Chronicle,* stated that "there could no longer be any doubt that a business reaction was well under way." During the year there were to be 23,146 mercantile failures, with liabilities of $520,000,000, the largest number, though not the largest liabilities, for any year since 1922. The stock market began to fall in January and February, higher interest rates were feared, and the normal processes of correcting an over-extended position began to operate.

MELLON FORESEES NO BUSINESS SLUMP; TAX SHIFT BY SMOOT

Secretary Is Optimistic Over Conditions Now and Finds No Sign of End of Prosperity.

SENATOR IS LESS SANGUINE

He Urged $300,000,000 Cut in Taxes, but Now Holds More Than $225,000,000 Unsafe.

FROM *THE NEW YORK TIMES,*
NOVEMBER 15, 1927

YOUNG FAVORS CHECK ON ABNORMAL CREDIT

Reserve Board Governor Tells Bankers System Can 'Properly' Limit Undesirable Growth.

BUT SPEAKS GUARDEDLY

And Declines to Answer Ten Questions on His Attitude on Brokers' Loans and the Like.

WARNING ON SECURITIES

ONE OF THE WARNINGS, FROM *THE NEW YORK TIMES* OF OCTOBER 3, 1928

COOLIDGE VISIONS NEW ERA OF PROGRESS IN AMERICA; HOLDS PROSPERITY A TEST

OUTLINES NATION'S NEEDS

President Urges Flood Control and More Ships for the Navy.

OPPOSES LOWER TARIFF

Photographs Encke's Comet, Barely Visible to Naked Eye

CHICAGO, Nov. 17 *(P).*—The first photograph to be obtained of the famous Encke's comet as it approaches the spot in its orbit nearest the sun has been taken by Professor G. Van Belsbroeck of Yerkes Observatory, University of Chicago officials announced to-day.

Using the 24-inch reflector, Professor Van Belsbroeck photographed the comet, which is

FROM *THE NEW YORK TIMES* OF NOVEMBER 18, 1927

301

Both the President of the United States and the Secretary of the Treasury, however, advised the people that
all was well. Coolidge apparently told the public what
Mellon told him to say, and between them they managed so to whet the public appetite for speculative profits,
that until after the end of Coolidge's term of office the
stock market with its gambling possibilties became the
chief centre of the interest of Americans of all social and
economic grades.

By January, 1928, the brokers' loans had risen to $4,-
400,000,000, but in spite of protests from leading bankers the President issued a statement to the public that
the amount of the loans was not too large. Newspapers
like *The New York Times* pointed out that no President
before had ever given out stock-market advice, but the
people, by then completely mad over the boiling market,
ignored the extraordinary fact that the President of the
United States and his Secretary of the Treasury should
be acting as market tipsters, and eagerly acted on the
tips. It did not seem possible to the people that the President and so wealthy and distinguished a financier as
Mellon might be wrong.

In spite of banking warnings, of the obvious fact that
the whirlpool of American speculation was sucking in
gold from all the world and seriously deranging world
finance, and of the successive sinking spells in the market
itself, the determined President and Secretary continued
to tell the public that all was well whenever the market

COOLIDGE SEES LOANS AS BUSINESS TREND

COOLIDGE'S OPTIMISM GIVES STOCKS A LIFT

President Not Disturbed by
$3,810,023,000 Held by the
Federal Reserve Members.

Market Booms and Sales Are
Second Largest on Record
for a Saturday.

INTERESTS WALL STREET

DURANT HELPS MOVEMENT

Financial Circles Have Been Discussing the Mounting Loans
for Some Time.

Predicts Brokers' Loans Will
Exceed $5,000,000,000 This
Year—Some Profits Taken.

WASHINGTON, Jan. 6 (P).—
The President, it was said at the White House today, believes that the increase represents a natural expansion of business in the securities, market and sees nothing unfavorable in it.

THE "BROKERS' LOANS" CONTROVERSY.

That President Coolidge should have allowed to be publicly quoted the remarks ascribed to him, regarding the unprecedentedly large expansion of bank loans to the Stock Exchange, can hardly be classed as wise or prudent. This judgment does not depend on the correctness or incorrectness of the White House view of such credits. But it was much like passing offhand judgment to describe that increase as a "natural expansion of business," in which the President could see "nothing unfavorable." Mr. Coolidge was described as not attempting "to qualify as an expert," or indeed to be in a position to say whether these brokers' loans had "reached a stage of disproportion." But if this was so, it would surely have been better to say nothing.

(Left) HEADING AND A PARAGRAPH FROM THE NEW YORK TIMES OF JANUARY 7, 1928. (Centre) THE RESULTS, FROM THE NEW YORK TIMES OF JANUARY 8, 1928. (Right) PART OF THE NEW YORK TIMES' EDITORIAL ON THE "BROKERS' LOANS"

needed a dose of such medicine. Under pressure it continued to rise to fantastic heights. Business leaders and many bankers lost their own heads. Many companies "split" their shares, giving their stockholders three, five, or, as in the case of the General Electric Company, even sixteen shares for the one share only previously held. These new shares rose rapidly in price, thus multiplying many times the price of the original shares. Every one, women with no knowledge of business, business men who ought to have had some, college professors, bootleggers and bootblacks, stenographers, the whole, it seemed, of the United States, had stocks on margin, and as they watched them rise in price felt that they had discovered a source of unlimited wealth. Personal expenditure, in view of such supposed profits and ease of money-making, became insanely extravagant. People bought as never before of all sorts of goods, which itself acted as a stimulus to trade. Aluminum Company of America, Secretary Mellon's own company, rose above $500 a share, although no one knew what it was worth and it was paying no dividends. Radio Corporation of America likewise crossed 500, and General Electric which could have been bought after the war for 110 sold at the equivalent of over 1600.

The newspapers, intent on circulation and quick to play up every story, whether a Hall murder case, a Lindbergh flight, or the public's stock-market insanity, to the utmost, gave the possibilities of fortune-making first-page space month after month, until, under the influence of the pronouncements of Coolidge and Mellon, the daily stories of winnings by friends, and the insistent headlines which could not be avoided in the daily papers, there must have been few individuals in 1928 and 1929 who had or could borrow money who had not found the combined psychological pressure too great for them and had not abandoned themselves to buying stocks at prices which bore no conceivable relation to values.

The rest of the world might be poor, and struggling to work out of the financial débris of the war. America had defied economic law to rise, apparently, to hitherto undreamed-of heights of wealth and prosperity. There seemed no end, no limit to possibilities of enhanced earnings and prices of securities. All one had to do was to buy and grow rich. Leading men of the nation assured the people that it was so. A "new era" had dawned in which all were to have money and poverty was to be abolished. As the decade drew toward its end, America was living in the fantastic dreams of opium or delirium.

In the mad decade, America was not wholly concerned with money-making, and the roll of accomplishment in the arts was a notable one. Eugene O'Neill in drama, Edwin Arlington Robinson and a host of others in poetry, Sinclair Lewis, Willa Cather, Sherwood Anderson, Thornton Wilder, Edna Ferber, and James Branch Cabell, to mention only a few in prose, and Frank Lloyd Wright in architecture, clearly indicated the stirrings of artistic life below the crass materialism of the period. In science, generally considered as rather peculiarly the province of America, our contributions were for the most part of a practical nature and in the first three decades of the new century, in proportion to population, we were far behind Europe. A rough indication of this may be found in the awards of the Nobel Prize which, on the above basis, went six times to France, eight times to Germany and eight times to England as contrasted with once to the United States. There was a leaven of noble and disinterested artistic and intellectual striving and achievement, but on the whole, as after the Civil War, and as in almost all post-war periods

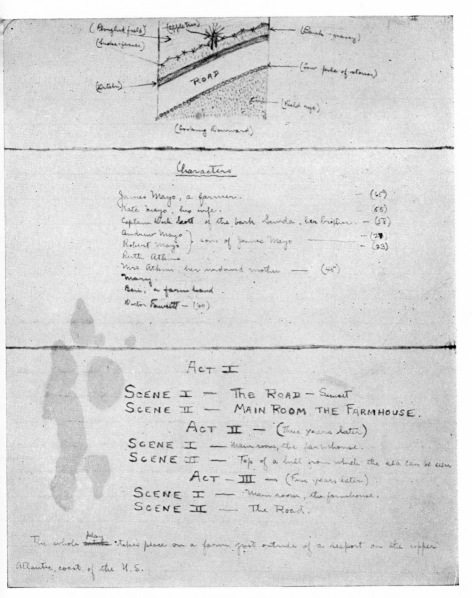

MANUSCRIPT OF "BEYOND THE HORIZON," BY EUGENE O'NEILL
A Pulitzer Prize Play, with sketches for the setting by the author.
From the Theatre Collection of the Museum of the City of New York.

Top: Orville Wright at Fort Myer, Virginia, September 9, 1908, delivering the U. S. Army's first airplane. *Centre:* The navy seaplane N-C 4, on the famous Trans-Atlantic flight of 1919. *Bottom:* M–130 type "clipper ship" designed by Glen L. Martin Co., 1932.

in all countries, life had become vulgarized, selfish, and material.

To realize the change which had come over the American people one has only to contrast the leadership of Roosevelt and Wilson with that of Harding, Coolidge, and Hoover. In spite of a certain lip-service to old ideals by the latter three, their real interest, as well as that of the people at large, lay in creating prosperity, it being assumed by all that happiness, contentment, and spiritual good would somehow automatically and inevitably follow in the wake of high wages, stock-market profits, and big dividends. By 1928 the good life had become synonymous with the possession of ever greater amounts of money by the individual, and identified with the person of the President even more than with the Republican Party. Both the genuine basis of good business and the false marshlight of stock speculation had become known as the "Coolidge Prosperity."

THE CAMPAIGN OF 1928

In the early summer of 1928 the party conventions met for the nomination of Presidential candidates. Months before, Coolidge had made his famous statement that he did not "choose" to run, and the Republican Convention, which met at Kansas City on June 14, nominated Herbert Hoover on the first ballot. Senator Charles Curtis, of Kansas, whose chief claim to fame was the fact that he was partly of Indian blood, was named for Vice-Presi-

dent. At the Democratic Convention at Houston, June
28, Governor Smith of New York was easily nomi-

THE CHOICE OF WEAPONS
—Thomas in the Detroit News.

THE 1928 PRESIDENTIAL CAMPAIGN
From the cartoon by Thomas in *The Detroit News*.

nated for President on the first ballot, with Senator
Joseph T. Robinson of Arkansas as his running-mate.

As usual, the platforms of both parties dodged the
chief issues, and there was little to choose between them
in the intentional haze of misleading verbiage. In the

campaign speeches both candidates declared for a tariff, and both promised relief to the farmers, but whereas Hoover stood for prohibition and private development of our water-power resources, Smith, although promising enforcement of the Eighteenth Amendment, counselled a modification of that experiment and the retaining in the hands of the Federal Government, for the benefit of all the people, of the great water powers already in its possession.

During the campaign Smith was bitterly assailed as a Roman Catholic, a "wet," a representative of the Irish immigration, and a tool of Tammany. He was also accused of favoring saloons and commercialized vice, and of being unfit for office. On the other hand, Hoover was proclaimed as the great organizer, executive, and engineer who would consolidate prosperity and lead the nation to yet greater wealth,—a description of his function and powers which the candidate himself accepted. Asserting that America was at that moment nearer to the abolition of poverty than any other nation had ever been, and that "the policies of the government bear an increasing responsibility for continued national prosperity," he also promised that "the victory of the [Republican] party will ensure stability of business and employment."

There was a much increased popular interest in the election as contrasted with that of 1924, as evidenced by the fact that 6,600,000 more votes were cast. Although Smith polled only about 1,000,000 less than Coolidge had in the former year in the great Republican victory, the 21,429,000 votes for Hoover as against Smith's 15,-000,000 gave the former a plurality of about 6,429,000. Hoover had been elected not only on the promise of

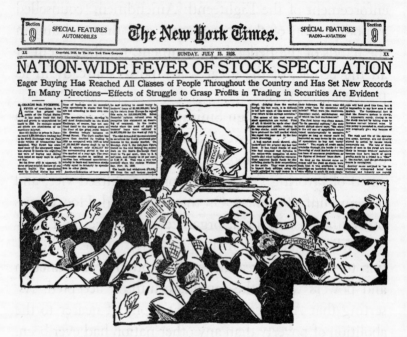

THE DANGEROUS AND FANTASTIC GAME OF WALL STREET
From "The New York Times," July 15, 1928.

continued prosperity but of a prosperity which should be in part manufactured by the government itself. If there were any failure in the continuous flow of business and stock-market profits, the President would therefore be likely to be held accountable for it and would find it hard to avoid the responsibility. Almost as soon as he had been nominated in June, talk began about a "Hoover market" to commence in September. During the summer, business improved and, under continued whipping of the public interest, participation in the delirious speculation had become phenomenal by the time September came. On the 13th, *The New York Times* noted that the public was so wild about stocks that it would believe any yarn, and the next day Secretary Mellon gave out an interview about the great prosperity of the country, adding that he saw no indication of a possible depression. The violent advance continued until October 26 when the American Bankers Association again issued a warning against the danger of the situation. On the 31st, however, President Coolidge tried to counter this with a public statement that the foundations of business were very strong.

The following week, Hoover was elected but Coolidge had still four months to serve. The dangerous and fantastic game went on in Wall Street. The entire nation was participating, and the United States was drawing money from wherever possible to aid it in carrying stocks. The whole world was becoming deranged by the process and in February, 1929, Governor Norman of the Bank of England found it necessary to come to Washington to consult with the Federal Reserve Board. Money was getting tight, interest rates rising to 12 per cent and more in New York, and responsible individuals and bodies were warning the public against the danger of the speculative orgy. The Bank of England rate had to be put up 1 per cent to 5½ per cent, and the strain on European money centres was beginning to tell.

On February 8, the Federal Reserve Board issued a

STOCKS SWEPT HIGH AS INAUGURAL NEARS

Lively Trading Brings Gains Up to 60½ Points in Renewed "Hoover Market."

$25,000,000 LOANS CALLED

But 10% Rate Fails to Check Buying Rush—Copper Shares Lead the List.

FROM *THE NEW YORK TIMES* OF MARCH 1, 1929

'INAUGURAL MARKET' BRINGS PUBLIC BACK, SENDS STOCKS HIGHER

Sustained Climb on Belief in an Extended 'Hoover Boom' Puts Gains Up to 25 Points.

6,021,300 SHARES DEALT IN

Increases Made Overnight and Blocks Up to 35,000 Are Sold at the Opening.

FROM *THE NEW YORK TIMES* OF MARCH 2, 1929

statement warning the American public and threatening that the Board would have to take measures if the brokers' loans were not reduced to a point which would no longer endanger the stability of the commercial and financial structure. Mr. Mellon then took it upon himself to issue a statement denying that the Federal Reserve Board intended to bring about a slump in stocks. A sudden reduction in loans, such as was absolutely essential, however, could mean nothing else, and stocks had slumped seventeen points after the warning. Indeed, the very day after, the New York Stock Exchange had to close for a day, the reason suggested being the need to catch up with the bookkeeping. In spite of Mellon, the Federal Advisory Council, on the 15th, recommended that the regional Federal Reserve Boards should ask all member banks to co-operate in the curbing of stock speculation.

After a break, the market started up again as wildly as ever, and on March 1 big headlines on the first page of *The Times* announced "Stocks Swept High as Inaugural Nears. Lively Trading Brings Gains Up to 60½ Points in Renewed 'Hoover Market.' " Although money was stiff at 10 per cent, the average price of industrial stocks rose to a new high of 366. Another heading on the same page of *The Times* read "First National Bank Stock Up $950 in 2 Days; Gain for Baker's Holdings Put At $13,000,000." That the market value of one man's holdings in one investment alone should rise $13,000,000 in two days made it seem as though we were indeed in a "new era."

The next day the first page of *The Times* carried the heading " 'Inaugural Market' Brings Public Back, Sends Stocks Higher. Sustained Climb on Belief in an Extended 'Hoover Boom' Puts Gains Up To 25 Points." On the 4th, Hoover, in his inaugural address, spoke of "our abounding prosperity" and of a future "bright with

313

hope," explaining again that the government should co-operate closely with business organizations to ensure the continuance of good times.

Although the new President stressed the growing lawlessness of the nation, the parts of his speech which struck the most responsive chord in the mind of the public were unquestionably those in which he discoursed of business and prosperity. As *The Times* said in the next morning's

A PAGE OF PICTURES OF PRESIDENT HOOVER'S INAUGURATION—PAGE 7

"All the News That's Fit to Print."	The New York Times.	THE WEATHER

VOL. LXXVIII...No. 25,973.   ● ● ● ●   NEW YORK, TUESDAY, MARCH 5, 1929.   TWO CENTS

HOOVER INAUGURATED BEFORE THRONG OF 50,000 IN RAIN; PLEDGES EFFORT TO ENFORCE LAWS, AID WORLD PEACE; PARTING WITH COOLIDGE IS CLIMAX OF DAY'S CEREMONY

THE NEW YORK TIMES OF MARCH 5, 1929

leading editorial, "the moving principle of Mr. Hoover's inaugural address, if it has one, is to be found in his assertion of what should be our 'larger purpose' at the present time. It is to 'establish more firmly stability and security of business and employment and thereby remove poverty still further from our borders.' This is the passage in his address which undoubtedly will be received with the greatest favor. Of course, he believes that incidentally this will yield moral and spiritual benefits of a high order. He thinks that individual betterment and social righteousness will go hand in hand with an enlarged prosperity. But prosperity is the great goal for which he will be found to be striving. Nor can it be said that in this he is not a true interpreter of the existing desires and plans of the American people." Opposed to the League of Nations, Hoover advocated our entering the Permanent Court of International Justice, but neither that nor his assertion that our increasing crime and lawlessness was the "most malign of the dangers" threatening the nation aroused much interest.

The continuance of Mr. Mellon as Secretary of the Treasury in the new Cabinet pleased the country, although the rest of the President's appointments were unexpected, and the Cabinet was not as strong as the public had anticipated it would be. Henry L. Stimson became Secretary of State, and Charles Francis Adams, representative of a distinguished family which had given the nation three Ministers to England and two Presidents, became Secretary of the Navy. Otherwise the public scarcely recognized the names of the new President's advisors. Almost immediately he disclosed his characteristic approach to problems in the appointment of commissions of enquiry, notably that headed by George W. Wickersham on law enforcement, including Prohibition, which was to be followed by almost innumerable other ones. In the complexities of modern life there is much to be said for fact-finding commissions. A year later, however, the country was to be somewhat shocked to find that although the President had abdicated leadership in order to allow the National Enforcement Commission to discover the facts and give its opinions, he declined to be bound by them when found. Of the eleven members who made their report in January, 1930, five advocated modification of the Eighteenth Amendment and two declared for straight repeal, leaving only four who wished to give the experiment further trial in its present shape, which they all agreed was eminently unsatisfactory.

Hoover, however, remained of the same opinion still. In spite of the year and more his commission had spent finding the facts, the President refused to face them. Meanwhile, the Jones Act, passed by overwhelming majorities in both Houses of Congress in 1929, had made certain violations of the Prohibition law liable to punishment of $10,000 fine and five years in prison, raising them to the rank of felonies. In view of the state of public opinion few laws could have been devised more calculated to bring law into contempt, and to add to that disrespect for law which Hoover had rightly declared to be one of the greatest menaces to the national life.

In this he was right, for lawlessness had been increasing to an extraordinary extent, and apparently with little or no recognition of its seriousness by the ordinary citizen, who so long as he was making money, and was not personally interfered with, paid slight attention to this hideous cancer in our social system. Although in such cities as London and Paris, millions of dollars in gold continued to be moved through the streets in ordinary trucks with no armed protection, New York City alone had to employ a fleet of 155 armored cars to carry pay rolls and any valuables that could not be concealed on one's person. The kidnappings, racketeering, and other evidences of violent crime had increased so rapidly as to make daily life in what we like to consider our civilized country take on the aspect of war in an enemy's territory.

From 1900 to 1930 the homicide record in thirty-one leading American cities had steadily mounted from 5.1 per 100,000 of population to 10.8, whereas in the latter year the rate for Liverpool was .5, that for London .8, for Canadian cities 1.6, and the average for the fifty-three chief cities of the entire world was 3.5. For every 109 homicides in the United States, Canada had 16 and London 8. In many of our States, although the honest citizen could frequently secure a permit to own a revolver only with the greatest difficulty, including perhaps the bribing of the police officer in charge of their issuance, criminals had no difficulty in providing themselves with entire arsenals of weapons, from pocket automatics to machine guns.

The public seemed to enjoy the show, much as they would a thrilling screen play, and to take no heed of the possibilities or to consider the situation as indicating a deep-seated disease in the body politic. The forces of municipal and State police appeared to be paralyzed, and our record of proportional captures and convictions was as small in comparison with European countries as our record of crimes was appallingly great. America's particular hero was the modest aviator Lindbergh, who properly occupied a position of peculiarly affectionate regard in the hearts of the public. Yet when his only child was kidnapped from its nursery in March, 1932, although a shudder ran through the country, nothing could be done about it, and our leading newspapers were soon treating every aspect of the case as a means of securing additional circulation, and the public read the story as a "thriller" with apparently little influence upon its attitude toward crime. In spite of a gesture of the Federal Government, which ·pledged its aid to the recovery of the child, precisely nothing was done. The Lindbergh case was spectacular only because of the prominence of Lindbergh himself. It was, however, but one glance at what was going on all over the country, in many different sorts of crime. For a few days it was hoped that the very prominence of the specific instance might awaken the public to existing conditions, but it did not, and after the one gesture, even the Federal Government relapsed again into supine surrender to the gangsters. The mention of this striking case is anticipating somewhat, and we must return to the beginning of Hoover's term.

In accordance with his pre-election pledge of a special session of Congress to do something for the farmers, Hoover called that body together on April 15, but nothing was accomplished, after much discussion, beyond the appointment of a Farm Board which was authorized to expend $500,000,000. In the course of the subsequent débâcle in American business, the Board was to prove extremely incompetent and ill-advised, and the several hundreds of millions which they expended in the purchase of wheat and cotton in a wholly vain effort to hold up prices were not merely wasted but, by creating hoards of vast amount of high-priced produce which overhung the market, continued to be a menace to the recovery of prices.

THE GREAT CRASH

The smash came in the autumn of 1929. By that time the forces which had been at work for nearly two years to bring about a normal and natural depression finally won over the official hypodermic injections given to speculation. The crisis of one of the greatest stock-exchange panics in the history of the world came on October 29. The "Coolidge Prosperity" lay buried beneath the smoking ruins of the inverted "Hoover Market." In one week, brokers' loans, which within a fortnight had stood at the fantastic figure of over $8,500,000,000, decreased nearly $1,100,000,000. Considering the character of the speculating public, which had come to include persons of every sort in every walk of life, such loans as are indicated by the above figures were bound to have enormous repercussions.

No individual or political party could have prevented the working out of the economic laws into an inevitable depression of the first magnitude following the war. Neither Mr. Hoover nor the Republicans can be blamed for that. What they can rightly be blamed for, and

BANKERS EMPHASIZE DANGER OF INFLATION IN SPECULATION RISE

L. P. Ayres Tells Convention "Stocks Are Selling on Expectation," Not Realization.

HE SAYS PRICES MUST FALL

And Predicts a "Sober Era" in Which "Hour of Old-Fashioned Virtues" Would Strike.

FROM *THE NEW YORK TIMES*,
OCTOBER 3, 1928

RESERVE BOARD WARNING SENDS STOCKS TUMBLING; LONDON RAISES BANK RATE

Senate Receives Resolution For 'Paper Trust' Inquiry

Special to The New York Times
WASHINGTON, Feb. 7 — Alleged control of white paper in the United States would be investigated by a special Senatorial committee under the terms of a resolution favorably reported to the Senate today by the Committee on Agriculture.

The resolution, originally introduced by Senator Schall of Minnesota, provides that the Vice President name five Senators to "investigate the activities of groups of American and foreign citizens controlling the supply of white paper in the United States with a view to determining whether such activities would have the result of creating a monopoly in the supplying of paper to publishers of small daily and weekly newspapers."

The committee would make a report, with recommendations, to the Senate.

BRITAIN WILL BUILD TWO NEW CRUISERS

"Big Navy" Group Wins and Bridgeman Announces the Decision in Commons.

DROP HERE UP TO 19 POINTS

List, Swept Down at the Opening, Rallies, but Closes Unsettled.

EXCHANGE SHUT TOMORROW

McFadden in House Questions Board's Right to Interfere— Officials Defend Step.

RATE RISE STIRS EUROPE.

British Business Dismayed— Repercussions Are Felt in Berlin and Paris.

The bottom dropped out of the stock market yesterday, and while there were fitful rallies during the day, stocks at the close were weak and unsettled, with declines of from fractions to more than 19 points through the entire list. Nothing was spared, the good going down with the rest.

Two developments from overnight brought about the break. The first and most important was the serious

FROM *THE NEW YORK TIMES* OF
FEBRUARY 8, 1929

---

heavily, was their stubborn resistance to facts and their insistence, against every indication to the contrary and the best advice, that all was well when the economic patient was becoming, in fact, very ill. When *The Commercial and Financial Chronicle* announced in January, 1928, that a depression was inevitably on its way, it was

WORST STOCK CRASH STEMMED BY BANKS; 12,894,650-SHARE DAY SWAMPS MARKET; LEADERS CONFER, FIND CONDITIONS SOUND

FINANCIERS EASE TENSION

Five Wall Street Bankers Hold Two Meetings at Morgan Office.

Wall Street Optimistic After Stormy Day; Clerical Work May Force Holiday Tomorrow

Confidence in the soundness of the stock market structure, notwithstanding the upheaval of the last few days, was voiced last night by bankers and other financial leaders. Sentiment as expressed by the heads of some of the largest banking institutions and by industrial executives as well was distinctly cheerful and the feeling was general that the worst had been seen. Wall Street ended the day in an optimistic frame of mind.

LOSSES RECOVERED IN PART

Upward Trend Starts With 200,000-Share Order for Steel.

From "The New York Times," October 25, 1929.

STOCK PRICES SLUMP $14,000,000,000 IN NATION-WIDE STAMPEDE TO UNLOAD; BANKERS TO SUPPORT MARKET TODAY

Sixteen Leading Issues Down $2,893,520,108; Tel. & Tel. and Steel Among Heaviest Losers

PREMIER ISSUES HARD HIT

From "The New York Times," October 29, 1929.

STOCKS COLLAPSE IN 16,410,030-SHARE DAY, BUT RALLY AT CLOSE CHEERS BROKERS; BANKERS OPTIMISTIC, TO CONTINUE AID

LEADERS SEE FEAR WANING

'Point to 'Lifting Spells' in Trading as Sign of Buying Activity.

GROUP MEETS TWICE IN DAY

240 Issues Lose $15,894,818,894 in Month; Slump in Full Exchange List Vastly Larger

The drastic effects of Wall Street's October bear market is shown by valuation tables prepared last night by THE NEW YORK TIMES, which place the decline in the market value of 240 representative issues on the New York Stock Exchange at $15,894,818,894 during the period from Oct. 1 to yesterday's closing. Since there are 1,279 issues listed on the New York Stock Exchange, the total depreciation for the month is estimated at between two and three times the loss for the 240 issues covered by THE TIMES table. Among the losses of the various groups comprising the 240 stocks in THE TIMES valuation table were the following:

CLOSING RALLY VIGOROUS

Leading Issues Regain From 4 to 14 Points in 15 Minutes.

INVESTMENT TRUSTS BUY

From "The New York Times," October 30, 1929.

THE SAD STORY OF OCTOBER, 1929

right, as were the various bankers, singly or in groups, who endeavored to stay the madness during the rest of that year. By the end of 1928, however, the spectacle of the wildly rising stock market, which had been evoked by the government, had become too much for ordinary cool heads, and many bankers and business leaders, as well as the rank and file, lost their balance then who had maintained it hitherto.

When in 1930, 1931, and later, the depression deepened, it became clear that the nation's incredible losses in the stock market in 1929 were as much responsible for the complete pessimism, loss of confidence, and slowness of recovery as was the business depression itself. Large sections of the public, indeed, should have been better off in 1931 than in 1928–29, as their salaries or wages had been little reduced, if at all, whereas the cost of living had gone down nearly 25 per cent. Unlike former panics, such as that of 1873 and 1893, the great bulk of conservative bond investments continued to pay interest. Had the nation owned sound securities, it could have stood reduced business incomes considering reduced living costs. The trouble was, to a considerable extent in countless cases, that pay cuts were mild compared with the loss of a lifetime's savings. It is those losses which can fairly be laid at the feet of those in the administration who did all they could to whip the people into a frenzy of stock speculation which they called "prosperity."

Throughout the early part of 1930, Mr. Hoover and

most government officials kept repeating that all would
be well in a few weeks or a month or two, regardless of
the fact that the depression was steadily becoming worse.
In his message to Congress in December, the President

---

r, DECEMBER 3, 1930. TWO CENTS In Greater | THREE CENTS | FOUR CENTS Elsewhere

HOOVER ASKS $150,000,000 TO AID IDLE;
WARNS OF DEFICIT AND END OF TAX CUT;
HIS CONTROL OF WORKS FUND OPPOSED

OPPOSE HOOVER METHODS

Democrats and Some Re-
publicans Disagree With
His Relief Program.

PARTY REGULARS PRAISE IT

Most of Leaders Are for Putting
the Proposals Into Force
Without Delay.

WALL STREET IS PLEASED

Holds Ideas for Business Sound
—Press Hails Avoidance of
Controversial Matters.

Bills Laid Before Congress on Employment Relief And to Deal With Country's Economic Recovery

Special to The New York Times.

WASHINGTON, Dec. 2.—Measures on employment relief and economic recovery introduced in the Senate and House today included the following:

By Senator Glenn—A resolution to carry out President Hoover's recommendation for an emergency fund of $150,000,000 to accelerate public works.

By Senators Robinson of Arkansas, McNary and Caraway—Resolutions to provide $60,000,000 to aid drought-stricken farmers.

By Senator Blaine—Bill for creating a Federal Industrial commission to study the stabilization of employment.

By Senator Capper—Resolution to distribute 40,000,000 bushels of the Farm Board's wheat surplus to relief organizations for food.

By Senator Brookhart—Bill increasing appropriations for public roads from $125,000,00 to $500,000,000 for two years.

By Senator Keyes and Representative Elliott—Twin bills to expedite work on Federal buildings.

By Senator Reed—Bill to suspend immigration for two years from all countries on this hemisphere and from Europe.

By Representative Cable—Bill to exclude all immigration of laborers until the Secretary of Labor decides they are needed.

By Senator Oddie—Bill to embargo the importation of all products' from Soviet Russia.

By Representative Huddleston—Bill to appropriate $50,000,000 to be used by the President as a "destitution fund."

MESSAGE READ TO CONGRESS

President Asks Speed on
Bills to Create Work in
Next Six Months.

URGES PUBLIC COOPERATION

He Advocates Federal Loans to
Farmers—Hits at Speculation
as a Cause of Depression.

TREASURY LOSS $180,000,000

Action on Muscle Shoals and
Inquiry for Changing Anti-
Trust Law Recommended.

PRESIDENT HOOVER'S MESSAGE TO CONGRESS, DECEMBER 2, 1930
"New York Times," December 3, 1930.

---

continued optimistic, although he admitted that the
number of unemployed had been 2,500,000 "on April
1" and had increased since. Had Mr. Hoover made no
impossible promises in the campaign in the year 1928, he
would have been pitied more and criticised less, but as
unemployment rose to six, seven, and even eight mil-

lions, it could not be forgotten that the President when candidate had declared that the only way to ensure employment had been to vote for him. When with wearisome sameness, month after month, and year after year, his promises of immediate betterment in business, whether based on mistaken facts or a mistaken notion as to the necessity of a false optimism, were proved wrong, the public grew more and more irritated. Moreover, in spite of certain excellent qualities as an executive and administrator, the President had always found it difficult to work in harmony with others, and the rift between him and Congress steadily widened.

In June and July, 1930, two important measures were passed, both destined to bring trouble on the country. The Hawley-Smoot Tariff Bill, which raised duties to the highest point yet attained, was passed by both Houses and signed by the President, June 17. In view of the fact that we had already drained the rest of the world of half its entire supply of gold, and that we insisted upon the payment of war debts, the Chinese Wall against imports of foreign goods, the sale of which to us constituted the only method possible of debt payment, alarmed all the debtor nations. It was clear that others could not pay us in more gold. If we did not allow them to pay us by selling us goods, there could be nothing left but bankruptcy if we still insisted upon being paid at all. It was no solution to the problem to point to the fact that a very large percentage of total imports still came in free. If

we levied prohibitive duties on the goods which our
debtors could ship to us, it did them no good if we allowed free entry to certain goods from other countries.
At the very moment when the world needed to build
up its foreign trade again, the new tariff bill not only
hindered us from doing so but in the way of reprisal or
self-defence brought into being such a vast number of
retaliatory tariffs in other countries as to bring the trade
of the world almost to a stand.

If the world crisis demanded as free a flow of goods
through normal trade channels as possible, so it also demanded the saving and creation of new capital, the
reduction of expenditure and taxation, and the balancing
of budgets. Congress took the moment to pass a new
pension measure for the veterans of the Spanish War,
which provided pensions up to sixty dollars a month for
soldiers who were disabled, the disability not being required to have anything to do with the war. A man, for
example, who had come out of the war perfectly sound
but who thirty years later might, from immoral habits,
have acquired a loathsome disease, could claim a pension
from the United States Government. It is difficult to conceive of a more unjust or indecent measure, but both
Houses of Congress, for the sake apparently of buying
themselves votes, passed the bill by large majorities over
Hoover's veto, as they also passed a liberalizing pension
bill for the World War veterans which the President
signed.

The hopes which had been expressed both by the administration and many economic experts and business leaders that business would improve were wholly falsified, and the depression merely deepened as the months passed. The year 1931 was indeed to witness what may be considered as a financial panic superimposed on the already existing commercial depression, with a resultant new crash of American security prices which carried them by June, 1932, to depths undreamed of even in 1930.

THE DEPRESSION IS UPON US

Up to the close of the Seventy-first Congress, which ended its sessions on March 4, 1931, the administration and the people at large had assumed that the United States could maintain its complete isolation and in some way pull itself out of the slough by its own bootstraps. The more important measures which the government had taken had indicated clearly the acceptance of that view. The ill-fated and uneconomic efforts of the Farm Board to maintain the prices of American farm products in the face of the world decline, the Hawley-Smoot Tariff Bill which built a wall against imports around us, the bills restricting immigration, and others all showed our belief, as did Hoover's own pronouncements, that we could play a lone hand and avoid the evils from which the world system was suffering. Nor were the various disarmament conferences in a different category.

Congress in the winter had seemed to have little realization of the situation, and on February 27 had passed over the President's veto a bill which gave the World War veterans the right to secure loans against their bonus certificates to the extent of fifty per cent of their face value, although the Treasury pointed out that this might involve the government in expenses amounting to over a billion dollars.

From April onward, the commercial depression deepened throughout the world, and the movement of gold was rapidly draining most nations of the metal, which flowed only to France and the United States. On May 11 the Austrian Government announced that the *Kredit Anstalt,* one of the great banking institutions of Europe, controlled by the Rothschilds, was in serious difficulties, and the second phase of the world panic set in. It is impossible to tell in any detail the spread of the trouble, but by this time it had become clear, even to the administration, that the United States could no longer isolate herself. All the nations of Central Europe were threatened with bankruptcy, including Germany, to the governments and private concerns of which latter country Americans had loaned about $2,500,000,000. In an effort to stave off complete disaster which might tear down the financial structure of the whole world, Hoover, unfortunately without consulting France, proclaimed a moratorium on all international war debts so as to give the world, and particularly Germany, a breathing spell.

The good effect of the one-year postponement was largely lost by the delays and objections interposed by France, which, as always, insisted upon keeping up the fiction of the integrity of the Versailles Treaty.

Although this might possibly have been avoided had Hoover consulted the French Government as to his intentions, he had consulted the leaders and many of the other American congressmen in order to ensure their endorsement of his action when Congress met. Not only, however, had Hoover and Congress been growing more antagonistic toward each other, but the November elections had resulted in a Democratic majority in the House. When Congress met in December, they did indeed ratify what the President had done, but, returning to isolationist principles and desirous of retaining all initiative in their own body, they so tied Hoover's hands as to make it practically impossible for him to recommence any negotiations or even conversations with our debtors. The various starts which we had made toward taking official part in international conferences, such as the appointment of Secretaries Stimson and Mellon as delegates, and not merely "official observers," to the economic conference in London in July, appeared to have been effectually quashed by the reactionary attitude of Congress.

Meanwhile our own situation as well as that of the world was growing steadily worse. The earnings of practically all of our great business enterprises of all sorts seemed to be melting down to nothing. Even the New York Central Railroad, which had paid continuous dividends for 60 years, suspended them, and its stock which had sold over 300 two years before dropped to 25, and was to sell under 9 in the next spring. The end of September the New York stock market recorded new and alarming low prices, and the leading New York bank stocks, which many thought thoroughly deflated when selling at an average price of 114 in February, had dropped to 44 ten months later. Banks throughout the entire country had been failing by hundreds, and many communities, even some of our larger cities, were left without any banking facilities at all. In their efforts to prepare for runs, institutions had been forced to sell their holdings of bonds at any prices obtainable, and the drop in prices of first-class securities added to the growing mistrust, and in turn caused more runs.

Mistrust in the ability of even the British Government to weather the storm had already caused that nation to go off the gold standard with resultant shock to the rest of the world, when our own situation became so alarming as to lead the President to summon a hasty meeting of the leaders of both Houses of Congress and other officials and advisors at the White House on October 6. Our Federal deficit for the year had already reached $600,-000,000 as against the Treasury's estimate of a surplus at the beginning of the fiscal period, and fear of the safety of the banks had led people to hoard another $600,000,-

ooo by October 1. European nations, led by France, which country, as she had done in the case of England, took action calculated to bring about the very condition she feared, hastily rushed to draw gold against their balances with us, until $588,000,000 was shipped in three weeks.

Fearing that we ourselves should be forced off the gold standard and that with continued runs and failures our entire banking structure might collapse, it was agreed at the White House conference to form a national corporation to help keep the banks solvent and to ask Congress, when it should meet, for further legislation. Pending the assembling of that body, the banks agreed among themselves to assist their weaker members.

On the meeting of the new Congress, both Democrats and Republicans joined to pass the needed legislation, and on January 22, 1932, the Reconstruction Finance Corporation Bill was signed by the President. The Corporation, which was to some extent modelled on the lines of the War Finance Board, was provided with a capital of $500,000,000, all to be subscribed by the government, and permitted to lend three times that amount if necessary. It was authorized to make loans to banks and other fiscal institutions and to aid in "financing agriculture, commerce, and industry." This included making loans to railroads, which it was hoped might thus be saved from defaulting on their obligations and going into bankruptcy. The management of the Corporation's business

330

was put in the hands of a board of seven members, our Ambassador to England, Mr. Dawes, resigning that post to become the head of the new agency.

Although the runs on the banks stopped to some ex-

DRIVE OPENS IN CITY TO CHECK HOARDING

200 Business and Civic Leaders Spur Effort to Return Idle Money to Circulation.

WILL PUSH "BABY" BONDS

Gen. Harbord, Miller and Others Warn Prosperity Waits On Liquefied Credit.

FROM *THE NEW YORK TIMES* OF MARCH 1, 1932

PRESIDENT INVOKES GOLD HOARDER LAW

Orders Return to Banks of $1,000,000,000 in Certificates, Coin and Bullion.

DEADLINE IS SET AT MAY 1

Way Paved to Ease Embargo on Domestic and Foreign Transactions.

FROM *THE NEW YORK TIMES*, APRIL 6, 1933

tent, hoarding was only slightly relieved and the general situation continued to be critical. The Federal deficit between June 30, 1931, and the end of February, 1932, had risen to $1,781,000,000 and was calculated to amount to nearly $3,000,000,000 by the end of the fiscal year. Leading cities of the country, such as New York, Chicago, Detroit, and Philadelphia, as well as numberless smaller municipalities, were on the verge of bankruptcy from a

331

combination of graft, mismanagement, and the effects of the depression on the raising of taxes. In two years the inventory value of live stock alone on our farms had dropped nearly $3,000,000,000, and the farmers were worse off than ever, after the expenditure of about $500,-000,000 on their behalf by the Farm Board.

On February 10, a non-partisan meeting was again held at the White House to consider further measures. That week, in spite of the operations of the Reconstruction Finance Corporation, hoarding of currency had risen to $1,300,000,000, with a consequent restriction of credit of five times that amount, or $6,500,000,000.

As a result of the conference, Congress passed an Act, signed by the President February 29, known as the Glass-Steagall Bill, which permitted member banks to borrow from the Federal Reserve on paper which had previously been ineligible under the earlier Federal Reserve Act. The several objects of the bill were to assist banks in trouble by making the conditions of borrowing easier; to attract hoarded money back into banks and circulation; to free more gold for foreign demands; and to help in financing the Treasury deficit. It was estimated that the possible additions to the currency under the terms of the Act might run from two to two and a half billion dollars, but although many considered that this might bring about dangerous inflation of the currency, the bill met with little serious opposition. In the same month in which this Act was passed, Secretary Mellon retired from the Treasury and was appointed Ambassador to England at the unusual age, for that post, of seventy-seven.

Having maintained strict allegiance to their party

WILL THE SKY NEVER CLEAR UP?
Fitzpatrick's cartoon in *The St. Louis Post-Dispatch.*

leaders and made a notable show of non-partisanship patriotism, Congress soon ran wild, and threatened, even against the vote of the American Legion itself, to pass a new Bonus Bill which it was estimated would take another $2,000,000,000 from the Treasury to add to the already appalling deficit. As always in hard times, all

333

sorts of heresies as to the nature of money were abroad, and in the spring of 1932 business, struggling hard with almost unparalleled world conditions, began to fear in addition radical legislation which might still further de-

BALL AND CHAINS THAT DRAG

As *News of the World* (London) regards hindrances to World Recovery.

range conditions and make any return to a sound basis more difficult if not impossible. The debates over the problem of meeting the hitherto unheard-of deficit in the Treasury by taxation became so wild and acrimonious that Congress had to be adjourned for tempers to cool and reason to reassert itself.

Although it had become more and more evident that there could be no recovery for the United States without a readjustment of the international exchanges and a reasonable improvement in economic conditions in the rest of the world, Congress still set its face resolutely against any possibility of further discussion of the war debts, and the end of the period of the Hoover moratorium hung over the heads of business men everywhere as the possible precipitation of more national bankruptcies and general financial chaos. In June representatives of England, France, Italy, and Germany met at Lausanne and settled the reparations question by a practical cancellation of all future payments due to any of them from Germany, although as payment of war debts to the United States from the first three would depend to some extent on payments from Germany to them, final ratification of the cancellation had to be made to wait upon action by us on the debt problem. Owing to the fact that our Presidential election was to take place in November there was no possibility of favorable action by Congress until at least the December session, but much interest was aroused by the fact that the former irreconcilable Senator Borah came out in July for cancellation under certain conditions, thus indicating that possibly America was at last willing to take a responsible position again in world affairs.

Meanwhile, we had been forced again to take some part in international affairs by the attack on China by Japan, both in Manchuria and at Shanghai. Although we declined to participate in the League of Nations, we did consult with that body and, invoking the "Kellogg Pact" and the Nine-Power Treaty, succeeded, with the help of the League, in staving off a Sino-Japanese war of magnitude. Little by little, it was becoming evident that, if we were to do business with the rest of the world, it would be necessary for us, whether we wished to or not, to assume some of the responsibility for international stability, either by joining the League or by working with it from the outside. In the long run one of the most lasting effects of the world depression beginning, for us, in 1929 may well be the enforced change from our old policy of isolation.

THE CAMPAIGN OF 1932

The nominating conventions of the two greater parties met in the early summer of 1932 when panic and depression had reached the most alarming point yet attained. The prices for securities in Wall Street appeared to indicate universal bankruptcy for even the strongest of business concerns; and conditions were unprecedented in some of the agricultural States. In one day, in April, one quarter of the entire State of Mississippi is said to have been sold at auction for non-payment of taxes and debts. The lands sold included 20 per cent of all the farms in the State and from 12 to 15 per cent of all town property. Almost 40,000 farms were sold by seventy-four sheriffs, and the State itself had to take over as owner 400,000 acres, raising its ownership to more than 1,000,000 acres formerly owned by individual farmers. In addition, vast tracts had been turned over to

1932's SOAP BOX

Cartoon by Fitzpatrick in *The St. Louis Post-Dispatch.*

insurance companies, loan agencies, and mortgage holders. One of the causes, apart from the drop in the prices and lessened demand for farm produce, had been the enormous increase in taxation. Between 1913 and 1930, not only had the bonded debt of the Federal Govern-

337

ment risen from about $1,000,000,000 to over $16,000,-000,000, but that of the States had grown from $300,-000,000 to $1,800,000,000, and that of smaller political divisions from $3,500,000,000 to $12,600,000,000. In other words, besides all the huge sums which had been raised in those seventeen years by annual taxation, we had increased our permanent governmental debts from $4,800,000,000 to $30,400,000,000. Both the industrial and agricultural sections of our nation were in despair. In 1928 we had been told we were within sight of perpetual prosperity and the abolition of poverty. By 1932 we seemed to see nothing but poverty and to be faced by stark ruin on every side. Few nations, if any, have ever had to drop with such appalling swiftness from superhuman hopes to blank despair.

In spite of the great unpopularity of Hoover, it was evident that the Republicans would renominate him, although both the candidate and the party appeared to be doomed to certain defeat. In June he was given the nomination on the first ballot and the Vice-President, Curtis, was named again for the same post. There was no interest at all in the convention, its results being a foregone conclusion.

There was more excitement when the Democrats met in Chicago on June 27. Governor Franklin D. Roosevelt of New York, a fifth cousin of former President Theodore Roosevelt, had been the leading candidate, with Al Smith as his only serious rival. In view of factional feeling within the party, however, it was thought that unless Roosevelt could secure the nomination by the fifth ballot many of the delegates pledged to him without enthusiasm would swing into some other column and a dark horse might receive the nomination. Three ballots had been taken when the convention adjourned for the night. Before it reconvened in the morning a deal had been made by which John N. Garner of Texas, Speaker of the House of Representatives, and William G. McAdoo of California decided to support the Roosevelt candidacy, and the governor was nominated on the fourth ballot, Garner later receiving the nomination for Vice-President. Little need be said about the platforms, which differed chiefly on the tariff, the Democrats standing for a revision downward whereas the Republicans upheld the standard of high duties. The Democrats also came out more clearly for a repeal of the Eighteenth Amendment than did the Republicans, and for non-cancellation of the war debts, though they wisely said nothing about reduction. On the whole the Democratic platform was the more clear-cut and satisfactory of the two documents.

In June, while the European nations were meeting at Lausanne trying to disentangle the problem of reparations and debts, a so-called army of ex-service men marched on Washington, encamping there with the avowed object of forcing Congress by their presence to pass new legislation in their favor at the expense of the already so deeply suffering public. After some weeks and when efforts proved unavailing to get them to return to their homes at the expense of the government, they were finally driven out of the city by the use of Federal troops and the local police.

THE ELECTION OF FRANKLIN D. ROOSEVELT

A slight slackening of the depression during the summer had no effect on the election in November, and as was to be expected, the Democrats won an overwhelming victory at the polls, the Republicans losing the electoral vote of all but six States—Maine, New Hampshire, Vermont, Connecticut, Delaware, and the rock-ribbed Republican stronghold of Pennsylvania. In the Electoral College Roosevelt received 472 votes to Hoover's 59, and his popular majority of over 7,000,000 was crushing. His party also gained control of the Senate and a huge majority in the House, a number of prominent Republicans of long service going down to defeat, led by Senator Smoot, who had been the chief sponsor of the Smoot-Hawley Tariff Bill.

In domestic affairs, one of the results of the election had been to open the way at last to submitting the repeal of the Prohibition Amendment to the people, two thirds of the new Senate being apparently "wet" and 343 "wet" members being found in the new House. Various polls taken in the preceding months, notably that of *The Literary Digest,* which latter had been found accurate on

GOVERNOR FRANKLIN D. ROOSEVELT ARRIVING AT THE DEMOCRATIC CONVENTION, JULY 2, 1932

All precedent was broken by the Democratic nominee when he flew to Chicago to receive notification of his nomination.

From a photograph by Kaufmann and Fabry.

THE FEDERAL AND STATES BUILDING, CHICAGO'S CENTURY OF PROGRESS FAIR, 1933

former occasions, had indicated that the sentiment of the voters had become preponderantly in favor of doing away with Prohibition, and this had brought about a change of position in candidates.

Neither the new President nor the new Congress, however, could come into office until March 4, 1933, and meanwhile Hoover and the "lame ducks" in the legislature would have to carry on, while both our domestic affairs and foreign relations needed definite policies. Never before has the clumsiness of our form of government which requires such an interregnum between election and inauguration of a President been so clearly demonstrated. Fortunately in the election which we had had to hold during the Civil War there had been no change of party. The crisis would have been great had Wilson been defeated in 1916 when war with Germany was hanging in the balance. In 1932, however, we felt to the full the effect of passing a vote of confidence in one administration without having the power to install the new one except after months of delay.

We have now traced the history of our nation from the earliest discovery of the continent upon which that nation has evolved until the very day of our present confusion. There have been high lights and deep shadows, much in which we can take a legitimate pride and much which we would wish to efface from the record. That is true of the history of any people. What is often forgotten by ourselves as by others is that in the short period in which we have spread across a wilderness 3000

NOW LET'S GET BACK TO WORK

President Hoover's offer of co-operation with President-Elect Roosevelt after the election.

A cartoon by Sykes in "The New York Evening Post."

miles wide, American morality and culture have both been subjected to extraordinary and peculiar strains. The world is just beginning to realize that much of

Chief Smiling-Roosevelt Breaks a Hole in the Dry Armor.
From "De Notenkraker," Amsterdam.

End of the Big Scrap.
From "Daily Express," London.

AS THE PRESIDENTIAL ELECTION OF 1932 WAS VIEWED ABROAD

343

that debasement and vulgarization of old values which it has been fashionable to consider as "Americanization" is in truth but the working out everywhere of the results of a too-rapid development of the mechanization due to the industrial revolution and of the modern democratizing of political machinery. In Europe, there were innumerable dykes of old customs, institutions, classes, privileges, ways of life and thought, which for long helped to keep the new flood from obliterating the values of an earlier and different age.

In America there was, to a great extent, an absence of such protecting dykes, and also, in the unparalleled opportunities for economic exploitation of natural resources and in the incomparable increases in population, there was a greater sweep and power in the encompassing flood. We felt the effects of machinery and democracy sooner, and to a greater extent, than did Europe. It is possible that in the new civilization to arise, whatever it may be, America may emerge first, as it has so often done from the lesser world depressions of a mere economic sort.

This is, perhaps, to take too hopeful a view, and, in any case, prophecy is no part of the task of the historian. One of the great problems of the world is how to preserve, in a mechanized and democratic order, those higher human values which have been slowly evolved in the past 2000 years or more of European civilization, and which, to a considerable extent, were based upon an

344

Top: Elgin Botanic Garden, Fifth Avenue, New York, about 1816. In 1802, the Common Council granted Dr. Hosack, a professor of Columbia College, fourteen acres of land for a botanic garden. The garden was purchased by the State in 1814 and presented to Columbia College. Part of the land is now the site of Rockefeller Center.

Below: The proposed buildings of Rockefeller Center, New York.

THE FIRST YACHT RACE AT NEW YORK
Colonel Morris's *Fancy* turning to the windward of another sloop.
Redrawn by F. S. Cozzens from the rare view of New York by William Burgess in 1717, in the Library of Congress.

THE DEFENSE OF THE AMERICA'S CUP IN 1930
After the start of the first race. *Left to right: Enterprise, Vanitie, Whirlwind, Resolute,* and *Weetamoe.*
By courtesy of Harold S. Vanderbilt.

aristocratic and not a democratic form of society and upon an economic order which is fast disappearing into the irrecoverable past. As yet, the cleavage between that past and the chaotic present is less complete in Europe than in America, leaving Russia out of the European picture. So far as we can understand the mind of western, or European, man, it is incredible that he will be able to scrap all the values he has so hardly evolved in the past few thousand years. The problem is not one of starting entirely fresh, but of a deep and radical readjustment to a changed social environment without sinking into a new dark age as a period of transition.

Europe, as we have said, had many anchors which held it to its old moorings in spite of the fact that it, and not the United States, initiated the industrial revolution. Europe thus swung out into the uncharted sea upon which all of us in the world are now afloat, more slowly than did our America which had few or none of such anchors. Moreover, we in this new world encountered in our frontier and the riches of a virgin continent, the electrical storms of unlimited economic opportunity which too often set the compass of our life spinning toward strange quarters. Europe is only just beginning to have its own compass of spiritual life deflected in the same way by the unlimited opportunities and problems of the new economic order which now embraces the markets and raw materials of the entire world. The "old Europe" is rapidly passing, though in some ways the safety of its readjustments may be greater than our own.

If, however, there was much in the old order the passing of which would be an irreparable loss to mankind, a study of that older order, as contrasted with what has so far emerged of the new, makes it clear that there are values evolving in the latter which are also of supreme importance. America has played no small part in the creation of these, and although there is ample ground for pessimism as we survey the moral and cultural life of the United States today, there is also much that is hopeful.

Such a statement is no less true because it is a mere commonplace. It is impossible for any one man to know the whole of American life in its vast and quickly shifting currents as we watch them swirl from day to day. There would seem, however, to be as little cause for despair of the future as there is for a shallow and unthinking optimism. The frontier has been closed to us. The unceasing streams of fresh and alien blood have been cut off in the closing of our ports to unrestricted immigration. The needs of the new economic order are insistent upon our taking our part in the affairs of the world. Isolation is now as impossible for us as for China or Japan. The economic barriers of the world have been broken, however politicians may try feverishly to reconstruct and patch them up. A new era is dawning, the nature of which no man can forecast. For good or for evil, the United States will be forced to play its part.

346

The most interesting, the most important, and, let us at least hope, the greatest, pages in our history are those which must await the hands of the historian of the future. We can but end our own task here.

On January 23, Missouri, the last of the necessary thirty-six States had approved the XXth Amendment to the Constitution which provided that in future the President should be inaugurated on January 20 instead of March 4, and the newly elected Congress convene January 3, so that Roosevelt was the last President to be inaugurated on the historic date. Meanwhile, in 1933, the now powerless President Hoover, had to struggle along with the lame-duck Congress. The executive and legislature had long been at loggerheads, and although in the country's crisis, Hoover suggested that Roosevelt, as President-elect, should co-operate with him, the latter declined for the most part to do so. Everything in the future, for the nation as well as himself, would depend on his establishing his own prestige by his own methods. It would have been folly for the new President to court defeat at the hands of Congress before he had even entered upon his new duties.

By March 4 the country was in the midst of a banking panic and a crisis of the first magnitude. In State after State the governor had been forced to declare banking

349

"holidays" and to close the banks under his control. The American people were bewildered and completely discouraged. The Hoover administration was on the defensive. Congress was discredited as were also the big bankers and other business leaders. Nothing much was known about Roosevelt, except his smile. As William Allen White wrote at the time of his inauguration, "we are putting our hands in a grab-bag. Heaven only knows what we shall pull out." With the disingenuousness apparently required of a Presidential candidate, his campaign speeches had not disclosed his real views, and confidence in him had been gradually waning until the, for him, lucky attempt at his assassination in Florida on February 15, which resulted in the death instead of Mayor Cermak of Chicago. Roosevelt's superb behavior on that occasion, and the sudden realization that he was all that stood between the nation and possible choas and ruin, rallied public opinion behind him as behind no other President-elect since Washington. The people were demanding some one to lead them, some one with character, some one who, whether wise or foolish, would at least try to *do* something. They had grown perhaps a little suspicious of Roosevelt's extremely charming personality, but when in the few minutes after the bullet was fired, Roosevelt showed himself wholly careless of his own safety, thoughtful only of his doomed friend, the people realized the courage and character behind the urbanity, and their confidence suddenly went out to him. Between a thoroughly discredited Congress with no ideas beyond the pork-barrel, and a popular hero, who was realized to be the only possible savior, if there was to be one, of society, there was no longer any question as to which would be master.

Roosevelt was inaugurated on Saturday, March 4. During the preceding days not only had banks been closing wholesale but gold had been steadily withdrawn on a large scale. The day before the inauguration the New York banks alone had lost over $116,000,000. On the day the new President took office all the banks of New York and Pennsylvania were added to the closed list, as were also all the principal stock and commodity exchanges. Stories had begun to leak out of colossal losses and scandalous mismanagement of the people's money by such men as Charles E. Mitchell at the head of the National City Bank of New York and Albert H. Wiggin at the head of the Chase National of New York, two of the largest banks in the world. In his Inaugural Address, Roosevelt lashed out at the "money changers," promised "action and action now," and stated that if no other way were feasible he would ask war-time powers from Congress.

By six o'clock in the afternoon he had secured from the Senate confirmation of all his Cabinet appointments without even the usual reference to a committee. The more notable appointees were Cordell Hull, the first Secretary of State from the South since Calhoun; William H. Woodin, Secretary of the Treasury; Harold L. Ickes, Secretary of the Interior; and Miss Frances Perkins, Secretary of Labor, an extremely able woman and the first to sit in an American Cabinet.

At the Cabinet meeting next day, Sunday, the imme-

ROOSEVELT ORDERS 4-DAY BANK HOLIDAY, PUTS EMBARGO ON GOLD, CALLS CONGRESS

FROM *THE NEW YORK TIMES* OF MARCH 6, 1933

diate problem was what to do about the banks. Attorney-General Cummings assured the President that the "Trading with the Enemy Act" of the World War had not been repealed in full and that he could use it. Roosevelt had already considered this and immediately issued a proclamation closing all the banks in the country for four days, placing an embargo on gold and silver for either export or domestic use, and imposing a penalty of $10,000 fine or ten years' imprisonment for violation. Monday morning the American people woke up to find themselves limited for the time being to the cash which they happened to have in their pockets on Saturday. The spell of panic, however, was broken. The psychology of the nation was changed in an instant. A wave of good humor swept over it. Every one, rich or poor, was in the same boat, and the sudden discovery that no matter how much you owned you had nothing to spend was treated as a huge joke. After three years' gloom and fear, the

It's a Matter of CONFIDENCE

Credit is based on confidence. We have full confidence in the integrity of our patrons and continue to solicit their patronage on a charge account basis.

If you do not enjoy this credit relationship with us, our **Credit Manager** will be pleased to discuss the opening of a charge account with you.

Checks will be accepted in payment of merchandise or charge accounts subject to collection.

RETAIL BUSINESSES EXPRESSED THEIR CONFIDENCE IN THE GOVERN-MENT BY ADVERTISING THEIR WILLINGNESS TO EXTEND CREDIT TO CUSTOMERS

American spirit, responding to new leadership, suddenly found itself again.

The new Congress had been called in special session for March 9. Meanwhile the President had been at work on measures to reopen sound banks as quickly as possible —money to be advanced by the RFC; the President's right of action under the doubtful Trading with the Enemy Act to be confirmed; war-time powers over gold

353

to be granted to him. On the evening of the 8th he called together the leaders of the new Congress and received their reluctant consent. In the early hours of the dawn Secretary of the Treasury Woodin was asked by newspapermen as he left the White House if the bill were finished. "Yes," he answered, "both bills are finished. You know my name is Bill, and I'm finished too." [1]

The following day Congress met, was organized in three hours, and in less than forty minutes after the House had begun consideration of the President's banking measure it was passed by acclamation, the Senate passing it by a vote of 73 to 7 after three hours' debate. Roosevelt signed it that evening. No such speed in peacetime legislation had been known before. An hour later, the same night, the President announced to a stunned meeting of the leaders that he wanted authority to cut $100,000,000 off government salaries and $400,000,000 off veterans' pensions and compensations, about 2,500,-000 persons being involved. The next day he sent a special message to Congress showing that passage of the bill was necessary or the deficit would be $5,000,000,000 by June 30, 1934.

Two days later, March 12, he gave his first Presidential talk to the people over the radio on the subject of the banking situation. It explained the position in the sim-

[1] Ernest K. Lindley, *The Roosevelt Revolution* (London, 1934), p. 81.

354

plest terms, as well as what he was trying to do, and made a tremendous popular hit. It has been said that the permanent officials of the Treasury sent him a draft of a speech, which was full of involved statistics, and which no one but a banker could understand. Roosevelt at once said it would not do, and then sitting a few minutes before a blank wall he visualized the ordinary Americans who would be listening to him—tradesmen, farmers, mechanics, clerks, professional men, and others with no technical knowledge of banking, and decided what he would say to them. The next day he sent another special message to Congress urging the immediate modification of the Volstead Act so as to permit, within constitutional limits, the sale of beer of higher alcoholic content in order that new revenues could be collected. The succession of short, sharp, and most incisive messages indicated to the public that the President had a well-defined policy which he was unfolding step by step, and public confidence rose rapidly, reflected in rising prices on the stock and commodity exchanges.

This was only in part true, though in the next few weeks more bills were sent to the obedient Congress, which promptly passed them—bills for the protection of the investor in securities, for mortgage relief, and other purposes—and on April 19 the President definitely carried the United States off the gold standard. He was, in fact, with the help of what he considered the best expert advice, although always making final decisions himself, trying experiments, and occasionally he frankly said so. In these experiments he has been motivated by two objects—one the overcoming of the depression, and the other the making over of the economic organization of the nation, the latter being what he called in his campaign speeches "the New Deal." It is this which appears —it is too soon yet to speak positively—his chief objective, and it is difficult as yet to judge what his conception of the new society may be. In his first year he has shown enormous courage but has, apparently, not seldom changed his point of view, as well as his advisers.

As the latter loomed large in the administration, to a considerable extent displacing the regular Cabinet in public sight, the so-called "brain trust" requires some comment. Of recent years college professors have been more and more frequently called into consultation as "experts." Hoover made frequent application to them when President; Roosevelt did the same as Governor of New York; and foreign governments have done likewise. However, they have never been so in the forefront of affairs as since Roosevelt entered the White House, and this, together with the vagueness of what the "New Deal" might signify, helped to hinder the restoration of confidence. The lack of ability to foresee the future, to say nothing in too many cases of the absence of personal integrity, had indeed thrown the "big business men," the bankers and captains of industry, into the discard, but on the other hand the American has never had much belief in the practical ability of a professor, and the "experts" have disagreed among themselves as notably as doctors are said to do.

JUST OILING THE CLOCK A BIT

A cartoon by Carlisle on the "Brain Trust" in "The Des Moines Register."

Moreover, Roosevelt chose many of his advisers from the distinct radical or left-wing group, the names of most of them being utterly new to the public. At first among the chief of these appear to have been Professor Raymond

Moley, Doctor R. G. Tugwell, and A. A. Berle, Jr., all of Columbia University, New York. In the summer of 1933 there were added to these and many others, Professor G. F. Warren of Cornell, a leading advocate of the "commodity dollar," and Professor J. H. Rogers of Yale. At least twenty to thirty others could be mentioned. It is to the "brain trust" that we owe the carrying out of the vague "New Deal," or as a great admirer of the President prefers to call it, "the Roosevelt Revolution." What the final result may be, no one can yet say, but as we shall see at the end of the chapter, they have presented a staggering bill for the American citizen to pay.

In May, in spite of somewhat improving conditions, it appeared as though the forces of disorder were gathering strength. The strongest two political groups with us are the veterans and the farmers, and both of these threatened trouble. A new Bonus Expeditionary Force marched on Washington, but Roosevelt had made preparations in advance and the disgraceful scenes of the previous year were not to be re-enacted. He had already organized his Civilian Conservation Corps, as one of his favorite relief measures, and thanks both to his personality and the evident lack of sympathy throughout the country with the demonstration being made by the ex-soldiers at the Capital, the march ended in a peaceful settlement. By August 1 over 30,000 veterans were working with 210,-000 other young Americans, in the Corps, building 50,000 miles of roads and trails, 12,000 miles of telegraph lines between fire lookouts, and improving conditions on some 15,000,000 acres of our forest lands.

The project for such a Corps of young men had long been a favorite one with the President, and may likely prove a lasting organization in our national life. Without general training in the army and with the practical disappearance of frontier experience, the opportunity offered by the Corps for a large number of young men to spend some time in at least a semi-disciplined life in the open appeals to many as an admirable thing. Adding educational features and the genuinely useful work in conservation of our forest and other resources, the objections to such an organizing of young men for temporary training are slight and the advantages are many. The future of this work holds many possibilities if properly and wisely handled.

The farm problem was more serious and cannot be said to have been settled yet. The farms of the nation were burdened with a mortgage debt alone of between $8,000,000,000 and $9,000,000,000, largely incurred when farm products had been at extremely high prices, whereas they had now fallen to equally extreme low prices. The farmers, unable to pay their interest and other debts, had united here and there, as they had done a century earlier, in attempting to prevent foreclosure and the loss of their homes, but the country was suddenly shocked into a more acute awareness of the situation when a farmer mob at Le Mars, Iowa, carried a judge out of the court room, abused him, put a rope around his neck, and threatened to lynch him unless he would agree not to sign any more orders for foreclosures.

One of the chief features of the depression throughout the world has been the maladjustment between the prices for raw products, that is commodities of all kinds, and of finished goods, the former having fallen much lower in proportion than the latter. Moreover, the farmer in general for the past few decades had been allowing himself to become less and less self-supporting. The old-fashioned farm with not only its chief crop but also its pigs, chickens, cows, and so on, had been, even in bad times, a fairly self-sustaining unit, but the modern farmer with his tractor instead of plow and often having to buy practically all he uses, even his eggs and milk, has become in innumerable instances almost as dependent on a constant inflow of money income as a city dweller. Caught with heavy debts and to a great extent unable to sell his crops for even the cost of production, his plight had become pitiable, although it must be confessed that he was not altogether blameless, for during the years of prosperity instead of reducing his mortgages and other debts he had increased them. The war had brought him high prices and a much extended market, and he had joined in the general American delirium of believing in the permanence of the "new era." Great industrial corporations had likewise increased their plants and debts to find themselves suddenly without the demand counted upon.

At such times of stress the farmer has always insisted upon an inflation of the currency, "cheap money," so that he may pay his debts more readily. It is an interesting point, which should have a strong bearing on the possibility of managing a currency in America, that the demand for a changed dollar never occurs except when prices are falling. When prices are rising, and therefore it is easier for a debtor to pay, it never occurs to him that he should offer his creditor a larger sum than called for in principal or interest to offset the creditor's loss, but always—in the 1830's, 1850's, 1870's, 1890's—when prices fall, then comes the inevitable demand for a cheap dollar. The lesson would seem to be that with our temperament we shall never make a dollar dearer though we may from time to time make it cheaper. But a stable dollar, which shall always have the same purchasing power, entails the altering of its content or value so as to halt rising prices as well as falling ones. On the other hand the psychology of the American people will have to be completely altered if we are to witness them deliberately trying at any time to halt rapidly rising prices for farm produce, stocks, real estate or other things.

The old dispute as to inflation was one of the marked features of the year's history, and the creation of a dollar with a higher purchasing power became a fixed part of the President's policy. The Farm Relief Bill sent to Congress by Mr. Roosevelt, and finally accepted by him with what was known as the Thomas Amendment, gave the

President varied and enormous powers of inflating the currency. He was permitted to reduce the gold content of the dollar up to 50 per cent; to issue $3,000,000,000 in paper money; to provide for the unlimited coinage of silver at the Bryan ratio of 16 to 1; and in other ways to cheapen both credit and money. Without going into details, the President's own part of the bill had provided for lowering the interest rates on farm mortgages, for a government guarantee of the interest on $2,000,000,000 of mortgage debt, and the revolutionary idea of paying the farmer for reducing his planted acreage in the hope of reducing output and so raising prices. In fact, the farmers, as in cotton for example, by an increased use of fertilizer and perhaps more intensive work, have actually raised a larger crop on the reduced acreage. The government had made the incredible error of paying out taxpayers' money to the farmers not for a smaller crop but merely for cultivating fewer acres.

The year's history has raised some very pretty ethical problems, of which the plan just noted and the currency question are two of the most interesting. Necessity knows no law, but it may be asked what are the possible limits of paying a man *not* to work? If in a period of glutted markets and low prices a farmer is to be paid not to raise crops, why should not a copper mine owner be paid not to mine copper or an author not to write books? It is impossible that the farm problem, which is one of the most serious in America, can be settled in that way, and

362

unless the markets of the world are again opened the plight of the farmer is likely to become even more difficult, especially in such crops as cotton which chemists are now threatening to produce synthetically with more ease than the manufacture of artificial silk. Meanwhile, the farm problem remained one of the most baffling in the President's first year.

The history of that year is essentially economic and it is impossible to describe all the measures taken by the administration or to describe all the agencies set up to carry them into effect. These became known by the initials of their names until the alphabetical jumble became bewildering, as is evident from the following list of the chief new bureaus created:

GOVERNMENT RECOVERY AGENCIES OF 1933

AAA —Agricultural Adjustment Administration.
CCC —Civilian Conservation Corps.
CCC —Commodity Credits Corporation.
CSB —Central Statistical Bureau.
CWA —Civil Works Administration.
ECNR —Executive Council for National Recovery.
ECPC —Executive Commercial Policy Committee.
FACA —Federal Alcohol Control Administration.
FCA —Farm Credit Administration.
FCT —Federal Coordinator of Transportation.
FDIC —Federal Deposit Insurance Corporation.
FESB —Federal Employment Stabilization Board.
FERA —Federal Emergency Relief Administration.
FHC —Federal Housing Corporation.
FHOLC—Federal Home Owners' Loan Corporation.
FSHC —Federal Subsistence Homestead Corporation.

FSRC —Federal Surplus Relief Corporation.
NEC —National Emergency Council.
NIRA —National Industrial Recovery Act.
NLB —National Labor Board.
NRA —National Recovery Administration.
PAB —Petroleum Administrative Board.
PRA —Presidential Re-employment Agreements.
PWA —Public Works Administration.
SAB —Science Advisory Board.
TVA —Tennessee Valley Authority.

One's mind goes back at once to the Washington of war times, and indeed the city was humming with an activity and the rapid growth of a bureaucracy such as it had not known since the days of Wilson and the European conflict. Of a few of these new activities we shall speak later, but must now consider the currency problem which was so closely allied to that of the farmer.

When Roosevelt agreed to the Thomas Amendment to his Farm Bill on April 19 and took America off gold, the British Prime Minister, MacDonald, and the representative of France, M. Herriot, were on the ocean on their way to Washington whither they had been invited by Roosevelt to consult on means of world co-operation in re-establishing stability and trade. They were stunned by the news which they received at sea that America had abandoned the gold standard, and were resentful at what they considered a trick merely to place a strong weapon for bargaining in the hands of the President. Reassured as to the American domestic necessity of the action when they reached the Capital, plans were made for the assembling in London in June of representatives of sixty-five nations in a world Economic Conference.

Perhaps the most disastrous feature of the depression

A POSSIBLE ADDITION TO THE LINE

A cartoon in "The New York Herald Tribune" on the costs of the many Government Relief Agencies.

had been, as we have said, the enormous drop in the prices of raw materials in every country producing them, whether farm produce and metals in America, copper and nitrates in Chili, coffee in Brazil, rubber in the Far East or what not. At going prices, the producers of commodities could no longer exchange their depreciated

365

products for the manufactured goods they desired. Added to this was the complete demoralization of the foreign exchange markets in money and the impossibility of those who did an international business figuring costs or profits. Moreover, the growing international deadlock was made worse by the increasing economic nationalism—the effort of each nation to save itself regardless of the international situation which was one of the root causes of the internal troubles of each.

Roosevelt had had from the beginning, as one of his chief aims, the raising of commodity prices by whatever means possible. He appears to have wavered between national and international action until after the Economic Conference had actually got started on its work in London. It is certain that after the Washington meeting both MacDonald and Herriot expected that he would assist in the effort to stabilize the foreign exchanges and thus render the international flow of goods and services, so essential to recovery, easier. It is also certain that when the American delegation sailed, they understood that one of their most important duties would be to stabilize, even though only partially and tentatively, the dollar with other currencies. There was a choice of two methods. Each country might try to raise its internal level of prices by currency manipulation regardless of other countries and of international trade; or the assembled nations of the world might try to raise world prices by some common agreement which would involve some more stable relation of the currency of each to all the others. The two methods were obviously mutually exclusive, for if each country tried to raise its internal prices by lowering the value of its currency regardless of others, the international chaos could only grow worse.

Roosevelt and his advisers had either not grasped this inherent incompatibility of methods or the President was wavering between two sets of advisers and the two methods of procedure. In any case, he suddenly made up his mind to keep a free hand to play with the American dollar and to decline any resort to international stabilization. His cable of July 3 to the Conference stating his determination with great abruptness astounded the world and torpedoed the Conference. With his instructions suddenly torn to bits, Secretary Hull labored manfully to save America from the not unwarranted anger of the other nations who had assembled with us for joint action, and to secure at least some results from the meeting. In this he was eminently successful, and the fact that the Conference did not at once break up with extremely bad feeling was due wholly to him. Meanwhile, Moley, who had been the original head of the "brain trust" and very helpful to Roosevelt during his campaign and early days as President, had turned up in London. Although only Assistant Secretary of State, his actions there with reference to his chief were such as to bring to a head a situation that had long become impossible. It was clear that Mr. Hull could no longer retain both his dignity and his

office if Moley remained, and the latter was soon removed.

When the United States had gone off the gold standard in April it had been confronted by a problem which,
in its immensity, was peculiar to itself. Not only was the
government honor pledged to pay the interest and principal of the national debt in gold coin but, largely dating
from the fear of inflation in the Bryan campaign of
1896, the greater part of all municipal, railroad, and
other bonds and mortgages was also so payable. In
most foreign countries such contracts were payable merely in "sterling," "francs," "marks," and so on, so that
no question arose when one country or another had gone
off gold, except in a few cases which called specifically
for gold payments. In such cases the highest Court in
England, the House of Lords, decided late in the year,
that payment would have to be made either in gold or
in its equivalent value in the paper money of the country, and the British Empire has honored such clauses.

The almost universal insertion of the gold clause in
the United States undoubtedly constituted a grave danger, and it may have been against public policy. The
fact remained, however, that the debtors had for years
been getting better terms for their loans because of it, and
now when at last the creditors found themselves in the
position against which they had been insuring themselves it was a distinct blow to public confidence to have
Congress pass, and the President sign, June 5, an Act

From a Wide World photograph.

THE NRA WAS INAUGURATED WITH PARADES IN VARIOUS PARTS
OF THE COUNTRY

In New York City 250,000 marchers representing numerous branches of business, took more
than ten hours to pass the reviewing stand.

THE WILSON DAM AT MUSCLE SHOALS, PART OF THE TENNESSEE VALLEY PROJECT

abrogating all these contracts and cancelling the obligation to pay in gold or its equivalent. In view of the rising price of gold and the vast mass of debt in the country, the measure was probably necessary but the fact that it marked a breach of good business faith on a hitherto unprecedented scale could not be concealed. This, with the failure of the Economic Conference, made men realize even more fully the far-reaching possibilities of the depression and of the as yet undefined "New Deal." In his cable to London the President had spoken of a "commodity dollar," and business was getting more and more at sea as to the monetary policy of the government, and as to what all contracts and property might be worth in the future. The first burst of optimism was over, and during the summer both the markets and the volume of many lines of business dropped somewhat alarmingly again.

Moreover, new developments had come throughout the spring with a rapidity and on a scale which had taken people's breaths away. Since the World War the government had owned the immense power resources of Muscle Shoals, for which it had paid about $165,000,000. As part of his public works programme, which was eventually to have $3,300,000,000 allotted to it for expenditure, the President got a bill passed not only for the development of the power of the Shoals but for a corporation which, under the name of the Tennessee Valley Authority, was to develop a whole area of 640,-

ooo square miles and lead, as he said, to "national planning for a complete river watershed involving many States and the future lives and welfare of millions." If the project should prove successful, he indicated that he had it in mind to duplicate it in other parts of the country. Naturally this threatened competition of the government with private enterprise on a colossal scale alarmed many, particularly the holders of public utility securities which, next to governments and railroads, had been considered the safest in the country. Largely held by savings banks, life insurance companies, trust funds, and private investors, the threat to one of the greatest industries in America had a depressing effect for the remainder of the period under review.

Of the various new government agencies set up, however, that which became known as the NRA evoked the most public interest. The National Industrial Recovery Act, passed in June, was made up of two distinct parts, the second granting the President control of the $3,300,-000,000 already mentioned for public works, which he might use at his discretion interpreting the words in their very broadest meaning. Although this was the greatest effort made by any nation to try the experiment of recovering from a depression by use of public money, it was the first part of the Act which was the most interesting.

The American has always been an individualist but as the wealth and opportunity of the individual grew on a national scale, and the great corporations arose, we have seen how the ordinary American felt it necessary, in order to preserve his own opportunity as an individual, to curb that of the trusts and great wealth. Hence came the Sherman Anti-Trust Law and other efforts which we have already noted in preceding chapters. It was evident, however, with 12,000,000 unemployed, that the evils of uncontrolled competition could be as great as those of combination in restraint of trade. Employers might try to keep on employees, to maintain wages, and in other ways to soften the effects of lack of business, but with cut-throat competition for what little business was doing there was in every trade at least a minority who would stop at nothing to cheapen costs and thus take business away unfairly from the better employers.

The first section of the Recovery Act aimed to correct this situation. As the Sherman Anti-Trust Law was constitutional and had to be got rid of, the President declared a "state of emergency" to exist, which he could declare terminated at any time. According to the terms of the Act any representative trade could draft a code of fair competition, which could be altered or amended by the President and which, when he had signed it, would become binding law on *every one* engaged in the trade. The President could force the drafting of codes even if an industry preferred not to do so. The right of both employers and employees to organize was recognized and the codes had to contain agreements as to

371

maximum hours, minimum wages, and other details. The Act was, in most of its features, to remain in force for two years, unless the President terminated the "emergency" sooner. It became evident, however, from his statements that he considered the new framework of industry would in many of its features be a permanent change from the old.

The first code to be submitted and accepted was that of the textile industry, which incidentally abolished child labor, but it soon became evident that the drafting of codes would be slow work, and on July 20 Roosevelt issued by decree a blanket code to shorten hours and raise wages, pending the formulation of codes for individual industries. Gradually these were submitted and signed, those for oil, steel, and lumber on August 19, and for the automobile trade a week later. General Johnson had at once been placed in charge of the NRA and realized the slowness of the voluntary drafting of the codes, which led to the President's issuing his blanket code, for which there was no legal basis and which had to be accepted voluntarily. At once Johnson swung into a campaign like that for the Liberty Loans in the war. The "Blue Eagle" was to be displayed by all joining and it was somewhat too clearly indicated that employers or shops which did not display it were to be boycotted. Mass emotion was played upon, and such great enthusiasm was worked up that Johnson predicted the return of 6,000,000 workers to employment by September, though, in fact, only about 2,000,000 additional were then employed. It is too soon yet to calculate what may be the final result of the NRA. It has worked in many cases rather hard on the small business man, and has accomplished considerably less than was hoped. On the other hand, we shall probably not go back to the old conditions, and some permanent as well as temporary gains may be anticipated from it. If a reasonable degree of prosperity returns once more, as it probably will, the attitude of the average citizen toward all these amazing powers which have been bestowed upon the government may change to a great extent. What people are willing to do and submit to when frightened is quite different from what they will accept when self-confident. It is too early as yet to speak of a permanent "revolution" as having been accomplished.

Toward the end of the year confidence was growing somewhat greater, and this was in one way evidenced by a freer discussion of the policies of the "New Deal," and especially of the President's attitude, so far as it was inferred or known, on the currency question. The effort to raise prices by buying gold, which is supposed to have been the idea of Professor Warren, proved a somewhat absurd failure. Late in November, the resignation of Doctor O. M. W. Sprague as adviser to the Treasury, a post in which he had been far from happy, became the signal for more general criticism of the government's wavering course on money. In the next few weeks, to mention only a few incidents, the Advisory Council of the Federal Reserve Board went on record as opposed to it; the American Economic Association did the same; a group of Yale professors of economics published a manifesto against it; a group of Harvard experts published a book condemning it. Finally, on January 31, 1934, the President issued a Proclamation devaluing the dollar by close to 40 per cent in gold, agreeing to purchase all gold offered at $35 an ounce, and also to sell gold to foreign central banks whenever it reached the export point.

Without attempting to enter upon the intricacies of the gold standard and exchange, it may be said that this action put the United States partially on a gold basis again and definitely reduced the value of the dollar, which the President reserved the right to reduce further to 50 per cent of its former worth in gold if he considered it necessary. The government had taken possession of all the gold in the banking system, and the Treasury figured that by reducing the gold content of the dollar from 25 and 8/10ths grains to 15 and 5/21sts, it would make a "profit" of approximately $2,670,000,000. Of course, taking over all the gold and reducing the amount in each dollar would leave the government in possession of the balance, but instead of a "profit" it must be considered, whether wise and necessary or not, as confiscation of the property of the government's citizens rather than a "profit" in the ordinary sense. Let us suppose that

From an Underwood and Underwood photograph.

PRESIDENT ROOSEVELT PRESENTS THE FIRST CHECK TO A TEXAS FARMER FOR THE DESTRUCTION OF HIS COTTON

Forty-seven acres had been plowed under in accordance with the government plan for reducing crops.

WITH REPEAL, CAME OUT-OF-DOORS DINING AND THE SIDEWALK CAFÉ, A
POPULAR CONTINENTAL FEATURE, NEW TO NEW YORK

the government had seized all the land in the country —so many acres from each owner. Then suppose it decreed that henceforth an "acre" should contain not 43,560 square feet but only 26,136, and returned to each owner the same number of "acres" it had taken from him. By this process it would have come into possession of 40 per cent of all the land in the United States, but no one would claim that it had done anything but confiscate it.

What the ultimate effects of the depreciation of the dollar will be yet remains to be seen. It should benefit exporters and hurt importers, and as domestic prices gradually rise some classes will gain and others lose. There would seem to be little doubt, however, that as one blow after another has been given to good faith and the sanctity of contracts, far-seeing investors have become less inclined to place their money in fixed or long-term investments, and that recovery has to that extent been retarded. On the other hand, the belief that the President has considered a return to a gold basis and that the depreciation will now be held within the limits of a fifty to a sixty cent dollar, has helped the growth of confidence.

Meanwhile Roosevelt had met Congress on January 3, delivering his message in person, and the nation was stunned when told the bill it would have to meet. The deficit for the current fiscal year was given as approximately $7,000,000,000, and the budget for the year as over $10,500,000,000. The President estimated that the government would have to borrow $10,000,000,000 in the next six months, and that by June 30, 1935, the total debt would be nearly $31,000,000,000, when he hoped the budget might become balanced. In his campaign speeches he had advocated "sound money" and an immediate balancing of the budget. The measure of the anxiety through which the nation had been passing for months may be taken from the fact that it felt a certain relief in January in finding itself with a fairly definite fifty to sixty cent dollar, and a budget which might be balanced in another two years after colossal taxation.

Economics are dull reading, and we have been able to touch upon only some of the more important economic measures in a year, the whole history of which was almost entirely economic. It is impossible as yet to say what the effect of the many experiments on a hitherto undreamed-of scale may have on the depression, and how much of the "New Deal" may prove permanent. In the space left we can merely glance at a few of the other events in what may prove to be one of the most important and significant peace-time years in our history.

As we noted in the preceding chapter, the way had at last been opened for the people to pass on the Prohibition experiment, and with unexpected and remarkable speed State after State voted for repeal until by December 5, thirty-six States, the number necessary for the adoption of the XXIst Amendment, which repealed the XVIIIth, had voted in favor. Only the two Carolinas had voted against the measure, and on December 6 President

Roosevelt issued a proclamation repealing the Prohibition Amendment while the Acting Secretary of State
announced the adoption of the XXIst. The settlement of

ISN'T THE BLAMED THING EVER GOING TO TAKE OFF?
A cartoon by Carlisle in "The Des Moines Register" in the summer of 1934.

the long vexed controversy brought general satisfaction
to the country, and none of the disorder the Prohibition-
ists had feared. In fact, New Year's Eve in New York
was one of the most orderly, although jubilant and
happy, in years.

As we have seen, the codes under the NRA brought about the abolition of child labor, though if the codes should lapse at the end of the "emergency" of two years, it is possible, though unlikely, that child labor might come back. Another significant experiment at the other end of the age scale has now come into play by law in twenty-five States—the substitution of old age pensions for the former "poor house," a movement which is likely both to spread wider and to be extended in scope. During the year also, there was inaugurated what Miss Perkins considers one of its "real achievements," the establishment of a national employment service under the charge of the Department of Labor and now operating over 2400 employment agencies scattered through every State in the Union. On the other hand, there has been a notable antagonism shown to the granting of huge salaries and bonuses to corporation officials. The various investigations of the year into the private affairs of many of the members of leading banking houses added to the feeling which was already rapidly growing. The bonuses, running in some cases into the millions, which had been paid to some corporation officials, had become a disgrace, both to the Boards of Directors who granted them and to the officials who received them. The RFC set a salutary example when it refused to advance money to certain railroads until the official salaries had been reduced to reasonable limits, and it is said that when Mr. Schwab was arguing with Mr. Roosevelt over the steel code and

378

remarked that he must look after the interests of his stockholders, the President smiled ingratiatingly and asked "were you looking after the interests of the stockholders when you paid those million-dollar bonuses to my friend 'Gene Grace'?"

Foreign affairs throughout the year were subordinate to domestic problems. We cannot, however, live wholly to ourselves. No progress was made with the problem of war debts or disarmament, and we have already spoken of the Economic Conference. For us directly, the most menacing situation of the year developed in Japan, whose seizure of Manchuria and antagonism to China raised difficult problems. The Act passed by Congress to give independence to the Philippines after a period of years was rejected by the Filipinos themselves, and thus became void. The fact is that much as a certain class in the islands clamors for independence, if the islands should become independent and consequently a foreign country, the withdrawal of American subventions and the necessary application of the tariff against the Philippines as against any other country would ruin them economically, to say nothing of the dangers to their independence from Japan if we withdrew.

In Cuba one of the periodical revolutions ran its course for six months, though this time it was a more genuine revolution than most of the mere political overturns. In spite of the immense amount of American capital invested in the island, we refrained from using our powers

379

under the Platt Amendment and maintained a position of neutrality until January 23, 1934, when we recognized President Mendieta's government with hopes that it might prove stable. Meanwhile Secretary of State Hull had been attending the Pan American Conference held at Montevideo, and had made a "good will" tour of South America, which was highly successful in bringing about a better understanding between ourselves and our important southern neighbors.

In New York City the overthrow of the shameless government of Tammany Hall and the election of Mr. La Guardia as Mayor was a significant event, and on the whole, in spite of colossal burdens assumed and much uncertainty as to the future, the first year of the Roosevelt administration marked a considerable advance in the national life. Not only had hope and vigor replaced the despair and lack of initiative of the preceding three years but we had come to occupy ourselves with the genuine betterment of conditions for all. In his speech to Congress on January 3, 1934, the President admitted that much which had been done hurriedly under the spur of necessity might have to be altered but that nevertheless progress had been made toward a better organization of the life of the nation. "We have undertaken new methods," he said. "It is our task to perfect, to improve and to alter when necessary, but in all cases to go forward," and on the whole the country did go forward in the first twelve months of his term.

CHAPTER IX

THE RECORD OF 1934

THE year 1934 was filled with striking events both at home and abroad. Our domestic affairs, with which we are chiefly concerned here, were set against a world background of political uncertainty and violence unexampled since the end of the World War. In France the scandals growing out of the Stavisky murder and other cases resulted in the fall of the Cabinet on January 28, and early in February a week of rioting and bloodshed in Paris caused the gravest crisis since the establishment of the present republic. The following week there was rioting in Vienna against the government, resulting in large loss of life. On the 17th of the month the world was stunned by the news of the death of King Albert of Belgium, killed while mountain climbing, and the European situation became tense, though it quickly cleared. In June occurred the shocking wholesale murders committed by the Nazi government in Germany in Hitler's "purge," soon after which he assumed supreme power as a dictator, following the death of General von Hindenburg. At intervals there were bloody upheavals in Spain. In July the Chancellor of Austria was assassinated, as were the King of Yugo-Slavia and the French Foreign Minister, Barthou, in October. The year ended with a renewal of mass murder in Russia. In the Far East, Japan continued to exploit Manchukuo and

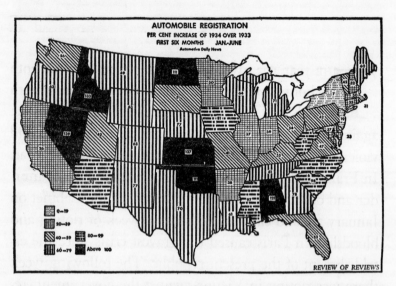

THIS TABLE COMPILED BY *THE REVIEW OF REVIEWS* SHOWED THAT THE MIDDLE WEST, GEOGRAPHICALLY SPEAKING, LED THE REST OF THE COUNTRY WITH AN INCREASE OF 95.7 PER CENT IN THE CARS REGISTERED DURING THE FIRST SIX MONTHS OF 1934

disregard world opinion, while at our own doors, the revolution in Cuba became more Communistic and violent.

In spite of these and other happenings in many countries, threatening the stability of individual nations and world peace, the United States, though suffering from sporadic violence in a series of strikes, which will be noted later, proceeded in an orderly fashion with stupendous plans for recovery. We have no exact figures in our country for unemployment or for those receiving various forms of Federal, State and local relief, but at one time the estimate of those being thus helped ran as high as 20,000,000. Although this figure, to be surpassed in 1935, may have been exaggerated, the proportion of our citizens ordinarily self-supporting who had to ask aid before the end of this fifth year of the depression was staggering, and considering the genuine sufferings of the people the patience and good sense manifested were remarkable.

This has probably been due to several causes. In some respects the American people is a lawless one. In the past all too many, from the great business leaders down to the smallest individual, have chosen for themselves from among the innumerable wise and unwise laws of the nation and its forty-eight States which they will obey and which they will not. As a result partly of national character and partly of the unique conditions of our national development, this fact has bred disrespect for law, and incidentally the rise of a genuine criminal class. But the American people have at the same time never been revolutionary. They have indeed been extraordinarily conservative in their fidelity to established forms of government. So much so that we are far behind many other countries in social legislation. Another point in the present depression as contrasted with earlier ones in

which greater violence occurred has been the unprecedented scale on which individuals of all sorts have been
helped by the governments, state and national, as noted
above. A century ago, in the great depression of 1837 to
1841, men and women froze and starved to death in the
streets of even New York. By gigantice efforts that sort
of thing has not been allowed to happen this time. Just
as the dole in England, however much deplored, is
acknowledged even by die-hard Tories to have saved
that country from social revolution in the past decade,
so the enormous sums for relief of all sorts under which
we have staggered probably account for the comparative
lack of trouble during these terrible five years among
ourselves.

As a third point, we must accept as a great stabilizing
factor socially the leadership of President Roosevelt,
whether we agree or not with many of his experiments
and specific policies. Personally, I disagree with many,
but the belief on the part of the great majority of the
people that he is doing his best for *them* has undoubtedly kept down a large amount of discontent which
under a less popular and trusted leader might easily have
smouldered into fierce flame. Undoubtedly some of his
policies have considerably retarded the rate of recovery,
which with us has lagged rather conspicuously behind
that of the British Empire and some other countries. It
is also a question whether, if recovery is too slow, the policies may not lead us into worse conditions owing to a

384

heavily depreciated currency which would overwhelm all, rich and poor alike, in common disaster.

As we noted at the close of the preceding chapter, Congress met on January 3, 1934. The President presented the figures for government expenses, stating that the deficit for the fiscal year would be around $7,000,000,000 but that he hoped to balance the budget by June 30, 1935. The nation was stunned but the President's control over Congress was as notable as in the preceding special session, the famous "hundred days," and the legislature offered little or no opposition to the program of the administration. So far from reducing any of the extraordinary powers granted to him in the emergency of the preceding year, his hands were strengthened and the legislation consisted largely in rounding out the main features of the New Deal.

One of the first of the important measures passed by request of the President was the Gold Reserve Act. This forbade the coining of gold and gave the government title to all the monetary gold in the country, including all the reserves of the Federal Reserve Banks. Under the Thomas Amendments to the Agricultural Relief Act, noted in the preceding chapter, the President had been given power at his discretion to reduce the gold content of the dollar by 50 per cent. The Gold Reserve Act now specifically gave him the power to reduce it to between fifty and sixty cents, and it was in accordance with this new Act that he established it temporarily at 59.06, as already described. The Act also transferred some of the powers properly belonging to the Federal Reserve system to the Treasury, that is, unfortunately, to a purely political instead of a banking agency.

As a further inflationary measure, Congress passed, on June 19, a silver purchase act which it was estimated might entail the purchase of a billion ounces and gave Roosevelt the power to place the country on a bi-metallic basis. As has been shown over and over again in history when two metals form the basis for a nation's money, one always shoves the other out of circulation, depending on which is the cheaper commercially. Another element of uncertainty was thus introduced into our monetary system. On August 9 all the stocks of silver in the country were nationalized and owners were forced to sell to the government at 50.01 cents an ounce and turn their holdings over to it. Although as yet, except as a potential source of possibly great future inflation, our new silver policy has had little effect on our domestic situation, it has had serious results for the countries which have a silver currency, such as Mexico and China. By forcing up the price of the metal we have raised the value of their currencies while all the rest of the world, except the small "gold bloc," has been reducing the values of theirs. This has put the silver countries at a great disadvantage as to foreign exchange and naturally reduced their purchasing power abroad. It may be noted here that the silver question, intruded constantly into our political life, has to a great extent been an off-shoot of the "great compromise" in our Constitution which gave each State two senators while basing representation in the lower house on population. Had it not been for the abnormal political influence thus given to the only seven, mostly thinly populated, states which produce silver, the silver currency question would have always had less power to disturb us. The influcence of the silver group has not been based on the number of ounces produced but on the number of senators involved, the total value of silver production being less than half the value of our peanut crop.

Before mentioning other Congressional measures we may stop to consider some of the effects, actual or potential, of the currency measures taken during 1933 and 1934. In actuality thus far they have not brought about the results for which they were designed. The measures were all aimed at bringing about a rise in prices. Professor Warren's gold purchase scheme proved farcical, and prices instead of rising actually declined somewhat while it was being practised. Again, after the gold value of the dollar was cut by about 41 per cent, wholesale prices rose only about 26 per cent and retail prices less than that. Moreover, a large part of both these rises can be directly attributable to the increased costs of production due to N.R.A., the A.A.A. and other parts of the New Deal. Yet if prices rise promptly in proportion to depreciation of the currency, they should have risen 70 per cent. The fact is that unless a person feels that his money is going to depreciate constantly on his hands he will not buy goods simply because some of the purchasing power of his money has been taken from him, any more than he will borrow money simply because he can do so at the low rate of 1 per cent. Until he feels confidence in the general business outlook and in his own personal one he will continue to limit commitments and act with caution. As a means of raising prices to lift us out of the depression the methods taken with the currency have thus largely, if not wholly, failed.

On the other hand, the measures taken, besides having caused us to break the national faith, may be laying up much trouble for us in the future. Owing to the enormous amount of promises to pay in gold dollars or the equivalent at the old value, estimated as high as a hundred billion dollars, the catastrophe would be so great if the Supreme Court decided that the Act of Congress abrogating the "gold clause" were unconstitutional that it is probable that body may have to find some way of validating our breach of faith. The number of gold clause contracts in other countries have been so small that their problem is quite unlike ours but it is not pleasant to go back on all our contracts while the courts of such nations as Holland and England are declaring that their business men must pay in full in such cases. On March 1, the Republic of Panama, with which we had a treaty guaranteeing that small country as rent for the Canal zone $250,000 a year in the value of our former gold dollars, returned the check sent, demanding that we pay them what we had promised and not the equivalent of only $150,000.

On the other hand, Canada, which has outstanding in the United States alone gold obligations to the extent of about $2,000,000,000, would find itself, in proportion to its resources, in almost as awkward a situation as the United States if the Supreme Court uphold the gold clause.

The scale on which the gold clause has been put into contracts, public and private, in America has created an entirely different problem from that existing with regard to a comparatively small number of contracts in Europe. Congress has the unquestioned constitutional power to regulate the value of money. But if the citizens at large create such a mass of future contracts payable in money of a value of their own choosing as to force the country into bankruptcy if Congress alters the value and the Supreme Court at the same time upholds the contracts, then Congress has practically been deprived of its constitutional power. There is no question that the gold clause on the scale we have used it has been against public policy. The decision of the Supreme Court belongs to the history of 1935 but we may note here that the President, Congress and the Court were placed in a most difficult, if not dangerous, position by the vast outstanding mass of gold contracts.

Apart from this question of honesty, other serious

problems loom. If sooner or later we have a sustained rise in business, the effect of the depreciated dollar will then be felt on prices, not now when wanted but just when it will not be wanted. When business and speculation become active, prices will rise of themselves but they will rise far more rapidly, possibly to the full 70 per cent extra, with a sixty-cent dollar than they would have done with a hundred-cent one. In addition, with the huge increase in government bond issues, with the possibilities inherent in the Thomas Amendments, the Silver Acts and others, and with the now practically complete dominance of politics in the Federal Reserve Bank System, the difficulty of preventing a huge inflation of both currency and credit would seem to have become almost insuperable. The result might well be such a boom as would be followed necessarily by a collapse which, as President Angell of Yale writes, would make "the events of 1929–1933 seem trivial." Thus far, therefore, it would seem as though the financial and currency policies of the government had not brought about the expected result of a rise in prices, have not "primed the pump," and have not restored confidence but on the contrary retarded its growth. Yet they have set forces in motion which may do incalculable harm. It is impossible to predict and one can consider only what has—or has not—in fact been achieved and what the possibilities may be for the future.

Among other important bills passed was the Bankhead

Bill which gave the government compulsory power to limit the production of cotton not only in the nation but on each individual farm. After a summer's trial this was endorsed by the farmers themselves by an overwhelming majority in a referendum vote in the autumn. This is not altogether surprising as the system would seem to have given the farmers who are now raising cotton a monopoly of that branch of agriculture.

A number of bills were passed for increase of the revenue, among them a new Income Tax Bill increasing returns by about $300,000,000. As part of the New Deal, Congress also provided for the control and regulation of the Stock Exchange, a wise action considering the magnitude of the interests now involved however the details may work out. The fact that changes were also enacted making the Securities Act of the preceding year more workable would indicate that such controls would in time be placed on a practical footing. Another action taken which may be considered as part of the New Deal program was the National Housing Act. By the terms of this it was hoped to reorganize the financing of private homes by those in need of assistance, and to stimulate the greatly lagging building trades. It provides that a home owner can repair or improve his house up to the amount of $2000 by discounting his note at his bank without security, the government guaranteeing the bank up to 70 per cent of the loan. If a person wishes to build a house he may get a loan from his bank on one mortgage payable in twenty years at a low rate of interest instead of first and second mortgages for short terms at high rates. The government undertook to guarantee the mortgage up to 80 per cent or $16,000, thus hoping to release bank funds for this purpose. For various reasons the law expected to put about $1,500,000,000 into circulation has not accomplished as much as was hoped, either in relief or recovery, but has been helpful.

Another Act which was a hopeful sign of increasing understanding of our economic situation in relation to the outer world but from which the results thus far have been meagre was a Tariff Bill which gave the President power to negotiate and conclude agreements with foreign nations, permitting him to raise or lower existing duties by 50 per cent. Mr. George N. Peek, the President's special adviser on foreign trade, calculated that from 1914 to 1933 the debt owed to us by the rest of the world had been increased by over $20,000,000,000. Of this the "War Debts" represent about $10,300,000,000, but it is evident that apart from them we cannot expect to continue to sell to other nations or get returns on our foreign investments unless we consent to buy more goods from them. It was not unexpected when in June Great Britain joined the other foreign nations (except Finland which continued to pay) in default on its War Debt to us. The British had been making "token" payments as an acknowledgment of their recognition of the obligation pending a possible re-settlement of the whole problem, but decided to suspend even this as a result of the absurd Johnson Bill, passed in April, which forbade Americans to lend money to any foreign country which might be in default of all *or even a part* of the money due us.

In an effort to put an end to the seemingly endless and bloody war between Bolivia and Paraguay, Congress prohibited the export to them of arms or ammunition and we requested that other nations would do the same but the munitions interests were too strongly entrenched in Europe for the most part and we were left with only the moral satisfaction of ourselves not aiding the conflict without being able to stop it although England joined us in May. Two other interesting actions were taken outside our own borders. A new treaty was made with Cuba by which we gave up our right of intervention under the Platt Amendment. This was in line with our efforts to establish better relations with all South America which Secretary Hull had worked for on his trip to the Montevideo Conference. A new Philippine Independence Bill was also passed, in much the same terms as the one of the preceding year except that it gave the Filipinos until fall to decide whether or not to accept. Beneficial as their independence may be for the American sugar grower it may well prove disastrous for the islands as many of the best leaders there now recognize. In the three hundred years of Spanish rule the population had increased approximately from only 3,000,000 to 6,000,000, whereas in the thirty years of American rule it has risen to over 12,600,000. Nearly half of these people are dependent on the production of sugar, hemp, tobacco and cocoanuts, which in turn are dependent on a free entry into the United States. If the Filipinos accept independence—or have it thrust upon them—they will be outside our tariff wall and the economic crash will probably result in intense misery.

By the end of March, the President, who had been handling Congress with consummate skill, was showing signs of strain, and went on a fishing trip on Mr. Vincent Astor's yacht for a fortnight. Congress had also felt the strain of being restrained, and in his absence proceeded to pass the Independent Offices Bill over his veto, a bill which called for additional payments to war veterans of $228,000,000 and provided for replacement of two-thirds of the 15 per cent reduction in Federal salaries, including those of the Congressmen themselves. Having behaved like mischievous schoolboys when the teacher has left the room, they suddenly became frightened, and marched in a body to greet him on his return at the Union Station. The humor of the situation was not lost on the President, who made a three minute speech to them from the platform of his private car, one of the most amusing and adroit of his whole political career.

The matter would have been sheer farce had it not been so serious. What appeared was the incapacity of Congress when left to itself and not any relaxing of Executive control, the only other failure of the President to get what he wanted throughout the long session being the rejection by the Senate of his St. Lawrence Seaway Treaty with Canada. He had declared, however, that the passage of the Offices Bill would destroy the savings effected under the Economy Act and upset the financial plans of the administration.

Both in his veto and later in the year Roosevelt made clear his stand on the question of the bonus and veterans' relief. As for the veterans themselves he has no wish to deprive of their pensions those whose disabilities came from service but he does object to setting up what is practically a relief bureau on special terms for a particular group of able-bodied citizens. As he put it at Chicago, he believes that "no person because he wore a uniform should thereafter be placed in a special class of beneficiaries over and above all other citizens." The problem of continual pressure by so large a group is, indeed, one of the most serious dangers which we face in the future. Almost every President has fought against the scandals of the Civil War pensions, yet although that war cost approximately $3,250,000,000 the American people have already paid out $7,370,000,000 in pensions to men who fought or did not, who were injured or not, and to their widows, children, and every one else who can claim a blood or pension relationship to them. For the comparatively small Spanish War we have paid out in pensions over $800,000,000 although less than 400,000 men took part. General Hines, of the Veterans' Bureau, has estimated that by 1966 this little war will have cost the nation in pensions about $3,700,000,000, although the war itself cost only $584,000,000. When we consider that we had over 4,000,000 men in the World War, and its enormous cost, the prospect ahead of us is staggering. In fifteen years its veterans have already received approximately $6,000,000,000 and incessantly the clamor continues for more. If the eventual payments bear any such relation to the cost of the war as in the case of the previous two wars the cost in time to the nation for this particular group of citizens, and every one who can be worked in as related to them, becomes unthinkable.

In this connection we may note that although in many ways, such as old age pensions, the social services in England have been far more largely developed than with us, yet from March 31, 1922, to March 31, 1934, the number of pensioners of the World War fell from 2,890,000 to 1,053,000 and the cost of pensions from £95,559,000 to only £45,051,000, due mostly to deaths, children attaining the age of sixteen, and the re-marriage of widows. The contrast with our own figures and their upward trend is notable.

One serious mistake the President made at the beginning of the year was in connection with the air-mail service. It was claimed that there had been graft and favoritism on the part of the Postmaster General in the previous administration, and Postmaster Farley suddenly cancelled all contracts with the private companies and turned the service over to the army to run. The army proved badly equipped for the work and in the little over three months, from February 9 to June 1, that it carried the mails, twelve army fliers were killed, though in a brief review of this work in *The New York Times* the Secretary of War made no reference to these men who had fallen in line of duty and merely noted that "not a single pound of mail was lost." The people, however, had been shocked by what they called "legalized murder," and a demand went up from the country, notably voiced by Colonel Lindbergh, for stopping the slaughter. The administration had to turn the business back to private companies which were equipped to handle it. They were, in fact, extraordinarily well equipped. It is not perhaps generally realized what a great change has come over aviation and that America now leads the world. At the time of writing this chapter figures are not yet available for 1934 but in 1933 they were as below:

	Mileage flown	Passengers carried	Goods and mails carried (tons)
U. S. A.	54,642,545	568,940	4,584
Germany	6,580,035	108,535	1,861
France	5,986,011	52,179	1,706
Italy	2,960,133	43,126	1,039
Great Britain	2,638,000	79,080	913
Netherlands	2,615,469	43,258	1,137

Of course the American continent, with its huge area and population, is peculiarly fitted to develop a great system of overland air routes, but the comparison with the rest of the world is no less striking if we consider our Pan-American service which links together thirty-four nations and colonies in the Western Hemisphere. That service, maintained by the government-subsidized Pan-American Airways, operates more than 26,600 miles of air routes, more than twice that operated by Imperial Airways, which is the British Empire service. In 1933 it operated also a fleet of 139 air liners as against only 37 by the British. In 1933 this American service, now the greatest in the world, maintained an efficiency rating of 99.5 per cent for schedules, and beat the British by a considerable margin in its safety record,—2,700,000 miles flown to every fatal or serious accident against 2,330,000 miles for the British.

The report on the working of the N.R.A. which had been asked for from a committee headed by Clarence Darrow was given to the public on May 20. It was, for the most part, a scorching criticism, laying particular stress on the hardships which the codes entailed upon the little business man in small communities.

After the end of the Congressional session, the President left on July 1 for a month's holiday, and on the cruiser *Houston* visited Haiti, Porto Rico, the Virgin Islands and Colombia. Having passed through the Panama Canal, he proceeded to Hawaii, and landed in the

Courtesy of Pan American Airways.

THE "BRAZILIAN CLIPPER"

A giant modern flying boat which carries forty-four passengers, as well as mail and cargo, and makes an average speed of 150 miles an hour and is capable of 192 miles an hour.

United States again at Portland, Oregon, on August 5.

Meanwhile a colossal physical disaster had overtaken the country. There had been a cycle of sub-normal rainfall in the central west lasting since 1909, and the dramatic sequel occurred on May 11, when, after scorching heat, a dust cloud 1000 miles wide suddenly carried 300,000,000 tons of formerly fertile soil off the surface of Trans-Mississippi farms eastward across 1500 miles of land and far out into the Atlantic. New York and other eastern cities were darkened at mid-day by the dirt from far beyond the Mississippi.

It was one of the great disasters of history. The drought and burning heat lasted until the showers of September. Cattle died by tens of thousands for lack of grass and water. In June the government hastily undertook to slaughter over 1,000,000 head to put an end to their sufferings. Of these more than 500,000 had to be buried as unfit for food. Streams disappeared, and even the Missouri River shrank to one-third of its normal size. Crops were the smallest since the bad year of 1893, and the A.A.A. had suddenly to reverse its policy of crop reduction. It was a striking example of what can happen to a "planned economy." In addition to the unemployment already existing, the government had to aid 400,000 families owing to the disaster. The loss to the country was estimated at $5,000,000,000. Fifteen states and approximately 10,000,000 people were affected.

The catastrophe served to call public attention to what

has long been going on due to soil erosion. All over our nation wasteful forms of farming and the cutting down of forests have resulted in the rain carving gulleys in the soil and ruining rich lands. The director of the Soil Erosion Service, H. H. Bennett, stated last summer that at least 3,000,000,000 tons of soil are washed out of the fields and pastures of America every year, and that we have already created, in the President's phrase, a "man-made Sahara" out of good farming lands which in the aggregate equals in extent the combined States of Connecticut, Massachusetts, and Illinois. From our great Mississippi Valley alone over 400,000,000 tons of soil are carried into the Gulf annually, a loss every year of the equivalent of enough good soil to make 1250 unusually rich farms of 160 acres each. Wind erosion is now being added to that from water, and America is confronted by a problem of such magnitude as can be handled only by the wise planning of the Federal Government. One suggestion has been to plant a forest 100 miles wide and 1500 miles long stretching from the Canadian boundary of North Dakota south to Texas.

It was evident on his return from Hawaii that the President's popularity had been in no way diminished, and in his addresses to crowds on his way back to Washington, notably in that of August 9 at Green Bay, Wisconsin, he gave a ringing defense of the New Deal. A month later the normally Republican State of Maine went Democratic, which was considered as a portent of the national

election to be held in November. At the same time as
the Maine election, Upton Sinclair, Socialist of California, announced himself as a candidate for governor on the
Democratic ticket, winning at the primaries over the
other Democratic candidate by 125,000 votes. His
"EPIC" (End Poverty in California) plan was so radical and unsound as to make his adherence to the party
of no little annoyance to its leaders. Other plans, even
wilder than Sinclair's, were proposed by others in California and capital began rapidly to leave the State.

At the beginning of October, the President in a broadcast to the people defended the administration, and particularly the N.R.A., although he admitted that it had
gone too far in such matters as price-fixing and the limitation of production. He also frankly pointed out other
defects, and suggested that he was considering a revision
of its provisions with a view to "legislation which will
determine its permanent form." Speaking of the claim
made by business men that his policies were preventing
the restoration of confidence he said nothing as to the unbalanced budgets, the possible reduction of expenditure
or a stabilized dollar. Instead he laid the blame for the
failure of confidence to return at the door of labor, and
promised to hold conferences with labor leaders to seek
some means of establishing an industrial truce. His acceptance of the resignation of General Johnson, the head
of the N.R.A., indicated there were considerable changes
to be expected. Donald R. Richberg took his place and

the general remarked that the "N.R.A. is as dead as the dodo." It was not, but was to be modified in the next few months, and probably in 1935, on more workable lines for business. Another important resignation was that of Lewis W. Douglas who had performed notable service as Director of the Budget. In view of the huge unbalanced budgets in prospect the loss of Douglas was felt by many conservative people as indicating a danger to sound finance. On the other hand the President's address to the members of the American Bankers' Association, gathered in Washington on October 24 for their annual meeting, and the speeches of leading bankers there, were considered as the signing of a "truce" between business and the administration. Although in the continued attacks on public utilities the "truce" was distinctly not in evidence, on the whole the relations between Roosevelt and business took on a more hopeful aspect for genuine co-operation, which continued from that time to the end of the year.

One of the most disputed points in the N.R.A. had been the celebrated 7A clause which, both in itself and as interpreted, gave, in the eyes of employers, too great power to the labor leaders of the large organizations. So far from smoothing relations between employers and labor it had made them more difficult, and the year had been marked, as the President admitted, by extensive and frequent strikes. In March had come the strike in the automobile industry which threatened to paralyze one of the key industries of the country and one on which the restoration of prosperity chiefly depended. This had been averted by the direct and successful intervention of the President. In June another important industrial conflict, this time in the steel industry, was prevented by William Green, the head of the American Federation of Labor.

On the Pacific coast a longshoremen's strike, combined with sympathetic action by maritime unions, had been in progress from May until the port was again opened in July, and there was much rioting and considerable loss of life. A general strike was then demanded but not called, though the teamsters joined the longshoremen, and the next week the general strike was on as the result of the votes of 115 unions. There was panic in the city and the militia were called out. The strike had spread to Oakland, and to Portland, Oregon. After 4600 militiamen had been called into action, and it was also evident that the longshoremen were losing the sympathy of the public, they agreed to arbitrate, and the general strike was over by July 19. There had been much unjustified violence on both sides.

In September 800,000 workers were called out in the textile industries, the biggest single walk-out attempted in our history. Among other demands was that for a five-day, thirty-hour week with no reduction in pay from that received for forty hours, but the 7A clause was also, as usual, one of the chief causes of the trouble. The cotton garment industry had not been affected by the strike but it also threatened a walk-out for October 1. In the South 15,000 militia were called out, and there was violence both in that section and Rhode Island. The conflict was marked by bitter feeling shown between the president of the United Textile Workers and General Johnson, then still head of the N.R.A., the latter claiming that the strike was "in absolute violation" of the agreement made by the textile workers with the Federal government when they had discussed the textile code. The number of workers out was variously estimated in the papers as from 500,000 to 800,000, but apparently 400,-000 would be more nearly correct. Again the President intervened, and with the promise that a Textile Relations Board would be created to protect labor's right to bargain collectively, and that certain claims with regard to wages and other matters would be investigated, the leaders called the strike off toward the end of the month.

In October the Great Atlantic and Pacific Tea Company closed its 428 stores in Cleveland owing to labor troubles and threatened to leave the city for good as it was claimed they could get no protection from violence. After ten days' negotiations and Federal mediation, order was restored and the stores remained.

The great event of November was naturally, however, the national election. Although polls taken by *The Literary Digest*, which have proved remarkably accurate in the past, forecast a great victory for the administration, it had been so frequently the case in the mid-term elections to have the administration defeated that no one could be sure what would happen until the votes were counted. The result was a staggering blow to the Republican Party. It was found that the Democrats had 69 seats in the Senate to only 25 for the Republicans, and one Progressive and one Farmer-Laborite. In the House the Democrats had 322 seats to the Republicans' 103. To find one party in possession of 72 per cent of the strength of the Senate and 74 per cent of the House one has to go back to the immediate post-Civil War period when as a result of the war the Democratic Party had almost ceased to exist.

It is true that, as in the last English election, the number of the winning party in the legislature was out of all proportion to the comparative strength of the voters at the polls. In the popular vote the Republicans had polled about 12,145,000 votes against the Democrats' 15,397,-000. As compared with 1932 the Democrats lost approximately 7,400,000 votes against a Republican loss of only 3,600,000 but even so the result for a mid-term election was practically unprecedented. In fact, it was almost too much for the Democrats for a too unwieldy majority is hard to keep in order. There was, however, little question that the popularity of Roosevelt was the chief factor in the victory. It must not be lost to view, however, that the vast number of people in one way and another getting money from the government may also have had much to do with the result. The temptation to Congress to continue pouring out the golden stream of billions will be very great. The result showed, nevertheless, that whatever conservatives might fear as to the possible ultimate results of the New Deal policies these appealed to the rank and file in their immediate effects.

That confidence had made great gains during the year was shown by the fact that although a few days after election, November 12, the Treasury lifted all restrictions on the export of gold and allowed any citizen to transfer his capital abroad if he chose, few seem to have taken advantage of the opportunity. No flight of capital occurred, and no necessity appeared of again putting into effect the restrictions which had lasted from the banking crisis of 1933.

During the latter half of the year, the question of war material became of interest from two different angles. On July 16 the Japanese Ambassador in London had intimated that his country would withdraw, as entitled to do after two years' notice, from the naval treaty of 1922 which prescribed a ratio of 5-5-3 for the naval strengths of Great Britain, the United States, and Japan. After prolonged but futile negotiations between representatives of the three powers in London, it was clear that Japan would not reconsider, and on December 29, the Japanese Ambassador in Washington formally denounced the treaty. In the Far East Japan has no neighbor to compete with her on the sea. Considering her

Photograph by Underwood and Underwood.

U. S. BATTLESHIP *CALIFORNIA*, IN NEW YORK HARBOR DURING THE NAVY CRUISE OF 1934

MINER'S CHILDREN LIVING IN FILTH AND POVERTY, SUBJECTED
CONSTANTLY TO DISEASE AND CORRUPTION

MINER'S CHILDREN LIVING IN PLEASANT SURROUNDINGS IN ONE OF
THE MANY SUBSISTENCE HOMESTEAD HOUSES OPERATED
BY THE GOVERNMENT

group of islands remote from both the United States and the British Empire, the former having to defend two coasts, 3000 miles apart, and the latter to maintain its intercourse with all its parts which encircle the globe, it is difficult to understand why Japan should require as large a navy as either of the other two powers. In March the Vinson Bill, passed by Congress, authorized the President to build our navy up to the full strength permitted under the treaty, but a race between ourselves and Japan to build up to unspecified limits would be a very different matter. There is no question that we could build faster than she but our whole policy, honestly pursued, has been the limitation of armaments; and it is to be hoped that some agreement may be reached by 1936 when the field for a race will be open.

During the fall, a Congressional Committee investigated the munitions industry, and brought out many disturbing facts as to the influence of the international group of producers on the provocation of wars, so much so that a similar inquiry for England was proposed in Parliament. No action has been taken as to the matter in America, and the army is itself opposed to the nationalization of the industry. The President has suggested, however, that in future wars private profits from the industry should be eliminated, and late in December appointed a committee, headed by B. M. Baruch, to prepare legislation which would, as he said, "take the profit out of war."

The arms manufacturers have also been accused of blocking helpful legislation in our internal war—that against crime—it having been said that legislation by Congress to control the traffic in revolvers and other portable weapons has been defeated by those interested in the profits derived from them. It is asserted that since the last war the United States has imported 1,000,000 revolvers and manufactured 500,000. The Attorney-General has said that "it is a conservative estimate that there are more people in the underworld carrying deadly weapons than there are in the army and navy of the United States." The year was marked by a series of spectacular kidnappings and other crimes, and it may be noted that although the homicide rate for the 31 largest American cities was 5.1 per 100,000 population in 1900 it rose to 10.7 in 1933, or more than doubled. The rate across the border in Canada for its largest 14 cities is only 1.5 per 100,000.

The situation had become such that Congress passed several laws breaking down State boundaries for the purpose of ensuring the safety of the citizens, and since the Federal Government took hold there has been a marked advance in the process of cleaning up the criminals. The question of States' rights has been left in abeyance in the crisis, as has the legality of declaring certain persons "Public Enemies" to be shot at sight. We have accepted the fact that crime has become so extensive that it is now war between the decent citizen and the underworld, and that when a well-known criminal is seen there is no more need for a trial than there would be for an enemy seen in real war. It is a confession of the break-down of the orderly process of the law but has to be acquiesced in temporarily. The first Public Enemy Number One was the notorious murderer Dillinger who was tracked down and slain by Federal agents on July 22. Since then we have also rid ourselves of Clyde Barrow, Bonnie Parker, "Pretty Boy" Floyd, "Baby Face" Nelson, and many others. The fact that under modern conditions with hand machine guns, fast cars and other equipment, a criminal could commit crimes and escape over the boundary into another State, has made Federal control inevitable. Moreover, Federal agents do not have the same relation to the underworld as do too often the local police forces. The most interesting capture was that of Bruno Hauptmann, the alleged kidnapper and slayer of the Lindbergh baby, who at the end of the year was being held for trial in New Jersey, and was convicted and sentenced to death in February.

Other evidence that Americans are waking up to the moral evils which the war and the post-war orgy brought to us are not wanting. Figures for 1934 are not yet available but those for 1933 show that in that year there was an increase in church membership of more than 800,000, bringing the total to over 60,000,000, an increase in seven years of nearly 8,700,000. During 1934, war was also started against indecent films, and although ignored at first it became of such proportions as to alarm the Hollywood producers. The lead was taken by the Catholic Church, and it is said that practically all of its 22,000,-000 membership enlisted for a year in the crusade, and the Protestants have joined heartily in the movement. It is little use to try to instil ideas of decency and clean living in children at home if you then take them to look at films on which crime and vice are made as glamorous as Hollywood can make them. This fact at last seems to be sinking into the minds of the American public.

On the whole, although recovery had not been as rapid as had been hoped and there was ample cause for anxiety as to both the present and the future, the year ended with a more hopeful spirit than it had begun. The Christmas trade was the largest since 1929, and the spirit of the people was both calmer and stronger.

In this brief survey it has been impossible even to mention many of the important measures taken or to describe at length the effects of all the forces put into operation or the experiments tried. Many mistakes have been made, many heavy risks taken. Both business leaders and the President have learned much. There is a better sense of co-operation throughout the entire nation and an appreciation of the fact that we are not merely trying to get out of the slough of depression but to build a better America. There is a sense of courageous adventure and endeavor. Unfortunately there is as yet no prospect of balanced budgets nor a halt to spending. At the end of the year the American Federation of Labor estimated that the unemployed numbered 11,459,000, and the burden is still tragically heavy and the suffering great. Nevertheless, the nation is considerably better off than at the end of 1933 in spite of the added blow delivered to us by nature in the great drought, a blow, however, which

IS IT GOING TO EXPLODE AGAIN?

A cartoon in the early part of 1934 by Fitzpatrick in "The St. Louis Post Dispatch" on the threat to World Peace.

was much intensified by our own wastefulness and carelessness in the past. If we are to remain a great and self-sustaining nation the time has come, as we have this year been sharply warned, when we must preserve those natural resources which are still left to us.

At the end of the year there were also signs of distinct

improvement in the world at large. December brought to Europe the almost sudden realization that, in spite of all that had happened to cause anxiety, nevertheless crisis after crisis had been surmounted and that instead of war the structure of peace was really stronger than when the year began or than any one had imagined. Not only were international relations, on the whole, felt to be on a firmer basis but in the democratic countries there had been a marked loss of interest in the various forms of dictatorships as the only means of solving national economic problems. In spite of much of both anxiety and bitterness, Europe was in better psychological condition and more hopeful and confident. Owing to wise handling of finances and to a rise in commodity prices, conditions were distinctly improved in Australia, South Africa, and several of the leading countries of South America. No nation can prosper by itself alone, and although much remains to be done to restore international trade, the improved condition of many parts of the world augurs well for our own improvement. One of the most encouraging signs, however, was the renewed hope of Americans themselves. Whatever we may think of individual measures adopted, or methods of carrying them out, America has been engaged for two years in a colossal effort at co-operation, and the stark despair of 1932 has now at last given place to courage, and the nation is once more finding itself and looking forward to accomplishment and not back to loss.

CHAPTER X

THE RECORD OF 1935

ALTHOUGH it is difficult to appraise rightly the ultimate importance of exciting events while living in the midst of them, I think it safe to say that the year 1935 will eventually be considered as one of the most important in the history of the Republic. It was a year which answered no fundamental questions for the American people—in spite of the Supreme Court decisions which we shall note in the course of this chapter —but which so placed issues before us that they must soon be settled one way or another; and the entire course of our civilization may depend upon how they are settled.

The significance of the year is that it has posed such important questions for us, and that America is forced to decide. It may be, for example, that toleration of opinion and the personal liberties of freedom of speech, press and action may be compatible with the extreme form of political and economic centralization and control desired by many, though both ancient and modern history, notably that of our own day in a number of great countries, would appear to teach otherwise. If they are not, then men and women will have to decide which of these

413

goods (if extreme centralization *is* a good) they most desire, and cast their ballots or perhaps, in time, fight for those they most desire.

Fortunately our decision cannot be made hastily. In the great populations of our modern democracies false information and emotion derived from newspapers, the moving pictures and the radio, acting upon all of us simultaneously, may cause us to advocate a course of action which we may later regret. The example of the Hitler régime in Germany shows us how even a sober, orderly, and highly cultured and intelligent nation may embark upon a course which ends in economic, spiritual and intellectual ruin, and once embarked finds it impossible to turn back. In our own form of government, perhaps the most useful function performed by our Supreme Court is that of preventing us from suddenly changing our institutions in their fundamental form, and of at least giving us time to consider whither we are bound. What even the friends of the present administration like to call "the Roosevelt Revolution" involves a large alteration in our relations to one another, in the relations of the citizen to his government, and possibly even in the choice of goods as noted above.

Many of the most radical, indeed almost revolutionary, measures passed by the administration in the three years it has been in power has been declared unconstitutional by the Supreme Court in 1935. This does not mean that the Court is oblivious to the social ills of our time or heedless of a humanitarian program. It does mean, however, that the methods of solution for our problems, proposed in haste and without due consideration, have not been in accord with the fundamentals of our form of government. These include certain defined relations of the citizen to his State and national governments. They also include certain relations between the States and the Federal Government which latter was erected to bind the States together, to perform certain functions for all better than the individual States could do, and also to guarantee certain personal liberties to all citizens. Decisions by the Court, although binding, are not final settlements of the problems involved. Either of two things can be done. More carefully thought-out solutions might be found or less carelessly drawn laws enacted which might better meet the constitutional test; or the Constitution itself, if a real majority of the American people and not a mere minority group wish to do so, could be amended. This is not, as some loud voices claim, necessarily a lengthy process. When the opinion of the people was finally consolidated, the amendment repealing Prohibition was put through all its stages in about nine months. The "lame-duck" amendment took only about eleven months. If the people do not take interest in a proposed change in our fundamental institutions or if a majority is opposed to such change, it would seem unwise that such change could be made by the Executive or a mere majority of one Congress. A very active minority may object strenuously to a delay of a few months before they can attain their objects, and indulge in recrimination against the Court, but, as just noted, if the people really wish the object to be attained the delay need not be more than a few months. Such a delay is surely better than to force a change, perhaps little understood or even undesired, on the nation without giving it time to think or express its genuine opinion.

The fact that such a "breathing space" has been forced on the people in 1935 is the most significant characteristic of that year. The American people may or may not as a whole approve of the New Deal and the methods adopted to put it into practice. If they do not, they should be thankful to the Supreme Court. If they do approve, the road is open to them to propose and pass amendments which will enable them to draft laws in accordance with an amended Constitution. At least they have been given time to think, and they have, under the present Constitution, the power to act. So long as that Constitution lasts and the Supreme Court carries on its present function of interpreting it, they cannot be swept along in a resistless current as have all classes in Russia, Germany and Italy. To one who has watched events in those countries, to some extent at first hand, that would appear to be something to be grateful for rather than to condemn.

We may now pass on to consider some of the more

specific important events of the year which bear on the generalizations of the preceding pages.

By Fitzpatrick in The St. Louis Post-Dispatch

TAKING CARE OF OUR 10,000,000 UNEMPLOYED WAS THE MOST PRESSING PROBLEM OF THIS PERIOD

Congress, the first to be elected since the inauguration of the New Deal, met on January 3, and on the 4th the President, in person, delivered his message on the state of the nation, his message on the budget following a few days later. In both of these he again emphasized his policy as trying to lead America toward a "new order of things" but "under the framework and in the spirit of the American Constitution." The keynote of the first message was "the security of the men, women and children of the nation," toward which goal the entire program of legislation should be directed. Somewhat better business had almost wholly failed to reduce unemployment, and during the year the number of unemployed was variously estimated at from ten to thirteen million. In January there were about five million on the Federal payrolls alone, of whom the President estimated 1,500,000 as unemployable. The remaining 3,500,000 he planned to take off ordinary relief and set to useful work as rapidly as possible. Instead of a dole, which would have been financially much the less expensive method, he wished to set the unemployed to work on such projects as slum-clearance, reforestation, road building, and so on. For this purpose he asked Congress for $4,000,000,000, and in spite of a heated contest between those who favored the dole system and those in favor of the works system, Congress finally appropriated $4,880,000,000 "subject to allocation by the President." No such sum had ever before in the history of the world been voted to be placed at the disposal of one individual.

The task of spending such a huge amount not only

wisely but as rapidly as possible—as it was largely to provide for those out of work and without means of support—was obviously a most difficult, and as was to be proved, an impossible one. Clearly the work to be provided would have to be of a sort in which labor costs would exceed the cost of materials as largely as might be. The object was not to provide the nation primarily with new roads, buildings and other things which it might or might not need but to provide penniless people out of work and out of luck at the very moment with means of subsistence. Moreover, the work was stipulated to be of a sort which should compete as little as possible with private industry so as not to cause further unemployment by forcing private business to turn off employees, by the government undertaking work which would have otherwise been handled by private concerns.

Undoubtedly it is far better for the morals of a man or woman to be paid for doing useful work than a mere sustenance dole in idleness. It was this aspect of the case which appealed to the President. The conditions of the problem, however, as has been noted, were extremely difficult. To a great extent the authorities in Washington consulted the local ones throughout the nation. Haste was essential, yet haste, in many cases, precluded careful consideration and detailed examination of plans suggested. Moreover, local politicians were anxious to bring as much money into their own communities as possible. As a consequence, sums were spent in many places for work which could not be classed as necessary or useful, and the term "boon doggling" became popular to describe such enterprises. For the most part the amounts involved were comparatively small although in the aggregate they have been considerable.

Looking at the problem merely from the economic and not from the human side, it is obvious that the "works" plan is far more costly than the "dole" plan. In the latter the government, which means in the end the taxpayer (as the government can raise money only by taxation or borrowing, and borrowings have also to be paid eventually out of taxes), has to pay only the cost of feeding, clothing and sheltering those without means of their own. On the other hand, the works plan calls for large outlays in addition, such as the cost of drawing plans, legal expenses, cost of materials, and the overhead which any ordinary business has.

Americans are a kindly and helpful people, and those with jobs or money assuredly did not wish to allow other Americans to be without food or shelter in the emergency, but as the year progressed the realization sank deeper that the eventual bill to be footed, whether taxes should be increased before the election of 1936 or postponed until after, would be a staggering one.

In his budget message, the President, who as we noted in the preceding chapter had announced in January, 1934, that he hoped to balance the budget by June, 1935, stated that the budget for the fiscal year ending June,

1936, would still leave an additional deficit of $4,500,000,-
000, and that by June 30 of that year the national debt
might stand at over $34,000,000,000. In fact, it did reach
an all-time high of over $30,000,000,000 by December,
1935, and it was then freely predicted that it would rise
to $38,000,000,000 in another two years. People began
to realize that unless the government went bankrupt
and merely repudiated these huge debts (which as the
debt has largely been carried by the banks for the government would mean their bankruptcy also and bring
our whole business system crashing about our ears), they
will eventually have to be paid either by ourselves or our
children.

On January 17, the President sent to Congress his
message on social security which resulted in the passage
of the Act of August 14, although Congress was much
overburdened and many Congressmen favorable to the
object of the Act strongly desired to hold it over for
more careful and mature consideration. When signing
the bill the President expressed his belief as to its fundamental importance, and remarked that if Congress in its
session had done nothing else, the passage of this bill
would make it "historic for all time."

Just as every one agrees that those injured in war, the
widows of those killed (until remarried), and the minor
children should be assisted by the State, so most now
agree that the State should provide a greater degree of
security for the old and for those injured, so to say, in

the economic life of the modern world. In theory, social insurance is correct, but in America just as the cost of war pensions exceeds the cost of the wars themselves, there is danger, as we do things, lest the cost of social security might approach perilously near the value of the social product. It all depends on how we administer the system chosen; whether we make it honest and scientific or whether we handle it as we always have the war-pension scandals. Even at present no one knows what it will cost. It is estimated that almost immediately 25,-000,000 people may become beneficiaries, with 50,000,-000 on the payrolls in less than twenty years more. If our handling of war pensions forms any criterion as to what may happen, we may also expect constant demands for increasing the amount of pensions and also the number receiving them, by lowering the age limit and in other ways.

This comment is not directed against the need of increased social security for our citizens. It is an open question, however, whether the matter should be handled by the Federal Government or by the States, and we certainly have to take into account the corruption of our politics as noted above. During the nearly three centuries of settlement and westward migration, from the founding of Jamestown in 1607 to the presidency of Theodore Roosevelt in 1901, Americans had been accustomed on the whole to doing much as they liked in exploiting the resources of the continent. The American temperament, character and outlook, as we have known them, were formed during that period which embraces nine-tenths of our entire history. Ordinary life was bare, meager and hard, but the prizes to be won were colossal. Economic success seemed to bring with it all the other desirable goods, and men as a whole devoted themselves to achieving that, and not mere security and contentment, with a vigor and buoyancy of spirit never known elsewhere.

The striving for this single goal, however, brought many evils in its train. In most of America, scholarship, letters, the fine arts, even the art of living a happy and fully rounded life were sacrificed to the striving for "success." To a great extent even government was sacrificed, and the man who saw, or thought he saw, the way to millions with their attendant prestige, power and luxury, did not care to become a government official or employee. Even such giants in Congress as Daniel Webster obeyed attentively the business desires of their constituents. It is true that many of those who reached the highest pinnacles of material success were of the coarser and more ruthless sort, far from admirable as men or citizens. But it is a mistake to think that these formed a small class apart from the rest of us. Almost all the founders of great fortunes rose from poverty and obscurity, and it must be recalled that for one who succeeded there were tens of thousands like-minded in their ambitions and methods who failed. For these and other reasons we have developed the politician and spoils system as known among us, rather than a government machine composed of trained men in the Civil Service. This has made it difficult under the New Deal properly to plan, carry out and co-ordinate the work of all the new bureaus. This has called for an enormous expansion in the number of Federal employees, which is said to have increased by over 200,000. Indeed, it was estimated by the end of the year that 16 per cent of all workers in the nation were on the government payrolls.

It is impossible to follow in this brief review the increase and frequent changes in the bureaus, commissions and departments, some thirty of the leading ones of which were listed in the preceding chapter. From various public utterances, the President had evidently considered that the strongest two pillars of the New Deal were the NRA, which regulated industry, and the AAA, which regulated agriculture. Both of these had many good ideas embodied in them but both proved unwieldy in practice. For example, the hundreds of codes under the NRA became increasingly annoying to business men, especially to the smaller ones who could not afford costly legal advice at every turn. Some features of the NRA, such as the abolition of child labor, had met with pretty general approval throughout the nation, and would be desirable to retain permanently in some form. Nevertheless, the constant interference with the running of business of all sorts by Executive Orders from Washington which were claimed to have all the validity and force of law, aroused much opposition, and the whole system by which Congress had delegated excessive powers to the President had always been considered unconstitutional by many of our leading legal minds and others.

The AAA had also become infinitely more complicated than had been intended or planned at first. Both that and the NRA were based on a philosophy of controlling (largely raising) prices, and of reducing production so as to create an artificial scarcity. The leading problem of our day, which had been widely discussed, had been considered to be how, in the midst of a vast potential plenty for all, that plenty could be best distributed so that all might share to a greater extent than hitherto. We had solved the problem of production, both agricultural and industrial. The unsolved problem was how to bring about a more just distribution. After three years of the New Deal many people who believed in its humanitarian objective came to be more and more sceptical as to its method of attacking the problem of plenty by the creation of artificial scarcity.

Whatever the solution may be, the year 1935 was notable for bringing large numbers of citizens to a new realization of the difficulties and complexities involved in trying to regulate the entire economic life of a nation of 125,000,000 citizens, each one of whom is naturally primarily concerned with making his own living if possible and as good a one as may be. In the beginning, the

AAA had started to regulate only one basic crop, cotton. Growers were to be paid for reducing the amount raised, being paid for what they did not raise by money derived from a "processing tax" to be passed on to the ultimate consumer of manufactured cotton goods. It was hoped that prices would rise, the income of the farmers would be increased, and a better balance established between them and the manufacturers whose goods they bought. At least two unexpected results had become clearly evident by 1935. One was that by raising the price of American cotton artificially above the world price, we heavily damaged and greatly endangered for the future our foreign markets for selling our surplus crop, cotton having been one of our most important exports, and the growers largely dependent upon such exports for their prosperity.

The other discovery had been that in a complex, closely interwoven agricultural-industrial nation such as ours, the artificial control of the price of one basic commodity leads practically inevitably to the control of others, and, in time, possibly to that of practically all. One crop, for example, can be restricted but the repercussions from this control spread in all directions, like the circles on water when a stone is thrown into it. The farmer may be paid for not raising cotton but other crops can be raised on the acres left idle. That makes a sudden increase in the new crop raised, and a glut ensues which hurts those who had been raising it before, so that the newly enlarged crop has to be taken under control in its turn. Tobacco was thus taken over and made basic. But when cotton and tobacco were limited, peanuts could be raised, and peanuts became basic and controlled when the peanut growers of North Carolina were threatened with ruin by the sudden increase in production in other parts of the country. So it goes. Moreover, in this day of synthetic products given to us by modern chemistry, there are many substitutes for vegetable products. An enforced scarcity of one of the latter leads to an increased manufacture of its industrial substitute, and control has to be widened to include those.

To a considerable extent, however, the policies of the government have been altered, or at least their application has been halted, by the action of the Supreme Court. The decision by the judges that the AAA was unconstitutional belongs to the history of 1936, as it was not handed down until January of that year, but from the beginning of 1935 there were accumulating evidences that many of the policies of the New Deal were unpopular whether in accord with the Constitution or not. By January some cases had advanced far enough for decision by the highest tribunal, and on the 7th the Court, by a vote of eight to one, decided that Section 9C of the NRA (the clause involved in the case) was unconstitutional. In that clause, the Court stated, Congress had transferred part of its lawmaking function, set down in the Constitution as its alone, to the President. If Congress could do that, then it could go on and transfer other legislative powers, not only to the President but to other officials or individuals. In a word, it would open the way to the abdication of Congress and the transfer of all its powers to a dictator. In another decision, May 27, the Court declared practically the entire NRA unconstitutional and the whole fabric crumbled. The Blue

ALL NRA ENFORCEMENT IS ENDED BY PRESIDENT AS SUPREME COURT RULES ACT AND CODES VOID; WHOLE OF NEW DEAL PROGRAM IN CONFUSION

THE HEADLINE ON THE SUPREME COURT RULING ON THE NRA
"The New York Times" of May 28, 1935.

Eagle was dead. However, business men and politicians had already come to the conclusion that the NRA had outlived its usefulness, such as it had been, and had rapidly been becoming both a business and a political liability. For easily understood political reasons it would have been difficult if not impossible to legislate it out of existence. The Supreme Court had cut the knot. The President expressed much concern as to the result on the nation's business but fortunately his fears were unjustified. Indeed, the destruction of the NRA marked the beginning of genuine business recovery. The economic life of the nation took a fresh start. This may have been in part due to the fact that forces of recovery may already have been well in motion. It would seem more

THE JUSTICES OF THE SUPREME COURT

This body is the highest Court of Appeal in legal matters and determines the constitutionality of laws passed.

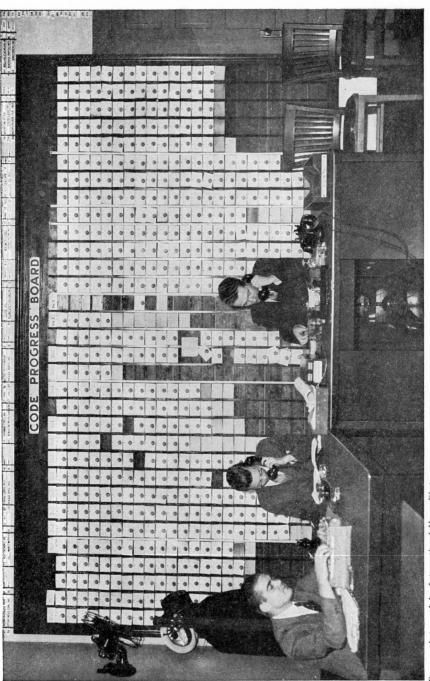

From a photograph by International News Photos.

THE NRA INTRODUCED SO MANY CODES THAT IT BECAME NECESSARY TO DEVISE A PROGRESS BOARD SIMILAR TO

likely, however, that there was genuine economic advantage in the abolition of the codes, and more especially that there was a considerable restoration of the feeling of confidence, without which there can be no genuine revival of business, due to the fact that the decision of the Court showed that there was still a bulwark between the people and the increasingly mistrusted ideas and experimentation of the New Deal. The NRA was finally dissolved by the administration on January 1, 1936. It may be noted that by that time the poll being taken by *The Literary Digest* showed that of the 1,370,000 answers received 60 per cent were opposed to the New Deal, a marked change from 1934 when practically the same people addressed had voted 60 per cent in favor of it. The figures must be taken only for what they are worth but in the past the *Digest* polls have been remarkable for their accuracy in indicating general public opinion.

Early in the year, on February 18, decisions were handed down by the Supreme Court on a group of cases involving the repudiation by the government of its promises to pay holders of government bonds in gold coin of the former weight and fineness existing before our depreciation of our dollar to approximately fifty-nine instead of one hundred cents, and the abrogation of the gold clause in all private contracts as described in Chapter One.

This decision—rendered five to four—was hailed by

the government as a victory though it was really a moral defeat. The Court generally agreed that Congress had power to regulate the currency and hence could devalue the dollar. It was further agreed that there could not exist a sort of double system of money in the country, the dollars in private contracts being valued at 100 cents while the government dollar was 59. But a very sharp line was drawn between the power of Congress to regulate the currency and the right of the government to go back on contracts previously made with the people who in good faith had loaned their money to the government when the government had needed it and who would now have their money paid back to them shorn of about 40 per cent of its previous value in gold. Even among the five judges who upheld the administration in the main and as to the power of Congress to regulate the currency and the value of the dollar, this point was strongly stressed.

Thus Chief Justice Hughes, one of the five, said in his Opinion that a promise solemnly made by the government to repay money borrowed by one Congress could not be altered by a later one merely because it found repayment under the agreed terms inconvenient. "On that reasoning," he said, "if the terms of the government's bonds as to the standard of payment can be repudiated, it inevitably follows that the obligation as to the amount of payment may also be repudiated. The contention necessarily imports that the Congress can disregard the obligations of the government at its discretion and that, when the government borrows money, the credit of the United States is an illusory pledge." He pointed out that there were no remedies the citizen could invoke unless Congress provided them but that, nevertheless, if Congress failed to provide them, "the contractual obligation still exists, and, despite infirmities of procedure, remains binding upon the conscience of the sovereign."

So far from providing remedies, the government later passed legislation preventing suits from being brought against it in this connection. The whole proceeding of the government, which brought such a sharp rebuke from the Court as to its morality, had not even benefited the government as had been hoped. As we noted in an earlier chapter, devaluation and repudiation had not attained their object of immediately raising the level of prices when a price rise might have been helpful but had merely piled up trouble for the future when the full effects of the policy may be felt in an abnormal speculation and rise in living costs when not wanted.

Much the same must be said of the government's policy as to silver, which by the end of the year, in spite of having caused much suffering among the peoples which have a silver currency, and demoralization in the silver markets of the world, had had no such beneficial effect among ourselves as had been anticipated by those favoring it.

431

On May 6, the Railway Pensions Act, which had placed a peculiarly heavy burden upon one industry arbitrarily selected, for pensions to workers, was declared unconstitutional by the Supreme Court, and during the year lower Federal courts declared other Acts unconstitutional, though many of these cases had yet to reach the Supreme Court at the end of the year. In fact, before it was over, some 2000 suits had been started involving almost all aspects of the New Deal. In spite of many of its ideals and aspirations, with which a large portion of forward-looking Americans must agree, so much of its legislation had been prepared so hastily, crudely and apparently regardless of the Constitution that few of us engaged in agriculture, commerce, industry and other pursuits could tell where we stood at the end of this momentous year. Indeed, in July the President had pressed for the passage of the Guffey Coal Bill, requesting that the Committee of Ways and Means would allow no doubts as to its constitutionality to "block the suggested legislation."

Earlier in the year, the President had failed to get favorable action on our joining the World Court. This, unlike the more debatable and contentious subject of joining the League of Nations, which might easily involve us in the quarrels of the Old World, would not lead us into international complications and would make for peace rather than for war. So far, however, though successive recent Presidents have all asked for the same action as did Roosevelt, the Senate has blocked the way. In view, nevertheless, of the alarming outlook abroad, notably in the Italo-Ethiopian dispute, Congress passed a bill, later subject of much dispute, looking toward preserving our neutrality in case of war.

An excellent recommendation by the President was that the government accounts should show clearly what subsidies are being paid to shipping companies under the guise of padded costs for carrying the mails, so that we may really know to what extent this particular industry is being subsidized. It is one of the serious drawbacks to government operation of any business that it is far more difficult for the citizen to know actual costs than in the case of private business. The accounts of all large-scale businesses are of necessity complicated, but the government is now the biggest business of all, and unlike private concerns, it audits its own books as each department pleases. No outside auditing firm is employed to check figures or suggest methods of cost accounting. This gave rise during the year to a considerable political controversy as to whether the Post Office had shown a large surplus or a large deficit. Spending as we are now a half score or more of billions every year, it is hard to determine what undertakings are profitable and what may not be. This is one reason why it is hard to determine whether a government charge for any service is really a "yardstick" or not. Any suggestion, therefore, such as noted above by the President for a clearer accounting system

433

should be welcomed, and it is to be hoped that such suggestions may in time be made for other government enterprises and expenses.

In spite of much continued crime in the United States, one of the matters accomplished by the Roosevelt administration, on the value of which all can agree, has been the fine work done by the "G-men" under J. Edgar Hoover, at the head of the Federal crime bureau. Only a year or two ago it seemed as though we had become helpless before the group of leading criminals and organized crime, with its keen minds and vast financial resources. The police of our great cities and forty-eight states seemed unable, as separate units, to compete with them. It is said that the criminals themselves gave the nickname to the Federal officers of "G-men," meaning government men, and it is certain that criminals fear them as they never did local officials. As a result of captures and prompt sentences or the killing of leading criminals resisting capture, many of the most notorious criminals are now out of the way, and there seems a fair chance of stamping out the most infamous of crimes for which our America has unhappily been noted: Kidnapping for ransom. Even huge ransoms look small as compared with almost certain tracking down and prompt conviction. Moreover, there seems to be a healthy change in public interest. The most notorious criminals, because of their daring and the risks they took, acquired not only public interest but a certain misplaced pub-

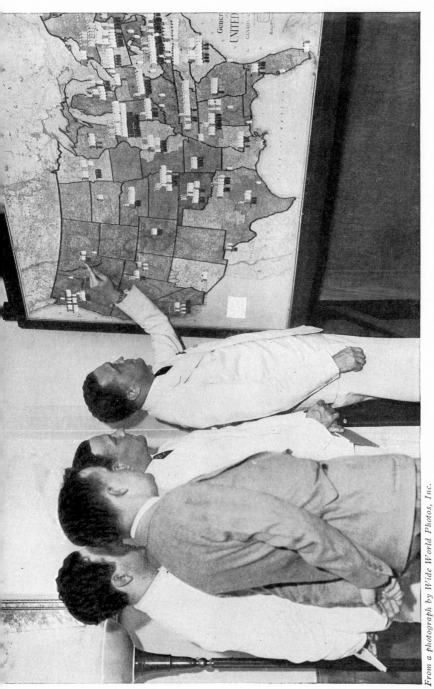

From a photograph by Wide World Photos, Inc.

J. EDGAR HOOVER WITH HIS ASSISTANTS STUDYING THE CRIME MAP ON WHICH IS INDICATED THE POSITION OF
EVERY "G-MAN" THROUGHOUT THE UNITED STATES

From a photograph by U. S. Forest Service.

WORK DONE BY THE CCC HAS BEEN PARTICULARLY OUTSTANDING IN THE FIGHTING OF FOREST
FIRES AND REFORESTATION

lic sympathy. The G-men, however, are quite as daring and take as many risks in protecting homes and society as the criminals did in bringing anxiety and sorrow to them, and now bid fair to become the public heroes in place of the gangsters. They are beginning to occupy the place in story and public imagination that the long-noted Northwest Mounted Police have in Canada, and there could be no happier augury for a period of better law enforcement in our country in this and the next generation than this shift in interest, particularly for the young. There will be less juvenile crime and creation of potential gangsters when boys learn to admire the G-men rather than the enemies of society they track down. Although so many of the measures of the Roosevelt administration are controversial, and intelligent men honestly differ about their value, the establishment of the G-men, as also of the CCC, mentioned in the review of the previous year, has met with the approval of all Americans regardless of party or economic views.

On May 22 the President appeared before Congress in person to deliver his Veto Message against the latest Bonus Bill. By the end of 1934, during which year about $700,000,000 had been paid to the veterans, they were again demanding immediate payment of the adjusted certificates due only in 1945. In spite of much murmuring among Congressmen about "mail order legislation" and "government by telegraph," direct pressure upon members of Congress proved successful, as usual, and the measure was passed.

In his Veto Message, the President calmly gave his reasons for refusing to sign the bill. America, he said, had been generous to the veterans. Up to June 30, 1934, it had spent in various ways more than $7,800,000,000 upon them, and by 1945 the figure would have reached to $13,500,000,000. The immediate payment, as called for in the bill, of the face value of the certificates not due until 1945 would entail a clear gift of $1,600,000,-000 more. He also pointed out that the veterans would share in the benefits of the Social Security Act, and that they had already shared to a greater extent than any other group of citizens in the money spent by the PWA. It may be noted that in addition to what they have received from the Federal Government, the veterans have also received large sums from the individual States, ten of which have given bonuses costing the taxpayers approximately $350,000,000. Other States have granted money in other forms, such as Kansas, which in fifteen years has expended over $6,000,000 on her veterans; or New York, which, under certain circumstances, exempts the real estate of veterans up to $5000 from taxation. Maine has a local pension system which in six years up to 1934 cost that far from rich State $500,000. Oregon, in addition to the bonus given, created a revolving fund for loans to veterans amounting to about $31,000,000. The insurance offered during the war, and the bonus and other benefits granted by the Federal Government were given in the belief that the nation might avoid such pension systems as have followed previous wars. For 1935, the Patman Bill failed of passage over the President's veto by only nine votes in the Senate.

Business improved during the year, the decisions of the Supreme Court having helped to restore confidence, so that the so-called "heavy industries," which had seriously lagged in recovery, began to gain ground at last. The huge sums poured out by various government agencies had been felt mostly in increased purchases of consumers' goods, but fear of what might still be in store, from either economic or political causes, had continued to keep capital timid about investments in building new plants or otherwise developing industry. A broad and sustained recovery cannot be based merely on arranging that by government borrowing the people, or a portion of them, shall have more to spend on clothes, cars, entertainment, food and other perishable commodities. Relief is necessary, but pouring government funds into the business well in certain lines has apparently not worked as the alluring metaphor of "priming the pump" suggests it might. The business of the country cannot get under permanent headway until large numbers of men, large and small, have determined to spend or borrow money for the creation of durable goods, such as dwelling houses, enlargement or modernization of plants and machinery, and so on. This can come only from a reasonable confidence in the future—hence the value of the Court decisions—and this confidence may be shaken by either economic or political causes.

The failure of the heavy industries to get a start was particularly notable in the utility industry, which, except for lack of confidence, would have invested huge sums in new plants and modernization. Although during the year, the gross business of this industry rose to an all-time record, its securities remained far below the level of prices which mere business conditions would have caused them to attain. Few investors were so hardy as to put new money into enterprises to which the administration had shown itself distinctly hostile. The willingness of the government to make gifts to localities to build their own plants at about half actual cost rendered deadly destructive the competition of such fifty-cent plants with even the most honest, efficient and public-spirited private plants which had had to provide the entire cost of construction for themselves, and at interest rates governing money borrowed for private industry and not at rates ruling for governments or municipalities. The claim of the TVA to be a "yard stick" for the price of electric current, even though it later claimed in 1936 that it sold its current merely as a by-product of other enterprise, had been pretty well shattered before the end of the year.

Nevertheless, private capital was naturally shy of investing in enterprises which might be run out of business any moment, and so one of the greatest industries of the country did not provide its share in general recovery. Just as toll roads have gone and we now travel freely on roads provided by public authority and at public cost, and just as for the most part we cross free the bridges which used to charge for the privilege, so some day the government may decide to provide electric current at half the cost of production or free. The public demand and the tendency of the present government seem to point in that direction, but we are apt to make such changes without reimbursing those who have formerly provided services, just as, when Prohibition came in, the values of breweries and distilleries were destroyed without compensation. The unwillingness of private capital to pass into an industry so threatened can be well understood, but is unfortunate as greatly retarding the possible rapidity of general business recovery.

Meanwhile, the CCC, already mentioned, continued its excellent work, especially in reforestation, which adds a very important item to the genuine and permanent wealth of the nation, not merely in standing timber but in the preservation of the soil. In a short summary, it is impossible to write of all the activities of the government, which have come to an astounding degree to overshadow the daily life of every citizen. It is also too soon to give a fair appraisal of the New Deal. It may well prove that in the long run we may judge President Roosevelt less by the successes or failures of his individ-

439

ual acts as by the new social outlook which he insisted upon, as we now do Wilson and Theodore Roosevelt. Perhaps we should not say a new outlook, for it is as old as the Christian religion, but we need at times some leader to bring us back from a rampant materialism. In practical measures the New Deal cannot be called a success. In fact, to a large extent its measures lie around it in ruins. Nevertheless, after the twelve years of crass materialism following as a reaction the abortive idealisms of the war, we needed to return to the search for a better social order.

By the end of 1935 scarcely any one could deny that the ordinary American citizen was taking a much keener, and, let us hope, a more intelligent interest in public affairs as contrasted with his private ones. As usual, however, a prolonged depression brought forward all sorts of quack schemes, and promises by leaders enjoying a temporary popularity of things impossible to perform. Among the more picturesque of these leaders for a time was U. S. Senator Huey Long, who succeeded in making himself practical dictator of the State of Louisiana, the only dictator of quite that sort we have yet had in the United States. His assassination on September 7, though deplored on account of the method of combating such an assumption of power, was generally accepted by the nation as fortunate. Both his rise and fall may have represented a passing phase of our political life or, more ominously, the beginning of a new era in our politics.

By Morris, George Matthew News Service

BUSINESS REACHES OUT FOR THE RECOVERY APPLE ATOP THE POLE,
WHILE THE BUGBEAR OF INFLATION SEEKS TO PULL HIM DOWN

The waning power and influence of Father Coughlin of
Detroit would seem, however, to mark a returning san-
ity. Toward the end of the year, on the other hand, the
Townsend plan to give every person over sixty at least
$200 a month provided the money were spent within

441

that time became regarded as possibly a dangerous political issue.

The year was also marked by the passing of two men
of typical American personality. On August 15, Will
Rogers, flying northward to Alaska with the aviator
Wiley Post, was killed by the plane crashing. Rogers,
who had begun a picturesque career as a cowboy, ending
as Hollywood actor and best known commentator on
world affairs, had endeared himself to the American
public by his quaint humor and piquant comments. He
left a large fortune, cleanly won, and a place in American life and humor not easy to fill. Naturally, writing
a daily article for the press, his wit occasionally ran thin
and his views were not shared by all his readers but he
was the friend not only of the mass of Americans but
of statesmen and others in high places, and like the
court jesters of old, he was privileged to make many a
shrewd thrust at shams, whether in private or public life
or international policies. Another man, of a different
type but who had filled a considerable place, was the
Reverend William Ashley (Billy) Sunday, the evan-
gelist, who died on November 6.

It is impossible to appraise the future value of the
advances in science made during the year but the possibilities are enormous. The lens cast for the new and
largest telescope yet made by man will enable astrono-
mers to see four times as far into the vast spaces of the
universe as has hitherto been possible. The telescope

itself has not yet been completed and no one can tell what results may follow. New methods of splitting atoms have been developed and new elements unknown to nature have been created as well as immense potential sources of energy. In the more immediate practical field perhaps the greatest advance, both for possible good and ill, was made in the field of aeronautics. The influence of air power rather than sea power undoubtedly was determining in certain European international complications, and the recognition of this fact will change the history of the next few years. In the Italo-Ethiopian war, the British navy, more than a match for the Italian, was stalemated in the Mediterranean partly by reason of the superior Italian air forces. History in the past two centuries has been largely determined by the "mistress of the seas," but in the future it appears it may be determined by whatever nation may be mistress of the air. The opening of a new and more horrible period of wars seemed to be indicated soon after the year closed in the placing by the British Government of an order for 30,000,000 gas masks to protect the population of the British Isles, no longer protected by the navy.

During the year the public was intensely interested in the trial of Bruno Hauptmann for the kidnapping and murder of the Lindbergh baby. He was finally condemned to death but the trial was marked by an almost incredible exhibition of sensationalism, and it has been estimated that some 400 newspapermen and scores of cameramen, telegraphers and radio reporters "covered" what should have been a solemn proceeding in the court at Flemington, New Jersey. Among decent people a good deal of resentment was aroused, which was much increased by the sudden forced flight of the Lindberghs to England to avoid further publicity and its dangers. There were threats against their second child, and although Lindbergh was perhaps the ideal of American youth, he and his wife had been unable to live the quiet home life, away from the constant blaze of the spotlight, which they had asked for and desired. They are both as fine types as our country can produce, and the fact that they had almost literally been driven from it to seek a more normal, quiet life in a foreign land bit deeply, for the time at least, into our American consciousness.

On the whole, however, America ended the year in a distinctly sounder condition than at the beginning. Business had improved; confidence had to a considerable, though far from complete, extent been restored; and many Americans at least had learned as a result of the experience of the preceding five years that quick easy money, bull markets and good tips are not all that is requisite for the good life. A saner and more wholesome atmosphere had replaced the feverish excitement of the pre-depression years and the extreme hopelessness of 1932.

CHAPTER XI

THE RECORD OF 1936

THE events of 1936, including the all-important one of the Presidential election in November, can best be treated in part chronologically and in part by topics. In this chapter we shall, for the most part, use the first method.

The new Congress convened on January 3 and for only the second time in the history of the country a President delivered his message in person and at night. Woodrow Wilson had done so on the evening of April 2, 1917, when he asked for the Declaration of War against Germany and felt that under the existing conditions not a moment was to be lost. Mr. Roosevelt's reason was different but of interest as showing the importance of the new force which has entered into the political life of our day, that of the radio. The Constitution provides that the President "shall from time to time give to Congress information of the state of the union." That is the origin of the "President's Message" as we call it. Between John Adams and Wilson every President had sent it to Congress in writing, but both of them had read it. The delivering it in person was thus not an innovation, but for

445

the first time it was arranged to have it broadcast to the entire nation, instead of merely being delivered to Congress, and Mr. Roosevelt chose the hour of nine P.M. as the best for broadcasting purposes.

The innovation is of importance because it would seem that the type of address intended to produce the greatest effect over the radio on citizens of every rank and sort would be different from that which would soberly present to the legislature that state of the nation which they have to take into consideration in drafting legislation. Many Congressmen felt that the President had in fact chosen the occasion of performing a constitutional duty to Congress to make, instead, a political speech to the nation. There was much protest, and the Chairman of the Republican National Committee, Henry P. Fletcher, demanded of the two leading broadcasting companies that they provide facilities and time on the air for an answer to be made by the opposing party. The incident, which had no other immediate result, brought out clearly the problem of radio technique in politics which caused trouble more than once in the course of the year.

The speech did seem to have been affected by the new audience for which it appeared to have been primarily intended, and was not in the best vein of the President. The passage in it which has been most quoted and which gave a genuine shock to many citizens was that in which the President said, speaking of his administration, that

446

"in thirty-four months we have built up new instruments of public power. In the hands of a people's government this power is wholesome and proper. But in the hands of political puppets of an economic autocracy such power would provide shackles for the liberties of the people." In a self-governing democracy, necessarily working through parties and periodic elections, it is obvious that those in power will be changed from time to time, and many even of those sympathetic with the aims of the President's New Deal asked themselves why it had been needful to build up such instruments of power as with a possible change of administration might, as he said, "shackle the liberties of the people"? Americans had generally understood that the system of government had provided such checks and balances that no one man or group of men temporarily in office could deprive the nation of its freedom. Although the statement did not lessen Mr. Roosevelt's popularity among the great mass of his followers it did undoubtedly deepen the mistrust with which his methods rather than his aims were to be regarded by a large body of conservative—not reactionary—opinion.

Meanwhile, the President had begun to liquidate the NRA, which, as we saw in the last chapter, had been declared unconstitutional by the Supreme Court in a 9–0 decision. Not only had the Court been unanimous but in a poll taken of more than 10,000 manufacturers 82% had voted against the revival of the NRA in any form.

447

On January 6 the President submitted the budget to Congress for the fiscal year 1936–37. Largely from the necessities of the case it was only a part of a budget and not a real forecast of expenses, although the nation was asked to raise $6,752,000,000. This did not take into account the enormous sum which might be needed for relief, and which could not yet be determined, though the President thought it would not run over $2,000,000,-000 more, of which he said he had $1,100,000,000 left from the previous year. Nor did it take into account what might happen if the AAA were declared invalid by the Court and from which the government expected to derive over $500,000,000. Nor again did it provide for any funds to pay the Bonus should it be voted.

The same day that these figures were submitted the Supreme Court did declare the AAA invalid by a vote of 6–3. In effect the Court stated that the Act was unconstitutional because it laid taxes, not for the general welfare as required, but for the benefit only of classes, groups or regions; and that it invaded the reserved powers of the States. Farming was not interstate commerce, and a Federal officer could not go to a farmer in a State and order him to cut down his crops, and what could not be done to him by force could neither be done by offering him money. Meanwhile, of course, contracts amounting to many hundreds of millions of dollars had been entered into with individual farmers, a considerable number of whom, as it later turned out, were getting

$10,000 and upwards for not raising crops, although the vast number were getting much less. Farmers themselves were more or less divided as to the effects of the ending of the AAA although probably the large majority wished to have the plan continued in some form. Professor Warren, the agricultural expert who had been consulted by the government, said, before the decision, that the farmers might find themselves better off without the Act just as the manufacturers did not regret the passing of the NRA with the emergency for which it had been designed. Nevertheless, the situation, which involved such vast numbers of people and huge sums, was chaotic as a result of the decision, and the President asked Congress for $200,000,000 to take care of the pressing demands. A new Act, known as the Soil Conservation Bill, was also hurriedly prepared, passed by Congress and signed by the President on March 1 in the hope that it might be more legal and at least take care of the emergency. At one time farmers had suggested "picketing" Congress until it provided the $280,000,000 due them and passed a new bill estimated to cost the people $500,000,000.

January was a bleak month for the Treasury. The same day that the just-mentioned item of news was carried by the papers there also appeared the request of the United States Conference of Mayors that Congress appropriate $2,340,000,000 for WPA relief; and that the Senate had agreed with the veterans' organizations for anticipating the payment of $2,491,000,000

449

bonds not due for some years. When Congress met no less than eight bonus bills had been offered, and the one finally agreed upon was passed by overwhelming majorities in spite of the protests of the Secretary of the Treasury. The President, who had not taken an active part in the opposition, vetoed the bill when sent to him but it was again passed by the necessary two-thirds vote and became law. Morgenthau estimated that by the end of the next fiscal year the government debt would have risen to an all time high of $36,500,000,000. Meantime, the President had asked for and received power for another year to again devalue the dollar.

The financial condition of the national finances brought clearly to the front the possibility of inflation, which had been largely discussed in relation to the Bonus. How inflation, and consequently lowered purchasing power of the dollar, might affect all charitable and educational institutions, as well as the ordinary citizen, was brought out clearly by Herbert Hoover in February, not as a politician but as a trustee of Leland Stanford University. The $24,000,000 endowment of that university, which had steadily grown without loss for fifty years, was by law invested in bonds and mortgages, but in case of serious inflation the purchasing power of the income would be greatly curtailed. Hoover on behalf of the university applied to the courts in California to allow the trustees to invest a portion of the funds in common stocks and real estate as a safeguard. To a large extent, the same worry as to future purchasing power of invested funds was felt by all trustees of colleges, hospitals and others having endowments invested in what had in the past been considered the safest form, just as individual investors had struggled with the problem.

In the same month, the government won a victory in the Supreme Court in the Tennessee Valley case, which was decided in its favor by a vote of 8 to 1. The scope of the decision, however, was very limited, as the Court said that it applied solely to the case then before it. That case involved only the Wilson Dam at Muscle Shoals, which had been built primarily for the purpose of manufacturing nitrates in the war with Germany. The Court ruled that as a by-product the government, *at that dam,* could sell its excess production of power. It did not rule, however, that the government could build dams anywhere for any purpose and sell unlimited power in competition with private companies. The question of whether the Federal Government could go into the power business, any more than the canning, clothing or other businesses, was not before the Court. The real problem of the validity of the greater TVA project was thus left unsettled. Meanwhile the President had asked Congress to repeal the Bankhead Cotton Act, the Kerr-Smith Tobacco Act, and the Potato Act, anticipating having them invalidated by the Court. Especially among the supporters of the New Deal, there had been much adverse comment on the Court's decisions, and it began to be thought that the question might be one of the leading ones in the fall campaign. The reaction of the people in general, however, as in the preceding year, appeared to be in favor of supporting the Court and retaining its powers unimpaired, although over forty bills were introduced into Congress to curb them in one way or another.

On the 10th of February the Court had handed down a unanimous decision of great importance. So far in this country we have had only one dictator, the late Huey Long, who was assassinated in September, 1935. Like all dictators he felt the need of controlling the public press, and his subservient legislature in Louisiana had passed a law giving him practical control over all newspapers in the state having a circulation of over 20,000. In a resounding decision the Supreme Court, when the case reached it, threw out the law, stating that "a free press stands as one of the great interpreters between the government and the people. To allow it to be fettered is to fetter ourselves." Long's dictatorship was only state-wide but if he had not been assassinated or had left a successor, the people of that sovereign State would have had no recourse against his tyranny except the Supreme Court. It is also natural that officials and legislators frequently become irritated by criticism, and the freedom of the press might some day get short shrift if it were not for the courts and their independence.

In connection with this topic we may note that in March the activities of the Senate Committee headed by

Senator Black received very severe comment. The Committee was ostensibly named for the purpose of investigating the utility industry lobby in Washington, but so wide was the dragnet thrown out that it was stated by responsible commentators and members of Congress that over 5,000,000 telegrams had been seized, a large part of them from organizations and individuals having no connection whatever with the avowed purpose of the investigation. In some cases injunctions were secured from courts to prevent this "prying" into private affairs. Senator Black is reported as saying that if any court should grant such an injunction Congress should immediately deprive the courts of such power. The question was left open as to whether, as *The Philadelphia Record* put it, "the specific right of the Senate to investigate denies the individual right of the citizen to immunity from reputed 'unreasonable searches and seizures'" as guaranteed to him in the Constitution.

In February two moves had been made in the sphere of foreign relations. The uncertain situation in Europe, much aggravated by the Italo-Ethiopian war, brought prominently before us again the problem of our neutrality. As noted in the last chapter a Neutrality Act had been passed in August, 1935, though admittedly imperfect. The problem, in fact, is of extreme complexity, and it may be questioned whether any law rather than wise diplomacy could keep us out of a general war. Many sincere and able thinkers, in Congress and out, who are

453

wholly opposed to war, still doubt that the making of hard-and-fast rules to apply to situations in the future, the intricacy of which cannot be foreseen, may not be more likely to involve us than to leave us free. However that may be, the Neutrality Act of 1935 was renewed for a year, with slight modifications. The President also sent out an invitation to the nations of South America for a meeting later in the year to consider joint problems, especially that of maintaining peace in at least the New World. The invitation, accepted, was to have happy results at a meeting in December which we shall note later.

Meanwhile, although the year was to witness a very marked revival in business it opened badly. On March 1, the American Federation of Labor reported that January had seen a drop of employment of nearly double that of the year before, and a despatch to *The New York Times* said that government payrolls were running at the rate of $11,000,000 a day. It estimated, counting government employees, those on various forms of relief, pensioners, war bonus beneficiaries and others, that by summer one-third of the entire population would be deriving the whole or a part of its support from the Federal Government. This unprecedented situation clearly held dangers of many sorts.

On March 3 the President in a special message to Congress urged the passage of a new tax law which may prove revolutionary in American business. In brief it relieved corporations of previous taxes bringing in approximately $1,000,000,000 and instead imposed a tax on a sliding scale of from 20 to 40% on undistributed corporation profits. It was considered that as the size of the tax made it practically imperative that corporations should annually pay to their stockholders all they earned during the year, the new tax, paid either by the corporations or the stockholders through their income tax, would bring in about $1,600,000,000. What the final results of this change may be cannot yet be determined, but there are a few points which seem clear. Many corporations, such as the American Telephone and others, have attempted in the past to maintain regular dividends. They have not paid out all their earnings in flush times, but have kept a reserve for the "rainy day." If they now have to pay out each year what is earned in that year, they will pay higher dividends in good years and smaller, if any, in bad ones. In other words, the irregularity of the stockholder's income will become much greater. He or she will have more to spend in good times and less in bad times than in the past, which would seem to tend to emphasize instead of to flatten out the economic curve. There are many other points to be considered but we here mention only two.

The other point is that if companies have to pay out every year what they earn that year, the income of the government will, like that of the individual, be subject to much more violent fluctuations than before. There will be a tendency on the part of both to live up to the income of boom years and be very surprised when there is little or no income in bad years.

In the same month, March, the President asked for another $1,500,000,000 to carry on relief work for another year. Counting the $8,570,000,000 for the years 1934, 1935 and 1936 this made over $10,000,000,000 and there was much discussion in Congress over relief methods, particularly the WPA, but the problem still remained unsettled at the end of the year.

In March and April two of the WPA projects which had come in for most criticism were both killed by Congress, the Florida Ship Canal and the Passamaquoddy project for harnessing the tides of the bay, after expenditures amounting to approximately $12,500,000.

An ominous item in the news for April was the announcement by *The National Tribune,* originally founded as the organ of the Grand Army of the Republic, that it would fight for a full pension system for all veterans of the World War, and asking the aid of the various veterans' associations, in spite of the fact that they have already received over $15,000,000,000. Considering the number involved, together with their possible wives and dependents, the cost in the future of any such system might well be as staggering as that of the Social Security Act. It may be noted that the veterans of earlier wars received no such bonus as did those of the last one, nor have we before had an old-age pension system available to all. The demand made was, though not then endorsed by the heads of the associations, that the three million or more veterans who served ninety days or more should form a select group in our population and receive pensions for disability, whether traceable to the war or not, and a special old-age pension over and above that paid to the citizens in general.

In May there was another adverse decision by the Supreme Court on the Guffey Coal Act. This had been considered by many unconstitutional when it was passed, as noted in a previous chapter, even the President having had his doubts. After the decision there was again talk of amendments to the Constitution, and it is interesting that the head of the American Federation of Labor, Mr. Green, although disappointed in the decision, hesitated about an amendment for fear lest it would "establish the autocratic power of Congress" to fix wages, establish hours of labor and perhaps destroy the right of collective bargaining. "In seeking a remedy," he said, "we do not want to propose something that in actual operation will be a restriction and limitation of the free use of our economic powers." That is a far-sighted view to take, but it might appear that if the Court had decided the Act constitutional the power of Congress which Mr. Green feared might come from an amendment would have been declared already to exist in the Constitution as it is. The Guffey Bill had been intended to set up a little NRA within the coal industry alone. There is no doubt that conditions are bad in that industry, and were so long before the depression, especially in the soft-coal fields. This situation is not confined to the United States but exists almost everywhere. The supply of soft coal is almost unlimited, and there is much competition with a large variation in the cost of production from one mine to another. On the other hand, the new forms of generating heat or power, such as gas, oil and electricity, have lessened the demand for soft coal. A rise in wages will mean a rise in price, and it is not unlikely that a rise in price would so cut down the market in competition with other fuels or powers as to reduce employment still further. The problem is one which no government has yet been able to solve satisfactorily, and this "sick industry" is nowhere more sick than in England, where Parliament has power to pass any legislation it wishes.

To complete the important decisions of the Supreme Court, we may note that in June it declared invalid the New York State Minimum Wage Law for women and children. With the exception of the National Women's Party, which expressed itself as "delighted" that women were free to compete on equal terms with men, the decision generally was received with regret. It was reached unfortunately by a majority of 5-4, though it should be observed that the oldest two members of the Court, Hughes and Brandeis, were both among the four who took the liberal and labor side. The Chief Justice was especially vigorous in its defence. Although it is necessary, he said in his Opinion, to preserve liberty of contract, "it is also necessary to prevent its abuse. . . . The test of validity is not artificial. It is whether the limitation upon the freedom of contract is arbitrary and capricious or one reasonably required in order appropriately to serve the public interest." He held that the law in question did this.

June was also notable for some huge figures in government finance, besides the political conventions to which we shall turn in a moment. On the 15th the Treasury delivered $1,600,000,000 in Bonus bonds and checks to about 3,000,000 veterans, and also announced financing of over $2,000,000,000. The former transaction, carried out through the Post Office, was the largest undertaking any such department in the world has ever been called upon to carry through. It was conducted admirably and the sudden inflow into the pockets of all sorts of persons of this huge sum produced no disorder of moment anywhere. On the same day the President signed a bill appropriating $272,000,000 for Mississippi flood control and a week later another flood-control appropriation of $320,000,000. He also signed a deficiency appropriation bill of $1,425,000,000 for relief, and on the 20th the Congress adjourned. It was the 74th Congress in our history and at its two sessions had made the record of $19,296,000,000 in appropriations and carried the national debt to almost $34,000,000,000. Just about a generation ago the country was aghast when a Congress, since called the "Billion Dollar Congress," appropriated that sum for the needs of government.

June has become the regular month for holding the national party conventions to nominate candidates and draft platforms. The Republicans met at Cleveland on the 9th and adopted their platform on the 11th. The gathering was notable for several reasons, among them being the fact that control had passed from the East to the Middle West. The "Old Guard" and former leaders had been almost completely ousted from power, and those in charge were mostly young in years or young in the political game.

After a detailed criticism of the Democratic administration, the platform proceeded to the specific pledges of the party if elected. Among others, it advocated a sound currency and opposed any further devaluation of the dollar; it promised to protect women and children with respect to maximum hours, minimum wages, and working conditions; it promised to balance the budget by cutting expenses; to repeal the reciprocal tariff laws; to provide old age pensions for those over sixty-five; and "to resist all attempts to impair the authority of the Supreme Court." There were also planks on agriculture and relief, which were rather vague. Governor Alf M. Landon (as he signs his first name), of Kansas was the chief candidate for leading place on the ticket, and before his name was placed before the convention he telegraphed from Topeka that he accepted the platform in full but

From a photograph by Underwood and Underwood.

POSTMEN LEAVING THE NEW YORK CITY POST OFFICE CARRYING THE BONUS CHECKS
TO WORLD WAR VETERANS

From a photograph by Acme Newspictures.

THE DELIVERY OF THE KEYNOTE ADDRESS OPENING THE REPUBLICAN CONVENTION IN CLEVELAND

wished to add to it so that those voting for him would know precisely where he stood. He clarified the platform as adopted by adding that if the laws for women and children could not be passed constitutionally he would favor a constitutional amendment; and that by "sound currency" he meant one convertible into gold, though not to be achieved until it could be done without injury to trade and agriculture. He also added that the civil service should be extended to every position below the rank of assistant secretaries of major departments and agencies, and that the inclusion should cover the entire Post Office department.

That evening he was unanimously nominated for President amidst the usual convention scenes. The young chairman of the party, John Hamilton, had failed in his effort to secure Senator Vandenberg for second place, the Senator declining anything but the first, and the followers of Colonel Frank Knox, a Chicago newspaper owner and editor, obtained the nomination for him. Mr. Roosevelt incurred considerable criticism from the fact that he chose the period of the Republican convention, which would ordinarily have provided the leading news, to make a speech-making tour of the West. Although he spoke to crowds in many cities he stated that the trip was "non-political."

June 23–27 the Democratic party held its convention at Philadelphia. For the first time in its history, the party abrogated the two-thirds rule and adopted, for that occasion only, majority rule in the choice of candidates. The South, which naturally opposed the change, was placated with the pledge that it would receive larger proportional representation in future conventions. It may be recalled that in 1912 Speaker Champ Clark had received a majority on eight ballots, but on account of the two-thirds rule lost the nomination when he could not climb higher, and it went to Woodrow Wilson when Bryan went over to him. The change in the rule at this convention must have been with an eye to the future, for there was no doubt that Roosevelt would be renominated, as he was by acclamation, together with Garner as running mate.

Postmaster Farley, acting as chairman, proclaimed that "the continuance of the New Deal is the issue," and this appeared in the platform, which had been first submitted to the President. It was a much longer document than the Republican one, and for the most part recited the changes and accomplishments under Roosevelt. Every group was promised something—the veterans continued "just treatment"; the farmers; labor; business; youth, and so on. There was much in the record of the New Deal which could be pointed to with pride. It had made successes and failures, and it was politically natural that the first should be stressed and the latter omitted. It was likewise natural that complete credit should be taken for the rise in commodity prices and increased business, though these were worldwide phenomena. The party further pledged itself to reduce the expenses of government and to extend the civil service. It also pledged itself to "maintain the letter and the spirit of the Constitution," and that if problems could not be settled within the Constitution to seek "clarifying" amendments to it. In addition, the platform pledged the party to a continued public-works program "at prevailing wages" to care for the unemployed.

For some time many of the leaders of the Democratic party had been opposed to the Roosevelt policies in many respects. Senator Tydings of Maryland, Senator Byrd of Virginia, Senator Carter Glass, former Senator James A. Reed, and former high officials such as Al Smith and Bainbridge Colby had sought to bring the party back to its earlier principles. During the convention Smith, Colby, Reed and others sent a message to the delegates but without effect. Some, like Smith, later bolted the party and came out for Landon, while others, like Glass, remained "regular" in so far as their vote was concerned but did not give Roosevelt support in the campaign.

Hard times always bring many radical and often foolish ideas into the political arena. Besides the regular parties, including the Socialist, which nominated Norman Thomas, and the Communist, which nominated Earl Browder, and which were expected to play their part in the election like the Democratic and Republican, there had been leaders of scattered groups whose real political strength with the electorate was uncertain. Father Coughlin, known as the "Radio Priest," claimed to have about 9,000,000 followers. There was also Doctor Townsend, whose old-age plan was thought to have won him a great following throughout the entire country in spite of the Congressional investigation into the finances of his organization, the results of which had alienated many. Again, there was the following of Huey Long and the late leader's Share Our Wealth Program. By the end of June these groups united, and the Rev. Gerald Smith, Long disciple, said in an address at Syracuse that "we are convinced that a Presidential candidate who will permit the Rev. Charles E. Coughlin to define his money plank—Doctor Townsend to define his old-age security plank—Gerald Smith to define his plank on labor, education and homesteads—the farmers' union to define their plank in agriculture—this man will be the next President of the United States." The man chosen to head this heterogeneous party was Representative William Lemke, and although most people disbelieved in the nine to twenty million votes promised for him by his followers, many did feel that the party might draw enough votes away from the New Deal to give the election to Landon. That even the Democrats were not too sure of their chances was shown by the desperate efforts to induce Governor Lehman of New York to withdraw his statement that he would not run again and to enter the race once more. The pressure brought to bear on him, and his final acceptance, were considered at the time to be indications that the Democrats felt they needed all the help they could get. In fact, in the early summer, the result of the November election was "anybody's guess," though the betting odds kept steadily in favor of Roosevelt.

Before considering the results we may turn to some of the events of the summer months. In June and July there was an exceptionally severe drought in the West and South. It did not prove as bad as that of 1934, although bad enough. In July the Department of Agriculture estimated the world wheat surplus at the lowest in nine years, and in August it was announced that the corn crop, the smallest in fifty years, would be 500,000,-000 bushels below the needs of our own people. The unexpected droughts of 1934 and 1936 indicate to some extent how difficult, if not impossible, long-range planning is in agriculture. Huge sums may be paid to farmers, facing presumed surpluses, to slaughter hogs and cattle or not to plant crops, only for the nation to find itself dependent on imported food. This does not mean that farmers should not receive assistance or that we should not attempt to solve the farm problem. It is merely an indication of how difficult that problem is. The drought also put the finishing touch to the projected great "shelter belt" of forest which had been started and which had been intended to stretch for about fifteen hundred miles north and south across the West and alter the climate. To make such an enormous forest grow in a semi-arid region would have required such an expenditure in care and watering, even when water could be obtained, as to make the scheme impracticable. Congress finally discarded it with Passamaquoddy and the Florida Canal.

In September the American Legion came out in favor of pensions for veterans' widows. We are still paying a few pensions to widows of men who fought in the War of 1812, which ended 121 years ago. The request may thus result in our paying pensions up to the year 2057 for World War widows.

The following month a step was taken, in the form of a tripartite agreement between Great Britain, France and the United States to further the stabilization of the foreign exchanges, and to that extent the rebuilding of foreign trade. Although no nation is as yet willing to stabilize its currency at any fixed ratio to gold, the step taken was of considerable importance as a milestone on the way.

In November came the Presidential election. Although as stated, the betting had kept steadily in favor of Roosevelt, in spite of fluctuating odds, and few people really doubted that he would win, the result was in many ways surprising. Out of the 45,812,155 votes cast Roosevelt received a plurality of 11,069,699, that is, 27,751,612 to Landon's 16,681,913. The minor parties, whose possible influence had been dreaded, almost disappeared. The Socialists received only a fraction of their vote of 1932; the Communists were negligible and in the great manu-

facturing State of New York received less than the 50,-
000 requisite to allow them to run a ticket in the next
election; while the Coughlin-Townsend party crumpled
ignominiously. It was a landslide for Roosevelt and a
great personal triumph.

As the contest may prove a turning point in our history we may analyze the results at some length. It is
impossible, of course, to discover the motives of the nearly
46,000,000 individual voters, but it is necessary to study
the results carefully in order to find as nearly as we can
what America wanted. In the first place we may note
that although the election *was* a landslide, every election
for the past twenty years has been one also, one way or
the other. That seems to be the way, since the war, that
our political contests go whichever side wins. Nor was
this last as great a landslide as others in our recent or
earlier history.

Two points tended to make it appear so in the newspapers and in the popular imagination. One was the
fact that Roosevelt piled up the largest majority in the
Electoral College since Monroe in 1820. This, however,
is very deceptive. It merely means that the majorities
in the several States fell in such a way geographically as
to give him a majority in all but two of the States. To
make the case clear we may note that a candidate could
receive a unanimous vote in the College, carrying every
single State, with a total majority in the whole nation
of only 48 votes provided that he had an ascertained

majority of one vote in each of the States. That is one of the peculiarities of our system of election. As a matter of fact Roosevelt received only 60.2 per cent of the vote cast for the leading two candidates in 1936 contrasted with Theodore Roosevelt's 60.02 in 1904; Harding's 63.8 in 1920; and Coolidge's 65.2 in 1924. These figures are altered somewhat, but not greatly, depending on votes cast for minor parties. They indicate, however, the comparative popularity of the two leading candidates and their avowed policies. Leaving out the geographical accident of the Electoral College result there was therefore nothing startling about the President's majority.

The other point about the landslide was the enormous Democratic majority piled up in Congress, but that has also to be analyzed if we wish to understand the possible shift in the desires of the nation. The Democratic tide has undoubtedly been flowing since 1930. The Democrats elected to Congress in that and the succeeding three elections to 1936 were 219, 313, 322, 334, which clearly marks a trend to be considered. However let us first turn to last year's election. It resulted in there being 334 Democrats to 89 Republicans in Congress. Owing to well-known factors connected with the Civil War and other matters, it is recognized that there is in the nation a special irreducible core of votes whatever happens or however the people may think as to current questions. That core is the 100 Democratic members of Congress from the South. The Democratic party always starts with these, which practically nothing can change. If we wish to consider shifts in public opinion, therefore, we have to eliminate this core of one hundred and take into consideration the remainder which is subject to alteration as public opinion alters. Considering the hundred as fixed, the ratio of free and alterable votes then stands at 234 to 89 in Congress. But after the Harding landslide in 1920 it stood at 300 Republicans to 132 Democrats, or taking out the fixed 100, 300 Republicans to 32 Democrats. In other words, both as regards the President and Congress, the landslide of 1936 was considerably less than that of 1920.

The above analysis is not made with the thought of trying to minimize the Democratic victory but merely with that of trying to understand it and to see it in perspective. We have also to consider that from one-quarter to a third of the people were receiving in one way and another help from the administration. While undoubtedly many of these voted from conviction and not, as the saying is, "from their pocketbooks," it is also, I think, unquestionable that many of these beneficiaries and of the unprecedented number of officeholders would naturally vote as their personal interest seemed to dictate. Moreover, as we shall note presently, business had been steadily getting better during the latter part of the year, before election, and it is a fundamental fact in American politics that just as no President can survive a crash so also his popularity rises if business does also.

Aside from other points which might be considered, we may mention only one other fact. As I have frequently pointed out, there has been from the beginning a rhythm in our national life. That there have been many evils in our *laissez-faire* system is unquestionable. Over a period of years they accumulate and fester in the body politic as poisons might in our own bodies. About once a generation there has resulted an uprising politically of the ordinary man, such uprisings usually coinciding with the regular depressions in the economic cycle. Thus we had the rising under Jefferson in 1800, under Jackson in 1828, Lincoln 1860 and Bryan 1896. Under any conditions we were due for another in the 1920's which I believe was merely postponed by the specious prosperity of the latter part of that decade, and which came with the crash.

Considering everything noted above, I would think that the election of 1936 was a normal incident in our national life in so far as its majorities and psychology are concerned. Looking at it in that light, however, we have also to consider the increasing complexity of our civilization, and the general instability of the world order, combined with the urge toward dictatorships and getting things done quickly regardless of retaining personal liberties. The periodic overturns in the past have all made for increased health in the nation. Essentially I believe that the Roosevelt administration and popularity conforms to type, and that the election indicated, after making all allowances for other factors, that the people are insistent, as on previous like occasions, on securing a greater and more direct voice in managing their affairs in all spheres and on getting a fairer deal in the division of the social product. The problem is whether in the present state of the world we can maintain the gains and consolidate them without attempting to go so far and so fast, that like some other nations we may be lured by the marsh light of a seeming security and better order based primarily on loss of freedom.

Throughout the latter part, especially, of the year, business, as stated above, rapidly improved with us as it did with many other nations. It became generally recognized, here and abroad, that the low point of the depression had been touched in 1932 in spite of the financial crisis of the following year. Measured by almost any standard, such as stock and commodity prices, national income, spending, and so on, the United States appeared definitely out of the depression before the end of 1936. Although more severe, it had lasted about as long as that of 1873–79. Indeed so rapid was the advance that action had to be taken to prevent inflation of credit and runaway markets. In the autumn the reserve requirements of the banks were raised by 50 per cent, and later the gold pouring in from abroad became a cause of anxiety, and steps were taken to "sterilize" it as far as forming the basis of new credits was concerned. There was, however, one disturbing factor, the persistence of unemployment. In spite of the long depression and the immense importance in financial and human terms of the unemployment problem it seems strange that, unlike some other countries, we have not as yet developed a national census of the unemployed. We have to rely on the very widely varying figures compiled by the Department of Labor, which usually minimizes the number, those of the American Federation of Labor, and others. The uncertainty is shown by the statement of Mr. Hopkins, the WPA Administrator, in the middle of November that the number was somewhere between eight and eleven millions! It was at least evident that with all the billions spent comparatively little impression had been made on this very human problem. There were various reasons for this. Undoubtedly, judging from cases under my own observation and from what is reported generally, although perhaps the great majority of those on relief or on WPA jobs remain only so long as they cannot secure jobs in private enterprise, great numbers also prefer not taking them when offered. But perhaps the chief obstacle encountered has been the fear on the part of business and investors to risk money in enlargement of plant, renewals or in new enterprises. In the first quarter of the year, for example, although securities were issued to the extent of about a billion of dollars, they were practically all to refund at lower interest rates former securities outstanding, and of the billion only about $75,000,000 could be considered as making jobs.

The great bulk of savings in this country is made by people of comfortable but moderate circumstances, whether they put their money in savings banks, life-insurance policies, annuities or securities direct. Compared with this great mass of savings, made up of the modest sums put aside by millions of ordinary people for their rainy day or old age, the accumulation of additional capital by the few of great wealth is a mere drop in the bucket. The constant uncertainty as to the future, the passage of new laws hampering business or laying heavy burdens on it, such as the tax on surpluses, the fear of eventual inflation, and so on, tend to make these people fearful of taking any risks with their hard-earned savings, as is partly testified to by the very low interest rates they are willing to accept on "seasoned" investments. There is probably also a larger amount of idle cash in banks awaiting investment today than ever before in the history of the country, earning nothing and making no jobs. There are only two ways to tap this vast reservoir of jobs, one of which is, so to say, no way. If confidence is restored, this money will flow into new business enterprises or the extension of old. That is one way. A man who has saved a thousand dollars cannot be forced to put it into this enterprise or that against his will and judgment. The other way, which is no way, is confiscation, under the guise of taxation or undisguised. But this means that savings will immediately stop. The man who denies himself for the sake of the future of himself or

473

his wife and children will not continue to do so if the government simply takes away his savings. At the close of the year the great problem was unemployment with its incalculable waste in human morale, and its waste of billions of dollars; and the key to the unemployment problem was confidence and the consequent flow of capital again into business enterprise instead of stockings.

The year was also marked by great disturbance in the ranks of labor. The Pacific dock strike which had hung over from the previous year, was settled early in the present one, but there were many others throughout the country, including, besides those at manufacturing plants, the strike of the elevator men in New York City which resulted in much suffering and discomfort, with some violence. The "sit-down" form of strike appeared in the troubles at the Firestone Tire and Rubber Company in January, and the next month there was an attempted general strike in Pekin, Illinois, the fourth time only that this has been tried in America. In September a dock strike started again on the Pacific coast, spread to the Atlantic, and in the months during which it lasted was said to have cost the country about $500,-000,000. In December the strike at the General Motors plants began, but its story belongs rather to 1937. Aside from these and other strikes, however, the main fact of great importance for labor in 1936 was the split between Lewis of the United Mine Workers, who formed the C. I. O., and the American Federation of Labor under

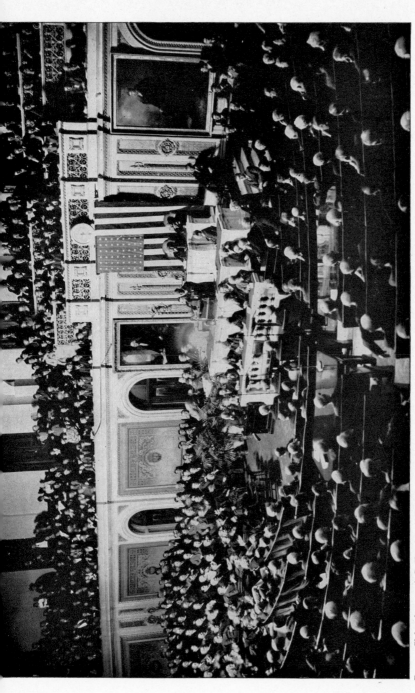

From a Globe photograph © Harris and Ewing.

ON JANUARY 3, 1936, AT NINE O'CLOCK IN THE EVENING, PRESIDENT ROOSEVELT'S MESSAGE TO
CONGRESS WAS BROADCAST TO THE NATION

From a photograph by Acme Newspictures, Inc.

ROOSEVELT'S TRIP TO THE ARGENTINE, FOR THE PAN-AMERICAN PEACE CONFERENCE, WAS HAILED BY ALL.

Green. Lewis, who wished to organize all of the workers in each industry into one big union to deal with the industry as a whole, was much more radical and aggressive in his theory and practice than Green. He fostered the sit-down strike and appeared to have little respect for the forms of law. Should he win it appeared that he might become one of the most powerful figures in the nation. In the November election he threw his whole influence on the side of Roosevelt and aided him largely in money and votes, particularly in the mining and normally Republican State of Pennsylvania. In fact so great was the assistance given that it was later to embarrass the President in spite of the semi-alliance that was built up between them. The year ended with the quarrel between the A. F. of L. and the new C. I. O. at its bitterest. Lewis seems to be honestly convinced of his mission, but the danger of his plans and methods may be no less on that account.

Soon after the election in November, President Roosevelt sailed for the Argentine, stopping in Brazil and Uruguay on the way, to act temporarily as head of the Conference of American Republics which he had called earlier in the year. The election had given him great prestige throughout the world, and in the weeks succeeding he had spoken much of the need of "making democracy work." In view of the almost universal menace of dictatorships to government by the people themselves, the President appeared in the rôle of the head of

475

one of the very greatest nations of all standing firm for the democratic and popular form of government as opposed to the autocratic. It was as such that he was received in South America, and in Buenos Aires the cheers of the populace, who gave him an enthusiastic welcome, were raised even more to "Democracy" than to the "President." It seemed as though freedom over all the earth took new heart. The meeting itself, in which the able American Secretary of State, Cordell Hull, took a leading part after the President left, was a distinct success. The better feeling between North and South America which had been fostered at Montevideo in 1933 was much increased, and machinery was set up for insuring as far as possible peace between the nations of the New World, all of which felt themselves menaced by the uncertain situation of the Old. While the primary undertaking was to avoid difficulties from arising between any of the nations of the western hemisphere, the same machinery is intended to be used in the case of a war starting in Europe which might menace the peace of the Americas. It was a cheering note on which to end a very mixed year marked by distinct improvement in business, a great natural disaster, labor troubles, and a national election which, although bitter feelings were involved, was one of the most orderly ever carried out in America. Many questions, however, particularly perhaps those of the Supreme Court and the Constitution, loomed for the year to come.

CHAPTER XII

THE RECORD OF 1937

THE YEAR 1937, with its episodes and contrasts, was one of the most dramatic and important which we have had to record and discuss. The constitutional controversy over the President's unexpected plan for changing the Supreme Court would alone have distinguished it among the important years in our history, but there were also unusual labor troubles, international complications, and the contrast between the prosperity with which it began and the deep economic gloom and anxiety in which it ended. The major topics with which we have to deal are politics (with the story of the Court including its decisions interwoven); labor conditions; the international situation; and business.

Congress, the 75th, met on January 3. It was overwhelmingly Democratic, there being 76 Democrats out of a total membership in the Senate of 96, and 334 in the House out of a total of 435. But the very size of the majority made it unwieldy, and because the party was to become hopelessly divided, the entire year was to prove singularly lacking in the enactment of any major Administration policies.

The President read his Message in person to the joint session of the two Houses, announcing, among other

477

points, that the nation had kept out of war in spite of provocations which in earlier times might have brought it on but that there was need for stronger national defence; that the permanent ordinary expenses of government could not in future be cut much below $7,000,000,-000 a year; and that labor must co-operate with capital because "the organization of thousands of workers creates a heavy obligation of public service" just as does the ownership of great properties and enterprises. According to the newspapers the President appeared in happy mood, the legislative year started auspiciously against a cheerful background of improving business and rising earnings and employment.

The following day the Supreme Court unanimously reversed the conviction and seven-year jail sentence of an Oregon Communist, asserting that the right of peaceable assembly was as fundamental as those of free speech and press. The decision, unanimous as it was, may be noted because in the controversy which later was to rage around the Court it was often ignored that the Court is the final guardian of individual liberty against the possible tyranny of local laws or local court decisions due to the passions of the place and moment.

On the 6th, Mr. Roosevelt again addressed Congress in a speech which was perhaps one of the most restrained and conciliatory in his career. He claimed, reasonably, that the main objectives of the New Deal were still seen to be desirable but that the NRA had failed because too

much had been attempted all at once; that it was to the interest of the nation to help business attain higher and
sound price levels; that we should develop intelligently a
social-security system; that the administrative machinery
needed overhauling; and that "means must be found to
adapt our legal forms and our judicial action into closer
harmony," although we "do not ask the courts to bring
non-existent powers into being." He also looked forward,
he said, to close co-operation with Congress on the basis of
"mutual respect for each other's proper sphere of functioning in a democracy." The address was extremely well
received throughout the country and press, and even such
a bitterly hostile anti-Administration paper as *The New
York Herald Tribune* praised it highly.

On the 8th in another Message, the President reported
on the budget situation. After saying that the programs
inaugurated to combat depression had been very costly
but worth-while, he stated that "we shall soon be reaping
the full benefits" and "shall have a balanced budget that
will also include provision for the reduction of the public
debt." It was indicated that the rise in government debt
would be stopped at the figure of $35,000,000,000, but
even at that figure the Federal debt (not counting the
huge amounts of state and other local debts) was $270
per capita, including all those on relief, as compared with
about $13 per capita in 1916, and $130 in 1930. Even to
attain partial balancing, the President counted on a large
decrease in relief and an increase in Federal income from

$4,000,000,000 to $7,000,000,000. But perhaps the most alarming feature was that he considered the necessary cost of government permanently stabilized at over $7,-000,000,000 though all during the post-war period up to the crash it had been only somewhat over half that figure. Fear of inflation and higher living costs was not lessened by the action of Congress on the 19th in extending the power of the President to June 30, 1939, to further devalue the dollar to 50 cents and to use the $2,000,000,000 fund, resulting from the previous devaluation, solely at his own discretion and that of his appointee, the Secretary of the Treasury.

The next day, in a downpour of rain, the President was inaugurated for the second time, being the first Chief Executive to have his term begin on January 20 instead of March 4 in accordance with the "lame duck" amendment to the Constitution.

The Inaugural Address contained no detailed outline of policies to be pursued but was rather a generalized expression of the President's political creed and humanitarian aspirations. He spoke of "one-third of a nation ill-housed, ill-clad, ill-nourished," and of what he hoped to do for them. He also stressed the need for additional power, stating that in a democracy safety depended not "upon the absence of power but upon lodging it with those whom the people can change or continue." A week earlier he had presented a plan to Congress for the reorganization of the government, which included placing all the 105 independent or semi-independent Boards, Commissions and so forth, such as the Interstate Commerce Commission and others, directly under control of the Executive, who was also to have six confidential assistants. The plan startled Washington because of the great increase and concentration of powers in the hands of the President, who had already been granted vaster powers than any other President, certainly in peace times, had ever dreamed of. The minds of many went back to Mr. Roosevelt's own words in his Inaugural Address of only a year before when he said that "in thirty-four months we have built up new instruments of public power" which in wrong hands "would provide shackles for the liberty of the people." Every one had long recognized the need for reorganizing the governmental machinery, which under Roosevelt had assumed a vastness and complexity unknown before, but although prompt passage of the Bill was asked it was evident that debate would largely center about the advisability of so greatly enlarging the power of the Executive, already overshadowing that of the Legislature. It is possible, however, that the President might have had his way, with some modifications, had it not been for the bombshell which he exploded little more than two weeks after his inauguration.

On the morning of Friday, February 4, the usual morning for his weekly press conference, the President called an emergency meeting of the Cabinet shortly after ten o'clock, and among those present were also included the chairmen of the House and Senate Judiciary Committees. What transpired is not known, but it appears that then for the first time the Cabinet was made acquainted with the President's Court plan. When the representatives of the press were admitted, a half hour later, the President read to them the message which he was sending to Congress. He then sent the Message, together with a letter from the Attorney General, Cummings, and a bill for the reorganization of the Judiciary, to the Capitol. Few, if any, bills submitted have so suddenly thrown the nation into turmoil and heated discussion. It provided for the addition of fifty Federal judges in the lower courts, for the speeding up of decisions and various other minor matters, but the chief point, one quickly realized by Congress and the country, was the section which permitted an increase in the membership of the Supreme Court, fixed at nine, to a maximum of fifteen if judges reaching the age of 70 did not care to resign. In that case the President was empowered to appoint one new judge for each over that age sitting on the Bench, of whom there were six, including the oldest and perhaps most liberal of all, Justice Brandeis. Leaving out the side issues it was at once recognized that if the bill were passed a President might pack the Court by placing six judges in it whose favorable opinions he could reasonably count upon. The nation was stunned by both the suddenness and the secrecy of the move. Apparently Roosevelt had consulted only three persons, the Attorney General, and two others guessed at but unnamed. Neither his official advisers, the members of the Cabinet, nor the leaders of his party in Congress had been approached. Roosevelt had not hinted at the measure during the campaign the preceding fall, and in fact the Party Platform had promised that legislation would be "within the letter and the spirit of the Constitution," and that if legislation not lying within these was desired an amendment to the Constitution would be sought.

Up to the November election the Supreme Court had been called upon to decide on the constitutionality of thirteen laws enacted by the New Deal. It may be noted here that the Court has no power to "veto," as it has been said, acts of Congress. It can only pass on the legal questions involved in certain kinds of cases which are permitted to reach it, and in doing so it has to decide, like any other court, whether the plaintiff or defendant has the law on his side. With our forty-eight state legislatures and the Federal Congress grinding out thousands of laws annually, the vast majority of cases before the Supreme Court do not involve constitutional questions or the validity of any Act of Congress. But it is stated in the Constitution (Art. VI, 1) that "this Constitution and the laws of the United States which shall be made in pursuance thereof and all treaties made, or which shall be made, . . . shall be the supreme law of the land, and the judges in every State shall be bound thereby, anything in the Constitution or laws of any State to the contrary notwithstanding." As it is thus clear that the Constitution is the "supreme law of the land" it is evident that the Supreme Court, like others, if a plaintiff claims that some particular law is not in harmony with the supreme law, must decide whether it is or not. Such cases, however, are usually very rare, and in its whole history, dealing with thousands of cases, the Court had declared only 77 laws to be unconstitutional, although Presidents had vetoed over 1100 acts of Congress.

During the Roosevelt administration, however, up to November 1936 when he was re-elected, the Court had been called upon to decide on the constitutionality of laws thirteen times, and in eleven had decided adversely, though only twice, in less important cases, by a five-to-four vote. In the three cases before it after election it had decided favorably. There had been much talk about the number of adverse decisions and the reason for them—whether the Court was out of touch with the times, whether the members were too old (although, as has been noted, Brandeis was both the oldest and most liberal), and what to do about it. Many thought that the reason was the hasty and careless way in which many of the laws had been drawn, or that in reality we were trying to legislate in ways not permitted by the Constitution. The overwhelming vote against some of the laws, such as the NRA, the first and second AAA cases and others, in which the poll of the Court showed 9–0 in five cases, 8–0 in two, 8–1 in two, and so on, would indicate that if we desired to keep the Constitution and the legislation both

From a photograph © by Harris & Ewing

ON OCTOBER 2, 1937, PRESIDENT ROOSEVELT INSPECTED THE GRAND COULEE DAM

Work is being rushed day and night to complete this power and irrigation project, the largest ever undertaken. It will provide power for homes and farms of the Pacific Northwest and will irrigate the arid Columbia River Basin.

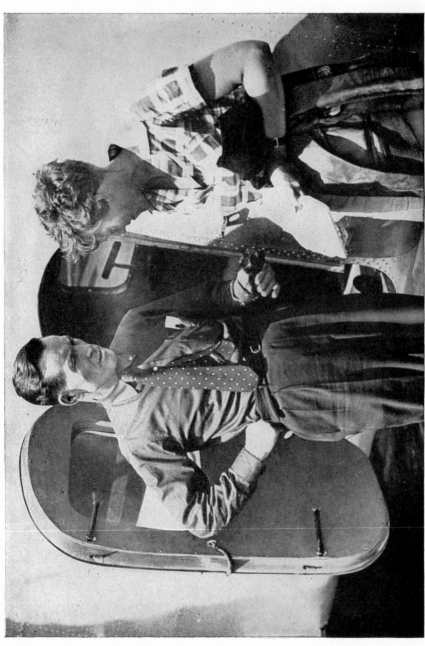

From a photograph by Wide World Photos, Inc.

ON THEIR LAST FLIGHT

Amelia Earhart and her co-pilot, Captain Frederick J. Noonan, at San Juan, P. R.,

we should have to amend the former or perhaps draw the laws more carefully. Discussion over the President's proposal raged until June in Congress and throughout the country.

The only immediate legislative effect of the President's Court message was the passage in the House, later also in the Senate, of a bill permitting the Justices to retire, if they so desired, on full pay when reaching seventy years of age. But, what was much more important, it was evident that the proposal to enlarge the Court had split both the country and the Democratic party wide open, and engendered an amount of bitterness which was to wreck the President's program. The question was recognized to be non-partisan, fundamental, constitutional, and party lines were ignored, such leading Democratic Senators as Burke of Nebraska, Byrd and Glass of Virginia, Clark of Missouri, Connally of Texas, King of Utah, Van Nuys of Indiana and Wheeler of Montana, swinging into line at once against the President and leading the fight which he was to lose. The Republicans refrained from taking any party stand, and the question was fought out in a great national debate without the contamination of party politics.

Before temporarily passing from this topic we may note that a Supreme Court with power of judicial review is not a peculiarity of our American system, as sometimes claimed. There are Supreme Courts, with similar functions, in all the British Dominions—Canada, Australia and the others—and a committee of the Privy Council in

England acts in the same way for the entire Empire. Such a body is imperative in any country or federal group having written constitutions. There must be some court of last resort able to determine whether particular legislation is in accord with the basic law.

On March 29, the Supreme Court handed down three important decisions in favor of the Administration, the same number it had so given before the controversy had started. In a 9-0 vote it ruled that the Federal government, in the Railway Labor Act, had authority to regulate industrial relations of a carrier engaged in *interstate* business. The earlier 9-0 decision against the NRA had been based on the ground that it could not regulate *intrastate* business, and the unanimous decision in each case made it clear the problem was not that of the age or conservatism of certain possible judges but of the nature of our federal government with its dual relationship between national and state powers and rights. Another decision upheld a revised Farm Mortgage Moratorium Law. The earlier one, which had been very hastily and carelessly drawn—even the President had said it was "loosely worded"—had been declared unconstitutional in 1935. Had it been properly drawn in the first place it would have been accepted then. In the third case, the Court to a considerable extent reversed its own opinion of fourteen years earlier, although the point it had to pass on was in some respects different. This was the New York State Minimum Wage Law. The Court agreed that a state has

486

the constitutional right to deal with the problem of minimum wages, and so obliterated the "no man's land" which the President had complained of as belonging to the jurisdiction of neither the state nor Federal governments. In all, the government had had seven favorable decisions since the election.

On April 29 both houses of Congress passed the Neutrality Bill, which had been opposed by such high authorities in international law as John Bassett Moore and others as being much more likely to get us into a war than to keep us out, however pacific the intention of the framers might be, and to give the Executive such new powers to undertake measures which would be considered "coercive" internationally as largely to transfer the real power to bring on war from Congress to the President.

Meanwhile the Supreme Court had handed down another decision favorable to the Administration in upholding the Wagner Act in four cases which had come before it, and the President had signed the Vincent-Guffey Coal Bill designed to set up a sort of little NRA in soft-coal mining, putting the industry under Federal regulation and heavily taxing such mine owners as might refuse to accept the code prescribed. In May the Supreme Court upheld the Louisiana Chain Store Act basing the tax levied not on the number of stores in a state but in the entire national chain, and later in the month approved the Social Security Act affecting over 26,000,000 workers and 2,-700,000 employers.

487

Meanwhile, owing to the Supreme Court debate and the increasing mistrust and animosity engendered in many members of Congress, that body had been making no progress in passing any of the Administration measures. In especial, the President's bill for the reorganization of the government departments was severely criticized in the light of his attack on the Supreme Court. It was pointed out by Senator Byrd (Democrat) who was chairman of the Senate Committee to draft a plan of reorganization, the independent Brookings Institution, and others that the President's plan would give immense added powers to the Executive and reduce those of Congress. Among other points the bill would have enabled the President (any President, it must be remembered and not simply Mr. Roosevelt) to alter a large part of the government at will and whenever he chose without consulting Congress. It was also felt by many that the diminished powers of the independent Comptroller General's office might much reduce the control of Congress over the purse strings, and the changing attitude of that body was indicated in the difficulty the President had in securing a $1,500,000,000 appropriation for relief to be expended at his sole discretion.

Two other points tended to increase the restiveness of many who had favored the relief and expenditure policies which the Administration had been pursuing during the depression. The nation appeared to have definitely emerged from that condition. Business was prospering, yet the number of persons on the government payroll was increasing. According to the Civil Service Commission's figures these numbered 824,259 (not counting those in the CCC, or persons on relief), as compared with 719,440 the preceding year and only 583,196 in 1932. If we add the legislative, judicial and military departments (but not the CCC nor those on relief), we had on April 1, over 1,-100,000 in government jobs, a figure never equalled before save in the World War.

Moreover the government debt was approaching an all-time high of $35,000,000,000. The theory of government spending in bad times to replace the decrease in private expenditure had been adopted by the Administration from the ideas of the English economist, John Maynard Keynes, but it had been a very essential part of his theory that as business improved the government should lessen expenditure, reduce its debt, and so restore its credit and resources to be used on some other occasion. This was not being done.

We may now come back to the dispute over the President's plan for changing the Court, which was rending the country. Few public questions in the past generation have caused so much discussion or aroused so much interest and passion. It was everywhere discussed in conversation, the press, on the air, while the Judiciary Committee of the Senate held public hearings for many weeks at which appeared scores of some of the best-known men and women in the nation, in favor of or opposed to the plan.

We need not here reopen the discussion, but in the course of it certain facts emerged. For example, the statement made by Justices Hughes, Brandeis and Van Devanter, at the request of the Committee, disproved completely the claim that the Court was behind in its work. Every case before it either had been, or would be, disposed of before the end of the term. Some of the congestion in some of the lower Federal courts was elsewhere shown to be due in part to the failure of the President to appoint judges to eight existing vacancies. Others, again, pointed to the danger of the government being able to send judges into certain courts and so perhaps influence such courts in its favor. Moreover, if one administration could appoint six judges to change the policy of the Supreme Court, other administrations could do the same, and the Supreme Court could thus be made completely subservient to the Executive and the Congress. It was pointed out that if the Court could be packed so as to alter parts of the Constitution none of it might be safe, and personal liberties, such as freedom of speech, religion and the press, might also be altered by some later administration hostile to them. The claim made that the right of the Court to "veto" legislation by Congress had been three times voted down in the Constitutional Convention of 1787 and that therefore it had no right to pass on the constitutionality of laws was shown to be an historical error. What had happened in the Convention was that it had been decided that the members of the Court should not be allowed to have a concurrent vote with the President because if this were done it would allow them not only to pass on the *constitutionality* of legislation, which it was expected as judges they would have to do, but also on the *policy* of legislation, which would properly be within the province of the Executive and not the Judicial department of government.

Meanwhile, a vacancy was created on the Bench by the resignation, May 18, of Justice Van Devanter, and the President thus had a chance to appoint a judge. Mr. Roosevelt had also come out bitterly against the Court, making support of his plan a test of party loyalty, and Mr. Farley had openly warned those members of Congress who opposed the plan that the party would not tolerate bolting.

Every aspect of the matter had been threshed out in the public discussions and before the Senate Committee in open hearings, when on June 14 the Committee gave its Report to the Senate, with a summary at the end which, in view of the great historical importance of the constitutional controversy, may be quoted in full. The Senate Committee had numbered eighteen, of whom five-sixths were Democrats, and the Majority Report was signed by ten, of whom seven were not only Democrats but had voted for practically every major policy of Roosevelt during their terms, except this issue of the Court. The Report stated that:

> We recommend the rejection of this bill as a needless, futile, utterly dangerous abandonment of constitutional principle.

It was presented to the Congress in a most intricate form and for reasons that obscured its real purpose.

It would not banish age from the bench nor abolish divided decisions.

It would not affect the power of any court to hold laws unconstitutional nor withdraw from any judge the power to issue injunctions.

It would not reduce the expense of litigation nor speed the decision of cases.

It is a proposal without precedent and without justification.

It would subjugate the courts to the will of Congress and the President and thereby destroy the independence of the judiciary, the only certain shield of individual rights.

It contains the germ of a system of centralized administration of law that would enable an executive so minded to send his judges into every judicial district in the land to sit in judgment on controversies between the Government and the citizen.

It points the way to the evasion of the Constitution and establishes the method whereby the people may be deprived of their right to pass upon all amendments of the fundamental law.

It stands now before the country, acknowledged by its proponents as a plan to force judicial interpretation of the Constitution, a proposal that violates every sacred tradition of American democracy.

Under the form of the Constitution it seeks to do that which is unconstitutional.

Its ultimate operation would be to make this Government one of men rather than one of law, and its practical operation would be to make the Constitution what the executive or legislative branches of the Government choose to say it is—an interpretation to be changed with each change of administration.

It is a measure which should be so emphatically rejected that its parallel will never again be presented to the free representatives of the free people of America.

The names of the Democratic Senators who by signing the Report took their political lives in their hand to save the constitution were King, Van Nuys, McCarran, Hatch, Burke, Connally and O'Mahoney.

Although the Judiciary Committee had thus reported adversely, the debate had to continue until a final vote might be taken. It was thought that it might be close and there was intense excitement. On July 13, Representative Sumners, chairman of the Judiciary Committee of the House, Texas Democrat and ordinarily a Roosevelt supporter, strongly denounced the measure. On the 14th Senator Robinson, Democratic leader of the Senate, and trusted lieutenant of the President, died suddenly, and the situation became more confused. On the 20th Lehman, Democratic Governor of New York and one of the President's strongest supporters, came out against the Court plan, but Roosevelt still insisted on a fight to the finish. On July 21, the vote in the Senate was taken, the administration leaders admitted complete defeat, and the bill was killed by a vote of 70–20, the 70 including 53 Democrats, and only 16 Republicans with one Farmer-Laborite. Amid cheering galleries the bill was sent back to the hostile Committee and permanently killed. Another court bill, drafted by the Committee, but having nothing to do with the Supreme Court and dealing only with certain minor improvements in the lower courts, was later passed and signed by the President. The last matter concerning the Supreme Court at this momentous session was the nomination by the President and confirmation by the Senate, 63–16, of Senator Hugo Black of Alabama to fill the vacant seat on the bench. Questions were raised as to Black's fitness for the post and especially as to his possible connection with the Ku Klux Klan but the Senate was assured that he had no such connection.

On August 21 Congress adjourned after, in some respects, one of the most remarkable records in our history. Notwithstanding the enormous popular majority given to the President in the election of the previous year, and the great majority of his party in Congress, not a single one of the major measures urged by him was passed. These, which were to build up a new New Deal or round out the old one, were five in number, namely those for reorganizing the government departments; the Supreme Court Bill; an Act embodying Wallace's plan for an "ever normal granary" as aid to the farmers; the Black-Connery Wages and Hours proposal; and one expanding the TVA idea to seven regional planning areas throughout the country. The measures which Congress did pass were not of the "must" sort, and included a housing Act; the amended Neutrality Act; and a few others. Meanwhile, the government debt had again climbed to a new high of $37,000,000,000.

On October 12 Mr. Roosevelt issued a call for Congress to assemble in special session on November 15, announcing over the radio to the nation that he wanted quick passage of bills providing for wages and hours regulation; the curbing of trusts; crop control; regional planning; and his government reorganization measure. Al-

494

though Congress met and remained in session until the end of the year, again not a single one of these measures was passed.

Meanwhile a sensation had been caused throughout the country by the publication of a series of articles in *The Pittsburgh Post-Gazette* purporting to show by reproduction of documentary evidence that Black had been a member of the Klan, resigned but had again become a member, and was so when placed on the Supreme Court. Black, who was in England, refused to affirm or deny anything, and finally sailed for home on a small steamer to Norfolk, Va. After arrival Justice Black admitted in a nation-wide broadcast, that he had at one time been a member of the Klan but that he knew nothing of the later membership card issued to him. It also transpired that instead of taking the oath of office before the Chief Justice when taking his seat, he had taken it secretly, though legally, before a minor official prior to his sailing for Europe in the summer.

The period under review was also a very disturbed one in the field of labor relations. Throughout the year the inter-labor split between the American Federation, with Green at its head, and Lewis's CIO continued unabated and with increasing bitterness. During the motor strike at Flint in January, Lewis startled the country by openly calling upon the President to side with the CIO and thus repay the campaign debt which he owed that organization both for its voting support and cash advanced.

495

Among other things, the Miners' Union had loaned the Democratic National Committee $50,000, but the country felt that it had been insulted by Lewis's crude demand upon the President.

Although Mr. Roosevelt issued a reply that was a scarcely concealed rebuke to Lewis, nevertheless it seemed to be the case that the Department of Labor was rather strongly during the year taking sides with Lewis against both the American Federation and employer concerns. One of the features of the labor disturbances during the year was the great increase in sit-down strikes, in which a comparatively few men by taking possession of a plant could stop operations. The method was entirely different from peaceful picketing outside a plant. Miss Perkins, the Secretary of Labor, without consulting the President or Cabinet, took the unprecedented step on her own initiative of asking Congress to give her Department the power to subpœna witnesses of either labor or capital to Washington to state the causes of disagreement, a demand which, partly from the extraordinary way in which it was made, met with no response. When her attention was called to the dangerous method of the sit-down strikes, which had been largely used by Communists in France in the preceding year, she merely remarked that it had not yet been decided whether they were illegal. In February, however, Judge Gadola in a decision enjoining the strikers to vacate the plants stated that "the legality of the sit-down strike is not an issue; only the right to hold property." Although after enormous cost to all concerned the General Motors strike was settled, or rather a truce made for six months, other strikes continued to harass all parts of the country, and the question of the sit-down remained serious. The method was again used in the strike against the Chrysler Company in March, when the American Federation of Labor came out in flat opposition to it, branding it as illegal, and certain, in the long run, to be highly detrimental to the cause of labor, in part because it was wholly disapproved of by public opinion. Nevertheless, Miss Perkins, although acknowledging the decision of the Michigan court, wrote to Congressman McCormack, in a letter made public, that it did "not reflect any wide-spread movement to defy law or impair civil government or change current conceptions of property rights. The objectives are the usual objectives in labor disputes." That, however, was not the general opinion apparently of the public. In Connecticut in March Governor Cross emphatically declared that there would be no sit-down strikes in his state so long as he was governor, and there was none. The next month the legislature of Vermont passed an Act outlawing the sit-down and imposing a penalty of $1000 fine or two years in prison for any one taking part in one. However, in Michigan sit-downers took possession of six General Motors plants at Flint and Pontiac, and the leading hotel in Detroit, while 400,000 men in the soft-coal industry were also going on strike. Demands were made on Congress to take action, and a number of Senators demanded that President Roosevelt come out taking a stand on the question, but no action was taken either by President or Congress, and strikes continued in many parts of the country, among the more important being the long docking strikes on the Pacific coast and the extremely bitter one at the plants of the Republic Steel, the United States Steel having come to terms. It was in connection with the Republic strike that when asked for comment the President made his famous answer of merely "a plague on both your houses." On the night before Labor Day Lewis replied to the President, after boasting that the CIO had 3,718,000 members, that "it ill behooves one who has supped at labor's table and who has been sheltered in labor's house to curse with equal fervor both labor and its adversaries." To this slur on the Chief Executive of the nation and repeated reference to the CIO's contribution to the Democratic campaign fund in 1936, the President made no reply, but the next day released a statement in which he said "the age-old contest between capital and labor has been complicated in recent months through mutual distrust and bitter recrimination. Both sides have made mistakes. . . . The conference table must eventually take the place of the strike." That both sides *had* made mistakes was clear but it was equally so that the Wagner Labor Act was not accomplishing its purposes, and *The United States News* estimated that there had been 2300 strikes in the first seven months of the year alone, nor did they greatly lessen as the year progressed. Many of the strikes had been

498

in the nature of fights between the two contesting labor organizations with both public and employers ground between them, but there was no sign of peace between Green and Lewis when the year closed. On the whole, the twelve months had been one of the most violent and disturbed in the entire history of American labor, frequently punctuated by the calling out of troops and serious rioting and bloodshed.

The sphere of international relations was also greatly disturbed during 1937. The civil war in Spain dragged out its weary length with marked ferocity. It is more than a civil war because it is openly acknowledged by all that Russians are fighting on the side of the Loyalists, and Germans and Italians on the side of the rebels, aiding them not only with troops but with munitions, planes and submarines. For some time the latter, belonging to an unknown nation, set up a reign of terror in the Mediterranean by sinking vessels of other nations without warning. The lawless sinkings showed how far back into barbarism certain nations had carried Europe. It had been over a century since pirates had similarly endangered peaceful shipping in the great sea, and then it had been the barbarians of the African coast and not European nations who had done so. In spite of protests these piracies did not stop until parts of both the British and French fleets joined in patrolling the waters. Fortunately no American vessel had been sunk and we avoided being embroiled in an incident, but during the whole year all matters had to be considered against the background of deep uncertainty and possible war in Europe.

The Neutrality Bill had been passed in the hope of keeping us out of war if possible should one come, though among those best qualified to judge there is much doubt, to say the least, as to whether the bill would have that effect or not. A further measure was suggested toward the end of the year in the Ludlow resolution which secured a surprisingly large number of signatures in Congress. Although well intentioned, this peace plan, as was pointed out by Henry L. Stimson, who in the past had been both Secretary of State and Secretary of War, would call for a huge enlargement of the American army, and perhaps to no purpose. In a word, the plan called for a Constitutional Amendment requiring a vote of the entire nation before we could take part in any war except to repeal actual invasion of our soil. In the past we have relied on two lines of defence, the diplomatic and naval. Both would be broken down, according to competent critics, by this plan. The first because diplomacy would lose its most important power in negotiation if other nations knew that no matter what the President or Congress might wish there could be no war except after the cumbrous and uncertain passing of the question through a plebiscite of so huge and mixed a nation. It would take the most important card in diplomatic dealings from our own hands and place it in those of our opponents. Secondly, the naval line of defence would become almost worthless because we could not go to war, if at all, until the navy had been passed and the foreign invaders were actually within the country. The chief interest in the support accorded to the plan was the indication of the deep desire of the people to avoid war at almost any price.

The most dangerous zone for us during the year, particularly the latter part, was the Far East owing to the great but officially undeclared war by Japan on China. Not only have our business interests in the latter country been very large, as in some other countries, but also our missionary and educational. Our relations with her have been different from those with any other nation. Not only have we long upheld the integrity of China and the policy of the "Open Door" but it is also the only nation in which we have extra-territorial rights long ago accorded to us legally by treaties and in which we have also maintained permanent garrisons of troops. In addition there has been a genuine international friendship of an unique sort between China and ourselves, and there have been large numbers of Americans living there permanently, not simply as business men but also engaged in the work of teaching, medicine and religion. Invasion of such a country on a vast scale by a hostile power would thus almost inevitably produce "incidents" which might be difficult of peaceful adjustment, but the difficulty has been increased because of the apparent supremacy of the military over the civil authorities in Japan. During the attack on Shanghai, we notified the Japanese Government (August 28) that we would hold them responsible for damages to American lives and property and that we reserved all our rights. A few weeks later the President issued a proclamation forbidding any American merchant vessels owned by the government to carry munitions or implements of war to either of the warring nations, and stating that any others would do so at their own risk.

On November 6 the members of the Nine Power Treaty Conference, of which Japan had originally been one, sent a message asking her to send representatives to Brussels to confer with the others with regard to the situation. Japan declined, and although some of the nations did join in the meeting it had to adjourn without accomplishing anything. Meanwhile in the East incident followed incident. The State Department had evacuated large numbers of Americans but many yet remained, as well as some of our war ships and our troops to guard our share of the international compound and for other purposes, all according to both treaty rights and duties.

Japan had done little but issue successive apologies for attacks on both British and Americans, including the severe wounding of the British Ambassador when on December 17 the culminating incident thus far for the United States occurred when Japanese planes sank the U. S. gunboat *Panay* in the Yangtze River above Nanking, killing several and wounding more. In addition they sank three vessels belonging to the Standard Oil Company, and attacked the British gunboats *Ladybird, Bee, Cricket* and *Scarab,* together with British merchant ships. Immediate demands were made through the State Department by Secretary Hull for apologies, compensation and a guarantee against such incidents in future. There had been too many of them. In view of the relation of the civil to the military parties in Japan and the peculiar position of the Emperor whose dynasty had been on the throne for nearly 3000 years and who is worshipped as a god by the people, Mr. Roosevelt made a shrewd move in demanding also that the Emperor be advised of the shock and concern felt by him as President over the indiscriminate bombing of "American and other non-Chinese vessels on the Yangtze." Japan had been counting on driving wedges between America and Great Britain but by her actions had brought them closer together. The American Note had been both dignified and firm, and the Japanese seemed to realize the gravity of the course they had been following. Apologies were made, but in addition a company of Japanese naval sailors were ordered to fire a salute of honor for the four American blue-jackets killed, and full indemnity was promised, which it appeared later might mount to a million dollars. The close of the year, however, was still marked by nervousness and tension.

We now come to the story of business during the year, which may be briefly told. Business had improved considerably in the latter part of 1936 and this improvement carried over into the first half or so of 1937. Both business men and investors, however, had received a very severe shock when the President presented unexpectedly his plan for destroying the independence of the Supreme Court, and as the case was argued before the country in the ensuing months and both the dangers of the plan and the insistence of the President became more apparent, distrust deepened. In addition, the international situation caused increasing uncertainty for those wishing to make long-term commitments. Moreover, the failure to reduce expenses or the number of persons in government employ, or the debt, in spite of rising prosperity also caused misgiving. In April a committee appointed by the Twentieth Century Fund (an independent Foundation), which was composed of business men, economists and labor and agricultural leaders, found that the total governmental debt in the United States, counting those of the Federal, state and local governments, stood at about $90,000,000,-000, "the largest that any nation has ever had," and pointed out the serious danger which would result if this debt were not to be gradually reduced. As the months went on, instead of reduction there came a steady increase. Once more, the constant strikes, as well as the higher wages demanded, and in many cases secured, in the face of rising costs of other sorts—notably increasing taxation—frightened both investors and those responsible for managing business. Investors asked themselves also in view of the forced distribution of surpluses under the Surplus tax what would happen to income if business should decline in profit with no accumulated reserves to draw upon. The whole price structure had likewise got out of adjustment. Although the aim of the administration had repeatedly been said to be to get prices up to the level of 1926, which they had not yet reached, the President announced on April 2 that they were too high, and that thenceforth government spending would be directed not at durable-goods industries, such as involved use of steel, copper, cement, etc., but at consumers' goods. The news was unexpected and stock prices dropped sharply.

In March, Mr. Eccles, Chairman of the Federal Reserve Bank, who had long been in favor of the deficit financing theory of the administration, announced that inflation, which all had dreaded, could be avoided only by increase of taxation and reduction of the government debt. Yet the end of the fiscal year in June found the government with a new deficit of about $2,500,000,000 instead of reducing the debt, and with no prospect of reducing expenses or of pursuing a reasonable tax policy. Senator Robinson, Democratic leader of the Senate and trusted friend of the President, himself said in the Senate late in the month that "we spend and we spend and we spend, and there are some of us who vote for all appropriations and also vote against all taxes." "In the time of prosperity," he added, "we ought to begin to put our house in order. Let me ask what would happen if another depression such as that which began in 1929 or 1930, and which has continued until recently should

505

strike the people of the United States and their affairs next year or the year following?"

Unfortunately it was not to be "the next year or the year following" for the appearance of at least a very severe recession, whatever it may develop into. By midsummer keen observers detected that business was slipping fast. Soon others began to realize it, and in the fall the market had a precipitate decline, after a fairly steady decline from February which had been considered only temporary. By the end of the year stocks had fallen 30–40 per cent since August, and business profits had followed suit. The recession was particularly severe in the steel industry, which, beginning the year with the best figures since 1929, was operating at less than 30 per cent capacity, making heavy losses instead of profits. Lewis of the CIO declared that the country was starting on another "tail spin," a "matter of life and death." Green of the A. F. of L. said that for labor the situation had "already assumed the proportions of a serious depression." Miss Perkins had to report, as quoted in *The New York Sun,* in November that 570,000 men had been laid off in October, the sharpest decline in the history of the Department except the similar period of 1920. Many economists looked back to 1907 for such a sudden and perpendicular drop in business. There was no sign of improvement at the end of the year, and on December 28 General Motors announced the laying off of 30,000 men.

Among the minor items of the year's history may be

ONE OF THE OUTGROWTHS OF THE ROCKEFELLER FORTUNE

Rockefeller Center, in the heart of New York City, continues to grow, and the beauty of its landscaping, its shops and many permanent exhibits attract thousands of people each day.

JOHN D. ROCKEFELLER ON HIS 97TH BIRTHDAY

Mankind has derived many benefits from the

From a photograph © by Brown Brothers

ANDREW W. MELLON, WHILE SECRETARY OF THE TREASURY

He gave to the nation his splendid collection of paintings and the funds

mentioned the attempted round-the-world flight of Amelia Earhart who, as a woman flier and attractive personality, had endeared herself to millions of Americans; and her disappearance in mid-Pacific while trying to reach Howland Island to re-fuel. Although the entire ocean area where she might be was quickly searched by vessel and plane, no trace was ever found.

On May 23 John D. Rockefeller, Sr., died at the age of 97. Owner at one time of the largest fortune in the world, his life span had covered the entire history of American business from before the Civil War. It was estimated that he left about $25,000,000, but he had made gifts to his family during his lifetime and in addition had given to various charitable, educational, medical, and other associations, and for other innumerable purposes all over the world, about $530,000,000, to which his son has since added some $170,000,000, making between father and son gifts for the benefit of the peoples of many nations of $700,000,000. Nearly $350,000,000 are handled by three of the Rockefeller Foundations for education, medical research and other uses. Whatever may be thought as to the methods of accumulating the beginnings of the fortune in a period of different business ethics and social outlook, no other man through his financial gifts has ever so widely benefited mankind. With our income and inheritance taxes no other such fortune will ever again be accumulated, and his death marked the end of an era in American history.

One other death in the year may be noted, that of Andrew W. Mellon, former Secretary of the Treasury and Ambassador to England. Before he died he had given his superb collection of paintings, probably the finest ever gathered by one individual collector, to the nation. He had also arranged for the building of a museum in Washington to house it, and building and paintings have been estimated at upwards of $50,000,000, a magnificent gift to the people. Shortly after his death, though too late for him to receive any satisfaction from it, the Treasury finally exonerated him of the charges which had been pressed against him on account of income-tax returns.

Finally, one or two trends in American life may be noted simply from statistics. That there is still much poverty and marginal or submarginal standards of living amongst us is true, but it is encouraging to compare ourselves with other nations and earlier times, and we may cite, to end, a few figures. On January 1, 1937, there were in the United States a total of 31,471,000 homes. Of these 11,500,000 had telephones; 18,000,000 had automobiles; and 21,800,000 were equipped with electricity. Although the figures for another trend are not available beyond 1935 we may note that between 1930 and that year the number of farms increased by nearly 524,000 up to a total of over 6,800,000. In spite of much justified self-dissatisfaction and the hope of still better living, what other nation could make such a showing as the above for tens of millions of its ordinary citizens?

A s WE saw in the preceding chapter, the year 1937 had been important and extremely dramatic owing chiefly to the fight over the President's plan to pack the Supreme Court, so unexpectedly thrust upon the country, as well as the later sharp reversal in the business trend. The high drama of 1938 was rather in international than in domestic affairs, but if less striking, the course of our history at home was perhaps in the long run no less significant. It centered largely about the person of the President, and in this respect was a continuation of our history since his election in 1932. Whatever may be the opinion of any citizen as to Mr. Roosevelt, there can be no doubt that he has been one of the most dynamic personalities ever to preside over the destinies of the nation, and the story of his two administrations must of necessity be largely written in terms of his acts and policies.

At the beginning of 1938 he was entering on his sixth year as President, and ordinarily we would have to recount a loss of popularity. By the middle of their second terms most Presidents lose a considerable part of their influence. People get tired of the same figure, issues often have changed, and the fact that, according to our tradition, no President has ever been elected for a third term makes him less powerful by the middle of his second term when politicians are thinking of the new President to come as a result of the conventions in a year and a half and the election in less than two. Taking the year as a whole, however, in spite of a slump for some five months, Mr. Roosevelt's personal popularity did not seem to diminish greatly, and in this respect his record is almost unique. Polls taken by the American Institute of Public Opinion, usually quite accurate, showed, however, early in April that 70% of the voters were against a third term, and also that 79% had grown in favor of trying to restore prosperity by helping business whereas only 21% still favored the "pump priming" method of spending our way out. Such signs as these, as well as the fall elections, appeared to indicate clearly that, on the whole, the country was heading for a period of cautiousness instead of experimentation. These periods of radical or conservative trend, if we choose to call them so, usually last for a number of years, and if it be a fact that the trend shifted in 1938, whether as voters we agree or not with the change of direction, it may well prove to be the most important happening in domestic affairs of the year.

At the beginning of 1938 it was evident to business men that the so-called "recession" had been fast deepening into a genuine "depression," in fact, one of the most sudden

THE OTHER PUMPERS ARE ALL SET

Brown in the New York Herald Tribune ©

ONE OF THE MANY CARTOONS WHICH APPEARED AFTER PRESIDENT
ROOSEVELT'S $5,000,000,000 PLAN TO MAKE THE PUMP OF AMERICAN
BUSINESS START FLOWING

and severe which the United States has experienced. For example, steel production, which had reached 92% of normal early in 1937, had dropped to 19% by the end of the year. Although this industry is always "prince or pauper," others had also failed heavily. Motor production was down about 35%, as were also cotton mill operations. Railway freight was about 17% lower and building had steadily slumped, owing partly to the high cost of labor and materials. Private investment in new enterprises or the extension of old was extremely disappointing in amount, and the increase of about $21,000,000,000 in government debt since the New Deal started had not brought about recovery. The steady increase in wages and taxation, as well as the political uncertainties and the attitude of government toward business, all engendered lack of confidence and hindered the risking of "venture capital," on which the expansion of business depends.

The address of the President to Congress on its assembling in January was generally considered as temperately worded, though it was lacking in specific suggestions as to how to meet the new crisis or in indicating any change from the methods already employed for five years without altering the situation. Possibly what attracted most attention was the President's statement that in future the national expenses could not be allowed to fall below $7,000,000,000 a year without "destroying essential functions or letting people starve." In order to provide such an amount from taxation, Mr. Roosevelt envisaged the necessity of a future national income of from ninety to a hundred billions, or some 15–20 per cent more than we enjoyed in the peak year of 1929.

In this respect the President's first address of the year, instead of helping to restore confidence, probably further undermined it. In another passage Mr. Roosevelt reiterated one of the basic ideas of the New Deal, with which perhaps most business men would agree but which also reveals the gulf between the President and the business man, large or small, as well as the private investor. "If private cooperative endeavor [business] fails," he said, "to provide work for willing hands and relief for the unfortunate, those suffering hardship from no fault of their own have a right to call upon the government for aid." The misunderstanding between the administration and a large part of the honest and humane business men and investors, which is inherent in the above statement, is worth noting, for even such an ardent New Deal advocate as *The London Times* pointed out that much of the difficulty in which America found herself lay in the inability of business and the administration to cooperate for the good of the country.

In his address to Congress and also at other times during the year, the President made several advances to business and also attacks on it, sometimes bewildering in the rapid passage from one to the other, but the main point in difference remained unaltered by the government. The difference is that the administration appears to believe

that business and capital are on strike and are deliberately
not going to work because for some reason they do not
wish to; on the other hand, business and capital feel that
it is a case, not of a strike but, of a lockout.

Thus, the difference between the administration and
business was not so much that business denied the President's statements that if business did not feed workers the
government would have to, or that if business did not
finance essential industries the government would have
to, as that business men and investors felt that they could
not take chances and make jobs with government attitude
and policies what they appeared to be. Further, they believed that as jobs dwindled, relief would become more
and more of a problem, and as private enterprise diminished, the sphere of government in competition with private business would necessarily increase, and the whole
evil process would continue in a vicious circle.

Although the President made a number of conciliatory
moves to confer with business leaders, on the other hand
there were incidents which seemed to indicate that the
administration was still opposed to cooperation. For example, in January Secretary Ickes made a somewhat violent speech in which he quoted at length from a recently
published book called *America's 60 Families,* which contained startling errors and was bitterly hostile to both
business and wealth. One sample, among many which
could be cited, of the inaccuracies as well as of the spirit of
the book, was the author's statement that by giving his

$50,000,000 art collection to the government the late Mr. Andrew Mellon had enriched his estate by the amount of the tax, estimated by the author at $32,362,000. Of course, the estate instead of being enriched lost $17,638,000, or what would have been the equity remaining to his heirs after the payment of the tax, if the author's figures were correct. This is characteristic of much of the book, which would not have attracted the attention it did had not a member of the Cabinet used it as the basis of a public address, which was what caused public uneasiness.

In the same month business was again alarmed by the attack by Mr. Lilienthal of the TVA on Mr. Wendell Wilkie, president of the Commonwealth & Southern utility system, for the latter's suggestion that the government pay a reasonable price for the properties which were being injured by TVA competition. Lilienthal's heated opposition to what he called this "radical" proposal seemed again to doom the utility industry, one of the three largest in the country, and, with other episodes, offset such advances as the President seemed to be making toward conciliation.

The muddle between business and the government was also exemplified early in February. The President had already had conferences with some of the big business leaders and had called a conference in Washington of the "little business men." Some thousand of them assembled for the meeting, a cross-section of America, little men in all sorts of business in all sorts and sizes of American communities. The confusion of the first session amused many who did not realize the importance of the opinions generally expressed in the gathering, but it gradually developed that the little business men had precisely the same grievances and wanted government to take the same course as the bigger men. They questioned, for example, the workability of a standard wages and hours bill on account of geographical differences; asked an investigation of NLRB, and that employer and employee be made *mutually* responsible; the repeal of the undistributed profits tax, and modification of the capital gains tax; agreed that social reform was necessary but that industry was being disrupted by the speed of changes called for; demanded a balanced budget, sound government finance, and less direct competition by government with private enterprise.

At the very time the little business men were voicing their grievances, Mr. Douglas, chairman of the SEC, delivered an address in Chicago in which he told investors that they had nothing to fear from the "death sentence" on holding companies, and that not only were the operating companies eager to go ahead but that the spending of the vast amounts of money then required, and which investors could supply, would be an enormous force in bringing about recovery and making jobs. But on that same day Secretary Ickes announced that new Federal loans and *grants* in sixty-one localities in twenty-one States were waiting to be poured into competition with

DELEGATES OF PRESIDENT ROOSEVELT'S "LITTLE BUSINESS MEN" CONFERENCE IN SESSION AT WASHINGTON

DOUGLAS CORRIGAN, THE YOUNG AVIATOR WHO HEADED FOR CALIFORNIA IN H
$900 PLANE, AND LANDED IN DUBLIN, IRELAND

local companies by the government to the amount of practically $100,000,000, and the investor, invited to come out of his cyclone cellar by Douglas, was frightened back into it by Ickes.

The need of jobs had been made evident at the beginning of the year when John D. Biggers made his first report as administrator of the new National Unemployment Census, which showed a *registered* number of wholly unemployed as 7,822,912 and a maximum total, as estimated by Biggers, of 10,870,000. But as uncertainty continued, business likewise continued to decline rapidly. A survey of 280 leading corporations showed that in the first quarter of 1938 they had earned net profits of about $100,000,000 as against nearly $310,000,000 in the same period the year before. The total investment of the people's $12,000,000,000 in railroads (either directly or through savings banks, insurance companies and other means of indirect investment) earned nothing as a whole and made the worst showing in the entire twenty-one years during which statistics have been kept.

Moreover, the strain on business was clearly indicated by the enormous decrease in the surplus of the nation's corporations, which had fallen from $21,000,000,000 in 1929 to $14,000,000,000 in 1935, and was still declining, especially rapidly after the passage of the law taxing undistributed earnings. At the beginning of the depression the corporations had been fortified to stand a siege and still pay out from surplus larger amounts in both wages

517

to workers and returns to owners than if there had been no surpluses, but that period had passed, for it must be noted that "surplus" means cash only to a moderate extent, and is also invested in buildings, machinery, necessary working balances, and other items which, unless used, can provide neither wages nor dividends. The change in the situation between the beginning of the depression of 1929 and the second depression may be expressed by the fact that in 1929 the surplus of business in corporate form available to be drawn on in bad times was about one-third more than the national debt. In 1938 the surplus had so dwindled from taxation and other causes, and the government debt had so increased that the latter was nearly three times the amount of the corporate surpluses. The government debt is a liability on which interest has to be paid. The surplus of the business corporations had been an asset which had helped to carry both workers and owners over hard times. As a cash resource it had well-nigh disappeared in 1938, and if we have continued hard times or a war, it will no longer be available.

In these years, so crowded with measures, largely economic, and with political events, it is impossible to mention all, and we can speak of some only, either as they occurred or carrying their stories through if they cover some months.

In January the Ludlow Bill, providing that a referendum of the people be held before war could be declared, was defeated in the Lower House of Congress, 209–188, after the President had sent a strongly worded letter opposing it as impracticable, incompatible with our form of government, and asserting that instead of keeping us out of war it would have the opposite effect. In February he signed the new Farm Bill which had been proposed as a substitute for the defunct AAA. Although it involved the payment of hundreds of millions and was a complex document of 62,000 words, the House was allowed only four hours for its consideration, scarcely enough time for the clerk to read it through, and was allowed to offer no amendments. If the "gag rule" thus afforded an example of how business should not be conducted in the House, there was at the same time proceeding in the Senate, under the rule permitting unlimited debate, an example in reverse of how business should not be conducted in that body. A filibuster, in which fifteen Southern senators took part, against the Anti-Lynching Bill lasted for forty-seven days, preventing the consideration of almost all other measures until the defeat of the Bill was finally conceded.

The agricultural problem is admittedly one of extreme difficulty. It is impossible to say as yet how far the new Farm Bill, which provides Federal control of the five major crops of wheat, corn, cotton, tobacco, and rice, may help to solve it. It carries regulation of the individual farther than any other measure yet passed, and later in the year there were various minor revolts against it, notably in the hard wheat, corn and cotton sections.

Among the difficulties are the impossibility of forecasting the crop yield merely from the acreage; the fact that the production of one crop may greatly affect the consumption of another; and that national prices cannot be held independently of world prices without perhaps losing the export trade and building up competition in foreign countries.

Throughout most of the year the affairs of the TVA provided anxiety for both business and the administration. In March the long quarrel between the chairman, Arthur Morgan, distinguished engineer and former president of Antioch College, and his two colleagues came to a head publicly owing to the request by Morgan for a Congressional investigation of the whole situation. The President preferred not to have an investigation but instead called the three directors to a hearing to be held by himself. Although, after several refusals, Morgan finally appeared he declined to admit the right of the President to hold such a court and insisted on an investigation by Congress to which body alone, he claimed, the TVA and its administrators were responsible. Called "contumacious" by the President, he was asked to resign, and on declining was discharged from his office. Some weeks before Mr. Roosevelt refused the request of Morgan for a Congressional hearing, Senator Norris, the father of TVA, had said that "the very theory of the TVA Act itself was to make the organization independent of any department, independent of any President, independent of any political change," a statement which sustained Morgan's position. Moreover, in the similar case of the President's discharge of Humphreys, the Supreme Court had ruled that he had no such power under the Constitution. Finally, Congress agreed to have an investigation, but it was still dragging along at the end of the year, and it was probable that it might be long before the case could reach the Supreme Court.

It had long been recognized, even under the previous Presidents, that the machinery of the Federal Government was clumsy and badly needed reorganizing on more modern and efficient lines. The vast extension of departments under Roosevelt had made the need more imperative than ever. By March Congress was debating the Reorganization Bill which had been introduced by the administration. At first there was not much criticism, but as the public came to understand better the sweeping powers which it gave the President, the opposition became as tremendous as it was unexpected. Congress was swamped with a deluge of letters and telegrams never before equalled unless in the Supreme Court fight of the previous year. Although the powers granted the President were very largely whittled down in both Houses, the nation had been so aroused over granting any new powers that the storm rose to hurricane force. In spite of the fact that the administration leaders told the Representatives and people that defeat of the Bill would be tantamount to repudiating the President and showing that he was "no longer the leader of the country," on April 8 it was killed for all practical purposes by being recommitted by a vote in the House of 204 to 196.

Early in the month at the height of the fight over the Bill during the President's stay at Warm Springs, his secretary, Mr. McIntyre, had suddenly called the reporters together at nearly one in the morning, to hand them a statement from the President, in which he said: "I have no inclination to be a dictator. I have none of the qualifications which would make me a successful dictator. I have too much historical background and too much knowledge of existing dictatorships to make me desire any form of dictatorship for a democracy like the United States of America."

Another incident connected with the Bill was an investigation by a Senate Committee, presided over by Senator Minton, which investigated what were claimed to be undue influences brought to bear by individuals and organizations against its passage. Nothing was found to sustain the charges, and the methods of the Committee, which resembled those employed by the earlier Black Committee which the Supreme Court had decided violated the right of the citizen to be protected against indiscriminate search and seizure, were in general condemned.

Questions of the rights of citizens were also raised by another Committee which had long been investigating the American Telephone Company at a cost to the public of $1,500,000 and probably as much to the Company.

Only a minority report of one member was made, making serious but unsubstantiated charges against the corporation. The company stated that it had not been allowed to cross-examine witnesses nor to disprove charges by placing witnesses of its own on the stand. This matter is still in abeyance.

A week after the defeat of the Reorganization Bill, the President asked Congress for an appropriation of $5,000,-000,000 with which to fight the depression, but there were signs that Congress was becoming restive. Among other factors, the little business men's convention had made an impression, many farmers were uneasy, and the Congressmen were just recovering from the almost unprecedented storm raised by the Reorganization Bill. A few weeks earlier, also, senators had listened with great attention to the testimony given before a Senate Committee by Bernard M. Baruch, a friend of the President, formerly one of his most trusted advisers and an ardent supporter of the earlier New Deal. In the course of his examination Mr. Baruch stated: "I say it with regret, but I would be less than candid if I failed to express my opinion that unemployment is now traceable more directly to government policy than to anything that business could or should do, and that if those policies are not changed neither business nor government can ever solve this most terrible of all our problems." He then outlined a constructive program which evidently impressed the Senate.

In April the first Third-party of the possible ones in 1940 was launched by the La Follette brothers, one Governor of Wisconsin and the other U. S. senator, but the movement was not taken seriously by the country at large, and as the year advanced little more was heard of it.

Early in May Congress passed both the Naval Expansion Bill calling for an expenditure of $1,100,000,000 and the $5,300,000,000 Revenue Bill, to which latter it attached important changes in the capital gains and undistributed profits taxes, to the evil effects of which business had long been calling attention. The President, in spite of his opposition to the changes, did not veto the Bill but allowed it to become law without his signature. In June Congress, in a panic over the result of the Florida primaries, which seemed at first to indicate that the good will of the President could swing elections, and with all the other primaries ahead, passed the Wages and Hours Bill which had been considered dead. On adjournment it had made an all-time record by appropriating over $12,000,000,000 for the expenses of government, presaging a possible accumulated deficit since 1932 of $25,000,-000,000 over income.

After the bitter fight over the Supreme Court Bill in 1937, there had been those who, like Senator Guffey of Pennsylvania, demanded that the Democrats who had shown their independence by voting against the President and the plan to pack the Court should be buried "in the oblivion of defeat" as "ingrates" when they should have

to go before the citizens in the primaries. This year came the chance and the idea seems to have been taken up by some of the President's inner circle—James Roosevelt, Tom Corcoran, Harry Hopkins, and Secretary Ickes being mentioned as most in favor of the experiment. On June 24 in a "fireside chat" the President broadcast that although "as President of the United States" he would not take part in the primaries yet as "head of the Democratic Party" he had every right to point to which Democrats he wished elected. The distinction was resented by many as was also the campaigning for or against senators in their home States.

After the Florida primary, in which young James Roosevelt had indicated his father's wishes as to which candidate he preferred, Harry Hopkins had gone to Iowa where he endorsed Representative Wearin. At the same time his assistant, Aubrey Williams, was telling WPA workers that "we've got to keep our friends in power." The country was shocked by the spectacle of the head of the vast system of relief taking an active part in influencing elections, and soon complaints came from several parts of the country as to the use of relief funds. Postmaster-General Farley, generally considered the most astute politician, with Garner, in the Democratic party, was said to have been strongly opposed to the whole idea of the "purge" (as it came to be called) and later came out in condemnation of it. But it went on, although the administration got a blow in the defeat of Wearin. According to *The United States News* the wages of 500,000 WPA workers in the South were raised, and the number of checks going out in the second half of 1938, about 12,750,000, would be by far the largest in the history of relief.

In July Mr. Roosevelt started on a long swing around the country. In all there had been nine foes slated for defeat, Senators Smith, George, Tydings, Gillette, Clark, Van Nuys, Adams, McCarran, and Lonergan, but although the President made his wishes known in various ways in various States, he staked his full prestige only in three, Georgia, South Carolina and Maryland, where the first three named senators were running. He spoke in all three States, and in Maryland the people were offered two new bridges at the last moment, a gesture that probably hurt more than it helped, but which was much in the news. Every one of the nine senators was re-elected, and the purge was a complete failure, except that Representative O'Connor, whom the President had condemned, was defeated in New York City.

The effects, however, were to be lasting. In innumerable communities voters had resented interference with their local politics and choices. In Georgia, for example, when Senator George, having been read out of the party, asked the voters, "Don't you want to choose your own representative? Don't you want him, once elected, to use his own sincere, God-given independent judgment?" he was not only cheered but overwhelmingly elected, as was

Tydings in Maryland. The effect in Congress was also to be lasting. The nine senators marked for defeat would naturally be resentful, and it had now been proved they could be independent and elected even with all the popularity, prestige and power of the President levelled against them. The lesson would not be lost on other members of the two Houses. Moreover the split in the party between the regular Democrats and the New Dealers had been made permanent. That Farley had disapproved of the whole proceeding had been clear, and when Roosevelt visited Texas, Garner, instead of meeting him, had gone fishing. Garner had, in fact, become alarmed not only over the purge and the spending program but a number of other policies of the President, and the split between the two chief officers of government had become definite, as was apparent to many then and as Mr. Elliott Roosevelt stated some months later.

The primaries had scarcely ended when the campaign for election was nearing its close. Election day, November 8, was to deliver another blow to the prestige of the President and greatly to strengthen both the independence of Congress and the fight for the control of the party in 1940 when the Presidential election will occur. There was evidently intense interest in the result on the part of the public, as about 2,000,000 more votes were cast than in the previous mid-term election of 1934, and the unusually heavy voting made the result more significant. For the first time since the New Deal began,

527

the Republicans polled more votes in the thirty-seven northern and border States than did their opponents, but the puzzle of the election was the big decline in the country at large of the Democratic vote, which lost 9,000,000. Did the relief and farm vote stay home or how many strayed to the Republican fold? It is impossible to say. Mr. Farley had declared the evening before election, that the issue of the campaign was the New Deal, but in spite of that there was a surprising overturn. Not only were all the senators to be purged re-elected, as we have noted, but many ardent New Dealers went down to defeat, such as Representative Maury Maverick of Texas and, more notably, Governor Murphy of Michigan, who had supported the administration in its attitude on the sit-down strikes, although New York was saved to the Democrats by the election of Governor Lehman. The campaign was notable, as most are in times of severe depression, for the number of movements which sprang up or were revived throughout the country of the type of the Townsend plan advocates. Senator McAdoo in California, a Presidential favorite, was defeated by a candidate who had in his platform "thirty dollars every Thursday" for the aged, and such lures had effect in many States, with varying results on the fortunes of candidates.

The new Congress showed 191 New Dealers in the House, 71 Independent Democrats and 170 Republicans. In the Senate the New Dealers retained 47 seats, while the Independent Democrats had 22 and the Republicans 23. In other words, in any combination against the New Deal policies there might be a voting strength of 46 to 47 in the Senate, and of 241 to 191 in the House, although the Republicans, in spite of their striking gains, were still heavily outnumbered. Had the President, by his Supreme Court fight, the purge, and other actions, not split his party into warring factions, the Democrats would still have been in unassailable control.

There were important deductions to be drawn from both the primaries and the election. The former had shown clearly that even a leader of the enormous popularity of Mr. Roosevelt could not transfer his popularity to others, and also that as Mr. Farley said after election: "The people of any State or city resent outside interference in local affairs." Moreover, it was shown by the election that in spite of fears to the contrary, the people would vote as they chose, or refrain from voting, even if some 20,000,000 of them were receiving money from the government. Another important inference to be drawn was that the people as a whole were moving to a "middle of the road" position. If they were expressing disapproval of the methods of the New Deal, it is to be noted that the greater number of successful Republican candidates were not reactionaries but expressed belief in the New Deal aims, just as did many of the Independent Democrats, though objecting to the methods, such as unsound government finance, concentration of too much power in the

Executive, and others, which they felt would defeat the objects aimed at and were dangerous for the future of the nation. The shift appeared to be not toward Toryism but toward a liberal Conservatism. One thing seemed certain, and that was that Congress would now take a far more independent position than it had for the previous six years, and that both primaries and the election had made the breach between New Dealers and straight Democrats wide and permanent.

The election had been fought while business, which had taken a turn upward in early summer, had been improving, though it halted and turned downward again in December, coincident with the announcement that the government debt had reached a new peak of over $39,-000,000,000, the amount of income and expenses having been respectively greatly over- and underestimated in the budget of January. Also, in spite of the fact that business had steadily improved since June, the number of workers on WPA had increased by 525,000 to a new high of 3,263,000 on November 5, and the administration announced that the balance of the appropriation of $1,500,-000,000 for relief which had been voted to last until March 1, 1939, would be exhausted by January 1. Partly as a result of these figures and of the general criticism during the campaign, it was evident that Harry L. Hopkins, who had resigned as Administrator of the WPA and been appointed Secretary of Commerce by the President, would face considerable opposition by the Senate to his confirmation, although eventual confirmation was generally conceded.

Among domestic happenings of a different sort which we may note was the hurricane of September 21 which swept the east end of Long Island and left a wide swath of destruction across New England from the Sound to Canada. It was the worst storm that district had experienced in considerably more than a century, and one of the worst in the country's history. The loss of life was nearly 700, and the property damage was variously estimated at from $300,000,000 to $500,000,000. In the path of the hurricane buildings were demolished and in many cases completely disappeared, blown to bits and scattered. Even the landscape was altered for a generation by the destruction of trees—the small city of Bridgeport, for example, losing over 20,000 on city property alone. Railway lines were heavily damaged and for nearly a week it was impossible to get from New York to Boston by accustomed routes, and roads were impassable even for automobiles. Cut off from transportation and even from communicating with the outside world by telephone or telegraph, one of the encouraging items in our year's story was the way in which all citizens of every sort turned out to repair damage and assist one another. No one who went through the experience could question that our new citizenry of all races could prove itself, when suddenly facing an emergency, just as robust and resourceful as the pioneers of old.

Two scandals may also be mentioned, the one for its political and the other for its human interest. In August, James J. Hines, one of the most powerful of the Tammany district leaders, had been placed on trial as protector of the policy and other rackets in New York. Although found guilty on all thirteen counts in a second trial in 1939, the Judge, Ferdinand Pecora, had ruled a mistrial in the first case owing to a technicality regarding a question asked by the District Attorney, Thomas E. Dewey. This was in mid-September. Dewey ran for Governor against Lehman and if one may judge from the election returns, and the immense acclaim that the later success in securing a conviction brought him, he would probably have been elected had not the first case gone against him during the campaign. If the above generally accepted surmise is correct, the ruling of Judge Pecora, an upright and able judge, gave New York State a Democratic instead of a Republican governor with possible considerable effect on national politics now and in 1940.

The scandal in which Hines found himself involved was in full, progress when another broke over the head of one of the best known and respected business men of Connecticut, reputedly "F. Donald Coster," who turned out to be the ex-convict Philip Musica, and who had been a daring swindler from boyhood. Securing control of one of the oldest and most reputable drug firms in the United States, he had, with his three brothers, all also living double lives under assumed names, falsified the firm's books to the amount of some $18,000,000. "Coster," whose career is one of the most fantastic in the history of crime, shot himself before arrest but at the end of the year his brothers were still awaiting trial. It may be said that the scandal was apparently wholly personal and financial and did not in any way affect the quality of the products in which the company deals.

In New York in July two picturesque events marked with unusually vivid contrast the change from old to new in world transportation. The square-rigged ship *Tusitala,* last but two of a vanishing race to sail under the Stars and Stripes, was towed from her berth on Riverside Drive to be broken up. Almost to a day, Howard Hughes alighted on Floyd Bennett Field on his arrival from flying round the northern hemisphere in just under three days twenty hours, having flown 15,000 miles at an average speed in the air of 208 miles an hour.

During the second half of the year a Committee, with Representative Dies as chairman, was holding an investigation into radical or "red" activities in the United States. It won the hostility, openly expressed, of leaders in the administration, but in spite of some rather absurd investigation, such as the Shirley Temple incident, and too limited funds, it disclosed enough facts to warrant its being continued when Congress met again in the next session.

As one of the indirect results of the depression with its

unemployment problem and the need for increased taxes by the States in competition with the Federal Government, a movement has been under way for several years to protect local business and raise taxes within each State at the expense of other States. It is similar to the unfortunate world movement since the war to make each nation self-sufficing. In 1938 it reached such proportions as to alarm the state governments themselves, and representatives of practically all of them prepared to attend a joint conference in Chicago early in 1939. One of the chief causes of American prosperity in the past has been the fact that we had the greatest free-trade area in the world, a single market of 3,000,000 square miles and 130,000,000 people, but if we "Balkanize" the United States into forty-eight water-tight communities as Europe is broken up, we shall lose this advantage with disastrous effect on the business of the nation as a whole. It is unconstitutional for any State to have a tariff barrier against the goods of others, but this is being got around in many ways, such as "use" taxes, agricultural quarantine laws, prohibitive "inspection" charges, truck regulations, and others. By the end of the year nine States had "ports of entry" through which goods coming in from other States in trucks had to pass almost as through foreign custom houses. One State alone had approximately seventy such "ports." Naturally States or sections discriminated against by others retaliate, and the danger is not only to our national business and the regaining of prosperity but

Courtesy of the artist, Carl Rose, and the "New Yorker Magazine"

A CARAVAN OF CALIFORNIA MILLIONAIRES, FLEEING EASTWARD FROM THE STATE
INCOME TAX, ENCAMPS FOR THE NIGHT IN HOSTILE WISCONSIN TERRITORY

even to our national union, for such discrimination and retaliation breed bad feeling and tend to divide us into hostile local groups, which is always a danger in so large a territory. Comparatively little noticed by the general public, the rapidity with which the movement advanced in 1938 may be considered as one of the important and ominous events of the year.

During 1938 there was much anxiety over foreign affairs. In March, Mexico confiscated the property of seventeen American and British oil companies. The year ended without our having been able to get any promise of compensation, although farm property was also expropriated and mining properties were threatened.

The Japanese-Chinese conflict brought a series of minor crises. In January our representative at Nanking was struck in the face by a Japanese soldier, and there was a raid on American-owned property. In February the United States, Britain, and France demanded of Japan whether she were building beyond the 35,000-ton limit for battleships under the joint treaty, and she refused to answer. It may here be noted that during the year the world armament race continued at an accelerated pace, the amounts spent by the six great powers in 1938 being approximately fifteen billions as contrasted with less than three billions in 1933 and scarcely over two in 1913. Our own expenditure for the past year was the most modest of all, about $1,066,000,000 as compared with $1,693,000,000 for Japan. During the European

THE HURRICANE

Streets in Massachusetts showing the destruction caused by the worst storm
New England has had in a century

Photograph by Acme Newspictures

SECRETARY OF STATE, CORDELL HULL, AND ALFRED LANDON, FORMER PRESIDENTIAL NOMINEE, AT THE

crisis in September we asked that country to aid in preventing the threatened war but she declined. In November, after waiting six weeks for a reply to our complaint of economic discrimination against us in China, Tokyo replied that Japan was "establishing a new order throughout East Asia," which indicated that she would pay no attention to our treaty rights in China or to our traditional policy—one of our most important—of the "Open Door" in that country.

In the European events of the year the chief point was our increasingly tense relations with Germany as Hitler first seized Austria, then threatened Czecho-Slovakia, and continued on his career which gradually became one of conquest with constant threat of embroiling the whole world. He discriminated against the United States in the payment of Austrian debts, and controversy over many matters in dispute finally led in November to the withdrawal of the Ambassadors of each country from the other, ostensibly "to report" but actually for an indefinite period. Relations were not severed but were greatly strained.

The main event in our relations with South America was the Eighth Pan-American Conference which was held at Lima, Peru, in December, our delegation being headed by Secretary of State Hull and including, by Mr. Roosevelt's appointment, his opponent in the last Presidential campaign, Mr. Landon. The Conference unquestionably had a good effect on our southern neighbors, and especially one of the great powers, Brazil. In November Mr. Hull had a success, long sought for, in signing a mutual trade pact with Great Britain, North Ireland, the Crown Colonies and Canada.

It was part, perhaps, of the trend toward conservatism noted in the United States during the year, that feeling against the totalitarian states increased. In this connection we may cite some figures published just as the year ended by the National Industrial Council Board which may indicate some basis for the swing away from complete government control back to the system of private enterprise.

AN HOUR'S WAGES WILL BUY

	Baskets of Food	Lbs. Bread	Lbs. Butter	Cigarettes	Pairs Socks
United States	2.83	7.5	1.6	112	4.4
Britain	1.26	5.2	0.8	21	1.7
France	1.23	5.0	0.5	40	0.9
Belgium	1.11	4.9	0.4	58	1.3
Germany	1.02	2.5	0.5	30	1.5
Italy	0.65	2.8	0.3	15	0.5
Russia	0.40	1.0	0.2	16	0.6

Put in another way, it takes to buy a pair of overalls, in

United States	1 hr. 11 minutes
Germany	10 hrs. 50 minutes
Italy	32 hrs. 56 minutes

To buy a pair of shoes the work called for ranged from three hours twenty-six minutes in the United States to twenty-four hours twenty-two minutes in Italy. In spite

STOCK MARKET CRASHES,
SELLING SETS NEW LOWS
-1929

GREAT BRITAIN OFF GOLD
STANDARD. £ AT $4.22
-1931

ELEVEN MILLION UNEMPLOYED,
ELECTION YEAR HITS BUSINESS
-1932

ROOSEVELT DECLARES BANK
HOLIDAY TO AVERT PANIC
-1933

OPPORTUNITIES FOR YOUTH
GONE SAYS NOTED LECTURER
-1935

BUDGET DEFICIT THREATENS
NATION'S CREDIT, SAYS SOLON
-1936

HOLDS RELIEF UNDERMINES
MORALE, DESTROYS CHARACTER,
1938

JANUARY 1939

Courtesy of the Crowell Publishing Company

IS THE CRYING JAG OVER?

A cartoon by Carl Rose which appeared in *Collier's Magazine* at the close of 1938

of our bad situation, the American of small income would seem still to have much to be thankful for as compared with those in the dictator countries, who in all cases, as would appear from the above and other figures, are worse off than in the democracies. In this regard we may also note, even in the midst of our great depression, the number of automobiles per 100 persons in the leading countries of Europe and America, excluding Russia, which in this respect is negligible:

United States . .	22
Canada	11
France	5
United Kingdom .	5
Germany . . .	2
Italy	1

During the year, the nation lost by death two of its most notable citizens. Colonel Edward M. House, the intimate friend and counsellor of President Wilson during the World War and one of the Commissioners to negotiate peace in Paris, died on March 28, and on July 9 a new vacancy on the Supreme Court was left by the death of Justice Benjamin N. Cardozo, a liberal and one of the ablest jurists who ever sat in that tribunal.

INDEX

INDEX

INDEX

Oriskany, I, 197; treason of, I, 203; escape of, I, 204, 207; II, 299
Arrears-of-Pension Act, 1879, III, 305 f.
Art, folk, I, 103
Arthur, Chester A., III, 254, 272, 301; for Vice-Presidency, III, 274; nominated for Vice-President, III, 289; becomes President, III, 292; change in, III, 293; and Civil Service, III, 294; courage of, III, 294
Arthur Mervyn, by C. B. Brown, II, 12
Articles of Confederation, in 1777, I, 228
Artisans, I, 115
Asbury, Bishop, circuit rider, II, 26
Ashburn, Colonel, record of Medical Department, I, 174
Ashburton, Lord, dispatched to Washington, II, 255
Ashley, III, 195
Associated Press, III, 236
Astor, John Jacob, II, 107, 220
Astor, Vincent, IV, 394
Astor, W. B., III, 164
Astoria, II, 107
Astronomy, advances in, IV, 442 f.
Atchison Railroad, IV, 42
Atlantic coast strike, IV, 474
Atlantic Monthly, The, III, 236
Audubon, J. J., ornithologist, II, 234
Aurora, The, by B. F. Bache, I, 294
Austin, Stephen F., leader in Texas, II, 188
Australia, IV, 412
Austria, IV, 199, 214; Austria *vs.* England, I, 77; Webster's note to, II, 306; archduke, assassination of, IV, 199; ambassador, recalled, IV, 203; Chancellor assassinated, IV, 381 f.
Automobile, IV, 18; number of, IV, 115, 270 f., (in 1937), 508; strikes, IV, 402
Aviation, IV, 396, 397; chart, IV, 397; British, IV, 398; Italian, IV, 443
Azores, wine from, I, 130
Aztecs, culture of, I, 9

Babcock, O. F., secretary of General Grant, III, 220; shielded by Grant, III, 230
Bache, B. F., Franklin's grandson, quoted, I, 294
Bacon, Nathaniel, leader of revolt, I, 57
Baer, George F., president of Reading Railroad, quoted, IV, 128 f.
Bahama, touched by Columbus, I, 7
Bainbridge, Captain, of the *Constitution*, II, 42
Baker, Newton D., Secretary of War, during World War, IV, 230

Baker, Ray Stannard, author of *Life of Woodrow Wilson*, IV, 116
Balfour, Lord, of England, arrives on War mission, IV, 224
"Balkanizing" of United States, danger of, IV, 534, 536
Ballinger, R. A., Secretary of Interior under Taft, IV, 164 f.
Baltimore, city of, II, 8, 13, 32; Union troops attacked, III, 28; Democratic Convention at, 1840, II, 240; 1848, II, 287; 1852, II, 310; 1860, III, 4; 1912, IV, 177
Baltimore, Lord, receives Charter, I, 31
Bancroft, II, 224; *History of the United States*, II, 225
Bank Bill, passage of, IV, 354
Bank notes, III, 278
Bank of England, in World War, IV, 225, 312
Bank of the United States, bill creating, I, 275; the second, II, 11, 178, 179, 186 f.
Bank questions, I, 123 f.
Bankers, I, 268; IV, 129
Bankhead Cotton Act, IV, 390 f.; repeal requested by Roosevelt, IV, 451
Banking, I, 55; reserve requirements raised, IV, 471; *see* also special acts
Banking "holidays," declared by State Governors, IV, 349
Banking panic of 1933, IV, 349 f., 350, 352 f.
Banking scandals, IV, 351
Banking system, II, 124 f., 185 f.
Banking warnings, IV, 302
Banks, I, 278; III, 155; IV, 151; failure of, in 1837, II, 186; IV, 42, 329; failure of, in 1933, IV, 351; closed by Roosevelt, IV, 352; government takes possession of gold in, IV, 374; investigation of members of, IV, 378; idle cash in, IV, 473
Banks, General N. P., III, 59
Baptist Church, missionaries, II, 25; split in, II, 261
Barbadoes, islands, I, 26, 33, 42
Barlow, Joel, poet, II, 4
"Barn Burners," faction of Democratic party, II, 288, 289
Barnard, reorganizes Columbia, III, 241
Barré, Colonel Isaac, speech by, I, 134
Barrow, Clyde, criminal, IV, 409
Barter, resorted to, I, 221
Barthou, French Foreign Minister, assassinated, IV, 382
Barton, Clara, service in Civil War, III, 118
Bartram, John, botanist, I, 113
Bartram, William, the naturalist, II, 11
Baruch, Bernard M., IV, 407, 523

543

INDEX

Bates, Edward, Attorney-General in Lincoln's Cabinet, III, 23
Battle of the Thames, II, 91
Battle Cry of Freedom, The, popular in Civil War, III, 144
Battleship, *Maine*, IV, 83 f.
Bayard, James A., United States Commissioner, II, 98
Bayard, Thomas F., Secretary of State, III, 283, 303
Beauregard, P. G. T., III, 30, 37, 52; in Mexican War, II, 281; forced to retire, III, 53
Beecher, Henry Ward, emotionalism of, II, 216
Beekmans, prominent New York family, I, 93
Behring Sea, I, 1; seal fisheries in, IV, 15
Belgium, in World War, IV, 199, 223; death of King Albert, IV, 381; IV, 538
Belknap, Jeremy, historical chronicler, II, 3
Belknap, W. W., Secretary of War, under Grant, resigns, III, 230
Bell, John, nominated for President by Constitutional Union Party, III, 5
Belleau Wood, in World War, IV, 237
Bemis Heights, in Revolution, I, 197
Benedict, E. C., IV, 41
Benjamin, Judah P., III, 16
Bennett, H. H., Director, Soil Erosion Service, IV, 400
Bennett, James Gordon, establishes *Herald*, II, 234; III, 21; IV, 81
Bennington, defeat of British at, I, 196
Benton, Thomas H., Senator, II, 144, 170, 293, 297; goes over to Crawford, II, 145; protests against spoils system, II, 166; demands of, II, 181
Berkeley, Governor, I, 47, 57; recalled by England, I, 58
Berle, A. A., Jr., of Columbia University, member of "brain trust," IV, 358
Bermuda, ship goes aground, I, 18; colony of, I, 22
Bernard, Francis, governor of Massachusetts, I, 147
Bessemer, Henry, inventor of manufacturing steel, III, 215
Bethlehem Steel Works, III, 215
Beveridge, Albert J., Progressive Senator, IV, 163, 172
Beverley, Robert, *History and Present State of Virginia*, I, 110
Beverleys, prominent Virginia family, I, 95
Bible, I, 12, 13; II, 228; distributing of, II, 118

Biddle, Nicholas, president of Bank of U. S., II, 178
Big business, IV, 120
"Big business men," IV, 356
"Big stick," the, IV, 139, 143
Biggers, John D., IV, 517
Biglow Papers, The, by Lowell, II, 285
Bill of Rights, the lack of a, in Constitution, I, 256
Bi-metallism, III, 280; IV, 386
Bingham, John A., for Johnson's impeachment, III, 196
Birney, James G., nominated for President, 1844, II, 246, 268
Bishopric of Durham, model for colonies, I, 53
Black, Senator Hugo, IV, 452 f., confirmed as Justice of Supreme Court, IV, 493 f.; and Ku Klux Klan, IV, 484, 495
"Black Friday," September 24, 1869, III, 220
Black Warrior, seized by Spanish, II, 324
Blackstone, laws, I, 34
Blaine, James G., candidate for Presidency, III, 253; hatred for Conkling, III, 259; denounces President Hayes, III, 261 f.; for free silver, III, 283; candidate for nomination, III, 288; Secretary of State, III, 291; expects to be the power behind the throne, III, 292; nominated for President, III, 296; declines to be a candidate, IV, 1; Secretary of State, IV, 7; leading figure of the administration, IV, 14; treaties with South America, IV, 15; his foreign policy, IV, 15; friends wish him to be a candidate, IV, 34
Blair, Francis P., II, 164; nominated for Vice-President, III, 198
Blair, John, I, 242
Blair, Montgomery, Postmaster-General under Lincoln, III, 23
Blake, Lyman R., invention of, III, 134
Blanco, General, replaces Weyler in Cuba, IV, 83
Bland, Richard P., I, 135; leader of silver forces, III, 283; quoted, III, 284
Bland-Allison Bill, III, 285, 293, 309; IV, 39
Bliss, Cornelius N., Secretary of Interior, IV, 75
Bliss, General Tasker H., at Peace Conference, IV, 252
Blockade, failure of, in Civil War, III, 44
"Blue Eagle," IV, 372, 428
"Blue-stockings," IV, 120
Boker, G. H., author, III, 144
Bolivia, at war with Paraguay, IV, 393
Bolshevism, IV, 248, 253 f.

544

INDEX

Budget, balancing the, IV, 376, 385, 420 f., 448, 479
Budget Burer , first director of, IV, 294
Buell, D. C., Union General, takes Nashville, III, 50
Buenos Aires, Peace Conference at, IV, 476
Buffalo, numbers killed, II, 7, 91; III, 212
Bulfinch, Charles, architect, II, 18
Bulgaria, in World War, IV, 224
Bull, William, only man in America who had degre , Doctor of Medicine, I, 113
"Bull Moose" party, IV, 180
Bull Run, battle of, III, 38; second battle, III, 65
Bunker Hill, battle of, I, 168, 169
Burchard, S. D., incident of, in Blaine campaign, III, 299
Bureau of Mines, established, IV, 164, 166
Bureau of War Risk Insurance, IV, 229
Burgesses, I, 21
Burgoyne, General, plans of, I, 194; captures Ticonderoga, I, 195; defeated, I, 196 f.
Burke, Senator, IV, 485, 493
Burnet, Governor of Massachusetts, I, 80
Burnham, Daniel, architect, IV, 19
Burnside, General A. E., succeeds McClellan, III, 68; failure of, III, 69, 86
Burr, Aaron, I, 296; II, 7, 52; selected as Vice-President candidate, II, 29; elected, II, 30; blocked by Hamilton, II, 53; duel with Hamilton, II, 53
"Burr conspiracy," II, 55
Busch, brewer, III, 214
Bushnell, Horace, quoted, II, 193
Business, competition in, IV, 371; NRA codes for fair competition in, IV, 371 f.; and inflation, IV, 390; hope for improvement in, IV, 410; recovery in, due to abolishment of NRA, IV, 428, 429; accounting system for government, IV, 433; improvement in, in 1935, IV, 437; and investment, IV, 437, 438, 439; improvement in, in 1936, IV, 471, 476; and capital, IV, 473; condition of, in early 1937, IV, 488, 503; distrust felt by, during 1937, IV, 504; recession of, IV, 506; "pump-priming" method of, IV, 390, 437, 510; recession of 1937 illustrated, IV, 512; misunderstanding with Roosevelt administration, IV, 513 ff.; "little business men's" conference, IV, 515 f.; profits in 1938, IV, 517; decrease in surplus of corporations, IV, 517 f.; Baruch on government policy toward, IV, 523; course of, during 1938, IV, 530
Butler, General Benjamin F., reaches New

Orleans, III, 53 f.; sent to take Petersburg, III, 94 f.; for Johnson's impeachment, III, 195 f.
Butler, William O., nominated for Vice-President, II, 288
Byrd, Senator Harry F., of Virginia, IV, 463, 485, 488
Byrd, William, of Westover, I, 97
Byrds, famous Virginia family, I, 95

Cabell, James Branch, author, IV, 306
Cable, the first, II, 206; influence on newspapers, IV, 17
Cable, George W., author, III, 240
Cabot, George, explorer, I, 8; II, 29
Cabots, prominent Boston family, I, 219
Calhoun, John C., II, 79, 81, 85, 120, 155, 170, 171, 181, 293, 302, 313; quoted, II, 117; Secretary of War, II, 104; nominated, II, 143; author of "Exposition," II, 157; influence of, II, 164; a massive egotist, II, 168 f.; toast at Jefferson dinner, II, 174; on nullification, II, 199; Secretary of State, II, 262; acknowledged leader, II, 285; speech of, II, 297; hears Webster's speech, II, 298; death of, II, 312
California, II, 137 f.; province of, II, 276; gold discovered, II, 283 f.; adopts Taylor's constitution, II, 295; question of slavery in, II, 318; problem of Japanese, IV, 195, 285 f.; election in, in 1934, IV, 401; Sinclair's plan to "End Poverty in California," IV, 401
Calvinistic theology, I, 94; II, 227
Cambridge, Mass., reached by Washington, I, 170
Camden, battle of, in Revolution, I, 206
Camera, portable, first used in 1888, IV, 19
Cameron, Simon, Secretary of War, III, 23; scandals of, III, 138, 218; makes trouble for Hayes, III, 262
Camp-meetings, II, 25, 216
Campaign of 1812, II, 68; of 1840, II, 242; of 1844, II, 264; of 1856, II, 331; of 1864, III, 99; of 1866, III, 185; of 1868, III, 198; of 1876, III, 251; of 1880, III, 288; of 1892, IV, 33; of 1896, IV, 58 f.; of 1900, IV, 100; of 1904, IV, 143; of 1908, IV, 158, 307; of 1912, IV, 177; of 1920, IV, 262; of 1932, IV, 330; of 1936, IV, 460 ff.; 466 ff.
Canada, I, 15, 123, 224, 233 f.; held by French, I, 10; France ejected from, I, 67; conquest of, I, 71; French in, I, 89; problem of, I, 160; boundary question, II, 43, 133; difficulty with, II, 253; revolt in, II,

546

INDEX

INDEX

campaign against, I, 207; at Yorktown, I, 207; difficulties of, I, 209; surrender of, I, 210
Corporations, dividends of, IV, 455; profits in 1938, IV, 517; surplus of, decrease in, IV, 517 f.
Corruption, disgusting honest men, III, 217 f.; in politics, IV, 422
Cosmopolitan, The, magazine, IV, 115
"Coster, F. Donald," *see* Musica, Philip
Cotton, I, 288; II, 8, 15, 121, 122, 247, 251; III, 151, 250; increase in, II, 15; importance of invention of cotton gin, II, 206; stoppage of exports, III, 72; need for, III, 31; textiles, III, 134; price of, IV, 31, 362, 363; production control of, by government, IV, 391; price question of, IV, 426
"Cotton belt," II, 108, 199
Cotton, Reverend John, I, 30, 37; death of, I, 41
Coudert, Frederic R., declines mission, IV, 78
Coughlin, Father Charles E., "Radio Priest," of Detroit, IV, 441, 463 f.
Coughlin-Townsend Party, IV, 464, 466
Council of Defense, in World War, IV, 228
Council of Safety of Pennsylvania, I, 221
Court of Arbitration, IV, 98
Court Improvement Bill, IV, 493
Court of International Justice, IV, 315
Court of International Settlement, IV, 296
Covenant, drawn up by Pilgrims, I, 25
Cowboy, III, 213, 243; IV, 103
Cowpens, battle of, in Revolution, I, 207
Cox, Jacob D., Secretary of Interior, in Grant's Cabinet, III, 200, 221
Cox, James M., nominated for President, IV, 266; defeated, IV, 267
Coxey, Jacob, "army" of, IV, 42
Crandall, Prudence, attacked by mob, II, 245
Crash of 1839, II, 187; the great crash in 1929, IV, 319
Crawford, William H., at the Treasury, II, 104; candidate for President from Georgia, II, 142
"Crédit Mobilier," scandal of, III, 221, 229, 290
Creek Indians, rising of, II, 94, 129
"Crime of '73, The," III, 283
Crimean War, mentioned, II, 199; III, 58, 118
Crimes in Early America, I, 115
Crimes, rise in, in 1933, IV, 408; kidnapping, IV, 408, 434; prevention of, by laws and Federal agents, IV, 408, 409, 434 f.

Criminals, "Public Enemies," IV, 408, 409
Crisis, The, novel by Churchill, IV, 115
Crittenden, Senator, III, 17
Croker, Boss, of Tammany Hall, IV, 60
Cross, Governor, of Connecticut, IV, 497
Crown Colonies, IV, 538
Crown Point, I, 77; capture of Americans, I, 168 f.
Crowninshields, famous family, II, 4
Cuba, IV, 76, 94, 136; junta in New York, IV, 79; achieves independence, IV, 95; intervention in, IV, 148; revolution in, IV, 379, 382; new treaty with, IV, 393
Cultural life in 1763, I, 114
Cumberland, Union vessel, III, 57
Cumberland Gap, I, 227
Cummings, Homer E., Attorney-General, suggests use of "Trading with the Enemy Act" by Roosevelt, IV, 352; quoted, IV, 408; IV, 482
Cummins, Senator, Progressive, IV, 163, 172
Currency, II, 123; III, 245 f., 289, 310; IV, 37; tobacco as, I, 57; in confusion, I, 237; inflation of, II, 181; crisis in, III, 277; inflation of, IV, 361; by Roosevelt, IV, 362, 364; national versus international stabilization of, IV, 366, 367; IV, 373, 374, 385, 386 (*see* special measures); effect of measures, IV, 387 f.; Great Britain, France and United States in agreement for stabilization of, IV, 466; IV, 480; Revenue Bill of 1938, IV, 524
Curtis, Justice Benjamin R., dissenting opinion of, in Dred Scott decision, II, 336; counsel for President Johnson, III, 197
Curtis, Charles, for Vice-President, IV, 307; renominated, IV, 338 f.
Curtis, George William, reformer, II, 207; III, 268
Curtiss, Glenn, maker of first successful hydroplane, IV, 115
Cushing, Caleb, chairman of Convention, III, 2
Cushman, Charlotte, celebrated actress, II, 234
Custer, General George A., overcomes Black Kettle, III, 212
Custom House, in Boston, attacked, I, 151, 158
Czar of Russia, Conference at the Hague, IV, 97

Da Gama, Vasco, explorer, I, 6
Daguerreotype, invention of, II, 232
Dale, Sir Thomas, as governor, I, 19

INDEX

Dallas, Alexander J., Second Bank of the United States, II, 123

Dana, Charles A., editor of *Tribune*, II, 234, 236; at Brook Farm, II, 207

Danish islands, I, 225

Dare, Virginia, first white child, I, 17

"Dark horse," the first, II, 265

Darrow, Clarence, heads committee to investigate NRA, IV, 398

Dartmouth College, I, 106; IV, 268

Daugherty, Harry, Attorney-General, forced out, IV, 289

Davenport, Reverend John, head of settlers, I, 40

David Harum, by Westcott, IV, 115

Davis, Henry Winter, III, 170

Davis, J. C. Bancroft, III, 224

Davis, Jefferson, II, 293; III, 14, 40, 49, 147, 171, 293; Secretary of War, II, 322; warning of, III, 1; elected President of Confederacy, III, 16 f.; character of, III, 16; removes Johnston, III, 96; refuses Lincoln's offer, III, 101

Davis, John W., nominated for President, IV, 295

Dawes, Charles, General, nominated Vice-President, IV, 294; head of commission, IV, 294; resigns as Amabssador, IV, 331; head of Reconstruction Finance Board Corporation, IV, 331

Day, William R., Secretary of State, IV, 75

Dearborn, General Henry, Secretary of War, II, 37, 87

Debs, Eugene V., IV, 43, 45; nominated for President by Socialists, IV, 159; sent to prison, IV, 246

Debt, suits for, I, 238; national, II, 181; III, 120; laws for imprisonment for, II, 212; *see* National Debt

Decatur, Stephen, daring exploit of, II, 42, 102

Declaration of Independence, I, 34, 188, 243, 260, 271, 297; II, 79, 140, 149; passage of, I, 190 f.; anniversary of, III, 241; quoted, III, 4

Declaration of London, IV, 203, 204

Declaration of Rights, I, 162

Declaratory Act of Parliament, I, 138

Deerfield, attack on, I, 71

De Grasse, Admiral, at the Chesapeake, I, 208, 209

De Kalb, Baron, General in Revolution, I, 199; death of, I, 206

DeLancey, James, delegate to Intercolonial Conference, I, 75

Delaware, I, 46 f., 59; divided, I, 190; population of, I, 245; ratifies Constitution, I, 257

de la Warr, Lord, arrives at Jamestown, I, 19

Delcassé, French Foreign Minister, IV, 147

Democracy, II, 119, 236; tendencies of, I, 37; limitations of, III, 124 f.

Democratic Convention at Baltimore, 1840, II, 240; Convention at Baltimore, 1848, II, 287; Convention at Baltimore, 1852, II, 310; Convention at Cincinnati, 1856, II, 331; Convention at Baltimore, 1860, III, 4; Convention at Charleston, 1860, III, 1; Convention at Louisville, 1872, III, 228; Convention at Chicago, 1884, III, 297; Convention at St. Louis, 1888, IV, 1; Convention at Chicago, 1892, IV, 35; Convention at Chicago, 1896, IV, 68; Convention at St. Louis, 1904, IV, 143; Convention at Baltimore, 1912, IV, 177; Convention at San Francisco, 1920, IV, 266; Convention at New York, 1924, IV, 295; Convention at Houston, 1928, IV, 308; Convention at Chicago, 1932, IV, 338; Convention at Philadelphia, 1936, IV, 461 f.

Democratic National Committee, IV, 496

Democratic Party, the new, II, 84, 154; III, 1; for poor man, IV, 64; adopts majority rule, IV, 462

Democrats, for tariffs for revenue, III, 250; nominate Samuel J. Tilden, III, 254; platform quoted, II, 267; platform of 1936, 462 f.; split in party, IV, 463; victory of, in 1936, 468, 469; ratio of votes, election analysis, IV, 405, 469

Denby, Edwin, Secretary of Navy, resigns, IV, 290

Denmark, and World War, IV, 200, 204

Department of Agriculture, IV, 465

Department, judicial, function of, I, 250, 265; *see* Judiciary

Department of Labor, created, IV, 135; employment service of, IV, 378; IV, 496

Department of State, I, 265

Department of the Treasury, I, 265; IV, 355, 373, 374, 400, 449, 450

Department of War, I, 265

Dependent Pension Bill, IV, 13

de Peysters, wealthy family, I, 121

Depression, *see* Panic, III, 208, 234, 274 f.; IV, 57, 321, 326 f.; in 1785, I, 226; and panic, 1894, IV, 48; beginning of great, IV, 277; causes of, IV, 360; IV, 365, 369, 376; factors offsetting moral ills of, IV, 383; near end at 1936, IV, 471; in 1937, IV, 506, 510

INDEX

Derbys, prominent commercial family, II, 4, 219
Detroit, post in Northwest, I, 128 *et passim*
De Vinne, Theodore, III, 241
Dewey, George, sent to Far East, IV, 88 f.; fight in Manila Bay, IV, 89; takes Manila, IV, 91, 133
Dewey, Thomas E., IV, 532
Diaz, Bartholomew, explorer, I, 6, 7
Diaz, Mexican dictator, IV, 174
Dickens, Charles, vogue of, III, 240
Dickinson, John, *Letters of a Farmer*, I, 145, 157, 162, 184, 189; quoted, I, 144
Dies, Representative, heads committee to investigate radical activities, IV, 533
Dighton Rock, inscription, I, 4
Dillinger, criminal, IV, 409
Dingley Tariff Bill, IV, 76
Dinwiddie, Governor, of Virginia, I, 74
Disarmament, IV, 282 f.; Conference, IV, 283; lack of progress, in 1935, in policy of, 379
D'Itajuba, Vicomte, Brazilian arbitrator, III, 224
Dix, Dorothea, reformer, II, 210
Dixie, written in 1859, III, 159
Dixon, Senator, Mason and Dixon Line, II, 321
Doheny, Edward L., involved in scandals, IV, 290
"Dollar diplomacy," IV, 175
Dolliver, Senator, Progressive, IV, 163, 165 f.
Dolphin, U. S. ship arrested by Mexico, IV, 192
Dominion of New England, I, 61
Donald McKay, "clipper" ship, II, 204
Donelson, Mrs., mistress of White House, II, 167
Dorchester, town of, I, 29
Dorr, Thomas W., governor, leader of revolt, "Dorr War," II, 258 f.
Douglas, Lewis W., Director of the Budget, resigns, IV, 402
Douglas, Stephen A., II, 293; III, 1; forces split, II, 322; debates with Lincoln, II, 339 f.; elected Senator, II, 343; nominated for President, III, 5; defeated, III, 7; prominence of, II, 319
Douglas, William O., Chairman of SEC, IV, 516 f.
Douglass, Frederick, prominent Negro, III, 99, 167
Dow, Neal, first prohibition law, II, 211
Draft Act, passed, for World War, IV, 232, 236 f.
Drafts, results of, in Civil War, III, 115 f.

Drago theory of non-intervention, IV, 142
Drake, Francis, explorer, I, 11, 209
Dred Scott decision, II, 335 f., 337, 339
Dress, after Revolution, II, 21 f.; in the West, II, 24
Drought, of 1934, IV, 399; of 1936, IV, 465
Duane, William, Secretary of Treasury, II, 180 f.
Duelling, never in vogue in America, I, 116
Duffield, George, minister, I, 184
Duke of Wellington, II, 92
Dulany, I, 93
Dunlap, William, adapter of plays, II, 5
Dunmore, Governor, I, 184
Durham, Bishopric of, I, 31
Dust storm of 1934, IV, 399
Dutch, I, 47, 95, 100; enterprise of, I, 15; ship with slaves, I, 22, 23; traders, I, 46
Dutch West India Company, I, 46
Dutton and Company, III, 237
Duty, upon tea, I, 143
Dwight, Timothy, one of the "Hartford Wits," II, 4, 65; quoted, II, 38

Earhart, Amelia, aviatrix, lost in Pacific, IV, 507
Early, General, Confederate, advance of, III, 94; near Washington City, III, 95
East Indian Company, formation of, I, 15, 155, 158
Eaton, Senator, Secretary of War, II, 164 f.; resignation of, II, 174
Eccles, Chairman, Federal Reserve Bank, IV, 505
Economic changes, in 1765, I, 136; after Revolution, I, 219; II, 247, 302; IV, 198; conditions, I, 240; II, 75, 258; IV, 23; factors, II, 237, 238 f.; IV, 376; forces, IV, 264, 366; laws, III, 231; level, I, 117; life of Colonies, I, 51, 96, 121, 124; questions in 1868, III, 199; system, II, 245
Economic Conference of World, plans for, IV, 364, 365; lack of success of, IV, 367, 369
Editorial, the, II, 236
Education, I, 106 f.; II, 17, the system, after Independence, II, 21; advance of (1830–1850), II, 231; after Civil War, III, 140; *see* Schools, Universities
Edwards, Jonathan, New England minister and writer, President of Princeton, I, 109, 111, 296
Eggleston, Edward, Hoosier author, III, 239
Egypt, overrun, I, 5
Eighteenth Amendment, the, IV, 269, 309 f., 316 f., 338 f.; repealed, IV, 376

553

INDEX

INDEX

involved in oil scandals, IV, 289; sentenced, IV, 290
Fallen Timbers, battle of, I, 291
Falmouth, town of, I, 70
Family influence, I, 121
Faneuil Hall, mass meeting in, I, 239
Far East, IV, 365, 382, 406, 501
Farley, Postmaster General, and Air-mail, IV, 396; Chairman Democratic National Committee, IV, 462; IV, 491, 525, 527, 528, 529
Farm Bill of 1938, IV, 519 f.
Farm Board, created, IV, 318
Farm lands, I, 118
Farm Loan Act of 1916, IV, 197
Farm Mortgage Moratorium Law, revised, upheld by Supreme Court, IV, 486; first, declared unconstitutional, IV, 486
Farm products, prices of, IV, 24, 359
Farm Relief Bill, IV, 361 ff., 364
Farmers, the, I, 103, 222, 232, 268; II, 193, 258; III, 132, 243 f.; IV, 25, 30, 318; mortgage debt of, IV, 359, 360, 361, 362, 363; indorse Bankhead Cotton Act, IV, 391; dust storm a tragedy to, IV, 399; contracts with, IV, 448 f.; demand money from Congress, IV, 449; IV, 465
Farmer-Laborite Party, IV, 405, 493
Farmers' Alliance, IV, 30 f.
Farming, changes in, II, 198; III, 129; machinery, II, 327; old-fashioned and modern, IV, 360
Farragut, David G., in command of Union fleet, III, 53; reaches Grant, III, 55; enters Mobile Bay, III, 97
Federal Agents, see "G-Men"
Federal appointments, question of, II₁, 268
Federal Constitution, I, 240: see Constitution
Federal Government, I, 229, 247; II, 2, 11; IV, 400, 415, 422, et passim
Federal Hall, I, 262
Federal Party, I, 293
Federal Reserve Act, IV, 186
Federal Reserve Board, IV, 311, 374, 386
Federal Reserve System, IV, 187, 279, 390
Federal Trade Commission, created for World War, IV, 196
Federalist Party, I, 285; II, 3, 36, 54, 65, 96, 103, 141
Federalists, the, I, 256, 264, 287, 296, 297, 298, 299, 301, 302, 306; II, 7, 16, 29, 31, 32, 44, 49, 52, 66, 67, 69, 102
Feke, Robert, portrait painter, I, 104
Ferber, Edna, author, IV, 306
Ferdinand and Isabella, King and Queen of Spain, I, 7

Field, James G., nominated for Vice-President, IV, 37
Fifteenth Amendment, passage of, III, 201 f., 265; IV, 9
"Fifty-four Forty or Fight," II, 264
Fillmore, Millard, nominated for Vice-President, II, 290; becomes President, II, 301; re-nominated for President, II, 331
Finances after Revolution, I, 272
Financial orgy in late 1920's, III, 214
Fine Arts, professorship of, at Harvard, III, 236
Finland, war debt of, IV, 392
Finney, Charles G., minister, II, 216
Firearms, manufacturers of, I, 225; IV, 407, 408
Firestone Tire and Rubber Company strike, IV, 474
Fish, Hamilton, as Secretary of State, III, 200, 222
Fish, Stuyvesant, financier, IV, 129
Fisher's Hill, Confederates defeated at, III, 95
Fisheries, I, 23, 55, 71, 214, 220; II, 327; disputes, III, 225
Fishing company, I, 27
Fishing fleets, I, 58
Fisk, Jim, notorious, III, 219; repudiates contracts, III, 220
Fitch, John, steam navigation, II, 111
Flatiron Building in New York City, IV, 19, 113
Flemington, New Jersey, Hauptmann trial at, IV, 443 f.
Fletcher, governor of New York, I, 93
Fletcher, Henry P., Chairman Republican National Committee, IV, 446
Flint, Michigan, strike at, IV, 495
Flint, Timothy, missionary, II, 25
Florida, I, 67, 86, 214, 279; II, 46, 48, 130; claimed by the French I, 9; Territory of, II, 252; secedes, III, 14; primaries, IV, 524; assassination of Mayor Cermak of Chicago in, IV, 350
Florida Ship Canal, a WPA project, killed, IV, 456
Florida case, the, III, 70
Floyd Bennett Field, IV, 533
Floyd, "Pretty Boy," criminal, IV, 409
Flying Cloud, "clipper" ship, II, 203
Flying Fish, "clipper," ship, II, 204
Flying Scud, "clipper," ship, II, 204
Food Administration, in World War, IV, 228
Forayers, novel by Simms, II, 219
Forbes, Charles R., head of Veterans' Bureau, resignation of, IV, 268 f.

555

INDEX

Forbes, General, march against Fort Duquesne, I, 77

"Force Act," passed, II, 177; III, 287

Ford Company, IV, 265, 270

Ford's Theatre, scene of Lincoln's assassination, III, 172

Foreign goods, exports of, II, 9

Forest Reserve Act of 1891, IV, 134

Forestry Service, IV, 164, 359

Forests, prevention of erosion of, IV, 400; "shelter belt" project abandoned, IV, 465 f.

Fort Duquesne, captured, I, 76, 77

Fort Frontenac, I, 77

Fort Jackson, III, 53

Fort Lee, in hands of British, I, 191

Fort Necessity, surrender of Washington at, I, 74

Fort Niagara, I, 77

Fort Pitt, I, 128

Fort St. Philip, III, 53

Fort Sumter, III, 23, 107, 162; bombarded, III, 25

"Forty-niners," II, 284

Foster, Stephen C., Old Folks at Home, II, 232 f.; My Old Kentucky Home, II, 233

Fourteenth Amendment, the, III, 193; IV, 9

Fox, Charles James, in the North Ministry, I, 211

Fox, John, author, IV, 116

France, see French, I, 14, 32, 53, 56, 123; II, 135; IV, 199, 214, 223, 297; claims of, I, 9; duel with England, I, 67; losses of, I, 77; longing for revenge, I, 198; at war with England, I, 199; policy of, I, 200 f.; makes treaties with us, I, 199; our obligations to, I, 213; our ally, I, 224; reduces our privileges, I, 225; our troubles with, I, 280 f.; relations with, I, 298; claims against, II, 182; agrees to make payments, II, 182; our debts to, II, 271; favorable to South, III, 72; in World War, IV, 214 ff. at Conference, IV, 255; at disarmament conference, IV, 282 f.; murder of Stavisky and fall of Cabinet in 1934, IV, 381; Foreign Minister assassinated, IV, 382; Air-mail of, in 1933, IV, 397; enters currency stabilization agreement with England and United States, IV, 466; IV, 536, 538, 540

Franco-Prussian War, III, 243

Franklin, Benjamin, delegate from Pennsylvania, I, 75, 242; early career of, I, 111; advice of, I, 134; disapproves confiscation of tea, I, 157; author of Articles of Confederation, I, 189; sent to Paris, I, 198; represents America in Paris, I, 211; character of, I, 244; quoted, I, 79, 246

Franklin, proposed state, I, 228

Fraud, after Civil War, III, 136, 230

Fraunces' Tavern, Washington takes leave of his officers, I, 216

Frederic, Harold, author, IV, 116

Fredericksburg, theatre in, I, 105; battle of, III, 69

Free lands, III, 128

Free schools, II, 231

Free silver, III, 309; IV, 57, 72, 100, 118

Free Soil Convention at Philadelphia, 1852, II, 312

Freedmen's Bureau, III, 168; bill passed, III, 183 f., 203

Freedom, bulwark of, I, 80

Freedom of conscience, I, 43, 65

Freedom of seas, IV, 249

Freedom of speech, I, 177; muzzled, IV, 246

Freedom of the Will, by Jonathan Edwards, I, 111

"Freemen," in the New World, I, 28

Freight rates, II, 194

Frelinghuysen, F. T., Secretary of State, III, 293

Frémont, John C., III, 59, 61; raises flag at Monterey, II, 276; nominated by Republicans f President, II, 331, 332; stubborn attitude, III, 44; nominated for President, III, 99

French, ships, I, 23; colonies, I, 32; empires, I, 49; population of, in America in 1690, I, 68; relations with the Indians, I, 68, 70, 86; families, I, 95

French and Indian War, I, 86, 125

French Revolution, American attitude to, I, 280

Freneau, Philip, poet in the Revolution, I, 186; II, 12

Frick, H. C., large coke manufacturer, IV, 23, 25, 26

Frobisher, explorer, I, 12

Frolic, British sloop, II, 88

Frontier, the, I, 44, 90, 100, 102, 119, 121, 122, 150, 264; our new, I, 226 f.; democracy of, II, 27; government of, II, 27; contributes to democracy, II, 236; at an end, IV, 20

Fuel Administration, in World War, IV, 228

Fugitive Slave Law, II, 157, 293, 296, 298, 301, 313, 314, 344; III, 20

Fuller, Margaret, leading reformer, member of Brook Farm, II, 207, 212

Fulton, Robert, makes trip on the Hudson in the Clermont, II, 112 f.

556

INDEX

Fundamentalism, II, 218

Funston, General Frederick, receives Aguinaldo's surrender, IV, 109; sent to Mexico, IV, 192

Fur trade, I, 10, 15, 23, 52, 81, 82, 233; II, 107

Fur traders, I, 125, 232; II, 263

Furniture, of early period, I, 100, 103; II, 18

Furniture making, I, 105

Furs, barter with Indians for, II, 4, 201

Gadola, Judge, IV, 496

Gadsden, Christopher, fellow radical of Samuel Adams, I, 137, 142, 148, 162, 165, 242; quoted, I, 132

Gadsden Purchase, II, 283, 304, 317 f.

Gage, Lyman J., Secretary of Treasury, IV, 75, 122

Gage, General, British commander, I, 143, 158, 165, 181; III, 54; made Governor, I, 160

Gallatin, Albert, Secretary of the Treasury, II, 37, 69, 98

Gallatin, *Report on the Subject of Public Roads and Canals*, II, 119

Galloway, Joseph, delegate to Continental Congress, I, 162, 186

Garfield, James A., connected with *Crédit Mobilier*, III, 229; nominated for President, III, 288; early career of, III, 290; elected President, III, 290; scandals raked up, III, 290; assassinated, III, 292

Garfield, James R., Secretary of Interior, IV, 164

Garland, Augustus H., as Attorney-General, III, 303

Garland, Hamlin, author, IV, 116

Garner, John N., nominated Vice-President, IV, 338; re-nominated, IV, 462; IV, 525, 527

Garrison, Lindley M., resigns as Secretary of War, IV, 208

Garrison, William Lloyd, abolitionist, II, 214, 243, 244, 245, 322, 332; quoted, 214

Gary, Judge, of Steel Trust, IV, 274

Gas masks, use of, to protect British Isles, IV, 443

Gaspée, revenue schooner, I, 154

Gates, General, commanding Americans in the South, I, 197, 206, 215; blunder of, I, 198

Gates, Sir Thomas, as governor, I, 19

General Court, constituted, I, 28, 30, 36, 133

General Electric Company, IV, 265, 304

General Federation of Women's Clubs, IV, 22

General Motors strikes, IV, 497, 506

Genêt, Edmond Charles, arrives in Philadelphia, I, 283 f.; marries daughter of Governor Clinton, I, 285

Geneva Award, III, 225

"Gentlemen," middle class of, I, 95 f.

George III, I, 128, 191, 278; II, 74

George, Lloyd, Prime Minister of England in World War, IV, 253, 255, 257 f.

George, Senator, IV, 526

George Washington, steamship, trip to France in World War, IV, 255

Georgetown, hamlet of, near Washington City, II, 14

Georgia, founded, I, 86, 90; ratifies, I, 257; secedes, III, 14

Georgian architecture of houses, I, 100, 102, 117, 118, 122; II, 17, 18, 99

Germans, I, 87, 91 f., 100; II, 256; III, 4; in Pennsylvania, I, 49; settlements, I, 86; numbers in colonies, I, 89; political troubles of, II, 196

Germantown, I, 102; defeat at, I, 195

Germany, IV, 132, 199, 214, 232, 257, 297, *et passim;* on blockades, IV, 204 f.; economic crisis in, IV, 327; *see* Submarine; air-mail in 1933 of, IV, 397; relations with United States, IV, 537; seizes Austria and Czecho-Slovakia, IV, 537; productiveness of wages in, IV, 538, 540

Gerry, Elbridge, envoy to Paris, I, 299

Gettysburg address of Lincoln, III, 145 f.

Gettysburg, battle of, III, 83 f.

Ghent, treaty of, II, 97 f.

Gibbons, John S., *The New York Evening Post*, III, 113

Gilbert, Sir Humphrey, discoverer, I, 9

Gilbert, Tennent, I, 108

Gillette, Senator, IV, 526

Gilman, Daniel Coit, president of Johns Hopkins, III, 240

Girard, Stephen, philanthropist, II, 107

Glass, Carter, the Democratic leader of the House, IV, 186; Senator, IV, 463, 485

Glass-Steagall Bill, passed, IV, 332

Glass blowing, I, 143

Glavis, L. R., charges of, in Taft administration, IV, 165

"G-Men," IV, 434, 435

Godkin, Edwin L., *The Nation*, III, 237

Goethals, G. W., engineer, work on Panama Canal, III, 148

Goethe, Wolfgang, German poet, II, 12

Gold, I, 11, 130, 131 f.; II, 186; III, 122, 152, 218, 246, 278, 281; IV, 11, 29, 33, 39, 48; from New Spain, I, 14; dreams of,

557

INDEX

I, 19; imports of, I, 54; discovered in California, II, 283 f.; basis, III, 123; yield of, III, 134; production of, III, 282; deposits, IV, 58; symbol of "money power," IV, 59; issue of 1896, IV, 60; standard, IV, 67, 68, 330; production of, IV, 100, 169; imports of, IV, 279; withdrawn from banks, IV, 351; embargo placed on, IV, 352; standard abolished, IV, 355; foreign reaction to abolishment, IV, 364; IV, 373, 374; government control of, IV, 374; coinage ratio of, IV, 374; export restriction lifted, IV, 406; steps to "sterilize" for credit basis, IV, 471; see special acts
"Gold bloc," IV, 386
Gold Clause, abrogation of, in financial documents, IV, 368 f.; IV, 387, 388, 389; upheld by Supreme Court, IV, 429 f.
Gold Purchase Scheme, IV, 376, 387
Gold Proclamation, by President Roosevelt, IV, 374
Gold Reserve Act, IV, 385 f.
Golden Circle, Knights of, III, 108
Gomez, Maximo, insurrection under, IV, 77
Gomez, Spanish discoverer, I, 8
Gompers, Samuel, great labor leader, IV, 30, 243
Good Hope, Cape of, I, 6
Gordon, Alexander, portrait painter, I, 104
Gorgas, Colonel, work on Panama Canal, IV, 148
Gough, John B., temperance orator, III, 240
Gould, Jay, financier, III, 214, 215, 216; corners gold, III, 219
Government, organized by Washington, I, 265; weakness of, I, 231; pay rolls of, IV, 424, 454; cost of, IV, 480; Roosevelt's plan for reorganization, IV, 480 f.; reaction to, IV, 481, 488, 494 *et passim*
"Government by telegraph," IV, 435
Government Recovery Agencies of 1933, listed, IV, 363 f.
Governor of colony, I, 65
"Granary, ever-normal," IV, 494
Grand Army of Republic, III, 304, 306 f.; IV, 465
Grand Central Station, IV, 114
Grand opera, II, 233
Grange, the, founded, III, 244 f.
Grant, Ulysses S., III, 44, 85, 97, 171, 224, 253, 268, 275, 279, 288; quoted, III, 50, 93, 105; in Mexican War, II, 281; becomes a brigadier-general, III, 48; early career of, III, 48 f.; captures Forts Henry and Donelson, III, 49 f.; captures Vicksburg, III, 84 f.; in command, III, 87 f.; made lieu-

tenant-general, III, 92; at Appomattox Court House, III, 104; report on South, III, 177; succeeds Stanton, III, 196; nominated for President, III, 198; scandals in administration, III, 218; relations with Gould, III, 219; his Cabinet, III, 200; his victory a tragedy, III, 200; exonerated, III, 220; re-nominated, III, 225; re-elected, III, 226; his second term, III, 228; weakness of, III, 230; panic under, III, 232; courage of, III, 248
Graves, British admiral, I, 209
Gray, Asa, botanist, II, 234
Gray, Robert, in the ship *Columbia*, II, 4
Great Atlantic and Pacific Tea Company, strike in, IV, 404
"Great Awakening, The," I, 108
Great Britain, IV, 392, 406, 407, 443, 466, 536, 538, 540; see England
Great Northern Railroad, IV, 124
Great Republic, ship built in 1853, II, 202
Great Seal of England, I, 64
Greece, descendants from, I, 4
Greeley, Horace, II, 236, 322; III, 40, 100; owner of *New York Tribune*, II, 234; opposed to Lincoln, III, 21; open letter to President, III, 73; nominated for President, III, 227; influence of, III, 227; death of, III, 228
Green, William, head of American Federation of Labor, IV, 403; quoted, IV, 457; IV, 475, 495, 499, 506
Greenback Party, III, 289
"Greenbacks," III, 123, 199, 246, 248; IV, 40
Green Bay, Wisconsin, IV, 400
Greene, General Nathanael, I, 192, 206; takes place of Gates, I, 207
Greenfield, Elizabeth, negro singer, III, 167
Greenland, discovered, I, 3, 4
Gregory Lode discovered, III, 135
Grenville, George, Prime Minister, hostility to colonies, I, 129, 130, 132, 134, 287, 288
Gresham, Walter Q., Secretary of State, IV, 39
Grey, Lord, Foreign Secretary in World War, IV, 216
Griffiths' "Birth of Nation," IV, 270
Griffiths, John W., designer of ships, II, 203
Groesbeck, Judge, of Illinois, counsel for President Johnson, III, 197
Grundy, Felix, leader of "War Hawks," II, 79
Guadaloupe, I, 123, 124 f.
Guam, ceded to U. S. A., IV, 94

558

INDEX

Guerrière, II, 88; surrender of frigate, II, 88
Guffey, Senator, IV, 524
Guffey Coal Act, IV, 432, 456 f.
Guide book, first American, I, 99
Guilford Court House, battle of, I, 207
Guiteau, Charles, assassin of Garfield, III, 292
Gulflight, sunk in World War, IV, 205
Gummere, S. R., IV, 147

Habeas corpus, writ of, I, 250; III, 125, 178, 206
Hague Tribunal, IV, 133, 145
Haiti, protectorate over, IV, 174
Hale, John P., nominated for President, II, 312
"Half-breeds," faction of Republican party, III, 253
Hallam, Lewis, Mr. and Mrs., actors, I, 105
Halleck, Fitz-Greene, poet, II, 220
Halleck, Major-General Henry W. H., commander of Union forces, III, 48, 52, 64, 82
Hamilton, Alexander, secures passage of resolution, I, 241; leading delegate from New York, I, 242; distinguished appearance, I, 243 f.; lack of actuality, I, 252; author of articles, I, 256; Secretary of Treasury, I, 265; early career of, I, 266; contrasted with Jefferson, I, 266 f., 270; views of, I, 267 f.; not an orator, I, 268; leader in Washington's Cabinet, I, 271; takes office, 1789, I, 272 f.; achievements as Treasurer, I, 273; acts to establish credit, I, 274; conflict with Jefferson, I, 275 f.; celebrated report on manufactures, I, 276; doctrine of implied powers, I, 276; how regarded by Madison and others, I, 277; does not conceal belief in necessity of corruption, I, 278; leader of commercial interests, I, 279; urges Washington to take third term, I, 280; regarding Treaty of 1778, I, 282; statement about imports, I, 285; interferes in all departments, I, 286; at the height of his power, I, 287; induces Washington to call out State Militia, I, 292; credit for new government to, I, 292; resigns his office, I, 293; dreams of, I, 301; disloyalty of, I, 302; split with Madison explained, I, 304; his pamphlet, II, 29; boss of the Federalist Party, II, 29; conflict with Jefferson, II, 29; plans of, II, 52; blocks Burr, II, 53; duel with Burr, II, 53
Hamilton, Doctor Alexander, Marylander, I, 101
Hamilton, John, Chairman Republican National Committee, 1936, IV, 461

Hamlin, Hannibal, nominated for Vice-President, III, 4
Hammond, George, British Minister, I, 284
Hampton Roads, scene of famous naval battle, III, 57; meeting of delegates, III, 101
Hampton, Wade, distinguished South Carolinian, III, 264
Hancock, John, fortune of, I, 97; character of, I, 146; breaks relations with Sam Adams, I, 154; English attempt to seize, I, 165; disappointment of, I, 170; on American side, an exception, I, 176; political deal of, I, 257
Hancock, General Winfield S., nominated for President, III, 289, 290
Hanna, Marcus Alonzo, Republican chairman, IV, 34, 71, 101, 105, 128, 143; character of, IV, 73 f.; elected Senator from Ohio, IV, 74
Harding, Sir John, Queens advocate, III, 70
Harding, Warren G., I, 231; nominated for President, IV, 266; elected President, IV, 267; character of, IV, 267; becomes President, IV, 275; opposed to League of Nations, IV, 282; and disarmament Conference, IV, 283; national budget under, IV, 287, 294; and the "Ohio gang," IV, 288 f.; scandals of administration, IV, 289; trip to Alaska, IV, 290 f.; death of, IV, 291; pity for, IV, 291 f.; mentioned, IV, 369, 468, 469
Hargreaves, inventions of, II, 15
Harlem Heights, battle of, I, 192
Harpers Ferry, III, 59, 61, 67; in possession of Union garrison, III, 66
Harriman, E. H., railroad financier, IV, 117, 118, 124, 129
Harriman, Kuhn, Loeb and Company, group of bankers, IV, 124, 125
Harrison, Benjamin, opposed to Constitution, I, 258
Harrison, Benjamin, IV, 14, 33, 34; nominated for President in 1888, IV, 1; election of, IV, 4; attributes of, IV, 5 f.; his Cabinet, IV, 7; favorable to bi-metallism, IV, 11; sends troops to Cœur d'Alene district in Idaho, IV, 27; renominated, IV, 34; defeated, IV, 38
Harrison, William Henry, chosen as agent, II, 23; Governor of Indiana Territory, II, 77; treaty with Indians, II, 77; takes command of force in West, II, 90 f.; nominated for President by Whigs, II, 183; nominated for President, II, 240; represented as candidate, II, 243; election of, II, 243; death of, II, 248

559

INDEX

INDEX

Hobart, Garret A., nominated for Vice-President, IV, 68
Holland, I, 14, 32, 53, 56; and World War, IV, 204; IV, 388
Holmes, Oliver Wendell, author, II, 226; III, 143, 238
Holt and Company, publishers, III, 237
Homer, Martin, III, 236
Homer, Winslow, American painter, III, 236
Homes, characteristics of in America, II, 19; government aid for improvement of, IV, 391; number in 1937, IV, 508
Homestead Act, passed, III, 128, 129, 185
Homestead strikes, IV, 26
Homicide, record of, in America, IV, 371; in England, IV, 317; rate for 1934 in America, and in Canada, IV, 408
Hood, General, Confederate, supplants Johnston, III, 96; abandons Atlanta, III, 96; defeat at Nashville, III, 96
Hooker, Joseph, Union General, "Fighting Joe," succeeds Burnside, III, 80; defeat of, III, 81; replaced, III, 82
Hooker, Thomas, leader of settlers, I, 38; preaches liberalism, I, 40, 42, 44
Hoover, Herbert, IV, 291; quoted, IV, 309, 314; Secretary of Commerce, IV, 268; nominated for President, IV, 307; elected President, IV, 310; "market," IV, 311, 313, 319; special session of Congress, IV, 318; optimistic statements of, IV, 320 f.; relations with Congress, IV, 328; moratorium, IV, 335 f.; renominated for President, IV, 338; defeat of, IV, 340; difficulties in last days of administration, IV, 349, 350; stand on inflation, IV, 450
Hoover, J. Edgar, head of "G-men," IV, 434
Hopkins, Harry, IV, 525, 530
Hopkins, Stephen, of Rhode Island, I, 75, 162
Hopkinson, Francis, poetry of, I, 186
Hospitals, in new possessions, IV, 110
Houqua, commanded by Captain McKenzie, II, 202
House, Colonel Edward M., member of Peace Commission, IV, 252; death of, IV, 540
House of Burgesses in Virginia, I, 22, 135
House of Lords, of England, IV, 368
House of Representatives, duties of, I, 249; mentioned, IV, 405
Houses, early, I, 99, 101
Housing Act, the National, IV, 391
Houston, cruiser, IV, 398
Houston, Texas, Democratic Convention of 1928 at, IV, 308
Houston, Sam, moves into Texas, II, 188;

President of Texas, II, 262; attitude toward Indians, II, 321
Howard, O. O., Major-General, head of Freedman's Bureau, III, 168
Howe, Julia Ward, *Battle Hymn of the Republic*, III, 144
Howe, General William, in command at Breed's Hill, I, 168; movements in Boston, New York and Philadelphia, I, 181 f.; ferries to Long Island, I, 192; goes into winter quarters, I, 193; lack of energy, I, 201; orders to, I, 195; with fresh troops, I, 191; orders to André, I, 204
Howells, William Dean, Consul in Venice, author, III, 20; *Life of Lincoln*, III, 144
Hudson, Henry, discovers river, I, 23
Hudson-Mohawk Valley route, I, 52, 82; II, 8
Hudson River, the, I, 46, 175, 191
Hudson River-Lake Champlain route, I, 194
Hudson's Bay, I, 4, 71
Huerta, Victoriano, Mexican leader, IV, 190 f.; abdicates, IV, 195
Hughes, Charles Evans, IV, 211, 257, 262; in charge of insurance investigation, IV, 149 f.; nominated for President, IV, 208; defeat of, IV, 209; Secretary of State, IV, 268; opens Disarmament Conference, IV, 283, 291; as Chief Justice of Supreme Court, quoted, IV, 430, 458 f.; IV, 490, 495
Hughes, Howard, IV, 533
Huguenots, French, I, 49
Hull, Cordell, Secretary of State, IV, 351; at World Economic Conference, IV, 367; "good will" tour of South America, IV, 380; at Peace Conference at Buenos Aires, IV, 476; IV, 537 f.
Hull, Isaac, friend and adviser of Andrew Jackson, II, 164
Hull, William, the first expedition in War of 1812, II, 85
Humanitarian reforms, II, 210, 212, 213
Humanitarianism, II, 214, 236, 238; III, 118
"Hundred," the, local organization, I, 21
"Hundred days," IV, 385
"Hunkers," split in Democratic party, II, 288, 289
Hunt, William, Secretary of Navy in Garfield's Cabinet, III, 291
Hunt, William Morris, American painter, III, 236
Hunter, General, takes place of General Frémont, III, 44
Hunter, William, publisher, I, 114
Hurricane of September 1938, IV, 531

561

INDEX

INDEX

INDEX

Labor, shortage of, III, 129; movement, III, 139, 163; versus capital, IV, 26 f.; unrest, IV, 274; strikes, IV, 401, 402, 403, 474; split in parties, IV, 474, 478, 486, 495 f., 495-499; *see* special unions
Labor Division, IV, 228
Labor Party, II, 197
Labor Reformers, new party, III, 226
Labor Unions, IV, 403; *see* special unions
Labrador, I, 3, 8
La Farge, John, artist, III, 236
Lafayette, Marquis de, inspired by dream of liberty, I, 199; on American side, I, 207, 213 f.; watches Cornwallis, I, 208; escapes from Paris, I, 281; visit of, presented with land, II, 140
La Follette, Philip, Governor of Wisconsin, IV, 524
La Follette, Senator Robert M., leader of Progressives, IV, 163, 172 f., 175, 290; nominated for President, IV, 295
La Follette's Seamen's Act, IV, 197
LaGuardia, elected Mayor of New York, IV, 380
Lake Champlain, I, 77, 180
Lake George, I, 180
Lake Superior, I, 74, 128
Lamar, L. Q. C., Secretary of the Interior, III, 283, 303
Lamont, Daniel S., Secretary of War, IV, 38
Lancaster, town in Pennsylvania, I, 121
Land, grant of, I, 73; in fee simple, I, 94; scarcity of, I, 119; drop of values, II, 125; price of, IV, 336 f.; loss of, due to wind and water erosion, IV, 400
Land Act, of Congress, II, 23
"Landholders," the, II, 259
Landholdings, huge, I, 119
Landis, Judge, decision of, IV, 150
Landon, Alf M., Governor of Kansas, nominated for President 1936, IV, 460 f.; 537
Landscape painting, I, 104
Landslides in elections, IV, 467, 468, 470
Lane, Franklin K., Secretary of Interior, IV, 184
Langdon, Cheves, II, 79
Lansing, Robert, Secretary of State, IV, 252
Larcom, Lucy, author, III, 144
Larkin, confidential agent, II, 277
Lawlessness, increase of, IV, 316, 408, 434
Lawrence, Captain, in *Chesapeake,* II, 90
Laws, need for carefully drawn, IV, 415; constitutionality of, IV, 483 f.
Lawyers, I, 115, 121
Leadership, lack of, in 1896, IV, 61; need of, IV, 350

League of Nations, IV, 211, 255, 262, 282, 296, 315, 335, *et passim*
Lease, Mary E., reformer, IV, 31
Leavenworth, II, 329
Le Clerc, General, II, 46
Lee, Fitzhugh, Consul-General, IV, 78
Lee, General Charles, turns traitor, I, 193, 201
Lee, Richard Henry, I, 134, 162, 258; introduces resolution, I, 188; famous words of, I, 306
Lee, Robert E., III, 30, 56, 59, 171; quoted, III, 105; in Mexican War, II, 281; captures John Brown, II, 344; succeeds Johnston, III, 62; movements against McClellan, III, 62 ff.; advances into Maryland, III, 65 f.; retreat of, III, 68; threatens Washington, III, 72; moves into Pennsylvania, III, 81; in Fredericksburg, III, 81; over-confidence of, III, 82; campaign against Grant, III, 92 f.; outflanks enemy, III, 93; outnumbered by Grant, III, 98; evacuates Petersburg, III, 104; surrender of, III, 104 f.
Lehman, Governor of New York, accepts re-nomination 1936, IV, 464; IV, 493, 528, 532
Leisler, Jacob, German leader, I, 62
Leland Stanford University, IV, 450
Le Mars, Iowa, farmers' rebellion against foreclosures at, IV, 359 f.
Lemke, Representative William, candidate for President 1936, IV, 464
Leonard, Daniel, takes Tory side, I, 186
Leopard, British frigate, II, 60
Letters of a Farmer, by Dickinson, I, 144
Levant, trading with, I, 14
Lewis, John L., forms C.I.O. Labor movement, 474 f.; influence of, IV, 475; IV, 495 ff., 506
Lewis, Sinclair, author, IV, 306
Lewis and Clark, route of, II, 116
Lewis, William B., II, 164
Lexington, I, 169, 177, 218; fight at, I, 166 f.
Leyden, emigrant from England, I, 23
Liberal Republican party, III, 221, 228
Liberalism, IV, 61
Liberty, I, 52; ideas of English, I, 78; fight for, not a New England product, I, 79; for individual, II, 213
Liberty, Hancock's sloop, I, 146
Liberty Bonds, IV, 243
Liberty Loan, IV, 276
"Liberty Party," II, 268, 269
Libraries, in New Spain, I, 10
Life, hard in the early days, I, 103
Life of the settlements, II, 26

565

INDEX

Life-insurance companies, III, 155
Lilienthal of TVA, IV, 515
Lima, Peru, IV, 537
Lincoln, Abraham, II, 241, 314; III, 8, 14,
90, 111, 112; quoted, II, 340, 341, 342,
343; III, 20, 24, 76, 145 f., 161, 171, 188;
debates with Douglas, II, 339 f.; defeated
for Senate. II, 343; nominated for President, III, 3; election of, III, 6; opposes in-
demnification, III, 18; Inaugural Address,
III, 18; prejudices against, III, 21; inaugural, effect of, III, 21; his Cabinet, III, 23;
caution of, III, 23; orders vessels to Sumter, III, 24; issues call for troops, III, 26;
insists on Union, III, 33; his assumption,
III, 35; is authorized to borrow, III, 36;
and *Trent* affair, III, 43; plans military
operations, III, 45; dispatches from Mc-
Clellan to, III, 64; gives command to Mc-
Clellan, III, 65; urges McClellan, III, 68;
intends to issue Proclamation, III, 73; his
position, III, 73; open letter from Horace
Greeley, III, 73; reads from Artemus Ward,
III, 76; replies to Greeley, III, 76; issues
proclamation, III, 77; troubles in Cabinet,
III, 78; calls meeting of Cabinet, III, 78;
handles situation with skill, III, 80; de-
poses Burnside, III, 80; ignorant of where-
abouts of Sherman, III, 97; renominated
for President, III, 98; Republicans opposed to, III, 99; seems impossible that he
can win, III, 99; overwhelmingly elected,
III, 100; assailed by Greeley, III, 100; offer
to South, III, 101; attends conference at
Hampton Roads, III, 101; insists Union be
saved, III, 110; difficulty to get men, III,
118 f.; difficult situation, III, 125; months
of anxiety, III, 126; signs Homestead Law,
III, 128; signs the bill authorizing Union
Pacific, III, 136; Gettysburg address, III,
145 f.; encounters defeatism, III, 147 f.;
resort to conscription, III, 151; concerned
with reconstruction, III, 167; theory of
seceded States, III, 168; attitude towards
ex-slaves, III, 169; vetoed bill on amnesty,
III, 170; second inaugural, III, 171; character of, III, 172 f.; assassination of, III,
172 f.; effect of his death, III, 174; Johnson selected by Lincoln, III, 175; suppression of freedom of speech, III, 178; his
plan favored by Johnson, III, 180
Lincoln, Benjamin, sent to South, I, 205, 239
Lincoln, Robert T., Secretary of War, III,
291
Lindbergh, Charles, flight across Atlantic, IV,
270, 304; child kidnapped, IV, 318; trial

of Hauptmann, IV, 443; forced flight to
England with family, IV, 444; protests
air-mail deaths of untrained army pilots,
IV, 397
Lining, John, studies problems of weather,
I, 113
L'Insurgente, French frigate, I, 301
Literary Digest, The, IV, 340; polls, IV,
404, 429
Literature, beginning in New England, I, 44;
flourish of, II, 232; after Civil War, III,
142; in the nineties, IV, 20
Little Belt, sloop of war, II, 80
Livingston, Edward, I, 7, 45, 46, 93; Secre-
tary of State, II, 175
Livingston, Philip, delegate to Continental
Congress, I, 162
Lloyd, Henry Demarest, and the "muck
rakers," IV, 20
Loan Certificates, I, 273
Loans, foreign, IV, 225
Locke, John, inspirer of Declaration, I, 190
Lodge, Henry Cabot, Senator, IV, 9, 63, 88,
94, 257, 296; quoted, IV, 56, 80, 89, 92,
94 f., 108, 130 f., 156 f.
Loeb and Company, bankers, IV, 124
Log cabin, II, 243
"Log rolling," II, 41, 272
Logan, James, botanist, I, 113
Logan, John A., III, 197; quoted, III, 188;
nominated for Vice-President, III, 296
Lôme, Depuy de, resigns, IV, 83
London, I, 11, 24; World Economic Con-
ference at, IV, 365, 367
London, Jack, author, IV, 116
London, new company, I, 16, 17, 18, 22
London Times, The, II, 203
Lonergan, Senator, IV, 526
Long, Senator Huey, power in Louisiana,
IV, 440, 452; assassinated, IV, 440; fol-
lowers of, IV, 464
Long, John D., Secretary of Navy, IV, 75
Longfellow, Henry Wadsworth, II, 223; III,
143, 238; most popular, II, 226; appeal to
sentimentalism, II, 232
Longstreet, General James, III, 83
Lookout Mountain, battle of, III, 88
"Lords of the Valley," I, 118
Loudon, English general, I, 76
Louisbourg, recaptured, I, 76
Louisiana, I, 227; II, 67, 324; ceded, I, 77;
Territory ceded to France, I, 303; comes
into our possession, II, 46; admitted, II,
115; Purchase, II, 132, 135; secedes, III,
15; after War, III, 169; under Huey
Long's dictatorship, IV, 440; Supreme

566

INDEX

Court's decision regarding his powers, IV, 440

Louisville, flourishing city, II, 117; Democratic Convention at, 1872, III, 228

L'Ouverture, Toussaint, Negro patriot, II, 46

Lovejoy, Elijah P., abolitionist, killed, II, 245

Low, A. A., owner of ships, II, 202

Lowden, Frank, Governor of Illinois, IV, 266

Lowell, James Russell, author, professor, ambassador, II, 223, 314; III, 43, 222, 238; quoted, II, 285; III, 144; service to democracy, II, 225; advocate of social causes, II, 232; *Biglow Papers*, III, 109

Loyalist, I, 205, 233, 264; treatment of, I, 177, 178 f.; heartily hated, I, 231

Loyalists, of Spain, IV, 499

Ludendorff, General, in World War, IV, 247

Ludlow Bill on war referendum, IV, 518 f.

Ludlow resolution for plebiscite on war, IV, 500

Lumber, I, 55

Lundy, Benjamin, *The Genius of Universal Emancipation*, II, 214

Lundy's Lane, battle of, II, 91

Lusitania, sinking of, IV, 205 f.

Lutherans, I, 51

Luxuries, extravagance of, III, 138 f.

Lyceum, success of the, III, 240

Lynn, city of, I, 29; II, 193

Lytton, Henry Bulwer, minister, II, 308

MacDonald, Prime Minister of Great Britain, arrives to plan World Economic Conference, IV, 364, 366

Machinery, manufacture of, II, 193; III, 133, 163, 242

Mackenzie, leader of revolt in Canada, II, 253

Macon, Nathaniel, called "last of the Romans," II, 72

Macon's Bill, II, 75, 79

Madeira, wine from, I, 130

Madero, Francisco, Mexican leader, IV, 174, 190

Madison, James, I, 241, 242, 243, 258, 285, 304; II, 50, 70, 81, 95, 120, 136; III, 13; quoted, I, 304; master spirit of Constitution, I, 252; *The Federalist*, I, 256; proposes a tariff, I, 272; disagrees with Hamilton, I, 277; Secretary of State, II, 37; becomes President, II, 66; choice of Jefferson, II, 68; warned by Adams, II, 73; issues Proclamation, II, 73; great mistake, II, 74; character of, II, 148

Mafia, operations of Italian, IV, 16

Magnalia Christi Americana, I, 110

Mahan, Admiral, mentioned, I, 289

Mail route, service of, II, 20

Maine, I, 33; winter of colony, I, 22; admitted in 1820, II, 116; part of Massachusetts, III, 132; goes Democratic in 1934, IV, 400

Maine, U. S. battleship, IV, 83 f.; sunk in Havana harbor, IV, 84

Maine Woods, III, 142

Malbone, Captain Godfrey, house of, I, 101

Malvern Hill, battle at, in Civil War, III, 63

Manchuria, seized by Japan, IV, 379

Mangum, Willie P., vote for, II, 183

Manhattan, merchants of, I, 46, 83

Manhood suffrage (*see* Suffrage), II, 119

Manigaults, I, 104

"Man-made Sahara," phrase of Franklin Roosevelt, IV, 400

Mann, Horace, educator, II, 231

Mann, J. R., Republican leader, IV, 188

Mann-Elkins Act, passage of, IV, 166

Manufacturing, growth of, I, 55; II, 195

Marblehead, architecture in, I, 101

Marbury *vs.* Madison, case of, II, 50, 51

Marching through Georgia, III, 144

Marcy, William L., II, 165; III, 288; instructions of, II, 326

Maria Teresa, Spanish war ship, IV, 93

Mariner's compass, II, 205

Marion, Francis, surprise of British, I, 206

Mark Twain, American humorist, III, 143; *Roughing It* and *Life on the Mississippi*, III, 239

Markets, problem of, III, 128, 131

Marsh harvester, II, 199

Marshall, John, I, 258; II, 16, 49, 83, 171; III, 13; quoted, II, 126 f.; envoy to Paris, I, 299; appointed Chief-Justice, II, 31, 56; decision of, II, 50; decision of McCulloch *vs.* Maryland, II, 125; importance of decisions, II, 127 f.

Martin, Homer, artist, III, 236

Martin, Luther, delegate from Maryland, I, 243

Maryland, I, 46, 49, 88, 90, 91, 93, 104, 110, 228, 241; II, 199; named for Queen, I, 31; revolution in, I, 63; Secessionist movement in, III, 28

Maryland, My Maryland, by James R. Randall, III, 159

Mason, George, I, 148, 242

Mason, James M., agent of Confederacy, III, 41; success of, in England, III, 90

Mason, Captain John, leader of attack on Indians, I, 40

Mason, John Y., represents America at Paris, II, 325

567

INDEX

Mason, Lowell, interest in music, II, 232
Mason and Dixon line, II, 246; III, 2, 30
Mass production, IV, 280
Massachusetts, I, 38, 41, 44, 56, 58, 105, 143,
155, 158, 160, 220, 228, *et passim;* coast
mapped, I, 23; population of, I, 30; bigotry
of, I, 37; charter, I, 59; expedition sent out
by, I, 70; payment to, I, 73; transfer of
Governor Burnet, I, 80; House of Repre-
sentatives, I, 147; population of, I, 245;
ratifies Constitution, I, 257; factories of,
II, 193; center of agitation, II, 299
Massachusetts Bay Company, I, 28
Massachusetts Institute of Technology, III,
140
Mather, Cotton, diary, *Magnalia Christi
Americana,* I, 110
Maverick, Representative Maury, of Texas,
IV, 528
Maximilian, set up as Mexican Emperor, III,
90, 191; executed, III, 191
May, S. J., urges secession of New England,
II, 333
Mayflower, the, sets sail, I, 23, 26, 43
Mayhew, Jonathan, minister, I, 184
Mayo, Admiral, sent to Mexico, IV, 92
McAdoo, William G., IV, 186, 187, 225, 266;
Secretary of Treasury, IV, 184, 186 f.; di-
rector General of Railroads, IV, 229; con-
flict with Alfred E. Smith, IV, 295; sup-
ports Franklin Roosevelt for Presidential
nomination, IV, 338
McCarran, Senator, IV, 493, 526
McClellan, George B., III, 58; in Mexican
War, II, 281; in command, III, 39; tactics
of, III, 39; policy of, III, 55; march up the
Peninsula, III, 59; plan of campaign, III,
60 f.; movements against Lee, III, 62 f.;
controversy about, III, 63 f.; over-estimates
enemy, III, 66; cautiousness of, III, 67;
deposed, III, 68; nominated for President,
III, 99
McClure's Magazine, IV, 115
McComb, John, architect in New York, II,
18
McCormack, Congressman, IV, 497
McCormick reaper, II, 129 f., 199
McCosh, James, President of Princeton, III,
240
McCulloch, Hugh, Secretary of Treasury, III,
246
McCulloch *vs.* Maryland, famous case of Su-
preme Court, II, 170
McDonough, Commodore, II, 92
McDowell, Union general in Civil War, III,
37, 56, 58, 60; defeat of, III, 39

McIntyre, Samuel, Salem architect, II, 18
McIntyre, Secretary to President Franklin
Roosevelt, IV, 522
McKay, Gordon, financial promoter, III, 134
McKean, Thomas, delegate from Delaware,
I, 162
McKinley, William B., IV, 7, 12, 13, 47, 83,
94, 121, 122, 169; quoted, IV, 112; free-
silverite IV, 66; nominated, IV, 68; elect-
ed, IV, 72; his Cabinet, IV, 74; the tariff,
IV, 75; sends ultimatum to Spain, IV, 85;
sends message to Congress, IV, 86; calls
for volunteers to fight Spain, IV, 88; popu-
larity of, IV, 101; election of, IV, 107;
character of, IV, 111; assassination of, IV,
112
McLane, Lewis, removed by Jackson, II, 180
McLeod, Canadian incident, II, 254; IV, 16
McNary-Haugen Bill, IV, 278
McPhaedris, house in Portsmouth, I, 101
McVeagh, Wayne, Attorney-General, III, 291
Meade, George G., in Mexican War, II, 281;
replaces Hooker, III, 82 f.; at Gettysburg,
III, 84 f.
Meat packing business, III, 164
Mechanical inventions, III, 129 f.
Medford, town of, I, 29
Medical Department during Revolution, I,
174
Medical schools, II, 21
Mediterranean, ports of, I, 5
Mellon, Andrew, Secretary of Treasury, IV,
268, 315; length of term, IV, 287; gives out
interview, IV, 311; makes statement about
Federal Reserve Board, IV, 312; resigns
from Treasury, IV, 332; becomes Ambas-
sador to Great Britain, IV, 333; death of,
IV, 508; benefactions, IV, 508
Melville, Herman, II, 224, 227, 230: III,
143; contrasted with Hawthorne, II, 221;
Moby Dick, II, 221; not mentioned by
Wendell, II, 222
Mendieta, President of Cuba, IV, 380
Mercantile class, I, 285
Mercantile theory, I, 54, 58, 123
Merchants, English, I, 179; Chinese, II, 4
Merrimack River, I, 27
Merrimac, re-christened *Virginia,* III, 57
Methodist Church, II, 26; missionaries II, 25,
263; split in church, II, 261
Metropolitan Museum in New York, I, 101;
III, 237, 241
Metropolitan Tower, in New York City, IV,
113
Meuse-Argonne sector, in World War, IV,
238

568

INDEX

Mexican War, movements in, II, 278 f.

Mexico, culture of, I, 1; independence recognized, II, 134; our relations with, II, 151; Emperor of, II, 188; government overthrown, II, 188; population of, II, 270; our relations with, II, 272; war with, declared, II, 275; treaty with, signed, II, 283; relations with, III, 289; IV, 191 ff.; resources of, IV, 190; IV, 386; confiscates oil properties, IV, 536

Mexico City, university, I, 41

Michigan, admitted as State, II, 75, 261; debt repudiated, II, 252

Middle Colonies, wealth in, I, 94, 188

Middle States, differences in, II, 2, 122; for protection in 1828, II, 155

Mifflin, Thomas, delegate from Pennsylvania, I, 162

Miles, General, receives surrender of Puerto Rico, IV, 93

Miller, Joaquin, Western poet, III, 239

Miller, Thomas W., Alien Property Custodian, IV, 268; sent to prison, IV, 289

Miller, William, preacher, II, 208

Millet, F. D., painter, III, 236

Milligan, L. P., case of, III, 126, 193

Millionaires, increase of, III, 164

Milton, John, poet, mentioned, I, 13

Mine-barriers, in World War, IV, 235

Miners' Union, IV, 496

Minneapolis, Republican convention at, 1892, IV, 33

Minnesota, I, 69

Minton, Senator, IV, 522

"Minute Men," in Boston, I, 165

Missionary emotion, III, 120

Mississippi, State, I, 102; admitted as State, II, 115; debt repudiated, II, 252; secedes, III, 15

Mississippi Valley, I, 9, 69, 74, 123, 175, 212, 279; II, 43; erosion of Trans-Mississippi farms during dust storm of 1934, IV, 399; yearly erosion in, IV, 400; et passim; bill passed for flood control, IV, 497

Missouri, admitted, 1821, II, 115, 328

Missouri Compromise, II, 132, 189, 261, 285, 295, 298, 316, 319, 320, 335, 336, 340

Missouri River, affected by 1934 drought, IV, 399

Mitchell, Charles E., head of National City Bank, money mismanagement rumored, IV, 351

Mitchell, John, first American treatise on the principles of science, I, 113

Mitchell, John, labor leader, IV, 128, 138 f.

Mitchell, Doctor S. Weir, author of *Hugh Wynne*, IV, 20

Mobile, in Federal possession, III, 98

Mobs in 1765, I, 136; attacks of, I, 146; in Boston, I, 157; in New York, I, 157

Mohawk Valley, I, 197; II, 22, 110, 198

Molasses, I, 129, 272

"Molasses Act," I, 84, 130, 145

Moley, Raymond, Assistant Secretary of State, member of "Brain trust," IV, 358; unpopular at World Economic Conference, IV, 367, 368

"Molly Maguires," secret Irish society, III, 275 f.

Monitor, meets *Merrimac,* III, 57 f.

Monmouth, battle of, in Revolution, I, 201

"Monopoly," cry of, I, 156

Monroe, James, Minister to France, II, 45; instructions from Jefferson to, II, 46, 61; Secretary of State, II, 69, 78; inaugurated as President, II, 103; in internal improvement bill, II, 120; messages of 1822 and 1823, II, 140; character of, II, 148 f.; product of Virginia, III, 13

Monroe Doctrine, the, I, 295; II, 89, 138 f., 307; IV, 52, 68, 131, 142, 200

"Monster, The," name for Bank of the United States, II, 125

Montevideo Conference, IV, 380, 393

Montgomery, Alabama, convention at, III, 15

Montgomery, General, captures Montreal, I, 180; quoted, I, 181

Monticello, Jefferson's home, I, 269, 293; II, 19, 36

Montreal, I, 81

Moore, John Bassett, IV, 487

Moore's Creek, defeat of British at, I, 183

Morgan, Arthur, Chairman TVA, IV, 520 f.

Morgan, Daniel, success of, in the South, I, 207

Morgan, J. P., IV, 23, 49, 119, 136; interview with Cleveland, IV, 49

Mormon, Book of, II, 208

Mormonism, spread of, II, 207, 209

Morocco, protectorate over, IV, 146

Morrill, Justin H., Representative from Vermont, III, 128

Morrill Act, passed in 1861, III, 122, 128

Morris, Gouverneur, delegate from Pennsylvania, I, 242

Morris, Robert, delegate from Pennsylvania, I, 189, 242

Morse, Jedidiah, *The American Universal Geography,* II, 3, 117; quoted, 117

Morse, S. F. B., inventor of telegraph, III, 163

569

INDEX

Morton, Levi P., Vice-President with Benjamin Harrison, IV, 1

Morton, Oliver P., war governor of Indiana, III, 261

Motley, John, historian, II, 224; III, 143; *John Barneveld*, II, 225; *History of the United Netherlands*, II, 225; *Rise of Dutch Republic*, II, 225

Motor-car industry, IV, 263

Motor production, drop in 1937, IV, 512

Mott, Lucretia, reformer, II, 212

Mount Airy, house on the James, I, 102

Mount Vernon, Washington's home, I, 239, 261

Movies, protest against indecency of, IV, 409 f.

Moving pictures, industry, IV, 263, 270

"Mugwumps," discontented Republicans in Cleveland campaign, III, 301, 302

Municipal Building, in New York City, IV, 113

Municipal government, efforts to clean up, IV, 120

Munitions industry, Congressional Committee investigation of, IV, 407

Munn *vs.* Illinois, famous Supreme Court decision, III, 309

Munsey's Magazine, IV, 115

Murfree, Miss (Charles Egbert Craddock), author, III, 240

Murphy, Governor, of Michigan, IV, 528

Muscle Shoals, bill for development of, IV, 369; Supreme Court decision on Wilson Dam project at, IV, 451

Muscovy, trading with, I, 14

Museum of Fine Arts in Boston, III, 237

Music, cultivated, I, 104

Musica, Philip, IV, 532 f.

Muzzey, Professor, quoted, III, 258

Napoleon, 44, 81, 83, 133, 182, 324; defied, II, 46; negotiations with, II, 47; supreme, II, 56; issues the "Berlin Decree," II, 57; his "Milan Decree," II, 57; confiscates every ship, II, 63; Decrees, II, 70; takes a hand, II, 72; abdication of, II, 92

Napoleon, Louis, our enemy in Europe, III, 89 f.

Narragansett Bay, I, 37

Nation, The, III, 236; quoted, III, 297

National Academy of Design, II, 232

National Association of Wool Manufacturers, III, 163

National Bank Act passed, III, 123

National City Bank of New York, IV, 351

National Cordage Company, failure of, IV, 40

National debt, III, 246; IV, 354, 375, 376, 385, 396, 420 f., 450, 459, 479, 489, 494, 504 f.; increase in 1937, IV, 512; deficit 1932–38, IV, 524; reaches new peak, 1938, IV, 530; see United States

National Democratic Party, IV, 70

National Housing Act, IV, 391 f.

National Industrial Recovery Act (*see* NRA)

National Road, II, 110, 114; Bill for the, II, 120

National Tribune, The, IV, 456

National Women's Party, IV, 458

Nationalism, III, 162, 164

"Natural rights," I, 139

Naturalization Act, I, 303

Naval Expansion Bill, IV, 524

Navigation Acts, passed in England, I, 56, 84, 143, 145

Navy Department, created, I, 301

Nazi government, beginning of, IV, 382

Nebraska, question of, II, 317 f.

Negroes, the first in America, I, 22; disposition of, III, 119; numbers of, III, 167; IV, 9; suffrage, III, 179, 198, 202, 207; IV, 8 f.; rights of, III, 181 f.

Nelson, T. R. R., counsel for President Johnson, III, 197

Netherlands, air-mail of, in 1933, IV, 397

Neutrality Act of 1818, II, 134

Neutrality Act of 1935, passed by Congress, IV, 433; renewed and modified in 1936, IV, 454

Neutrality Bill of 1937, IV, 487, 500; amended, IV, 494

Nevis Colony, I, 26

New Deal, IV, 356, 358, 369, 373, 376, 385, 387, 391, 400, 406, 416; *et passim*

New England, I, 30, 42, 58, 106; coast of, I, 23, 26; population of, I, 34; Confederation, I, 41; colonies, I, 70; mercantile scheme, I, 84; trade of, I, 85; character, I, 94; determination in, I, 95; different from South, I, 97; social class, I, 98; differences between New England and South, I, 98; mansions in, I, 101; literature of, II, 222; point of view, II, 222; contribution to intellectual needs, II, 229; historians of, II, 224; drift from main streams of American life, II, 230

New Hampshire, I, 106, 237; settled, I, 34 f.; population of, I, 245

New Harmony, community of, II, 207

New Haven, settled, I, 34; site of theocracy, I, 40 f.

570

INDEX

New Jersey, I, 46, 79, 92, 105; population of, I, 245; "Plan," I, 245; ratifies, I, 257
"New Lights," split in the Church, I, 109
New Mexico, Territory of, II, 318
"New Nationalism," programme of, IV, 170
New Netherland, Dutch claim to, I, 46
New Orleans, founded, I, 69 f., 227, 234, 303; II, 43, 46, 48, 113; battle of, II, 95 f.; merchants of, II, 186; occupied by Union forces, III, 53, 98; in carpet-bag régime, III, 203; murders in, IV, 16
New Spain, population of, I, 10
New World, I, 1, 11, 30; exploitation in, I, 15; English character in, I, 22; as asylum, I, 28; English colonies in, I, 32
New York, I, 46, 70, 92, 99, 106, 121, 143, 200 f., 227, 228; named for Duke of York, I, 47; colony, I, 53; added to New England, I, 61; colony best situated, I, 82; against Constitution, I, 190; agrees to, I, 190; ratifies, I, 259
New York Central, IV, 151; suspends dividends, IV, 329
New York City, I, 93, 102, 107; as trading post, I, 52; harbor, I, 240; the temporary capital, I, 260; early political life of, I, 266; intellectual life of, II, 5; commercial, II, 7; the leading commercial port, II, 8; population of, 1860, II, 195; shipping at, II, 202; talent in, II, 220; riots in, III, 115; Democratic Convention, 1924, IV, 295
New York Civil Service Reform League founded, III, 274
New York Custom House, III, 271
New York Evening Post, II, 288
New York Gazette, The, I, 114
New York Herald Tribune, IV, 479
New York Journal, The, IV, 83
New York State Minimum Wage Law, declared invalid, IV, 458; upheld by Supreme Court, IV, 486 f.
New York Stock Exchange (*see* Stock Exchange), IV, 19 f.
New York Sun, The, abuse of Cleveland, III, 229; IV, 35; quoted, IV, 506
New York Times, The, beginning of, II, 243; IV, 302, 311, 313, 314, 397, 454
Newfoundland coast, I, 8, 55; fisheries question, II, 132
Newlands Act, IV, 134
Newport, I, 200 f.; old mill at, I, 4; II, 7, 94, 101, 104
Newspaper, our first, *Boston News-Letter*, I, 113
Newspapers, IV, 17, 88, 288; increase of circulation, IV, 304

Niagara, Fort, II, 91
Niagara River, II, 86; crossing of, II, 253
Nicaragua, IV, 137; custom house in, IV, 173; our troops sent to, IV, 296
Nicaragua Canal, II, 307
Nicholson, Francis, Andros's deputy, I, 62
Nightingale, Florence, great service of, III, 118
Nine power treaty, IV, 283, 336 f.; Conference on, IV, 502
Nineteenth Amendment, IV, 269
NLRB, investigation asked, IV, 516
Nobel prize, IV, 306
Non-Conformist, in New England, I, 30
Non-Intercourse, II, 105
Norfolk, in possession of Confederates, III, 56
"Normalcy," coined by President Harding, IV, 263, 275
Norris, Frank, author, IV, 116
Norsemen, discoverers of America, I, 3, 4
North, Lord, of the Exchequer, I, 144, 149, 151, 155, 156, 158, 166; "It is all over," I, 210; resigns as Prime Minister, I, 211
North, contrasted with South, II, 9; antagonism towards South, II, 104; differences, II, 169; fear and passion of, II, 303; prosperity in, II, 304; III, 127; sentiment concerning slavery, II, 321; attitude toward South, III, 13; population of, III, 29; disasters of the, III, 37; affected by Proclamation, III, 77; conditions after Civil War, III, 106 f.; losses in Civil War, III, 148 f.; suspicious of South, III, 181; changes in, III, 208 f.
North American Review, II, 118
North Carolina, I, 48; ratifies Constitution, I, 259; secedes, III, 26; IV, 427
North Ireland, IV, 538
Northern Pacific, III, 234; IV, 42, 124 f.
Northwest, I, 233, 285, 288; plans for, I, 254
Northwest Mounted Police of Canada, IV, 435
Northwest Territory, I, 291; II, 23, 75
Norton, Charles Eliot, appointed professor, III, 237
Norton, John, leading Puritan minister, I, 42
Nova Scotia, I, 71
Noyes, John Humphrey, "perfectionist," II, 207
NRA, passed, IV, 370; IV, 371; codes, IV, 372, 378; blanket code issued by President, IV, 372; IV, 373, 387; report on, by Clarence Darrow and committee, IV, 398;

INDEX

Patents, number of, II, 205
Paterson, William, I, 243
Patman Bill, rejected, IV, 437
Patriots, I, 264
"Patroons," I, 93
Patterson, General, III, 37
Peace Commission at Paris, IV, 94
"Peace Conference," suggestion of Virginia, III, 18
Peace Conference after World War, IV, 251 f.
Peace Conference, at Buenos Aires, IV, 476
Peace of Utrecht, I, 70; IV, 212
Peace Treaty of 1763, I, 123
Peale, II, 117, 232
Peanut crop, IV, 427
Pearls, spices, etc., from East, I, 5, 9
Pecora, Ferdinand, Judge, IV, 532
Peek, George N., Foreign Trade Advisor to Roosevelt, IV, 392
Pekin, Illinois, general strike at, IV, 474
Pemberton, defends Vicksburg, III, 85
Pendleton, Edmond, I, 135
Pendleton Act, passed, III, 293
Penn, William, charter to, I, 48, 83; II, 10
Pennell, Joseph, artist, III, 236
Pennsylvania, I, 59, 79, 88, 92, 94, 95, 110, 121, 128, 235; II, 2 f.; charter granted, I, 48; colony, I, 53; frontier colonies, I, 87; Assembly, I, 188; against Constitution, I, 190; ratifies, I, 257; most democratic, II, 12; victory for schools, II, 231; banks closed, IV, 351
Pennsylvania, University of, I, 106
Pennsylvania Gazette, The, I, 114
Pennsylvania Railroad Union Station (1910), IV, 114
Pensions, roll of, III, 304 f.; scandals, IV, 286 f.; for Spanish War, IV, 325, 395; veterans, cut by Roosevelt, IV, 354; IV, 394, 395, 436, 456; Civil War, IV, 395; old-age, under NRA, IV, 378; IV, 456 f.
People's Party, the, II, 258; IV, 31
Pepper, George W., represents Pinchot, IV, 165
Pequot War, I, 40
Percy, Earl, I, 166
Perkins, Miss Frances, Secretary of Labor, IV, 352, 378, 496, 497, 506
Perkins, Thomas H., II, 4
Perry, Matthew, C., sent to Japan, II, 327
Perry, Oliver H., Captain, victory of, II, 90
Pershing, John J., IV, 237, 238, 294; despatched to Mexico, IV, 193; made commander in Europe, IV, 235
Peru, II, 134
Petersburg, I, 105; assault on, III, 94

Petition, to the King, I, 183
Petroleum, III, 134
Peyton, Randolph, I, 162
"Phalanxes," communistic associations, II, 207
Philadelphia, I, 94, 99, 105, 107, 111, 200 f., 227, 234; II, 42, 112; population of, I, 92; once more in our possession, I, 202; convention at, on May 14, 1784, I, 241 f.; outstripped by New York, II, 10 f.; population of, II, 195; riots at, II, 257; Republican convention at, 1856, II, 331; 1872, III, 225; Democratic convention at, 1936, IV, 461 ff.
Philadelphia & Reading Railroad, failure of, IV, 40
Philadelphia Record, The, quoted, IV, 453
Philippine Independence Bill, IV, 379; a new, IV, 393 f.
Philippines, IV, 79, 89, 92, 94, 101, 109, 156, 255; reject Independence Bill, IV, 379; IV, 393
Phillips Exeter Academy, II, 258
Phillips, Wendell, II, 322; quoted, II, 333; III, 99, 180; at Cooper Institute, III, 189
Phips, Governor, I, 70
Phonograph, IV, 19
Phyfe, Duncan, II, 18
Pickering, John, trail of, II, 51
Pickering, Timothy, in Adams's Cabinet, I, 298, 303; II, 52, 65, 96
Pickett's division, III, 83
Pierce, Franklin, nominated for President, II, 311; elected President, II, 312; offers to buy Cuba, II, 324; sends Minister to Spain, II, 325 f.
Pierce, William, quoted, II, 148
Pietists, I, 95
"Pilgrims" from Leyden, I, 24
Pillsbury, manufacturer, III, 214
Pinchot, Gifford, chief forester, IV, 164
Pinckney, Charles Cotesworth, I, 243; II, 29, 74, 81; envoy to Paris, I, 299
Pinckney, Thomas, nominated by Federalists for Vice-President, I, 296
Pit, The, by Norris, IV, 116
Pitt, William, Prime Minister, I, 76, 86, 127, 138, 143, 157
Pittsburgh, II, 110, 113, 195; renamed, I, 77; riots in, III, 276; steel mills, IV, 274
Pittsburgh Landing, attack at, III, 52
Pittsburgh Post-Gazette, on Hugo Black and Ku Klux Klan, IV, 495
Plan of Union, failure of, I, 75
"Planned economy," IV, 399

573

INDEX

Plantation, I, 20, 21, 32, 55, 90, 92, 93, 117; II, 109, 199; III, 30, 102, 208
Planters, I, 119, 235; II, 63, 122, 124
Platt, Thomas C., III, 254, 262, 290, 291; IV, 64, 103, 105, 160
Platt Amendment, IV, 95, 96, 380
Plymouth, company, I, 16, 17, 22, 34, 41
Poe, Edgar Allan, poet, lonely figure of, II, 219, 230
Political philosophy different from British, I, 142
Political rights, I, 120
Political theories, II, 206
Political thought, recent influences on, III, 165
Politics, I, 54
Polk, James K., nominated for President, II, 266; practically unknown before nomination, II, 266 f.; sends Slidell to Mexico, II, 272; declares war against Mexico, II, 275; instructions to consul at Monterey, II, 276; qualities of, II, 287, 324
Pollock vs. Farmers' Loan & Trust Company, IV, 47
Pontiac rebellion, I, 128
"Pony Express," the, III, 136
Poor, laws for the, II, 212
Poor Richard's Almanac, I, 112
Pope, General, III, 44; made commander, III, 64 f.
Population, distribution of, II, 1; beyond the Alleghenies, II, 22; distribution of, II, 160; shift in, II, 192; increase of urban, II, 194 f.; increase of, II, 200; in West, in 1790, I, 228; changes in, IV, 23
Populist movement, IV, 31, 37
Porches, I, 104
Port Tobacco, I, 105
Porter, Fitz-John, at Gaines's Mill, III, 63, 85
Porter, Horace, Grant's secretary, III, 220
Porter, Peter B., leader of "War Hawks," II, 79, 91
Portland, Oregon, IV, 399; strike at, IV, 403
Porto Rico, I, 255; IV, 76, 79, 92, 93, 94, 110; IV, 398
Portsmouth, New Hampshire, peace meeting at, IV, 146
Portugal, reached by da Gama, I, 7
Portuguese explorers, I, 6, 7, 15
Post, Wiley, aviator, killed, IV, 442
Postal Savings Bank, establishment of, IV, 37
Posts, on the American side, I, 233
Potato Act, repeal of, requested, IV, 451
Potomac River, I, 175, 274

Practical Navigator, The, by Nathaniel Bowditch, II, 3
"Prairie schooner," II, 201 f.
Preble, Commodore, II, 42
Precious metals, I, 54
Pre-exemption Act, II, 250
Presbyterians in Oregon, II, 263
Prescott, Colonel William, I, 168
Prescott, historian, II, 224
President, duties of, I, 248
President of Switzerland, III, 224
Press, censorship of, I, 61
Prevost, General, losses of, II, 92
Price-Fixing Committee, IV, 228
Prices, rise of, I, 221; in 1857, II, 338; decline of, IV, 29; in 1921, IV, 278 f.; maladjustment of, IV, 360; fluctuation of, IV, 361; effect of depreciation on, IV, 375; artificial control of, IV, 426; structure of, IV, 505
Princeton, I, 105; III, 156
Printing press, II, 237; IV, 17; in New Spain I, 10
Privateering, I, 220, 223
Proclamation, Gold, IV, 374
Proclamation Line of 1763, I, 226
Proclamation of Amnesty, III, 169
Proclamation of Non-Intercourse, II, 72
Proclamation of 1763, I, 128
Proclamation, repealing Prohibition, IV, 377
Proctor, British general, II, 91
Proctor, Senator, IV, 83
Production power, IV, 451
Products, substitutes for, IV, 427
Progressive Convention at Chicago, 1912, IV, 179
Progressive League, IV, 176
Progressive Party, IV, 172, 295, 405
Progressive Senators, IV, 163
Prohibition law, the first, II, 211; III, 11, 252; IV, 315 f.; repealed, IV, 376 f.
Prohibition Party, first appearance, III, 226; IV, 67; IV, 377
Propaganda, IV, 211, 244
Prosperity, II, 80, 181; III, 233; IV, 57, 154, 278, 279, 299, 310, 314; after Revolution, I, 218; in 1791, I, 226; end of, after Revolution, I, 237
Protestants, I, 12, 65; animosity toward Catholics, I, 63; IV, 410
Provincial Congress, of Massachusetts, I, 165
Prussia, I, 77; III, 223; IV, 200 et seq.
Public credit, I, 273
"Public Enemies," IV, 408, 409, 434, 435
Public lands, sale of, II, 185; III, 209
Public library movement, I, 113
Public utility securities, IV, 370

574

INDEX

Public works system, IV, 418, 419, 420
Publishing, IV, 115
Pulaski, Polish general, I, 199
Pulitzer, quoted, IV, 81
Pullman, George M., III, 213; strike in his company, IV, 43 f.
"Pump-priming," IV, 390, 437, 510
Purchasing power, II, 194
Pure Food Act, IV, 150
"Purge," advocated by President Franklin Roosevelt's friends, IV, 524 f.; fails, 525
"Purge," by Hitler, in Germany, IV, 381
Puritan New England, I, 110; II, 228
Puritanism, force of, I, 12 ff.
Puritans, the, I, 26, 34, 40, 108, 131; their beliefs, I, 29; their characteristics, I, 31; their legislatures, I, 118
Putnam, General, issues an army order, I, 220
Pyle, Howard, III, 236

Quakers, the, I, 43, 44, 47, 58, 92, 95; II, 12; persecution of, I, 42; retreat in Pennsylvania, I, 49
Quay, Matthew, III, 218; IV, 105
Quebec, I, 77, 129, 160, 180; post at, I, 11; attack on, I, 70
Queenstown Heights, II, 86
Quincy, Josiah, Jr., I, 152

Radicals, catchwords of, I, 235
Radio, IV, 19, 271, 446
Railroads, II, 111, 205; III, 130, 152, 155, 215, 234, 236, 244, 308; IV, 25, 33; surveys for, II, 318; mileage of, II, 338; prosperity for, III, 136; grants to the, III, 209; mileage of, III, 209; earnings, III, 276; mileage of, IV, 119; salary reductions demanded by RFC, IV, 378
Railway freight, drop in, 1937, IV, 512
Railway Labor Act upheld by Supreme Court, IV, 486
Railway Managers' Association, IV, 44
Railway Pensions Act, declared unconstitutional, IV, 432
Rain, shortage of, in 1934, IV, 399
Rainbow, "clipper" ship, II, 203
Raleigh, Walter, explorer, I, 9, 12, 17
"Raleigh letter," II, 265
Randolph, Edmund, I, 62, 242, 271; quoted, I, 245; Attorney-General, I, 265; Jefferson's successor, I, 287
Randolph, Edward, special investigator, I, 59
Randolph, John, II, 72; quoted, II, 157
Randolph, Peyton, I, 135

Ranger, I, 209
Ratford, II, 60
Ravenels, I, 104
Read, George, I, 162
Reading Railroad, IV, 128
Recall of judges, IV, 161
Recession, business, in 1937, IV, 506; of 1937–38, IV, 510
Reciprocity, IV, 15
Reconcentrados, IV, 78
Reconstruction Act passed, III, 193 f., 201
Reconstruction Finance Corporation (see RFC)
Recovery Agencies of Government, listed, IV, 363
Red Cloud, leader of Sioux, III, 212
Red Cross, IV, 242
Reed, James A., former Senator, IV, 463
Reed, Thomas B., elected Speaker, IV, 7, 8
"Reed Rules," IV, 8
Referendum, IV, 161
Reforestation, IV, 439 (see Forestry, CCC)
Reform Club, IV, 35
Refrigerator car, III, 213
Regional planning proposal, IV, 494
Registry fees, I, 61
Reid, Whitelaw, nominated for Vice-President, IV, 34
Religion, a moving impulse, I, 26; churchgoing after Revolution, II, 25; breakdown of the old, II, 208
Religious heresy, I, 13; beliefs of Puritans, I, 29; toleration, I, 37; life, in Early America, I, 108; ideas, II, 208
"Remember the Maine," IV, 85
Reparations Commission, IV, 294
Representation, idea of, I, 138; popular, II, 28
Republic of Panama, IV, 140, 388
Republic Steel Company, strike, IV, 498
Republican Party, I, 285, 293; II, 103, 142; III, 179, 185, 188, 201, 202, 226, 250, 257; formation of, 1854, II, 323; Convention at Philadelphia, 1856, II, 331; Convention at Chicago, 1860, III, 3; Convention of, 1864, III, 98; for sound money, III, 199; Convention at Philadelphia, 1872, III, 225; platform of 1872, III, 231; party of protection, III, 250; Convention in Cincinnati, 1876, III, 253; attitude of the South, III, 265; Convention at Chicago 1880, III, 288; Convention at Chicago 1884, III, 296; Convention at Chicago, 1888, IV, 1; platform quoted, IV, 2; defeat of, IV, 14; Convention at Minneapolis, 1892, IV, 33; conception of, IV, 63; Convention, IV, 68;

575

INDEX

President, IV, 111; is right about big business, IV, 120; love of fairness, IV, 121; his Cabinet, IV, 122; first message to Congress, IV, 126; control of business, IV, 127; undertakes settlement of mining dispute, IV, 130 f.; and the Venezuela question, IV, 133; and conservation, IV, 134 f.; and the Canal, IV, 136 f.; wields "the big stick," IV, 139; makes treaty with Santo Domingo, IV, 141; nominated for President, IV, 143; elected President, IV, 144; leads the country in idealism, IV, 144; and Russo-Japanese War, IV, 145 f.; arranges for conference at Algeciras, IV, 147; champion of doctrine of one law for rich and poor, IV, 151; hold on people, IV, 152 f.; his policies, IV, 156; contrast with Taft, IV, 156 f.; in Africa, IV, 162; met by Pinchot IV, 165; public regard for, IV, 168; return from Africa, IV, 169; no specific programme to offer, IV, 170; popularity of, IV, 175 f.; does not avoid the spotlight, IV, 176; nominated by Progressives, IV, 179; defeated for Presidency, IV, 181; request refused by Wilson, IV, 233 f.

Root, Elihu, Secretary of War, IV, 122, 257, 262

Root-Takahira Treaty, IV, 154

Rosecrans, General, defeat of, III, 86 f.

"Rough Riders," IV, 89, 92, 104

Roxbury, II, 29

Royal Academy, I, 104

Royal Charter for Massachusetts, I, 28

Rule of 1756, the, II, 56

Rum, I, 84, 272

Rush, Richard, minister, II, 136

Russell, Jonathan, II, 92, 98

Russell, Lord John, III, 22, 43, 70

Russia, IV, 199, 214, 223; offer of, III, 190; power of extending, II, 137; boundary in America, II, 139; fall of, IV, 221; mass murder in, IV, 382; IV, 538, 540

Russo-Japanese War, IV, 145

Rutledge, Edward, I, 162, 244

Rutledge, John, I, 162, 243

Sacco and Vanzetti, case of, IV, 273

Sackville-West, minister, mistake of, IV, 3

Sacramento, city of, III, 209

"Safety" bicycle, IV, 18

Sagasta, IV, 83

Sahara Desert, I, 6

"Saint Cecelia Society" in Charleston, I, 105

"Salary grab," III, 230

Salem, settlement at, I, 4, 27, 101

Salisbury, Lord, and the Venezuela dispute, IV, 53

Salmon Falls, attack by Indians, I, 70

Salvation Army, IV, 242

San Francisco, Democratic Convention at, 1920, IV, 266

San Juan Hill, in Spanish American War, IV, 92

"Sanitary Fairs" in Civil War, III, 118

Santa Anna, ruler of Mexico, II, 188, 278 f.; routed, II, 189; retreat of, II, 280; resignation of, II, 282

Sampson, Admiral, in Spanish-American War, IV, 91, 92; jealousy with Schley, IV, 93

Santa Fe Trail, II, 201

Santiago, port of, I, 225; assaulted in Spanish-American War, IV, 92

Santo Domingo, II, 44; III, 220; treaty with, IV, 141; election supervised, IV, 173

Saratoga, British defeat at, I, 198, 200 f.

Sargent, painter, III, 236

Saturday Evening Post, The, IV, 115

Savannah, II, 193; capture of, in Revolution, I, 205; evacuated by Confederates, III, 97

Savannah, first Atlantic steamship, II, 113

Savannah, Confederate schooner, III, 36

Savings banks, increase of, III, 140; failure of, III, 233

"Scalawags," after Civil War, III, 203

Scandals, of Reconstruction Days, III, 203; in Harding administration, IV, 151; banking, IV, 351; of 1938, IV, 532 f.

Scandinavians in the West, II, 196; III, 4

Schenectady, attack by Indians, I, 70

Schley, Admiral, in Spanish-American War, jealousy with Sampson, IV, 91 f.

School fund, I, 253

Schurz, Carl, III, 4, 221, 263, 268, 302; quoted, III, 187; service to country, III, 177; report of, on South, III, 177; Secretary of Interior, III, 261; free hand given to, III, 271

Schuyler, General Philip, in Revolution, I, 172, 180, 266

Schuylers, the, prominent New York family, I, 93; 121, 280; II, 7

Schwab, Charles M., steel magnate, IV, 378 f.

Science, interest in, II, 234

Sclopis, Count, III, 224

Scotch immigration, I, 87, 92

Scotch Presbyterians, II, 25; distress of, I, 87

Scott, Thomas A., vice-president, Pennsylvania Railroad, III, 233

Scott, Walter, popularity in America, II, 12

Scott, General Winfield, victory of, II, 91;

578

INDEX

sent to Charleston, II, 176; leadership of, in Mexico, II, 278; captures Vera Cruz, II, 280; armistice with Santa Anna, II, 281; movements of, II, 282 f.; nominated for President, II, 311; head of Union army, III, 37

"Scrap of paper," a, IV, 214

Scribner's, Charles, Sons, III, 237

Scribner's Magazine, III, 236

Sea Witch, "clipper" ship, II, 203

Secession, the leading issue, III, 9

Sectional characteristics, II, 2

Sectionalism, I, 296; III, 162

Securities Act, IV, 355, 391

Sedition Act, I, 303

Seldes, Gilbert, quoted, II, 211

Self-government begun in America, I, 22

Seminole Indians, in Florida, II, 129

Senate (*see* Congress), ratifies Alaska Purchase, III, 190; withholds confirmation of Hayes's Cabinet, II, 263; on Federal appointments, II, 273 f.; passes currency bill, III, 283 f.; fight on Spanish Treaty, IV, 94; opposition to Treaty of Versailles, IV, 251 ff.; confirms Roosevelt's Cabinet appointments, IV, 351; approves Roosevelt's banking bill, IV, 354; IV, 405; rejects St. Lawrence Seaway Treaty with Canada, IV, 395; Committee to investigate utility industry lobby, IV, 453

Separatists, religious group, I, 13, 23

Serapis, English frigate, I, 208, 209

Serbia, in World War, IV, 199

"Seven Days' Battles," in Civil War, III, 63

Seven Pines, battle of, in Civil War, III, 62

Sewall, Arthur, nominated for Vice-President, IV, 70

Sewall, Judge Samuel, *Diary*, I, 110

Seward, William H., II, 293; III, 3, 112, 222; Governor of New York, II, 254; Secretary of State, III, 22; chafing at delay, III, 23; negotiates, III, 24; fantastic plan, III, 24; object of attack, III, 78; proposal of Napoleon, III, 90; in charge of foreign affairs, III, 189; success of, regarding Alaska, III, 190

Sewing machine, II, 206; export of, III, 133

Seymour, Horatio, Governor of New York, III, 115; nominated for President, III, 198; for sound money, III, 249

Shafter, General, in Spanish War, IV, 92 f.

Shakespeare, reading of, in America, I, 12, 105

Shame of the Cities, The, by Lincoln Steffens, IV, 116

Shannon, British frigate, II, 90

Shannon, Wilson, minister to Mexico, II, 271

Shaw, Anna Howard, reformer, IV, 22

Shays, Captain Daniel, rebellion of, I, 238 f., 258

Sheffield, Lord, *Observations of the Commerce of the American States*, I, 224

Shelburne, Lord, I, 126, 128, 211, 224

"Shelter belt" project abandoned, IV, 465 f.

Shenandoah Valley, I, 87; in Civil War, III, 61, 66, 68, 94, 98, 154 f.

Shepherd, Elliot F., reformer, III, 302

Sheridan, General Philip, rides from Winchester, III, 95; victory of, III, 95; captures railway at Danville, III, 104; sent by President Johnson to Mexican border, III, 191

Sherman, James S., nominated for Vice-President, IV, 158

Sherman, John, III, 246, 261, 284, 285; IV, 11; Secretary of State, IV, 74; sends note to Spain, IV, 82

Sherman, Roger, I, 161, 242

Sherman, William T., march to the sea, III, 46, 92 f.; joins Grant, III, 85; in command of Army of Tennessee, III, 88; takes Atlanta, III, 100; leaves Savannah, III, 102; quoted, III, 97

Sherman Anti-trust Law, IV, 123, 126, 132, 196; found hindrance to competition, IV, 371

Sherman Silver Act of 1890, IV, 39, 40

Shiloh, battle of, III, 52

"Shin-plasters," in Civil War, III, 123

Shipping, II, 8, 258; profits, II, 107; losses, III, 136; subsidies, IV, 433

Shirley, Governor of Massachusetts, I, 75

Sigel, General, beaten by Early, III, 94

Silliman, Benjamin, geologist, II, 234

Silver (*see* free silver), I, 130; II, 186; III, 152, 281; IV, 11, 39; dreams of, I, 19; production of, III, 281 f.; stocks nationalized, IV, 386; foreign exchange affected by our policy on, IV, 386; embargo placed on, IV, 352; offshoot of "great compromise" in Constitution, IV, 386 f.; IV, 431

Silver Purchase Act, IV, 386

Simcoe, Lieutenant-Governor of Canada, I, 284

Simms, William Gilmore, notable writer of South, II, 219

Simpson, "Sockless" Jerry, IV, 31

Sinclair, Henry F., trial of, IV, 290

Sinclair, Upton, Socialist candidate for California governor, IV, 401; "EPIC" plan of, IV, 401

579

INDEX

INDEX

INDEX

Tempo of life, IV, 272

Tenure of Office Act, passed, by Congress, III, 303; III, 195 f.

Tennessee, and Western movement, I, 226; admitted as State in 1796, I, 291; secedes, III, 26; after War, III, 169

Tennessee Valley Authority (see TVA)

Tenth Amendment to the Constitution, I, 275

Territory, acquired by Spanish-American War, IV, 97

Texas, II, 48, 318; difficulties in, II, 188; annexation of, II, 190; size of, II, 190; attempts at annexation, II, 250 f.; recognized by some nations, II, 251; annexation discussed, II, 261; annexation defeated, II, 262; the burning question of, II, 265 f.; problem of governing, II, 271; annexation proposed, II, 269; admitted, II, 270; slavery in, II, 294; debt of, II, 296

Textile industry, code of, IV, 372

Textile mills, I, 225; II, 105, 121, 193

Textile Relations Board, IV, 404

Thackeray, W. M., in The Virginians, I, 92

Theatre, in New York, II, 5; in Philadelphia, II, 15; in Charleston, II, 15; little advance in, II, 234

Theocracy in New England, I, 30, 31, 65

Theuss, Jeremiah, portrait painter, I, 104

Third-party movement of La Follette brothers, IV, 524

Third term, poll on, in 1938, IV, 510

Thirteenth Amendment, III, 179

"Thirty Dollars every Thursday," IV, 528

Thirty Years' War, I, 88

Thomas Amendment to Farm Relief Bill, IV, 361 f., 364, 385

Thomas, General George H., in Mexican War, II, 280; "Rock of Chickamauga," III, 87; commander of Army of the Cumberland, III, 88; opposes Hood, III, 96

Thomas, Lorenzo, appointed by Johnson, III, 196

Thomas, Norman, Socialist, presidential candidate, IV, 463

Thompson, Richard W., Secretary of the Navy, III, 261

Thoreau, Henry D., author, II, 226, 227; Walden, II, 228; Week on Concord and Merrimack Rivers, II, 228; death of, III, 142

Thorwaldsen, Erik, discoverer, I, 3

Thurman, A. G., nominated Vice-President, IV, 1

Ticknor, F. O., Little Giffen of Tennessee, III, 159

Ticknor, George, History of Spanish Literature, II, 224

Ticonderoga, Fort, I, 77, 167, 169

Tilden, Samuel J., nominated for President, III, 253; controversy over election, III, 255 f.; character of, III, 257; death of, III, 258

Tillman, "Pitchfork Ben," Senator, IV, 31

Timber, I, 58

Timrod, Henry, writer, II, 219; Ode on the Confederate Dead, III, 159

"Tippecanoe and Tyler, too," II, 243

Tippecanoe Creek, battle of, II, 76 f.

"To a Waterfowl," II, 118

Tobacco, I, 55; II, 8, 65, 92, 108, 120, 122, 199; IV, 166; staple crop, I, 19, 52; as currency, I, 57; "aristocracy," II, 109

Tobacco Act, the, Kerr-Smith, IV, 427; repeal requested, IV, 451

Toombs, Robert, secessionist, III, 16

Toral, General, IV, 93

Torch-light processions, II, 242

Tories, treatment of, I, 177 f., 264; II, 136

Tower, the, in London, I, 28

Town schools, I, 106

Town-meeting, I, 44, 52, 154; II, 65

Townsend, Doctor Francis, IV, 464

Townsend Plan, IV, 441 f., 464, 528

Townshend, Charles, Lord of the Exchequer, I, 143, 151, 152; death of, I, 149

Townshend Acts, I, 147

Tracy, Benjamin F., Secretary of Treasury, IV, 7

Trade conditions, changes in, III, 140

Trade posts, IV, 538

Trade routes, I, 56

Trading centers, I, 10, 69

"Trading with Enemy Act," use of by Roosevelt, IV, 352

Tramp, Tramp, Tramp, the Boys Are Marching, III, 144

Transportation, II, 194; III, 163; problem of, II, 205; III, 130; system, III, 29; of troops in World War, IV, 229

Transylvania, I, 228

Travel between the colonies, I, 99

Treaty of Alliance, I, 212

Treaty of Amiens, II, 45

Treaty of Paris, 1763, I, 77

Treaty of Peace, I, 127

Treaty of Peace, after Spanish-American War, IV, 94

Treaty of Peace, of Revolution, I, 229

Treaty of San Ildefonso, II, 44

Treaty of 1783, I, 284

Treaty of Washington, signed, III, 223

INDEX

Treaty, signed at Versailles, IV, 257, 262 f.
Treaty with Cuba, IV, 393
Treaty with England, 1846, signed, II, 274
Treaty with England, terms of, I, 213
Treaty with the Indians, I, 291
Trent, British mail steamer, III, 42 f.
Tribune, The, established, II, 234, 236, 322; III, 40, 73, 115, 227
Trinity Church, III, 210
Triple Alliance, IV, 199, 212 f.
Triple Entente, IV, 199, 212, *passim*
Tripoli, II, 42
Trist, Nicholas P., succeeds in making treaty, II, 283; in charge of Mexican negotiations, II, 281 f.
Trolley, IV, 113
Troops, need of, by Allies, IV, 232
Trumbull, John, poet of Revolution, I, 186; II, 4
"Trusts," IV, 24, 73, 116
Tudors, English ruling family, I, 12
Tugwell, Dr. R. G., member of "brain trust," IV, 358
Tunbridge Wells, English Spa, I, 92
Tunnels, connecting New York with Long Island and New Jersey, IV, 113
Turkey, IV, 201, 224, *et passim*
Tusitala, sailing vessel, IV, 533
TVA, IV, 369 f.; as "yard stick," for electric current, IV, 438, 439; and Wilson Dam project at Muscle Shoals, IV, 451; validity questioned, IV, 451; IV, 494; quarrels and investigation by Congress, IV, 520, 521
Tweed, William H., III, 217 f., 254
Tweed Ring, III, 203
Twelfth Amendment, II, 32
Twentieth Amendment, IV, 349
Twentieth Century Fund, IV, 504
Twenty-first Amendment, IV, 376 f.
"Two Penny Act," I, 135
Tydings, Senator, of Maryland, IV, 463, 526
Tyler, John, II, 254; nominated for Vice-President, II, 240; becomes President by death of Harrison, II, 248; vetoes bank bill, II, 249; Cabinet resigns, II, 249; administration of, II, 250; difficulties with England, II, 250; appealed to for aid, II, 259; and annexation of Texas, II, 262; withdraws, II, 268
Tyler, Royall, *The Contrast,* II, 5
Type, movable, II, 205
Typewriter, IV, 19

Ultra-Loyalists, I, 149
Uncle Tom's Cabin, I, 184; II, 322
Underwood, Oscar W., IV, 178, 184

"Underground Railroad," II, 299
Unemployment, first appearance of, I, 14, 15; in 1838, II, 187; after World War, IV, 323; competition aided by, IV, 371; NRA as aid to, IV, 372 f.; IV, 384; increased by 1934 drought, IV, 399; estimated number in 1934, IV, 383, 411; dole and works system of relief, IV, 418, 419, 420; human element a factor in situation of, IV, 472; factors to remedy, IV, 474; census for, IV, 472, 517; IV, 523, 534
Union, the, II, 32; movement, II, 197; dissolution of, demanded, II, 244 f.; love for, II, 247; saved for the time, II, 302; constitutional question of, settled, III, 161; sentiment for, III, 162
Union Pacific Railroad, III, 136, 209; ceremony of completion, III, 210
Union Pacific Railway, scandals of, III, 229; IV, 42, 117
"Union Leagues," III, 203
Union Station at Washington, IV, 114
Union Trust Company, III, 234
Unitarianism, II, 3, 208, 227
United Mine Workers, IV, 474
United States, I, 1, 17, 32; population of, I, 3 f.; limits of, I, 4; hope of races, I, 51; not prepared, II, 84; new power of, III, 162; isolation of, IV, 263; debt of, IV, 277 f., 337 (*see* National Debt); attitude towards Cuba, IV, 380, 393; attitude on munitions export, IV, 393; and Philippines, IV, 393; dust storm of 1934 in, IV, 399; economic success the goal in, IV, 423; hope renewed in, IV, 410, 412; militia called in strike situation, IV, 403; and neutrality, IV, 453, 454; drought of, 1934, IV, 465; agreement with Great Britain and France to stabilize foreign exchange, IV, 466; trend toward better business, IV, 471; crusade against moral evils, IV, 499 f.; opinion on Roosevelt and policies, IV, 510; opposition to Government Reorganization Bill, IV, 521; danger from threatened "Balkanization," IV, 534; relations with Japan, IV, 536; with Germany, IV, 537; with South America, IV, 476, 537 f.; trade pact with Britain, IV, 538; productiveness of wages in, IV, 538, 540; feeling toward totalitarian states, IV, 538
United States News, The, estimate of strikes, IV, 498; IV, 526
United States Sanitary Commission, III, 118
United States Shipping Board, IV, 230
United States Steel Corporation, IV, 117, 159, 263, 274, 276 f., 498

584

INDEX

United Textile Workers, IV, 404
Universities, in New Spain, I, 10; English, I, 92
Upshur, Abel P., Secretary of State, II, 262
Utica, II, 7

Vallandigham, Clement L., III, 108
Valley Forge, winter at, I, 174
Van Buren, Martin, II, 168, 243; leader of New York, II, 154; Secretary of State, II, 164; supports Jackson, II, 167; offers resignation, II, 174; Minister to England, II, 175; Vice-President, II, 175; nominated for President, II, 183; elected, II, 183; an enigma, II, 184 f.; his rank today, II, 185; proposes bill for banks, II, 186; inherits problem of Texas, II, 189; delays annexation of Texas, II, 190; defeated, II, 243; probable candidate, II, 264; candidacy impossible, II, 265; nominated, II, 289; defeat of, II, 290
Vandenberg, Senator, declines presidential nomination, IV, 461
Van Devanter, Justice, IV, 490, 491
Van Nuys, Senator, IV, 493, 495, 526
Van Rensselaer, General, II, 87
Van Tyne, estimate of, I, 171
Vanderbilt, Cornelius, III, 164, 214, 216, 233
Vanderbilt, William H., IV, 23; quoted, IV, 25
Vans Murray, William, as American Minister, I, 302
Vassar, Matthew, III, 140
Vassall house in Cambridge, Mass., I, 101
Venezuela, IV, 131; the dispute with, IV, 51 f.
Vergennes, not trusted by America, I, 212
Vermont, intriguing with British, I, 233; property qualification in, I, 237; legislature outlaws sit-down strike, IV, 497
Verona, Congress of, II, 135
Verrazano, I, 8
Versailles Treaty, IV, 282, 328 f.
Veterans, IV, 354; march on Washington, IV, 358; bill for pensions of, IV, 394; pension figures for, IV, 395 f.; State and Federal aid to, IV, 436 f.; Bonus Bill, IV, 450; receive bonus checks, IV, 436
Veterans Bureau, scandals of, IV, 289; IV, 396
Vicksburg, III, 55; effect of capture of, III, 86
Victoria, Queen, III, 224
Vienna, riots in, in 1934, IV, 381
Villa, Mexican bandit, IV, 193

Vincennes, capture of, I, 205
Vincent-Guffey Coal Bill, IV, 487 (*see* Guffey Coal Bill)
Vinson Bill, IV, 407
Virginia, I, 11, 31, 44, 46, 48, 88, 90, 99, 102, 105, 110, 160, 241, 245; II, 1, 199; charter, I, 16; settlements in, I, 17; population in 1625, I, 19; charter, quoted, I, 21; becomes Royal colony, I, 21; stability of, I, 22; first settled, I, 23; goal of Pilgrims, I, 25; laws of, I, 30; in revolt, I, 57; "the Resolves," I, 135, 148, 304; Assembly, I, 188; passes Resolution, I, 188; population of, I, 245; ratifies, I, 258; House of Delegates, passes resolutions, II, 294; joins the Confederacy, III, 26
Virginia Gazette, The, I, 114
Virginia Military Institute, III, 158
Virginia, University of, III, 157
Virginians, The, I, 92
Volstead Act, IV, 269; modification sought by Franklin Roosevelt, IV, 355
Volunteers in Civil War, III, 110 f.
Von Bernstorff, German Ambassador, given passports, IV, 220
Von Diedrich, German Admiral, IV, 90
Von Holleben, IV, 132
Von Steuben, Baron, I, 199
Voters, foreign, III, 217; qualifications of, II, 241

Wade, Benjamin, III, 170, 196
Wade-Davis Bill, III, 169
Wages, I, 121 f.; in 1840, II, 196; III, 139; basis, III, 168; decrease of, III, 276; IV, 128, 159, 280; of WPA workers, IV, 526
Wages and hours bill, IV, 516, 524
Wages and Hours proposal, Black-Connery, IV, 494
Wagner Labor Act, upheld by Supreme Court, IV, 487; IV, 498
Walker, Governor, quoted, III, 155
Wall Street, I, 262; IV, 49, 59, 66, 123, 136, 152, 175, 311, 336
Wallace, Henry, Secretary of Agriculture, IV, 494
Wallace, General Lew, in Civil War, III, 52
Wanamaker, John, IV, 3
War of 1812, I, 288 f.; end of, II, 100; losses of, II, 104
War of Spanish Succession, I, 70
War debts, IV, 257, 265, 286, 288, 293 f., 299; conference on, IV, 335; IV, 392
War Department, scandals of, III, 138
War Finance Board, IV, 330

585

INDEX

War Finance Corporation, IV, 228
"War Hawks," II, 79, 80, 85, 87, 95
War Industries Board, IV, 228
War, Queen Anne's I, 70
War Trade Board, IV, 228
War, World (see World War)
Ward, quoted by Lincoln, III, 76
Warm Springs, Georgia, IV, 522
Warner, Colonel Seth, I, 196
Warren, Professor G. F., of Cornell, member "brain trust," IV, 358; and Gold Purchase Scheme, IV, 373; IV, 449
Warwick, Earl of, I, 13
Washburn, manufacturer, III, 214
Washington, George, I, 151, 173, 212, 241, 242, 244, 256, 292, 302; brothers of, I, 73; as Lieutenant-Colonel I, 74; with Braddock, I, 76; knowledge of Indian warfare, I, 79; character of, I, 146; introduces resolutions, I, 148; appointed Commander-in-Chief, I, 169; reaches Cambridge, I, 170; size of army at first, I, 170; his small army, I, 171; difficulty in keeping troops, I, 172; without efficient backing, I, 173; difficulties of, I, 180; determines to take Boston, I, 181 f.; on his way to New York, I, 182; moves to New York, I, 191; retreats across East River, I, 192; at Newark, I, 193; retreats across the Delaware, I, 193; attacks Hessians at Trenton, I, 193; pushes to Morristown, I, 194; makes surprise attack on Princeton, I, 194; moves to defense of Philadelphia, I, 195; winter quarters at Valley Forge, I, 196; destitute army, I, 200 f.; despatches General Lincoln, I, 205; sends Greene to South, I, 206; issues order against secret meetings, I, 215; greatness of, I, 216; returns to Mount Vernon, I, 216; refuses to accept paper, I, 222; fear of, I, 233; troubled at growing anarchy, I, 239; made chairman of Convention, I, 243; his great influence in Convention, I, 252; chosen President, I, 260; a world figure, I, 261; leaves Mount Vernon with regret, I, 261; his journey to New York, I, 262; inaugurated, I, 262; the first inaugural procession, I, 263; organizes government, I, 265; signs the bill for U. S. Bank, I, 276; rift in his Cabinet, I, 278 f.; unanimously re-elected, I, 280; urged by Hamilton, I, 282; adopts Jefferson's view, I, 283; assailed, I, 293 f.; declines to be a candidate, I, 294; his "Farewell Address," I, 294 f.; death of, I, 306; quoted, I, 172, 222, 244
Washington City, II, 16, 68, 107, 110; plans

for, II, 13; burned, II, 94; threatened in Civil War, III, 61
Wasp, sloop-of-war, II, 88
Watertown, protests of, I, 29, 36
Wayne, Anthony, protests of, I, 183, 291
Wearin, Representative, IV, 525
Weaver, James B., nominated by Prohibition Party, III, 289; IV, 38
Webster, Daniel, II, 178, 181, 254, 293, 302, 303, 322, 330; III, 25, 189; leader of New England, II, 140; turns political somersault, II, 141; for protection, II, 156; quoted, III, 157; famous reply to Hayne, II, 170; quoted, II, 171 f.; electrifies the nation, II, 173; scandal of, II, 179; complimentary vote to, II, 183; ability of, II, 183 f.; fails in nomination, II, 240; Secretary of State, II, 249; negotiates with Ashburton, II, 255; his position, II, 287; debate of, II, 296 f.; famous "Seventh of March" speech, II, 298; quoted, II, 298; "Reply to Hayne," II, 298; denounced, II, 299; Secretary of State, II, 306; death of, II, 312
Webster, Pelatiah, quoted, I, 222
Welles, Gideon, Secretary of Navy, III, 23
Welsh immigration, I, 92, 100
Wendell, Barrett, History of Literature in America, II, 222
Wesley, John, preacher, I, 109
West, national feeling of, I, 229; interests of, I, 234; lands, problem of the, I, 253; resources in the, II, 17; life in, II, 24; poverty in, II, 24; development of, II, 115; population of, II, 110; importance of in 1828, II, 160; intensity of life, II, 231; development blocked, II, 252; developed by railroads, III, 210 f.; primarily agricultural, III, 214; economic ideas of, III, 245
West, Benjamin, painter, I, 104
West Indies, I, 26, 42, 55, 58, 74, 105, 130, 224 225, 228, 288; slaves from, I, 46; possessions lost to England, I, 210
West Point, established, II, 41; III, 30, 39, 48
West Virginia, admitted to Union, III, 28
Western Union Company, founding of, II, 206; III, 163
Westover, in Virginia, I, 97, 102
Westsylvania, I, 228
Weyler, General, reports concerning, IV, 77, 82, 83 f.
Wharton, Mrs. Edith, author, IV, 116
Wheat, beginning of wheat growing, II, 199; III, 31, 151, 250; IV, 31; surplus diminished, IV, 465

586

INDEX

INDEX

Wilson Tariff Bill, IV, 47

Windom, William, Secretary of Treasury, III, 291; IV, 11

Wine, duty on, I, 146

Wine Islands, slaves from, I, 46

Winslow, John, arrives in Massachusetts, I, 61

Winthrop, John, first governor, I, 29, 30, 34, 36, 37, 44; death of, I, 41

Wirt William, Attorney-General, II, 104

Wirt, William, *British Spy,* II, 16

Wister, Owen, author, IV, 116

Witches, hanging of, I, 44, 94

Wolcott, Oliver, in John Adams's Cabinet, I, 298

Wolfe, capture of Quebec, I, 77

Woman's movement, II, 238 f.

Woman's Rights Convention, the first, II, 213

Woman's suffrage, IV, 161, 269 f.

Women, employment of, IV, 22

Women's Christian Temperance Union, IV, 22

Women's Clubs, IV, 120

Wood, Leonard, IV, 110; at San Juan Hill, IV, 92; service in Cuba, IV, 96, 103; candidate for President, IV, 266

Woodbury, Levi, Secretary of Navy, in Jackson's Cabinet, II, 175

Woodcraft, romance by Simms, II, 219

Woodford, Steward L., Minister at Madrid, under McKinley, IV, 83, 86

Woodin, William H., Secretary of Treasury, IV, 352; quoted, IV, 354

Wool, increased demand for, III, 132

Woolworth Building, in New York City, IV, 113

Workingman's Party, II, 197

World, The New York, III, 187; IV, 81

World Court, IV, 282 f., 432

World Economic Conference (*see* Economic Conference)

World War, the, I, 221; III, 111, 228, 277 ff.; beginnings of, IV, 198 f.; prices in, IV, 202; troubles at sea, IV, 203 f.; we enter, IV, 220; causes of, IV, 223; our troops in France, IV, 236; our operations in France, IV, 237 f.; Armistice signed, IV, 239; our part in, IV, 240; losses in, IV, 241; treatment of our soldiers, IV, 242; resolution ending, IV, 260; changes wrought by, IV, 264 f.

WPA, IV, 449, 456, 472; workers, IV, 525 f.; 530

Wright, Frank Lloyd, architect, IV, 306

Wright, Silas, reformer, II, 288

Wright brothers make first flight in air, IV, 115

Writs of Assistance legalized, I, 143

Wyoming, admitted in 1890, IV, 22

Wythe, George, opposes resolutions in Virginia House of Burgesses, I, 135, 242, 258

X, Y, and Z, I, 300

Y. M. C. A., IV, 242

Yale University, I, 105, 108; III, 240

Yancey, William L., III, 16, 40; quoted, III, 158

"Yard-stick," IV, 368, 369

Yeardley, George, I, 19, 21

"Yellow" journalism, IV, 81

Yorktown, I, 229, 266

Young, Brigham, successor to Joseph Smith, II, 209

Young, Owen D., on Dawes Commission, IV, 294

Zenger, Peter, I, 114

Zimmermann, note to Mexico, IV, 221

OUR country is rich in the men and women who have risen to distinction as workers and leaders. Our country is rich in natural scenes of beauty and grandeur. Our country is rich in buildings which have expressed the courage, tenacity, and imagination of our people.

The final pages of each volume of this edition of James Truslow Adams's *History of the United States* present in attractive form some of these outstanding personalities, some of the most thrilling moments of our history, some of our most beautiful natural scenes, some of the most conspicuous representations of our architectural imagination—a veritable panorama of American life.

THE PANAMA CANAL—THE S. S. *CALIFORNIA*
IN THE GAILLARD CUT

The construction of the Panama Canal was one of the world's outstanding engineering achievements. Long before the United States entertained the idea, Ferdinand de Lesseps, builder of the Canal at the Isthmus of Suez, organized a French company to cut a sea-level canal through the Isthmus of Panama and enable shipping to make this short route between East and West. Due to the ravages of yellow fever and malaria and due to the reckless extravagance of incompetent officials, the project met with defeat and was abandoned in 1889.

In 1904, prompted by President Theodore Roosevelt, the United States acquired the property from the French Panama Company, and through the efforts of General William C. Gorgas and others conquered the mosquito, carrier of yellow fever and malaria, and started work on the Canal. As work progressed slowly under too many leaders, the Army took over the job and, under Colonel George Goethals, successfully completed the task in 1914.

From the opening of the Canal on August 15, 1914, to June 30, 1932, 69,466 commercial vessels passed through the locks, and paid in tolls $292,864,830.

IRANISTAN—AN ORIENTAL VILLA

In 1846, Phineas Taylor Barnum, American showman and circus proprietor, found his fortune so large that he determined to gratify his somewhat exotic taste in the selection of a residence. Upon purchasing seventeen acres of land at Bridgeport, Connecticut, he engaged a London architect to draw up plans in the manner of Brighton Pavilion. The many spires and minarets of the Pavilion, one of the first examples of Oriental architecture in England, appealed greatly to Barnum's spectacular imagination. A showman even in his private life, he thought that a residence of a novel order might indirectly serve as an advertisement for his various enterprises. The materialization of his fancy, Iranistan, was a combination of Byzantine, Moorish, and Turkish architecture, and was completed in 1848.

BICYCLING ON RIVERSIDE DRIVE—THE CLAREMONT
IN THE BACKGROUND

Drawn by W. A. Rogers.

Bicycling played the part in the life of the nineties that automobiling does today. Every one had a bicycle who possibly could have one and used it. Livery stables suffered losses and health gained, according to a medical authority of the period. Clubs were organized and runs of all kinds became the order of the day. More and better bicycle roads were demanded in city and in country. Women found a new emancipation, and clothiers complained that their only orders were for cycling suits. Some women cyclists wore bloomers, a striking departure from the trailing skirts then in vogue. There were many types of bicycles. Among the most popular was the tandem or "bicycle built for two." Some of the better known makes were: Columbia, Imperial, Stormer, Sterling, Crawford, Spalding, Cleveland, Monarch, Stearns, Syracuse, Barnes, Featherstone, Pierce, Tribune, and Victory.

THE UNITED STATES FLEET JOINING THE BRITISH
AT SCAPA FLOW

From the painting by Francis Gribble in the Navy Department, Washington.

On December 7, 1917, Admiral Rodman's United States battleships united with the British at Scapa Flow, forming the Sixth Battle Squadron of the British Grand Fleet. The *New York* led, followed by the *Wyoming, Florida, Delaware, Texas,* and *Arkansas,* and were greeted with enthusiastic cheers by the British. It was the work of this fleet to keep the seas clear of the German High Fleet, and this they did, saving Allied and neutral tonnage, and affording safe transport to the American troops. In this, as in other cases, the record of the United States Navy in the War was one of which all citizens are justly proud.

TO THOSE WHO MADE THE SUPREME
SACRIFICE

COLUMBIA GIVES TO HER SON THE ACCOLADE OF THE
NEW CHIVALRY OF HUMANITY

The original was designed by Edward H. Blashfield in 1919.

COLUMBIA·GIVES·TO·HER·SON
THE·ACCOLADE·OF·THE
NEW·CHIVALRY·OF·HUMANITY

SERVED·WITH·HONOR·IN·THE·WORLD·WAR
AND·DIED·IN·THE·SERVICE·OF·HIS·COUNTRY

Woodrow Wilson

THE COUNCIL OF FOUR OF THE PEACE CONFERENCE

From the collection of photographs in the War Department.

In the picture are shown, reading from left to right: Signor Orlando, of Italy; Mr. Lloyd George, of Great Britain; Monsieur Clemenceau, of France; and President Wilson, of the United States. The gentlemen standing are confidential secretaries of Signor Orlando and Mr. Lloyd George.

The picture was taken in the room where the "Council of Four" held their meetings at the Paris home of President Wilson, 11 Place des Etats-Unis, Paris, France, May 27, 1919.

THE SINGING TOWER, MOUNTAIN LAKE, FLORIDA

From a photograph copyright by Van Natta, Lake Watts, Florida.

In 1929, the transforming of a dreary sandhill into a most beautiful expanse of verdure was completed, and the Bird Sanctuary at Mountain Lake, Florida, was presented to the American people. The idea was conceived and made possible by Edward W. Bok. The Sanctuary, by Frederick Low Olmsted, provides a haven for myriads of birds. In its rare planting and beautiful vistas it is of surpassing beauty.

The Singing Tower, designed by Milton B. Medary, is a carillon tower unsurpassed in the world. Standing in the middle of an area of fifty acres, and surrounded by oak and palm trees, it has rightly been called America's Taj Mahal. It is of pink Georgia marble with a base of native Florida coquina rock—a mixture that gives the tower its soft and unbelievable tone of beauty, particularly when seen at sunrise or during sunset.

In front of the tower is a reflection lake. There is a second lake, a pool for flamingoes. The carillon of bells is played at sunset each day. In surroundings of such beauties of trees, flowers, birds, and architecture, is fulfilled the wish of the donor as revealed in the words of John Burroughs at the entrance: "I come here to find myself. It is so easy to get lost in the world."

BUILDING BOULDER DAM, NEVADA

This view was taken looking up the Colorado River from Observation Point to the coffer dam location, and gives an idea of the tremendous task which faced the engineers of this project.

The dam creates a reservoir 115 miles in length, with an area of 145,000 acres and storing 30,500,000 acre-feet. This storage is for use in irrigation and regulates the flow of the river so as to improve navigation and protect from overflow, water shortage, and silt accumulation the lands in the valleys adjacent to the river below the dam and in the Imperial Valley in southern California.

In the upper centre is shown the overhead cable car which carried twenty men across the yawning chasm each trip. It was called the "skip" by the workmen who referred to "skipping across the river." On the left is the control station for the overhead cable car, while the location for the coffer dam is shown in the centre. This dam was used to divert the Colorado River through huge tunnels, during the construction of the dam from the solid rock base of the river bed.

THE CALIFORNIA MEMORIAL STADIUM, UNIVERSITY OF CALIFORNIA

The California Memorial Stadium occupies what was formerly the "Spooner's Retreat"—the lower reaches of beautiful Strawberry Canyon. Erected at a cost of over a million dollars, which was raised by subscription, the Stadium was dedicated to California's war heroes on November 23, 1923.

The Stadium is used for football, and for some years has been the setting for graduation exercises. It had originally a capacity of 73,000, which has since been increased to about 83,000.

In the background is the Sather Campanile. Built of steel and granite, with a height of 307 feet it becomes an outstanding landmark. In 1917 chimes were installed; the twelve bells, varying in weight from 349 pounds to 4118, play for ten minutes thrice daily.

WILSHIRE BOULEVARD, LOS ANGELES, CALIFORNIA

*From a photograph furnished by the All-Year Club
of Southern California.*

Ultra-modern Los Angeles, a city combining the old and the new, clings to its romantic and un-American past. Nuestra Señora la Reina de los Angeles (Los Angeles) was founded in 1781 by the Decree of Carlos III of Spain, upon the recommendation of Felipe de Neve, then Governor of the Californias, that Alta California must be colonized by permanent residents to protect it from the encroachments of France, England, Russia, and the new American nation. A year's recruiting produced twelve families willing to found the new city, and after a hazardous trip through the desert, the chosen site was reached. A flag was planted and the city founded with due ceremony. Changing from Spanish to Mexican rule, Los Angeles was the largest community in California when the American flag supplanted the Mexican in 1846.

Its history varies between prominence and oblivion; the boom period of the 1880's and the recent Hollywood boom, and quiet days of growth and expansion. All that is most modern in shops and buildings is blended with the old-world atmosphere of the Spanish and Indian quarters. In the photograph is seen Wilshire Boulevard, palm-lined and brilliantly lighted at night, which connects the heart of the city with dozens of southern California beach resorts.

MICHIGAN AVENUE, CHICAGO

In 1833, thirteen young men in Mark Beaubien's Sauganash Tavern voted to incorporate the frontier post of Chicago with its one hundred and fifty inhabitants. On July 4, 1836, during the celebration attending the turning of the first shovelful of earth in the work beginning on the Illinois and Michigan Canal, Judge Theophilus Smith's veracity was doubted and scoffers pulled him down from the barrel from which he made the statement that in a hundred years Chicago would boast a population of 100,000. The census of 1930 gave Chicago a population of 3,375,235.

Starting on the prairies, later filling in the streets near the river to a height of ten feet, and hoisting buildings eight feet to meet the new grading, Chicago advanced by leaps and bounds only to be burned out in 1871. Rising anew, this time in stone and iron and brick, Chicago grew to the glories of architecture and the civilization of the eighties, and was host to the World's Columbian Exposition in 1893. The Exposition brought realization to the city of the possibilities of its Lake Front and the Chicago Plan began to take form. This has resulted today in a new and transformed waterfront, lined with buildings designed to enhance its beauty, and a park which stretches from Michigan Avenue to the Lake Front—part of Chicago's deeds of a century which have made the Chicago of today.

THE *MANHATTAN*

In 1819 America electrified the world with the first transatlantic steamship. The *Savannah*, built as a small sailing vessel and later fitted with a steam boiler and engine, was the first vessel to brave the ocean voyage with steam, though she made the greater part of the trip under sail. She presented such an unusual sight that off the coast of Ireland she was pursued by the British revenue cruiser *Kite*, who thought her on fire.

A picture of the *Britannia*, a vessel similar to the *Savannah* and the first Cunarder to cross the ocean in 1840, is shown in Volume III. A comparison of the *Britannia* and the S.S. *Manhattan*, seen on the opposite page, will give some idea of the progress that has been made in ocean travel.

With the launching of the *Manhattan*, on December 5, 1931, a new era for American shipping began. She is the highest powered American-built merchantship, designed to carry 1250 passengers, and with a guaranteed speed of twenty knots. The *Manhattan* is equipped with the latest devices for safety, comfort, and convenience.

THE TWENTIETH CENTURY LIMITED

A monarch of the rails typifying the progress in transportation since the days of the *De Witt Clinton*. On her maiden trip in 1902, she covered in twenty hours the distance between New York and Chicago, which in thirty years has been reduced only two hours. The Twentieth Century, said to be the most popular de luxe train in the world, uses the Hudson type locomotive, which has great reserve power and is able to handle the heaviest train smoothly under all operating conditions.

THE CATHEDRAL OF LEARNING

Towering thirty to forty stories upward, the Cathedral of Learning at the University of Pittsburgh is the last word in modernism in academic architecture.

It is the design of Charles Z. Klauder, and is the embodiment of American dynamic vitality rather than the usual expression of academic background and learning.

THE STATE CAPITOL, LINCOLN, NEBRASKA

Photograph by courtesy of the Lincoln Chamber of Commerce, Lincoln, Nebraska.

In its new Capitol, Nebraska has given to the world a distinctive architectural contribution. Departing from the conventional State capitol in simplicity of style, it is considered by many the most vivid and original conception in the field of American art. The architects, Bertram Grovenor Goodhue Associates, have designed the building to symbolize the inherent power of the State of Nebraska and the purpose of its citizens, thereby forming a monument to the outdoor life of an agricultural State and to the aspirations of a pioneer community. The base of the building, in the form of a rectangle 437 feet square and two stories high, typifies the wide-spread, fertile plains of Nebraska, while the central tower, rising triumphantly to a height of 400 feet, expresses the aspirations and ideals of the citizens.

The sculptural wall decorations, always an integral part of the structure, are the work of Lee Lowrie and exemplify the power of the law, telling the story of its development from the earliest times.

THE UNION TERMINAL, CLEVELAND

Throughout the United States the dreary old railroad stations of a past era are giving place to fine new buildings.

The Union Terminal in Cleveland is considered one of the most beautiful of these modern terminals. Situated in the heart of the city at the junction of Ontario Street and Canal Road, it looks out upon the Public Square. It was completed in June of 1930 at a cost of $100,000,000. The architects are Graham, Anderson, Probst, and White.

THE CAPITOL AT OLYMPIA, WASHINGTON

From a photograph by Merle P. Junk.

Washington, the Evergreen State, in less than one hundred years has grown from wilderness to present-day civilization. Seattle, with its 400,000 inhabitants, its skyscrapers and modern activity, has grown up in the lifetime of one of its original twenty-four settlers. In contrast to this civilization is the hardy pioneer of today, living within the confines of the State a frontier life very similar to that of the blazers of the Oregon Trail.

On the opposite page is shown the new Capitol at Olympia. In the centre is the Legislative Hall with its 300-foot dome; at the left the Insurance Building; and at the extreme right, a corner of the Temple of Justice. These buildings were constructed mainly of materials native to the State.

NEW YEAR'S DAY IN PHILADELPHIA —
THE MUMMERS' PARADE

The advent of the New Year has been celebrated in Philadelphia since the post-Revolutionary period when the city was the capital and Washington received his friends on New Year's Day in the Morris Mansion on Market Street.

Originally, parties of the Mummers went around from house to house during Christmas week, asking dole.

In the nineteenth century, the Beelzebubs and Coney Crackers Clubs paraded in uniform and the volunteer fire companies joined in the celebrations. Later came the Mummers Clubs and on New Year's night in the nineties they, and most of Philadelphia's citizens, used to turn out for fun and frolic as thousands tried to jam in around Independence Hall and "shoot in the New Year."

For thirty-two years now these Sons of Mummers have been parading on Broad Street on New Year's Day with courtiers and clowns cavorting to the amusement of the crowds of onlookers.

THE MARDI GRAS AT NEW ORLEANS

The gaieties of social life in New Orleans reach their climax on Shrove Tuesday, the day preceding Ash Wednesday, which inaugurates the Lenten season each year. The first record of the celebration of Mardi Gras in New Orleans is in 1827; it was a simple procession of maskers—the processions of maskers which take place today in many parts of the city very closely resemble the original. In 1837, the first semblance of tableau was introduced, and in 1839 the dominant figure was an immense rooster, six feet high. A grand mask and fancy dress ball wound up the affair.

Today the public events of the Carnival begin on the Thursday night preceding Mardi Gras with a brilliant street pageant. On Monday night, there are another ball and pageant, and then on Tuesday, Mardi Gras day, comes the day pageant of "Rex" and his queen, rulers of the Carnival reign. In different sections of the city, merchant associations award prizes to maskers who pass before them in review. The maskers who ride in the floats of Rex's procession distribute favors along the route and a beautiful jewelled crown, sceptre, and necklace are presented to the queen and a mantle to Rex. The entire city plays in the street and the festivities carry on into the night when the Grand Concluding Pageant and Ball are given. At midnight the chimes of the 150-year-old St. Louis Cathedral ring out, ending the gaieties and ushering in the solemn season of Lent.

THE TOURNAMENT OF ROSES, PASADENA

The First Tournament of Roses was held in Pasadena, California, on New Year's Day, 1889. As a small village festival inspired by the Carnival of Roses at Nice, France, it consisted of a few residents decorating their private vehicles with flowers and driving through the streets to the community baseball grounds where amateur sports were held.

During eight subsequent years the Tournament grew to such an extent that a special organization was founded to conduct it.

A whole year of preparation now goes into the making of the Tournament. Only natural flowers are permitted to appear in the parade and they must be picked not more than twelve hours before the scheduled starting time of the pageant. In 1931 there were approximately 250 units in the parade which was five miles long. Each year the pageant has a definite theme. In 1933 Fairy Tales in Flowers was the subject, and the float pictured opposite was one of those in the parade. Instead of amateur sports in the afternoon, the annual East-West football game is held in the Pasadena Rose Bowl.

A THANKSGIVING DAY PARADE IN NEW YORK CITY

This Thanksgiving Day Parade has its place among America's pageants. It was inaugurated in 1924 to open officially the Christmas season in a large New York retail store's toy department. Thousands of people every year wait for hours to watch the floats, balloons, clowns, stilt-walkers, etc., pass, on their route from the National Academy of Design at 109th Street and Amsterdam Avenue, down Broadway to 34th Street. The outstanding feature of the parade are the balloons, which are designed by the artist Tony Sarg, in colorful and humorous figures, some of the best known being, the Turk (seen in the photograph), the Drum Major, Alligator, Dachshund, etc. They are of gigantic size, filled with non-inflammable helium, and in past years it has been customary to release them at the finish of the parade, prizes being offered for their return. This will not be repeated in coming years because of possible danger to aviators.

THE BRIDGE OF YESTERDAY

The old covered bridge is a quaint and picturesque landmark. A roughly constructed wooden shed on stone piers, its sloping roof protecting the floorboards from the weather, it has endured from generation to generation. Representative of a more leisurely age, when speed was not the god of travel, it recalls the days when horse-drawn vehicles travelled narrow dirt roads.

Opposite is a drawing, by R. Emmett Owen, of the old covered bridge at Campton, New Hampshire, which was swept away during one of the floods of 1928 and 1929.

THE BRIDGE OF TODAY

The George Washington Bridge spans the Hudson River from New York City to Fort Lee, New Jersey. A huge steel structure of the suspension type, it has 3500 feet of river span and two towers measuring 635 feet above water. It is a single deck structure consisting of four roadway lanes and two pedestrian sidewalks. Additional roadway lanes and a lower deck intended for rapid transit service can be added to meet future requirements. O. H. Ammann was the chief engineer and Cass Gilbert consulting architect. Ground was broken and construction started in May, 1927, and the bridge was opened to the public on October 25, 1931. It was built and is now owned and operated by The Port of New York Authority.

THE BRIDGE OF TOMORROW

Designed by Hugh Ferris.

The bridge of the future has been designed to alleviate congested housing, a problem becoming yearly more acute in large cities.

Like the bridge of today, it is a great span of the suspension type. The pylons are carried upward to form skyscrapers and apartment buildings, and the central roadway is flanked by dwelling accommodations which are hung from the cables. In this manner air space is put to practical use, and city occupants are afforded a maximum of light and air together with a fine water view.

STEEL WORKERS

From a photograph by Jeannette Griffith.

The skyscraper is peculiarly an American contribution to the history of building. The introduction of steel as a fundamental element of structure revolutionized the whole art and industry of building, making it no longer necessary to erect walls by piling stone on stone, brick on brick. Without steel the walls of our high buildings would have to be so thick at the bottom as to leave little or no space inside. The photograph opposite portrays a detail in the stirring drama of steel.

THE DOWNTOWN SKYLINE OF NEW YORK, SEEN
FROM BROOKLYN BRIDGE

From a photograph copyright in 1933 by P. L. Sperr.

The skyline of New York, one of the world's famous views, is constantly changing. Great skyscrapers spring up almost overnight to replace the quaint old buildings which represent a past age.

In the foreground of the picture opposite may be seen some of the old houses which have so far withstood the advance of modern architecture. In the left foreground is the Fulton Fish Market, while facing it across South Street is the Old Market Building. Meyers Hotel stands in the centre foreground at the intersection of South Street and Beekman Street. In the background at the extreme left is the first modern skyscraper on South Street. Continuing to the right, in the background, the tall building with a level top is the City Bank and Farmer's Trust. It is flanked, in the photograph, on the immediate left by the International Telephone and Telegraph, and on the immediate right by the Standard Oil Building. The very tall building in the centre background is the Cities Service, at 60 Wall Street. To its right is the Bank of Manhattan at the right of which is the Irving Trust Company. The Singer Building is the tallest building in the extreme right background.

THE EMPIRE STATE BUILDING, NEW YORK CITY

On August 30, 1929, former Governor Alfred E. Smith and the Empire State Directors published plans for the world's tallest structure, the Empire State Building. On May 1, 1931, the building was opened, nearly a month ahead of schedule. An average of 2500 men were employed daily in the construction work of the building. Ten million bricks were used, there are 200,000 cubic feet of stone, 730 tons of exterior chrome-nickel steel and aluminum, nearly 7 miles of elevator shafts, and enough floor space to shelter a city of 80,000.

The building towers 102 stories above the street, the tallest structure in the world. It is 1250 feet to the tip of the mast. There are observatories on the 86th and 102d floor atop the mooring mast. These attracted 1,130,000 visitors during the first year, who found scenes of interest and beauty spread for miles below them.

PART OF THE LINDBERGH COLLECTION
OF MEDALS AND TROPHIES IN THE
JEFFERSON MEMORIAL BUILDING,
ST. LOUIS, MISSOURI

This collection of medals, which organizations and countries throughout the world have designed and struck off, is the largest ever presented to one person.

Above: The aviator's portrait engraved in gold is seen here with the French Legion of Honor miniature button, and (*to the left*), French Legion of Honor medal, and U. S. Distinguished Service Cross; (*to the right*), Belgian Legion of Honor Medal, and a special medal from King Albert of Belgium.

Below: (*Upper left*) is the giant key to London, and below it is the almost invisible key to Paris. Surrounding them are gold medals presented by countries, cities, and organizations, too numerous to mention. Brooklyn school children presented the key to the right of the key to London. At the top left is a letter from Marshal Foch.

THE *AKRON* IN THE CLOUDS

From a photograph copyright 1933 by P. L. Sperr.

The Navy airship *Akron* was the first zeppelin-type airship built in America, and was launched on August 8, 1931. She was 785 feet in length, weighed about 240,000 pounds, with a gross lift of 403,000 pounds, and was regarded as the finest of all lighter-than-air craft in regard to safety.

After the launching, the *Akron* underwent extensive flights, including trips to California, Cuba, and the Canal Zone, and performed satisfactorily in storm and high winds.

On Monday evening, April 3, 1933, the *Akron* left her hangar at Lakehurst, New Jersey, on a regularly scheduled flight to calibrate New England radio stations. Encountering a violent thunderstorm at sea, the rudders broke, the ship was driven down and sank about twelve-thirty that night, twenty miles off Barnegat Light on the Jersey coast. Only three of the seventy-six on board survived.

THE STATUE OF LIBERTY

From a photograph copyright by P. L. Sperr.

The bronze Statue of Liberty is the work of Frédéric A. Bartholdi, and was presented to the United States by France on August 5, 1884. The figure was intended to symbolize the historic friendship between the two republics and the freedom and brotherhood underlying the republican form of government. It stands on Bedloe Island in New York Harbor.

Representative of all that the New World offers, Liberty welcomes the newcomer to our shores and fills the homeward-bound American with pride in his home, his country, and his government.

D